D1499719

Readings: A New Biblical Commentary

General Editor
John Jarick

A C T S

ACTS

F. Scott Spencer

Sheffield Academic Press

To Lauren Michael and Meredith Leigh,
who love reading

Copyright © 1997 Sheffield Academic Press

Published by Sheffield Academic Press Ltd
Mansion House
19 Kingfield Road
Sheffield S11 9AS
England

Typeset by Sheffield Academic Press
and
Printed on acid-free paper in Great Britain
by Bookcraft Ltd
Midsomer Norton, Bath

British Library Cataloguing in Publication Data

A catalogue record for this book is available
from the British Library

ISBN 1-85075-673-2
ISBN 1-85075-817-4 pbk

Contents

Preface

In previous publications on Acts, I offered detailed examinations of a few selected passages: a book-length treatment of the Philip material in 6.1-7, 8.4-40, and 21.8-14 (*The Portrait of Philip in Acts*, 1992); and related articles probing more fully the roles of 'Neglected Widows in Acts 6.1-7' (1994) and 'The Ethiopian Eunuch and his Bible' in 8.25-40 (1992). Each of these studies reflected a central concern to interpret particular texts of Acts in the light of both their wider Lukan narrative context and their sociocultural setting in the first-century eastern Mediterranean world. The current project afforded a welcome opportunity to extend such analysis to the whole book, to track the 'socio-literary' contours of the entire Acts journey from station to station rather than from intermittent vantage points.

In pursuing this reading adventure, I have benefited immeasurably from numerous expert guides, acknowledged in the bibliography, who have made their way through Acts before me. I owe particular thanks to Bruce Malina, Jerome Neyrey and other members of 'The Social Sciences and New Testament Interpretation' Task Force of the Catholic Biblical Association for their trailblazing cartography of the social world of Luke–Acts, and their gracious hospitality towards me as a fellow traveller. As a grateful 'client-friend', I hope that the present reading of Acts, with all its shortcomings, will 'honor' these scholars in some measure.

I am also indebted to Wingate University for supporting this project through the James L. and Christine McMillan Spivey Instructorship, a Jessie Ball duPont Summer Research Grant, and a Spring semester sabbatical. Along the way I received valuable encouragement from several colleagues in the university, especially from Provost Bill Christie; Jerry, Byrns, and Edwin in the Religion Department; Bob and John in English; and historian 'Father Dominic' across the hall. I was also stimulated by many fruitful exchanges with Wingate students in advanced seminars on Luke and Acts.

I have enjoyed lecturing on Acts in several area churches, including First Baptist Church and St Paul's Episcopal Church in Monroe, North Carolina; St John's Baptist Church and Sardis Baptist Church in Charlotte, North Carolina; and First Baptist Church in Pageland, South Carolina. Thanks to each of these congregations for their warm receptions.

It has been a pleasure once again to work with the editorial team at Sheffield Academic Press. Special thanks go to David Clines, for first inviting me to contribute to the *Readings* series, and to John Jarick (series general editor) and Eric Christianson (production editor) for superintending the commentary's final publication.

Scriptural citations come primarily from the New Revised Standard Version of the Bible (NRSV) and the twenty-sixth edition of the *Novum Testamentum Graece*.

Finally, words cannot express how much I appreciate the understanding and support, both personal and intellectual, of my wife and colleague, Dr Janet M. Spencer, who was busy completing her own work on Shakespeare's history plays as I was writing mine on Luke's dramatic history of the early church. Our two daughters, Lauren Michael and Meredith Leigh, also deserve special mention for putting up with our scholarly preoccupations, enriching our lives in countless ways, and keeping our feet on the ground. Some of my happiest hours have been spent reading and discussing books with them. Appropriately, then, I dedicate this 'reading' of Acts to my bibliophile daughters, in the hope that they might be not only readers, but prophetic speakers of the word, as Acts envisions (2.17).

F. Scott Spencer
Wingate University
Wingate, North Carolina

Abbreviations

BAGD	W. Bauer, W.F. Arndt, F.W. Gingrich and F.W. Danker, *Greek-English Lexicon of the New Testament*
Bib	*Biblica*
BTB	*Biblical Theology Bulletin*
CBQ	*Catholic Biblical Quarterly*
Int	*Interpretation*
JBL	*Journal of Biblical Literature*
JSNTSup	*Journal for the Study of the New Testament*, Supplement Series
NICNT	New International Commentary on the New Testament
SBLDS	SBL Dissertation Series
SBLMS	SBL Monograph Series
SecCent	*Second Century*
SNTSMS	Society for New Testament Studies Monograph Series

Introduction

The book of Acts presents a dynamic story of the spread of the Christian gospel from Jerusalem to Rome, propelled by the earliest followers of the risen and ascended Jesus in the power of the Holy Spirit. Its traditional designation—'The Acts of the Apostles'—accentuates the mighty *deeds* (acts) performed by an esoteric circle of *twelve* eyewitnesses (apostles) to the ministry and resurrection of Jesus (see 1.1-26; 2.42-43; 3.1-10; 4.33; 5.12-16). But such is not the whole story. The *words* of Jesus' witnesses, implicitly identified with the very 'word of God' (4.31; 6.2, 7; 8.14; 12.24) and crystallized into several extended *speeches* (e.g. 1.15-22; 2.14-40; 3.12-26; 4.8-12), are just as important as their acts, if not more so, in advancing the Christian mission. And as the story unfolds, various missionary-prophets, powerful in both word and deed *outside* the nucleus of the Twelve (e.g. Stephen, Philip, Barnabas and Paul), also play key roles by complementing and even surpassing (in Paul's case) the contributions of the earliest apostles. Moreover, guiding and energizing all missionary endeavor in the book of Acts is the figure of the Holy Spirit, arguably the chief protagonist in the narrative (see Shepherd). Not a few readers have suggested 'The Acts of the Holy Spirit' as a more apt title for this work.

Despite its size (28 chapters, ranking with Matthew and Luke as one of the longest New Testament books), uniqueness (unlike the Gospels, there is no collection of synoptic Acts), and lively, entertaining plot, the book of Acts has often been brushed over or even brushed off by Christian readers. Witness the report of the early church father, John Chrysostom (c. 347–407) concerning the reception of the 'strange and new dish' of Acts in his day: 'Certainly there are many to whom this book is not even known, and many again think it so plain that they slight it. Thus to some their ignorance, to others their knowledge is the cause of the neglect' (cited in Parsons and Pervo, *Rethinking*, p. 1). In the modern world, many Christians, both devout and nominal, also pay little mind to Acts. Certainly Acts receives short shrift in comparison with the higher profile Gospel narratives in both the church's lectionary and the secular press. (There is nothing like a titillating 'Acts Seminar' to rival the splash of the 'Jesus Seminar' in the US media.) Other Christians, more familiar with the content of Acts, effectively dismiss the book or relegate it to secondary status, mostly for its treatment of Paul, which fails to measure up, in their estimation, to his more robust self-image and deeper theological insight reflected in his own writings. Partly, then, Acts suffers in popularity precisely because of its uniqueness: it is not a Jesus narrative or a Pauline letter.

Still, in other quarters of the contemporary church—indeed, among those groups growing at the fastest rate—the book of Acts is alive and well and highly valued. Evangelical and charismatic believers throughout the world typically find in Acts an inspired blueprint for authentic Christianity. They nostalgically and zealously examine this work with the aim of recreating its portrait of the primitive church (getting back to the 'original' model), especially the aggressive pursuit of new converts (evangelism) and the dynamic experience of prophetic and wonder-working gifts of the Spirit (*charismata*).

The present reading is targeted for a broader audience, that is, for any serious student, Christian or not, seeking to gain a satisfying, although by no means exhaustive, understanding of the overall narrative of Acts in light of recent academic scholarship. While not aiming to proselytize readers into some form of modern Acts-style disciple, I do hope to win some sympathy for Acts as a volume worth investigating, partly for *cultural* reasons—enhancing our acquaintance with the first-century church in the Mediterranean world as well as helping us to appreciate and evaluate a thriving segment of the contemporary global church heavily influenced by this book—and partly for *literary* reasons: this intriguing, spirited account of early Christian origins makes for 'a good read'.

To prepare us for encountering Acts, we must position this particular reading in relation to current reading trends in professional biblical study. Before that, however, it will be useful to provide a brief sketch concerning what we know—and do not know—concerning the *writing* of the book we are about to read.

I. The Writing of Acts

The Author: Who Wrote Acts?

Although the addressee is identified by name (Theophilus) in the preface to Acts, the writer appears only as the anonymous 'I'. This anonymity continues throughout the balance of the work; as with his name, we learn nothing about the writer's appearance, family, occupation, or any other biographical details. The preface does disclose something, however, about the author, namely that he has written a previous treatise ('the first book') for the same addressee concerning 'all that Jesus did and taught from the beginning' (1.1). Almost certainly this former publication was the Gospel of Luke, also composed for 'Theophilus' (Lk. 1.3) and recounting the actions and teachings of Jesus of Nazareth ('a prophet mighty in deed and word', Lk. 24.19).

Since the Third Gospel is also anonymous, we still know very little about the particular identity of the author of Acts. Early tradition attributed both volumes to a physician named 'Luke' cited as a 'beloved' co-worker in Paul's letters (Col. 4.14; 2 Tim. 4.11; Phlm. 24). But the name 'Luke' never surfaces in this Gospel or Acts, and attempts to uncover specialized medical language in these works redolent of a surgeon's touch have failed to convince. (For convenience I will refer to Luke and Acts as the 'Lukan' narratives or writings, without assuming Dr Luke's authorship.)

Positing some association with Paul is more plausible. Following the preface, the body of Acts is narrated mostly from a distant third-person viewpoint. But at a few intermittent points in the latter half of the work (16.10-17; 20.6-15; 21.1-16; 27.1–28.16), a more intimate first-person perspective re-emerges, but now as 'we' (the plural form). Consistently this 'we'-company appears alongside Paul during some segment of his missionary journeys. A sober conclusion arising from this data suggests that the author of Acts, belonging to this occasional 'we'-party, was a 'peripheral participant' (Kurz, *Reading*, pp. 121-23) or 'sometime companion' (Fitzmyer) during the Pauline travels which he reports.

The Genre: How Was Acts Written?

In the preface to Luke's Gospel, the writer claims to have sifted carefully all available traditions handed down from eyewitnesses in composing his own 'orderly account' of events (Lk. 1.1-4). There is little doubt that in Acts the writer also utilized others' sources in producing his 'history' of the early church. The problem comes in determining precisely what those sources were and how they were redacted (edited) and incorporated into the final form of the book of Acts. We have no other extant versions of the same material with which to compare Acts' account as a basis for making hypotheses concerning layers of tradition, as with the Jesus-traditions in the synoptic Gospels. There is some apparent overlap between events reported in Acts and the letters of Paul (such as the 'Jerusalem Conference' in Acts 15 and Galatians 2), but such links are sporadic and reported in very different forms. Another impediment to distinguishing between source and redaction in Acts is the pervasive (albeit not perfect) thematic and stylistic unity which the material evinces. The speeches, for example, sound strikingly similar chords regardless of speaker or setting (see Soards).

Almost as frustrating as the search for discrete sources underlying Acts has been the quest for an overall literary model (genre) shaping its composition. Here, however, the nature of the problem is quite different. Rather than facing a dearth of comparative materials, scholars struggle to position Acts within a wide range of ancient Jewish and Greco-Roman literature. Amidst this embarrassment of riches a variety of theories have been spawned, classifying Acts alternately as a type of historical monograph (like Sallust's Roman history), a biblical history (like that of the Deuteronomist), an apologetic history (like Josephus's *Antiquities*), a biographical succession narrative (like Diogenes

Laertius's *Lives*), or a popular romance or novel (like Chariton's *Chaereas and Callirhoe*). The push to fit Acts into one of these slots—and in some cases to fit in the Lukan Gospel along with it—has fostered considerable debate, but little consensus (see Powell, *What Are They Saying*, pp. 5-13; Parsons and Pervo, *Rethinking*, pp. 20-44; and articles by Palmer, Alexander, Rosner and Marshall in Winter and Clarke, *Ancient Literary Setting*, pp. 1-82, 163-82). This state of affairs is hardly surprising, given the inevitable 'flexibility of and overlap between all the genres we or the ancients discern' (Downing, p. 99) and Acts' distinctive packaging (*sui generis*) of literary styles and conventions—even differing in certain respects from the preceding Lukan volume. Whereas the Gospel presents a more episodic series of events punctuated by numerous aphorisms and parables of Jesus, Acts unfolds more smoothly as a continuous narrative featuring extended journeys and developed discourses by Jesus' followers.

The Canon: Where Does Acts Fit in the Bible?
The content of Acts compels us to correlate this work with three other biblical writings: (a) the Jewish scriptures, especially the Greek version known as the Septuagint or LXX (the version of the 'seventy' supposed translators); (b) the Gospel of Luke; and (c) the Pauline letters.

(a) While we can only speculate concerning the sources of particular events reported in Acts, we know that much of the speech material derives from the Jewish scriptures. Throughout Acts, from the first chapter (1.20) to the last (28.25-27), clear citations appear from each of the major divisions of the biblical canon (cf. Lk. 24.44): *law* (e.g. Acts 3.22-23; Deut. 18.15-20), *prophets* (e.g. Acts 28.25-27; Isa. 6.9-10) and *psalms* (e.g. Acts 1.20; Ps. 69.25; 109.8). The speeches of Stephen and Paul in Acts 7 and 13 respectively, are predominantly rehearsals of biblical history. In the narrative segments as well as the speeches of Acts, scholars have detected the broad influence of scriptural patterns, such as the rejected-prophet or suffering-servant motif (Moessner), the faithful prophet vs. tyrannical king conflict (Darr, pp. 155-68), and the Elijah-Elisha template (Brodie; Evans). In short, as John Darr comments, the book of Acts (along with the Lukan Gospel) 'is saturated with the language, imagery, settings, and flavor of the Septuagint (LXX). It is hard to find a part of Luke's narrative that has not been affected by this intertextual linkage' (p. 28).

(b) Granting that the author of Acts formerly wrote the Gospel of Luke, questions still remain regarding the precise relationship between the two volumes. We have already suggested certain generic distinctions in how the two narratives are presented. What about the thematic and plot connections between the stories which they tell? Do they relate one continuous, unified story, a two-act drama, the story of 'Luke–Acts'? Or is Acts a more loosely-linked, self-contained sequel to the Gospel, written on a later occasion, having separate as well as shared interests with its predecessor? The emphasis in Acts 1 on furthering the global missionary agenda of the risen-ascended Jesus announced in the last chapter of Luke and the obvious characterization of the leading witnesses in Acts to match the profile of the Lukan Jesus (see Talbert) argue in favor of Acts as a direct extension of the Gospel: what 'Jesus did and taught from the beginning' in the first book (Acts 1.1) is now continued through Jesus' followers in the second volume (see Marshall, 'Acts'). On the other hand, in favor of 'loosening the hyphen' in Luke–Acts (see Parsons and Pervo, *Rethinking*), we must appreciate that we have no record of conjoining the two works in any canonical list (in the modern canon they are separated by the Gospel of John); that each work stands on its own as a complete narrative (distinct reports of the ascension both conclude Luke's Gospel and introduce Acts); and that differences as well as similarities emerge in the portraits of the Lukan Jesus and the Acts missionaries (for example, the 'high-society' image of Paul, which stands at odds with Jesus' profile; see Lentz). While the two Lukan volumes may be profitably correlated, specific links must be demonstrated rather than assumed and distinctive nuances appreciated rather than flattened.

(c) The large role Paul plays in Acts and the likelihood of the author's at least passing acquaintance with this historical figure invite a comparison with Paul's letters. As noted above, some see the Paul of Acts as an unfortunate distortion of the 'real' Paul. Others, however, view Acts as offering a distinctive, but complementary, portrait of Paul by no means inconsistent with his own writings. Strong emphases in Acts on Paul's reputation as a powerful worker of miracles, a friend of social elites and a gracious compromiser with traditional Jewish believers do sound very different tones from the 'weak' servant of the Corinthian correspondence in conflict with the 'super-apostles' and from the radical freedom-fighter of Galatians. But strains of Paul's suffering as the righteous servant of the Lord and his vigorous law-free mission to the Gentiles also come through loud and clear in Acts, quite consonant with the epistolary image. Differences in genre again complicate comparative analysis: crafted narratives about Paul's missions in Philippi, Thessalonica and Corinth (Acts 16-18), as part of a larger narrative framework, can be expected to offer a rather distinct perspective from Paul's own occasional letters to the Philippians, Thessalonians and Corinthians, dealing with specific issues at particular historical moments (Wenham, pp. 257). At no point does Acts offer a direct quotation from Paul's letters. Whether and to what extent the author of Acts was familiar with Paul's writings at any level remains a matter of conjecture. Bearing these problems in mind, an exploration of intertextual links between Acts and the Pauline letters can still prove to be illuminating. Again, rather than assuming wholesale harmony or dissonance, each comparative case must be carefully judged on its own merits (see the full discussion in Wenham).

The Date: When Was Acts Written?

Since the story breaks off with Paul's imprisonment in Rome, a few scholars argue that Acts must have been written shortly before his martyrdom in that city at the hands of Nero (c. 64 CE). This assumes, of course, that the author was providing an up-to-the-minute account of early Christian history. Most scholars, however, judging Acts to be a more selective and reflective look back on the impact of Paul's mission, place the book a generation after Paul's death, in the closing decades of the first century; some time after the destruction of Jerusalem and its temple in 70 CE—the memory of which seems to underlie the rhetoric of Stephen's speech in Acts (7.44-50) and several texts in Luke (13.33-35; 19.41-44; 21.5-6, 20-24; 23.27-31) (cf. Tannehill, *Narrative*, II, pp. 92-96)—and before the letters of Paul, which Acts does not allude to, were collected and circulated close to the end of the century. (It has even been suggested that the publication of Acts sparked the collection of Paul's writings.)

The Audience: For Whom Was Acts Written?

The reference to a specific addressee—Theophilus—does not take us very far in determining the audience of Acts. Outside his name, we know next to nothing about Theophilus' identity. The Lukan preface applies to him the same honorific title—'most excellent' (*kratistos*)—that Acts attaches to successive Roman governors of Judea, Felix and Festus, stationed in Caesarea (23.26; 24.3; 26.25). But this broad appellation was scarcely definitive of any particular office; it could easily apply to a variety of persons of some social distinction. In any case, if Theophilus did hold some key political post, we are not told what or where that might have been.

Whatever his identity, it is also unclear how Theophilus relates to the wider audience of Luke and Acts. His appearance in the prefaces of the two works may reflect nothing more than a formal acknowledgement of his literary patronage. While he would thus be expected to endorse the project on some level, he would not necessarily be typical of the original readers. From the internal evidence of the Lukan narratives, Philip Esler has surmised that the intended community of readers was a mixed lot both ethnically and economically, comprised of both Jewish and Gentile believers (including Jewish-sympathizing Greeks) both 'from the glittering elite and from the squalid urban poor' (p. 221). However, although each of these character groups—Jews and Gentiles, rich and poor—are featured in Luke and Acts, that does not guarantee that they represent mirror images of the first readers. Literary characters in the 'fictional' world of the story may or may not correspond in varying degrees to particular persons in the 'real' world. In the case of the Lukan narratives, the problem of matching specific characters and readers is heightened by the well-known universal focus on 'all' people as beneficiaries of God's salvation in Christ (e.g. Lk. 2.10, 30-32; 3.6; Acts 1.8; 2.17, 21, 38-39; 10.34-36). While it may be interesting and fruitful to read the Lukan story from the perspective of one or more of its characters—as Robert Tannehill has done with the Gospel from the viewpoints of 'Cornelius' and 'Tabitha' who appear in Acts—we must appreciate (as Tannehill does) that such a reader is an imaginative construct, plausibly suggestive of one type of first-century reader, but neither exhaustive of that type nor exclusive of others.

II. The Reading of Acts

Recent developments in the scholarly reading of Acts have followed two broad trends: one reflecting newer *literary-critical* concerns, the other *social-historical* interests. On the literary side, frustration with the traditional approach of mining Acts for underlying hypothetical sources and situations which then control interpretation of the text (the classic problem of circularity) has prompted a fresh focus on the text itself, in its final canonical form, and on strategies for reading this text drawn from secular narratological study (see Spencer, 'Acts'). Under the rubric of 'narrative' and/or 'reader response' criticism, this method has concentrated on explicating the developing *plot* of the Lukan story, the roles and relations of *characters*, both major and minor, within that story, and the connections among redundant literary *patterns*. Moreover, this approach pays special attention not only to the story's content, but also to various elements of its *discourse*—that is, *how* the story is presented rhetorically. On the whole, newer literary analyses of Luke and Acts—represented most fully by Robert Tannehill's landmark two-volume exposition of *The Narrative Unity of Luke-Acts*—treat these works together as one continuous, 'orderly' (Lk. 1.3), carefully crafted, tightly interwoven narrative. Thus the best commentary on Luke and Acts is *Luke-Acts*; intertextual parallels and sequences take precedence over extratextual comparisons and contrasts. Apparent breaks or gaps in the Acts story, which historical critics have typically exposed as 'seams' betraying the patchwork of discrete source and redactional materials, are deftly negotiated by narrative critics like Tannehill in the interest of depicting a coherent, consistent portrait.

In addition to exploring anew the narrative world of Acts, recent studies have also canvassed the first-century social-historical world of Acts in light of new discoveries and methodologies. More than antiquarian curiosity is at work here. The basic assumption is that no modern reader can hope to interpret Acts adequately without gaining a competent understanding of the ancient milieu in which the text was originally embedded. Increasingly, scholars have stressed that such an understanding stretches beyond a passing acquaintance with certain major political figures and events to which Acts refers, to a deeper familiarity with pervasive cultural (familial, environmental, ethnic, economic, symbolic, religious) patterns and values which Acts takes for granted. By necessity, the pursuit of this 'assumed knowledge' has led biblical scholars into fruitful dialogue with scholars from other disciplines.

One approach, reflected in the massive, six-volume project on *The Book of Acts in its First-Century Setting* edited by Bruce Winter, brings biblical critics together with ancient classical historians to illuminate many facets of the Jewish and Greco-Roman environment encompassing Acts. Particular energy is devoted to providing a 'thick description' of everyday social and cultural life in Mediterranean antiquity, drawn from a wide range of available literary, epigraphic, and archaeological data pertaining to such issues as 'transport and travel, roads, religion, urban élites, food supply and housing' (covered in Part 1 of volume II on *The Book of Acts in its Graeco-Roman Setting*, ed. Gill and Gempf).

Another approach, reflected in the groundbreaking collection of essays edited by Jerome Neyrey on *The Social World of Luke–Acts*, utilizes the methods and models of cultural anthropologists and other social scientists to produce typical 'scripts' or 'scenarios' of the core systems and values governing first-century, eastern Mediterranean society. Such scenarios include (a) the construction of personal identity in exclusively 'dyadic' or group-oriented terms relative to one's standing within kinship, patron-client, and other social networks, (b) the prevailing struggle within a 'limited goods' context to assert and defend one's honor in the public arena (and thereby avoid shame), and (c) the regulation of eating habits and other bodily activities along lines of 'purity' and 'pollution' to reflect vital social boundaries in the body politic. Since the book of Acts was originally written for readers immersed in this peculiar 'symbolic universe', a 'considerate reading' of Acts in the modern world requires our apprehending the alien codes and concepts which it assumes (see Malina, 'Reading').

While many Lukan and other biblical scholars have increasingly welcomed these newer literary-critical and social-historical methods over the past decade, some have cast a more wary eye. We have already noted the caution of Parsons and Pervo against presuming a facile generic and narrative unity between Luke and Acts. Proponents of various 'postmodern' perspectives have launched a more pointed critique of narrative criticism's preoccupation with textual unity and coherence. Stephen Moore, for example, contends that for all their supposed dependence upon contemporary literary theory, biblical narrative critics like Tannehill are most indebted to the formalistic 'New Criticism' of the 1940s and 1950s, which is scarcely 'new' any longer; in fact, recent literary study driven by 'deconstructive' and other 'poststructuralist' methodologies has reacted strongly against New Criticism's quest for thematic unity and poetic design in favor of more pluriform, destabiliz-ing, even subversive readings of texts (Moore, pp. 51-55). In their 1993 study of *Narrative in the Hebrew Bible*, David Gunn and Danna Nolan Fewell have expressly adopted this more radical approach:

> [W]e understand texts to be inherently unstable, since they contain within themselves the threads of their own unravelling... 'Decon-structive' criticism seeks to expound the gaps, the silences, the con-tradictions, which inhabit all texts, like loose threads in a sweater, waiting to be pulled (p. 10).

Concerning matters of social context, scholars from various ideologi-cal viewpoints argue that investigations of the social world of the origi-nal readers of ancient texts like Acts must be balanced by honest appraisals of the social locations and agendas of *contemporary* readers as well. As much as we may claim to distance ourselves from the inter-pretive process in the interest of producing 'objective', 'scientific' social-historical readings of ancient literature, we inevitably import our own prejudices, questions, and experiences into the process. There are no purely disinterested readings. Better, then, to lay one's interests on the table, as Ivoni Richter Reimer does in her careful social-historical study of *Women in the Acts of the Apostles*:

> Social-historical exegesis is thus an interdisciplinary effort that draws information from other fields of scholarship with two purposes in view: first, to tell the biblical story more vividly, and second, by means of these vivid and concrete biblical truths to supply people, in their present conditions of life, with strength to apply themselves on behalf of the reign of God... The present book attempts to reconstruct the various stories of women in the Acts of the Apostles from the perspective of Latin American liberation theology and its clarification through feminist liberation theology (p. xix).

III. This Reading of Acts

In articles on 'Neglected Widows in Acts 6.1-7' (1994) and 'The Ethiopian Eunuch and His Bible' in Acts 8.25-40 (1992), I endeavored to merge newer literary- and social-critical approaches to illuminate partic-ular characters and plot developments within Acts. The present reading aims to explicate the whole of Acts in light of these overlapping 'socio-literary' frameworks (cf. David Gowler's pioneering studies of the Pharisees in Luke and Acts from a 'socio-narratological' perspective [*Host*; 'Characterization']).

I embark on the reading of Acts as an *exploratory journey*, which seems to be an especially apt reading strategy for a book comprised of a series of missionary travel narratives. Literarily, I chart this reading journey step-by-step as it unfolds, paying special attention to the 'building' of characters (cf. Darr), the mounting and ebbing of conflict and suspense, the shifting of narrative viewpoints, and the fulfilling and frustrating of expectations created along the way. I maximize the element of discovery, approximating a first reading of the text and resisting the urge to peek ahead and foreclose the story's dramatic tension. This is by no means a 'naive' reading, however. I assume thorough prior knowledge of the preceding Lukan narrative (the Third Gospel) and of the Jewish scriptures in Greek (LXX) and regularly point out parallels and differences between Acts and these foundational documents. I also assume broad familiarity with the cultural codes and social-symbolic systems structuring the ancient Mediterranean world and frequently interpret scenes in Acts in light of typical first-century scenarios (for example, the conflict scenes as honor-shame contests).

A cursory reading of Acts may track a general missionary course (a) extending over a period of several years following Jesus' departure to heaven, (b) running through a number of eastern Mediterranean urban centers from Jerusalem to Rome, and (c) encountering many Jewish and Gentile respondents, both sympathetic and antagonistic. The present reading, however, conducts a more detailed, nuanced survey, mapping a variety of specific (a) *temporal*, (b) *spatial* and (c) *social* dimensions of each segment of the Acts journey. Such trifocal cartography is character-istic of both narrative criticism and social-science analysis in different ways. The former method, as sketched by Mark Alan Powell, seeks to place a literary scene within its temporal, spatial, and social 'setting' (*What Is Narrative Criticism?*, pp. 69-83), while the latter, as illustrated by Jerome Neyrey, delineates the standard 'maps of times, places, and persons' reflecting the cultural boundaries presumed in the text (Neyrey, 'Symbolic Universe' and 'Ceremonies'; cf. Rhoads).

As for the question of the unity and consistency of Acts, this commen-tary traces a number of recurring emphases, parallel events, and mimetic characters. A feeling of déjà vu regularly attends the traveller through Acts. But this is not to say we find ourselves running in monotonous cir-cles or drifting along dull, flat stretches where nothing much seems to change. While we encounter many similar situations, what often catches the eye is something new or different that develops within otherwise redundant scenes. While the path of the Christian gospel presses inex-orably out to the ends of the earth, it bogs down here and there in the face of stubborn opposition and takes several surprising twists and turns under the Spirit's spontaneous leadership. At times it even threatens to turn back on itself (deconstruct), as when Peter and the apostles appear reluctant to follow the Lukan Jesus' radical pattern of table-service (6.1-7) and table-fellowship (10.1–11.18) and when Paul curiously fusses and splits with his partner, Barnabas, just after winning a unanimous vote of confidence for their Gentile mission at an ecumenical council in

Jerusalem (15.36-40). In short, the dominant male heroes of Acts do not always appear so heroic.

What about the women of Acts? It has been commonplace to regard the Lukan writings as relatively supportive of women, due to the high percentage of female characters featured in these narratives, many of whom—especially in Acts—seem to be persons of some standing in the community. In recent years, however, feminist critics have argued that Luke and Acts present more of a 'double message' (Seim), if not an outright negative picture, concerning women's roles in the early church. Despite their high visibility, Lukan women are frequently subordinated to men, relegated to conventional domestic service, and rarely given a voice in community affairs (see D'Angelo; Seim; O'Day; Martin). These feminist-critical concerns have provoked me (as they have a growing company of other male scholars) to read Acts with greater precision and 'suspicion' regarding the characterization of women. For example, I am particularly interested in monitoring the extent to which the grand ideal of Spirit-inspired prophetic 'daughters' and 'maidservants' in Acts 2.17-18 is realized, modified, or nullified in the balance of the book.

Finally, some orientation must be provided to another sizeable character group encountered throughout Acts: 'the Jews'. In this post-Holocaust era, scholars have been rightly preoccupied with the treatment of Jews in the New Testament. A range of opinions have been offered on the Jewish question in the Lukan narratives (see Tyson), including the extreme position of J.T. Sanders, who views this material as representing thoroughgoing anti-Semitic propaganda. I follow the more moderate view that Acts paints a *mixed* portrait of the Jewish people. Many Jews welcome the witness of the early Christian missionaries, who themselves, after all, are Jewish disciples of the Jewish Jesus Messiah. In the context of Acts, I employ the term 'Christian' not to designate a separate religion over against Judaism but rather a messianic 'sect' (cf. 5.17; 15.5; 24.14; 26.5; 28.22) or movement within Judaism. The 'church' represents the community of believing disciples which may overlap with or be alienated from the synagogue, depending on the situation. Jewish opposition to Christian leaders—which can be severe—reflects in-house, intra-Jewish rivalry fomented typically by a cadre of temple or synagogue officials dubbed 'the Jews' in Acts, but not encompassing the whole Jewish populace. Counter-attacks—which can also be quite sharp—function much like the prophetic critiques of Israel's political and religious authorities in the Jewish scriptures. (Indeed prophetic texts are often cited in these attacks.)

To be sure, the influx of Gentiles threatens to pull the church apart from its Jewish roots. But such a break is decidedly resisted in Acts, as evidenced in key conciliatory summits in Jerusalem between James, the leader of Jewish disciples in Judea, and Paul, the chief architect of the Gentile mission in the Diaspora (see chs. 15, 21). The challenge to modern Gentile readers of Acts in a predominantly Gentile Christian context is to appreciate the cultural mix of Jews and Gentiles in the believing communities of Acts and the profile of many Gentile Christians—of whom Cornelius is the most outstanding example (10.1-48)—as 'God-fearing' devotees of Judaism both before and after their faith and baptism in the name of Jesus Messiah.

Acts 1-2: Orientation: The Journey Begins

Extraordinary events occurring in or near the city of Jerusalem on two momentous days inaugurate the journey through Acts and intimate the adventures which lie ahead for the alert reader-explorer. Both of these days became significant fixtures on the Christian calendar as a result of the unique New Testament reports presented in Acts 1-2. The first holy-day—*Ascension*—comes forty days after the resurrection of Jesus on 'the first day of the week' (Acts 1.3; Lk. 24.1). Although the narration of the ascension event is confined to a brief report in 1.9-11, references to 'the day he was taken up' appear before and after (vv. 2, 22) and tie the whole first chapter together around the ascension axis. The second banner day—*Pentecost*—marks a revitalized celebration of an annual Jewish harvest festival set, as its name suggests, on the 'fiftieth' day after the first day of Passover (cf. Lev. 23.15-21; Deut. 16.9-12; Tob. 2.1; *Ant.* 3.252; *War* 2.42). This festival provides the temporal setting for the entire narrative in 2.1-41 (cf. framing time-notes: 'the day', v. 1; 'that day', v. 41). It also signals the commencement of dynamic communal life which the fledgling Jerusalem church continues to enjoy 'day by day' following Pentecost (2.42-47).

Although in terms of 'real' chronology several days separate Ascension and Pentecost, in the 'story time' of Acts these two days are more directly connected both structurally and thematically. Structurally, the accounts of these days' activities are closely juxtaposed: only four verses separate 'the day he was taken up' in 1.22 and 'the day of Pente-cost' in 2.1; and thematically, the two narratives exhibit a number of common, interlocking features:

(1) Unusual manifestations of natural and celestial phenomena attend both days' events: a cloud and white-robed messengers usher Jesus *up into heaven* (*eis ton ouranon*, 1.10-11), and mighty gusts of wind and tongues of fire accompany the Spirit's outpouring *down from heaven* (*ek tou ouranou*, 2.2).

(2) The two narratives are also linked in a pattern of *prophecy* (1.4-5, 8) and *fulfillment* (2.1-13, 17-18), focusing on the effusion of the Spirit as a catalyst for inspired proclamation of 'God's deeds of power' (2.11).

(3) Both reports call attention to the *Galilean* provenance of the first disciples of Jesus (1.11; 2.7) who play a leading role in each day's events set in the heart of *Judean* territory (cf. 1.8; 2.14). Counterbalancing this emphasis on regional identity, however, is a universal dimension in both scenes, projecting a global extension of the gospel well beyond Judean

and Galilean borders: 'to the ends of the earth' (1.8) and 'every nation under heaven' (2.5).

(4) In both chapters, the twelve apostles emerge as the principal leaders of the earliest congregation of Jesus' followers in Jerusalem, with Peter as their chief spokesman (1.2, 13, 15-26; 2.14, 37, 42-43). However, each story surrounding Ascension and Pentecost also makes a point of enumerating the membership of the whole community (120/3000; 1.15/2.41) and disclosing the participation of all believers—including women—in decision-making and ministries of prayer, prophecy and charity (1.14, 23-26; 2.17-18, 44-45).

The Day of Ascension: 1.1-26

The first chapter, revolving around the day of Ascension, begins to define the group which will undertake the ensuing journey through Acts. The twelve apostles of Jesus are clearly slated to play a major role, but what about Jesus himself? The opening section in 1.1-11 climaxes with Jesus' dramatic *departure* from earth in full gaze of the apostles, raising important questions about who will now guide them along the Way. The concluding section in 1.12-26 reports another notable absence—this time within the ranks of the Twelve—prompting a necessary ('must' [*dei*], 1.16, 21-22) *regrouping* of personnel before the journey can proceed.

Departing: 1.1-11

In the opening paragraph (1.1-5), the narrator situates the starting-point of the Acts journey within three distinct time-frames:

(1) The beginning of Acts is presented not as an isolated new moment but rather as the next 'act' in a sweeping drama of salvation history, encompassing up to this point 'all' of Jesus' words and deeds until the day of his departure (1.1). This prior story of Jesus' ministry is published in a first volume which came to be known as the Gospel of Luke, dedicated to the same auditor and (perhaps) patron, Theophilus (cf. Lk. 1.1-4).

(2) The opening of Acts is also linked more narrowly to the immediate past period of *forty days* since Jesus' resurrection (1.3). Interestingly, this period marks a considerable extension of the temporal frame suggested in the final chapter of Luke's Gospel. There, Jesus' resurrection and appearances to his disciples are narrated at some length but compressed temporally into *one* very full day (cf. Lk. 24.1, 13, 29, 36). At the close of the chapter, Jesus' departure is recounted much more briefly but seems to be set at the end of the same day (24.50-51). In Acts 1, the prolonged duration of the period of Jesus' post-resurrection appearances (forty days) is accompanied by an attenuated, generalized description of these events (1.3). The reality of the period of Jesus' abiding presence with his disciples is emphasized here; exactly what the risen Jesus said

or did is not as important at this stage as the simple fact that Jesus stayed long enough among his followers to nurture, instruct and prepare them adequately for their upcoming mission (Tannehill, *Narrative*, II, p. 10). As for Jesus' departure, Acts elevates its importance by giving it its own day—indeed, the climactic day of Jesus' post-resurrection epiphanies—and by dramatizing it as a visible heavenly assumption. (This assumption is entirely unique to Acts 1.9-11 if 'carried into heaven' is a later gloss to Lk. 24.51, as Parsons argues, *Departure*, pp. 29-52.)

The forty-day period also connects the beginning of Acts with the scriptural story of God's dealings with Israel. During the Israelites' wilderness trek from Egypt to the promised land, Moses was 'taken up' to Mt Sinai for forty days of fasting and receiving the Lord's commandments for his people (Exod. 24.18; 34.27-28; Deut. 9.9-11; 10.10; cf. 1 Kgs 19.8; 2 Esdr. 14.37-48). The Lukan Jesus reprised part of this Mosaic role at the outset of his ministry, fasting in the wilderness for forty days and overcoming temptation by citing Deuteronomic teaching (Lk. 4.1-2, 4, 8, 12). In the final stage of the earthly sojourn leading up to his ascension, the risen Jesus again acts like Moses by issuing commandments (*enteilamenos*) to his apostles over a forty-day span. Here, however, important differences in location and action also emerge: Jesus is not isolated in the desert nor is he reported to be fasting. In fact, Acts 1.4 suggests that Jesus instructs his followers while 'eating with them' (*synalizomai*, lit. 'sharing salt together'; cf. Lk. 24.36-48; Acts 10.41). Jesus' last days on earth are spent in communion, not isolation; celebration, not deprivation—bolstering his disciples for the mission they will carry out in his (physical) absence.

(3) The final time-frame in the opening paragraph of Acts shifts from the distant and immediate past to the imminent future: 'you will be baptized with the Holy Spirit not many days from now' (1.5). Spiritual direction for the apostles will not cease with Jesus' departure. The same Spirit which inspired the teaching of the risen Jesus (1.2) will soon envelop Jesus' followers and continue to enlighten and equip them for ministry. This promise of the Spirit's descent is reiterated in 1.8 and fulfilled in the dramatic story in 2.1-41, set in Jerusalem at Pentecost.

The Jerusalem venue for the initial outpouring of the Spirit is already mandated by Jesus in 1.4. The earliest followers of Jesus must not bolt back to their Galilean homesteads, but rather tarry in the holy city (cf. Lk. 24.49). Although Jerusalem has recently spurned Israel's Spirit-anointed messiah, this most hallowed center of divine encounter since the Davidic period will still be the site for a new manifestation of God's Spirit and revitalization of God's people.

The relationship between the community of Jesus' followers and the nation of Israel centered in Jerusalem is developed more fully in 1.6-11, sparked by the disciples' urgent query regarding the restoration of Israel's kingdom (1.6). Restoration hopes were deeply rooted in classical prophecies of Israel's future and closely tied to the sacred space of Jerusalem/Zion. A typical perspective on the climactic 'days to come' (or 'that day') envisioned the mass return of scattered Israelites to the holy city/mount and establishment of a glorious new Israelite kingdom governed in peace and righteousness. This scenario also projected that the Gentile nations would concurrently stream to Jerusalem and acknowledge the sovereignty of Israel and her God, either voluntarily converting to Yahweh's ways (Isa. 2.2-4; Mic. 4.1-8; Zech. 8.20-23) or forcibly being brought to submission on the battlefield (Joel 3; Zech. 12.8-9; 14.1-3; cf. Psalm 2).

In the Persian period, dreams of exiles returning to the promised land and rebuilding the Jerusalem temple began to be fulfilled; but in the minds of many Israelites the prophetic vision was never fully realized in the Second Temple era. For example, the concluding message of the book of Tobit features a pious Galilean forecasting the glorious exaltation of Jerusalem and renovation of the *second* temple 'when the times of fulfillment shall come', accompanied by a great influx of Diaspora Israelites and Gentiles from the 'ends of the earth' who 'will all be converted and worship God in truth' (Tob. 13.1-14.7; cf. Sir. 36.1-17; Bar. 4.5-5.9; *Pss. Sol.* 11.1-9; 17.21-46).

Against this backdrop, the question of the Galilean apostles in Acts 1.6 reflects their anticipation that the 'time of fulfillment' had finally dawned with the resurrection of Jesus or, more precisely, that the risen Jesus was the divinely-appointed agent now poised to bring about the eschatological restoration of Israel. Jesus' response in 1.7-8 is both affirmative and corrective. On the one hand, Jesus does not deny that God's purposes for Israel have been significantly advanced through his own ministry, passion, and resurrection, and, indeed, he reminds the apostles that his mission is about to be capped by a mighty renewal of God's people through Spirit-baptism (1.8; cf. 1.5).

In other respects, however, Jesus reconfigures his disciples' conventional expectations. *Temporally*, he puts off the apostles and begins to open their minds to fresh perspectives on God's dealings with Israel. The precise timetable for Israel's salvation—set exclusively by the Father—remains outside their knowledge (1.7). What is also unknown to the apostles (or at least not fully acknowledged) is the *spatial* dimension of their involvement in God's kingdom, which Jesus now discloses. Rather than sinking roots in Jerusalem and waiting for the world to flood *in*, Jesus' followers are to move *out* from Jerusalem, through Judea and Samaria, and ultimately 'to the ends of the earth' (1.8). The flow is centrifugal instead of centripetal; the apostles are just beginning their journey, not ending it. And what will be the nature of this journey? Yet again Jesus redirects a typical line of thinking: he launches a mission of Spirit-motivated 'witness' and conversion, not nationalistic warfare and conquest.

After mapping the coming (down) of the Spirit and going (out) of the apostles, Jesus is lifted *up* in a cloud and taken out of sight (1.9-11). His followers are transfixed by this celestial spectacle until two white-robed messengers (Moses and Elijah?, cf. Lk. 9.28-33; angels?, cf. 24.4, 23) suddenly appear on the scene. In question form, these two 'men' challenge the skygazing preoccupation of the 'men of Galilee', implicitly reorienting them to their urgent task of going and telling about, rather than standing and looking at, the risen Jesus.

As for Jesus' destination, the narrative accentuates through repetition the fact that he has been transported 'into heaven' (*eis ton ouranon*, twice: 1.11). His disciples, of course, remain earthbound, indeed specifically commissioned to traverse all of earth's territory. Thus it may appear that Jesus and his followers are now heading in polar opposite directions. But in fact, Lukan cosmology, while generally dualistic, allows for periodic intersection between heavenly (holy, God-ruled) and earthly (evil, Satan-dominated) realms. For example, the heavens 'opened' to Jesus at his baptism, from which he received the power of the Spirit and assurance of the Father to defeat the devil and fulfill his earthly messianic mission (Lk. 3.21-22; 4.1-18). In the present text, complementing the two references to Jesus' departure 'into heaven' is a double mention of the disciples' peering 'into heaven' (*eis ouranon*, 1.10, 11). To be sure, they catch only a glimpse, nothing like the elaborate visions witnessed by certain apocalyptic seers on guided tours of the heavenly world. But in this glimpse the disciples receive a vital sign of heavenly blessing on their impending tour of duty throughout the earth, a sign soon to become reality in the Spirit's mighty rush 'from heaven' on Pentecost (2.2). Moreover, a parting word from the two white-clad attendants discloses that Jesus himself is destined to appear again on the earthly stage (1.11). The ascension marks an important shift in Jesus' relationship to the world, but not the end. Departure does not mean abandonment.

Regrouping: 1.12-26

In the wake of Jesus' departure, his followers must deal with the pressing business of regrouping as a cohesive community and mobilizing for their assigned mission. A variety of spatial, temporal and social factors structure the initial phase of this enterprise in 1.12-26.

Topographically, the journey begins to revolve around three 'high' points proximate to Jerusalem: two—Mt Olivet, just outside the city limits, and 'the room upstairs' within the city—are explicitly mentioned, and the other—the temple mount—is implied by association (1.12-13).

In certain Jewish circles *Mt Olivet* was envisioned as a base of operations for violent revolution against oppressive foreign kingdoms. For example, post-exilic Second Zechariah prophesied the Lord's mighty apocalyptic descent to the Mount of Olives, from where he would crush all the marauding nations gathered against Jerusalem (Zech. 14.1-4); and in the middle of the first century CE, a popular eschatological prophet from Egypt marshalled a sizeable Jewish mob at Mt Olivet, from where he planned (futilely, as it turned out) to launch a wall-smashing, Joshua-style invasion of Jerusalem to oust the Roman overlords and place himself in power (*Ant.* 20.169-71; *War* 2.261-63; cf. Acts 21.38; Horsley and Hanson, pp. 167-72). Such triumphal images of Olivet, however, are resisted in Luke and Acts. Jesus did make a grand entrance into the holy city from Mt Olivet, but he came weeping over Jerusalem's inevitable destruction, not warring against Rome's imperial rule (Lk. 19.28-44). And now in Acts 1, Mt Olivet provides the stage for Jesus' grand exit: his going up and away from the earthly arena instead of coming down to conquer as Zechariah predicted. While Jesus also dispatches his disciples from the mountain to the city, he sends them to wait for spiritual blessing, not to fight for political freedom.

Although not a center of resistance to the Roman garrison stationed in the Tower of Antonia, in the Lukan landscape Mt Olivet does represent a place of opposition to the Jewish religious establishment based in the *temple*. After approaching Jerusalem from Mt Olivet and weeping over the ill-fated city, Jesus headed directly to the temple to enact a provocative protest against the temple system (Lk. 19.45-47). During the ensuing week, Mt Olivet became the haven Jesus retreated to at night after tense days of teaching in the temple precincts amid mounting opposition from the priestly hierarchy (21.37–22.2); it was also a center of prayer for Jesus and his disciples (22.39-46), unlike the temple which Jesus regarded more as a 'den of robbers' than 'house of prayer' (19.46); and ultimately it marked the site of Jesus' betrayal by Judas and arrest by temple police, leading to his crucifixion (22.47-53).

In view of this background, it may seem strange, even foolish, for Jesus' disciples to leave the refuge of Olivet in Acts 1 and make their way back into the hostile environs of Jerusalem. But they do not initially 'go up' (*anabainō*) to the temple (cf. Lk. 18.10; Acts 3.1), the hub of official opposition to the Jesus movement. Rather they first 'go up' (*anabainō*) to an *upper room* (1.13), a secluded, relatively safe zone within the city, symbolically set apart once again from the threatening heights of the temple establishment. Earlier in the Lukan narrative, just after Judas had sealed the deal to betray Jesus to temple authorities (Lk. 22.1-6), Jesus and the apostles assembled in 'a large room upstairs' to share together their last Passover meal and the shocking revelation that a traitor was in their midst (22.7-23). Now in Acts, Jesus' followers gather again in a private loft—beyond the reach of temple rulers—to pray (the upper room is a true 'house of prayer', 1.14), replace Judas (1.15-26) and await the Spirit's arrival. This picture fits into a larger scenario in Luke–Acts, pitting the hospitable, honorable institution of the house/household (*oikos/oikia*) against a callous, discredited temple system (see Elliott and discussion below).

Beyond these spatial arrangements, the setting of 1.12-26 includes two temporal perspectives:

(1) The disciples' passage from Olivet to Jerusalem is measured as 'a sabbath day's journey' (1.12). The narrator thereby not only supplies information about the distance of this particular trip (about one-half mile) but, more importantly, orients the reader to the schedule governing the entire Acts journey. The clock is set to 'Jewish standard time', subjecting the travellers to the limits and opportunities of various fixed hours of prayer, days of consecration (such as the weekly sabbath) and seasons of pilgrimage and festivity.

(2) Membership in the apostolic circle is restricted to those who accompanied Jesus 'during all the time' of his earthly ministry, from the beginning at his baptism to the final 'day when he was taken up' (1.21-22). Once again, the narrator alludes to the previous account of 'all' (*pas*, cf. 1.1) that Jesus accomplished (Luke) as a key travel guide for the ensuing course of apostolic witness in Jesus' name (Acts).

The social structure of the developing Christian community may be glimpsed in the numerical groupings of 12 and 120 and the comparative characterizations of Peter, Judas, and 'certain women'.

The primary task of reorganization at this stage in Acts is filling the apostolic slot made vacant by Judas' recent apostasy. One and only one member must be 'added to the eleven apostles' (1.26), making the circle of *twelve* complete again. Within a Jewish context, the significance of such an action is obvious. The number twelve represents the whole nation of Israel under the ancestral headship of the twelve sons of Jacob/Israel. Thus the twelve apostles now take their place as appointed heads of a new Israelite kingdom inaugurated by Jesus and continuing to be restored after his departure (cf. Lk. 6.12-16; 22.28-30). The apostles' authority over the community is further certified by their priority listing *by name* before any other members (Acts 1.13) and by the size estimate of the larger congregation as a multiple of twelve (120; 1.15).

Still, certain elements within the narrative suggest a more inclusive, less hierarchical model of leadership and ministry. Although particular qualifications (male, early companion of Jesus) delimit the pool of apostolic candidates and only two candidates (Joseph and Matthias) are seriously considered, the final determination by *lottery* rather than fiat lends a degree of openness to the proceedings; theoretically, at least, anyone can draw the lucky number (Crossan, p. 73). Also, the process of selecting a new apostle is clearly a joint effort between the current apostles and the entire community. Although Peter emerges as the chief leader—beginning to fulfill Jesus' promise of rehabilitation in Lk. 22.31-32—he does not pontifically appoint Judas' replacement. After hearing Peter's guidelines, the *congregation*—'*they*'—propose the two candidates (contrast the Western text's '*he* proposed...', a correction designed to increase Peter's authority), cast the deciding lots, and pray together for divine insight (Acts 1.23-26). As in 1.14, 'all' members of this fledgling Jesus community enjoy unbrokered access to God through prayer.

Judas' failure provides an interesting counterpoint to Peter's. Both apostles turn their backs on Jesus—one through betrayal, the other through denial—but Judas is irrevocably lost while Peter is ultimately restored. Apparently, Peter's treachery is viewed as an isolated aberration, while Judas' is treated as symptomatic of his total apostasy from Jesus' way. Notice the dominant spatial/territorial thrust of Judas' negative appraisal in Acts 1, most of which is focalized (somewhat ironically) through Peter's speech: (1) Judas purchased a *field* with the proceeds from his sale of Jesus, a 'field of blood', as it came to be known, not only because of Jesus' innocent blood which was sacrificed to buy it, but also Judas' own guilty blood which was spilt upon it. (2) Whereas Jesus is vindicated—raised from the dead, taken up to heaven, having promised to pour out his dynamic Spirit—Judas is disgraced—brought down to death, 'falling headlong', pathetically pouring out his 'bowels' (1.18-19). (3) Although Judas had held an honorable 'place (*topos*) in this ministry and apostleship' of the Twelve, he tragically 'turned aside to go to his own place (*topos*)', a desolate, accursed spot where no one can survive (1.20, 25).

Although Judas' loss is both tragic and problematic for the early followers of Jesus, it is not the end of the world. Judas is not indispensable. Another can simply be chosen to take his place. Two acceptable replacements are put forward, and nothing in the narrative precludes the possibility that others might be available. In any case, at the same time that the Judas affair reinforces the importance of the twelve apostles as chief witnesses to Jesus' resurrection, it also begins to deconstruct this idea, opening the apostolic ranks to a new member and creating space for others, perhaps, to become partners in the Christian mission. A quick look forward in the Acts story confirms this possibility. Matthias does not fall away in apostasy, but he does fall into oblivion, never seen again after Acts 1; likewise, nine of the remaining eleven apostles receive their last mention in 1.13. (Only Peter and John appear again.) In their places, we encounter new witnesses such as Stephen, Philip, Barnabas, James, and, of course, Paul. We embark on an open journey to the ends of the earth, open to new companions as well as new territories, receptive to fresh voices and changing perspectives.

What place do *women* have on this journey? Acts 1.14 acknowledges women's participation in the upper room prayer group, which is scarcely surprising in light of their involvement in Jesus' ministry (Lk. 8.1-3) and witness of his death, burial and resurrection (23.27-28, 55-56; 24.1-10). Beyond their gender, the social status of these 'certain women' remains undefined. The Western text portrays them as the apostles' wives and childbearers ('with their wives and children'), but this seems to reflect a later tradition reinforcing apostolic authority and counter-balancing various non-domestic profiles of women's work throughout Luke–Acts (e.g. Lk. 8.1-3; 10.38-42; 18.1-8; Acts 16.3-15; 18.1-3, 18-26).

Mary is singled out by name and identified as 'the mother of Jesus', recalling not only her unique maternal role but also her prominent prophetic vocation at the beginning of the Gospel (Lk. 1.46-55). But, as with Matthias, this is Mary's swan song: she is never heard from again in the Lukan narrative. Moreover, Mary and the other women in Acts 1.14 are embedded in a rather androcentric story that threatens to squeeze them out and nullify their presence. Just before, in the ascension scene, 'two men' (*andres*) do all the speaking, and they direct their remarks to the 'men (*andres*) of Galilee' (1.11). And in the scene immediately following, Peter is the only character given a voice, and he addresses the congregation as 'males-brothers' (*andres adelphoi*, 1.16) on the matter of selecting a *male* apostle (*andros*, 1.21) to replace Judas.

In short, women will accompany the apostles and other male witnesses on the journey through Acts, but whether they will actively lead and shape the mission to any degree or just tag along for the ride remains to be seen.

The Day of Pentecost: 2.1-47

Taking a bird's-eye look at Acts 1–2, we previously noticed several common threads tying together the days of Ascension and Pentecost. As we now focus more directly on the second day, we are struck by a marked intensification as well as parallelism of events associated with the two occasions. The dramatic temperature rises considerably on Pentecost, and not just because of the 'fireworks' display. Extraordinary events erupt 'suddenly' (2.2) this time, and with greater force. The lone rising cloud and pair of white-clad messengers attending Jesus' ascension give way on Pentecost to tornadic sounds, flaming sights, and inspired utterance by 'each' and 'all' of the assembled believers (2.1-4). Inert spectators ('Men of Galilee, why do you stand looking?', 1.11) are transformed into energized prophets ('Are not all these who are speaking Galileans?', 2.7). The Spirit promised becomes the Spirit provided. The private business of a modest band of 120 turns into a bustling public affair attracting the attention of representatives from 'every nation under heaven' and the commitment of 3000 new believers (2.5, 41). The atmosphere changes; the journey now 'feels' different: less like a secret passage through backroads and alleyways, and more like a parade down Main Street.

Outpouring: 2.1-13

Seasoned travellers (informed readers) through biblical terrain immediately experience a sense of déjà vu upon encountering the sights and sounds of Pentecost. Peter will associate these phenomena with prophecies from Joel (2.16-21), but other well-known scriptural scenarios also spring to mind. The stormy blast and fiery blaze accompanying a dynamic manifestation of divine presence on earth recall the theophany to Moses and the Israelites at Sinai (Exod. 19.16-20), especially in combination with Pentecost—which became an occasion for celebrating the giving of Torah and renewing the covenant (*Jub.* 6.17-22)—and tongues-speaking, which denotes the Spirit-ignited ('tongues as of fire') proclamation of 'God's deeds of power' (Acts 2.3-4, 11; Exod. 20.1-2; according to Philo, the divine oracle proceeded directly from the fire at Sinai in language intelligible to the people [*On the Decalogue* 46-49]). However, along with these echoes of the Sinai story comes an important change of setting in Acts. The locus of divine revelation shifts from the isolated, liminal zones of mountain and desert (Sinai) to the populated, centralized areas of city (Jerusalem) and house (2.2, presumably the same upstairs apartment as in 1.13). These two areas—*polis* and *oikos*—represent the major sites of fellowship and witness throughout Acts. The course is now set for missionary journeys 'from house to house' (cf. 20.20) 'in every city' (cf. 8.40; 15.36), not a preparatory trek through the wilderness.

Other biblical images evoked by the Pentecost narrative surround the call of Isaiah. Like Jesus' appointed witnesses gathered in the upper room, the commissioned prophet of old encountered the awesome presence of God in thunderous voice and pyrotechnic vision *filling the house* where he was stationed:

Isaiah
The house was full of his glory (6.1 LXX).
The thresholds shook at the voices of those who called, and the house filled with smoke (6.4).

Acts
There came a sound like the rush of a violent wind, and it filled the entire house where they were sitting (2.2).
All of them were filled with the Holy Spirit (2.4).

Once again, however, a critical spatial distinction modifies the parallel. The house-setting for Isaiah's theophany is the house of the Lord, the Jerusalem temple; by contrast, the early church's house is a private residence set, as we have seen, in opposition to the temple within the Lukan narrative. Ironically and tragically, the Spirit/glory of God now finds a more receptive home in an ordinary domestic dwelling than in Israel's sacred cultic center.

Finally, as a foundational story about language and communication, preparing the way for effective witness, the Pentecost narrative resonates in different ways with two other biblical stories. The primeval tower of Babel myth explains the origins of multiple dialects and nations scattered throughout the earth as divine judgment on futile human attempts to reach up to heaven (Gen. 11.1-9). Pentecost completely redirects the Babel trajectory. The disciples build no towers or shrines; they simply wait in borrowed quarters for the Spirit to come *down from heaven* to them. And when this outpouring occurs, it generates a remarkable *ingathering* of people 'from every nation of heaven' and *translating* of God's message into their 'own native language' (three-fold repetition in 2.6, 8, 11 underscores the crowd's amazement over hearing their own dialects/tongues).

On a smaller scale but more closely tied to the overall Lukan plot, the experience of Zechariah the priest at the beginning of the Gospel provides an interesting counterpart to that of the early Jesus community on Pentecost at the beginning of Acts. On duty alone in the Jerusalem temple while 'the whole assembly of the people was praying outside', Zechariah received a heavenly visitor announcing the birth of a son who would be 'filled with the Holy Spirit' from the womb. Doubting this promise of Spirit-action, Zechariah was struck dumb in the temple and emerged utterly incapable of speaking to the crowd (Lk. 1.8-23). He remained in this condition until the time came to circumcise his new-born son. Then, upon signalling the revealed name for the child (John), 'his tongue freed, and he began to speak, praising God'; moreover, he himself became 'filled with the Holy Spirit' and burst forth with elo-quent prophecy regarding Israel's hope of salvation (1.59-67; interest-ingly, the setting for this incident seems to be Zechariah's *home*, not the temple; cf. 1.23). Once again, the Pentecost narrative echoes an earlier report but transposes it into a different key. The personal Spirit-filling and tongue-loosing enjoyed by a single Judean priest after a period of judgment become spontaneous gifts lavished on an entire company of Galilean disciples. And, of course, however amazing Zechariah's prophecy might have been, it was still uttered in his own tongue. The real shocker at Pentecost is that all these Galileans suddenly begin speaking a wide range of regional languages they have never learned!

This multilingual, interregional dimension of the Pentecost story merits further analysis beyond comparisons with scriptural precedents. First, there is the *Galilean* issue. The crowd is 'amazed and astonished' not only about what they are hearing (their native dialects) but also *who* is speaking, namely, a group of Galileans (2.7). Of course, such bewil-derment may have nothing to do with Galileans per se; any local group suddenly erupting in a chorus of foreign tongues would doubtless have prompted a similar reaction. But the explicit and emphatic reference to 'Galileans' at the end of the query in 2.7 suggests that the particular identity of these people is more than incidental. While Luke–Acts some-times treats Galilee as a part of the larger territory of Judea, the land of the Jews (Lk. 4.44; 23.5; Acts 10.37), more often it makes a clear regional distinction, separating Galilee in the north from Judea and its capital, Jerusalem, in the south, the seat of Jewish politics and culture

(Freyne, pp. 90-91). Underlying this distinction may be a popular stereotype of Galileans, like Jesus and his disciples, as backwater 'boorish dolts in the eyes of sophisticated Jerusalemites' (Malina and Neyrey, 'Conflict', p. 104; cf. Acts 4.13; Jn 1.46; 7.15, 52), not to mention the closer connection between Galilee and the Gentile world (cf. Lk. 6.17; 7.1-10; 8.26-39; Isa. 9.1; Mt. 4.15). For 'devout Jews...living in Jerusalem' (2.5), articulate, Spirit-gifted Galileans might appear to be a contradiction in terms; such an attitude certainly characterizes those scoffers in 2.13 who dismiss the Galileans' outburst as the product of a drunken binge.

Secondly, the Pentecostal display of glossolalia is remarkable for its *global scope* as well as its Galilean source. The narrator exaggerates the case, of course, in claiming representation from '*every* nation under heaven', but as the rough sketch below illustrates, the specific regions catalogued in 2.9-11 form a box around Judea and Jerusalem, suggesting a broad sampling of peoples from the four corners of the earth.

		Pontus		Mesopotamia	
Rome	Asia	Phrygia	Cappadocia	Parthia	Media
		Pamphylia		Elam	

JUDEA-JERUSALEM

	Crete		Arabia
Libya/Cyrene		Egypt	

And so the global mission outlined in 1.8 begins to be realized. But beginning must not be confused with fulfillment. Pentecost still belongs to the orientation phase of the journey, more adumbrating than actually advancing the gospel's proclamation throughout the earth. While the Jerusalem church's witness extends to many diverse language groups from various lands, ethnically it remains limited at this stage to *Jews* (including some 'proselytes' or full converts to Judaism, 2.10). Moreover, the mission remains confined to pilgrims ('visitors') and immigrants ('living in Jerusalem') who have travelled *to* Jerusalem from the Diaspora. The Spirit's propulsion of witnesses *from* Jerusalem out to the ends of the earth takes us beyond the Pentecostal experience.

Interpreting: 2.14-36

While some in the audience write off the tongues-speaking disciples as babbling drunkards, others respond to the Pentecostal demonstration with rapt interest, wondering: 'What does this mean?' (2.12). This question not only reflects the crowd's reaction within the Pentecost story but also marks an appropriate reader response to the story and an effective bridge to Peter's explanatory speech in the next scene. Although readers informed by previous narratives in the Lukan corpus and Jewish scriptures know something of Pentecost's significance at this stage in Acts, there is still much to learn.

Rhetorically, the narrator summons the reader's attention and stresses the importance of Peter's speech through a string of redundant introductory comments in 2.14-15 linked by 'and':

(1) [Peter] raised his voice *and* addressed them,
(2) 'Men of Judea *and* all who live in Jerusalem,
(3) let this be known to you, *and* listen to what I say'.

Early in the speech, Peter cites a prophecy of Joel about the outpouring of the Spirit as the key to understanding the day's strange events: Joel's announcement has just been fulfilled. Also, given its length and strategic placement at the beginning of a major introductory discourse, the Joel citation serves a programmatic function within Acts: what Joel announced sets the agenda for the entire Acts journey. Jesus' sabbath reading from Isaiah—focusing, like Joel, on the Spirit's activity—served a similar function in Luke's Gospel (4.16-19; cf. 7.21-22).

The narrator's *temporal* perspective, mediated through Peter, is manifest in a critical alteration of the very first line of the received Joel text. In place of the prophet's forecast about what 'will come to pass *after these things*' (Joel 3.1 LXX), Peter declares: '*in the last days* it will be' (Acts 2.17). Acts thus sounds a sharper eschatological note than Joel and injects a strong sense of urgency into the disciples' mission. The indeterminate 'times or periods' of 1.7, known only to the Father, have suddenly crystallized into the divinely decreed ('God declares', 2.17, also added to the LXX) 'last days' of the present age.

Accompanying this dramatic turning of the aeons, in which the Spirit of the new age breaks in to revitalize the old, is a collapsing of the natural day-night frontier: 'The sun shall be turned to darkness and the moon to blood' (2.20). Here day becomes night, as at Jesus' crucifixion (Lk. 23.44-45); conversely, the shock of inebriate activity at nine in the morning (2.15), whether provoked by the Spirit or spirits, suggests night's encroaching upon the day. In any case, the eschatological Spirit marches to a unique beat unrestrained by normal circadian rhythms. We must remain alert at all times on the journey through Acts. Who knows what other unusual happenings might crop up in the early morning or even at midday, midnight and other standard hours of repose?

As the Pentecostal Spirit knows no temporal bounds, so it transcends and bridges conventional *spatial* divisions in the cosmos. Generally, God's Spirit moves freely between and works wonders within both 'heaven above' and 'earth below' (2.19). More specifically, the Spirit will bring heavenly/divine knowledge and experience into the earthly/human arena through three means, accentuated in Peter's discourse by further adjustments to the Joel source (LXX):

(1) The Spirit-filled people of God will gain special insight into the heavenly world through *visions and dreams* (2.17). Placing young men's visions before old men's dreams reverses the Joel order and perhaps subtly reflects a Lukan emphasis. The elderly Zechariah and Simeon receive special epiphanies in the infancy stories (Lk. 1.8-20; 2.25-35), but for the most part, beginning with Jesus' baptism, visionary experiences come to younger men in Luke and Acts. Jesus' disciples have already seen the heavens open once in Acts (1.9-11), and we can expect further such revelations to emerge later in the narrative.

(2) The Spirit will also display divine power throughout the cosmos in the form of heavenly *wonders* and earthly *signs* (2.19-20). The Greek Joel text employs only one term—'portents' or 'wonders' (*terata*)—to designate the phenomena in both spheres and then describes such phenomena as unusual disturbances in the natural order (fire, mist, darkness). The Lukan change to 'signs' (*semeia*) in tandem with 'portents' or 'wonders' shifts the focus of the Spirit's work to miraculous deeds of mercy which meet human needs, such as those Peter associates with Jesus' ministry immediately after the Joel citation: 'Jesus of Nazareth, a man attested to you by God with deeds of power, wonders (*terata*), and signs (*semeia*)' (2.22). Although Jesus occasionally manipulated the forces of nature (Lk. 8.22-25), primarily he performed signs and wonders which liberated suffering humanity from the ravages of disease (healing), demons (exorcism) and death (resuscitation). Again, we can anticipate that the Spirit will enact similar signs and wonders through Jesus' followers in Acts.

(3) In addition to enabling earthbound people to *see* heavenly visions and *do* heavenly works, the Spirit will anoint them to *speak* heavenly words as well: 'and they shall prophesy'—a statement added to the Joel passage at the end of 2.18, reinforcing and extending the announcement in the previous verse ('your sons and your daughters shall prophesy'). As Peter proclaims these and other Spirit-charged words unveiling the purpose of God for the 'house of Israel' (2.23, 36), he demonstrates as well as describes the prophetic vocation envisaged by Joel. The stage is set for additional prophetic displays in Acts, not only by Peter, but also by other personnel who will serve as the Spirit's mouthpieces.

Further probing this question of Spirit-employed personnel, we detect once again a boundary-breaking agenda in the Joel passage. Just as the Spirit transcends conventional spatial limits in a dualistic cosmos, so it cuts across stereotypical *social* lines in a hierarchical culture. Framing the Joel citation in Acts is a striking universal emphasis: 'all (*pas*) flesh' will be engulfed by the Spirit in these last days, and 'everyone (*pas*) who calls on the name of the Lord will be saved' (2.17, 21). (Interestingly, the citation cuts off right before Joel returns to a more particular soteriology, limited to those whom the Lord elects to call in Jerusalem/Zion.) Such a perspective echoes that of another prophetic text which defined the scope of Jesus' ministry in Luke: 'all flesh shall see the salvation of God' (Isa. 40.5/Lk. 3.6). Also, we may hear in the more distant background Moses' passionate plea in response to Joshua's attempt to restrict the Spirit's influence: 'Would that all the Lord's people were prophets, and that the Lord would put his spirit on them!' (Num. 11.29). This dream, shared later by Joel, begins to come true at Pentecost.

Within its broad, inclusive framework the Joel passage makes it particularly clear that the Spirit will not discriminate on the basis of *gender* (sons/daughters; male/female slaves), *age* (young/old) or *class* ('even...my slaves') (2.17-18). However, to what extent this 'equal opportunity' scenario will actually be played out in Acts is complicated by certain gaps and tensions in the Lukan narrative up to this point. Elderly and/or female prophets figure prominently in Luke 1-2 (Zechariah, Elizabeth, Mary, Simeon, Anna) but then drop entirely out of sight (and hearing) in the rest of the Gospel. As we have already seen, Mary and other women resurface in the Jesus community in Acts 1, but they are given no voice and granted only the chance to eavesdrop on messages addressed by male speakers to male hearers. A similar androcentric pattern emerges in Acts 2, but with some progressive variations. Notice the sequence of Peter's direct audience appeals surrounding the Joel citation about prophetic women:

> Men (*andres*) of Judea and all who live in Jerusalem (2.14)
>> Your sons and your daughters shall prophesy (2.17)
>> My slaves, both men and women...shall prophesy (2.18)
> Men (*andres*) of Israel (2.22)
> Men-brothers (*andres adelphoi*) (2.29)

Although Peter never explicitly extends his words to 'ladies and gentlemen' to match Joel's reference to sons and daughters (women are still constructed by male discourse), he does increasingly expand his designations from *regional* (Judea/Jerusalem) to *national* (Israel) to *familial* (brothers) networks. The logical next step would openly endorse a gender-inclusive, 'fictive' household of God's people, like that intimated long ago by Joel and concretized in more recent memory by the Lukan Jesus ('My mother and my brothers are those who hear the word of God and do it', Lk. 8.21).

The last line of the Joel citation—'Then everyone who calls on the name of the Lord shall be saved'—raises two crucial questions which Peter addresses in the balance of his speech in 2.22-36: (1) Who is this saving Lord? and (2) Who is it that needs salvation (and why)?

In a Jewish context the answer to the first question would appear to be elementary: the only saving Lord is Yahweh, the God of Israel. Peter, however, has more to say on the matter. Although maintaining the traditional focus on the sovereignty of the one true God ('God' [*theos*] is mentioned eight times in 2.22-36), Peter radically defines and sharpens that focus in terms of God's purposes coming to fullest expression in the life, death, resurrection and exaltation of 'this man', 'this Jesus' of Nazareth.

Life:	Jesus of Nazareth, a man attested...by God with deeds of power...that God did through him (2.22).
Death:	This man, handed over to you according to the definite plan and foreknowledge of God (2.23).
Resurrection:	But God raised him up... This Jesus God raised up (2.24, 32).
Exaltation:	Being therefore exalted at the right hand of God... God has made him [this Jesus] both Lord (cf. 2.21) and Messiah (2.32.36).

The climactic presentation of Jesus' role as exalted Lord is vividly highlighted by a spatial image of Jesus' placement at *the right hand of God*. We can now complete the picture of Jesus' destiny begun at his ascension: after he was taken up into heaven out of the apostles' view (1.9-11), he took his place at God's right hand (2.25, 33-34). Within the wider scriptural and cultural context of Acts, this position reveals two aspects of Jesus' status. First, after suffering (unjustly) the utter *shame* of crucifixion, he was elevated to the place of highest *honor* in the universe, next to God himself—a place of consummate regal authority even above that enjoyed by the most venerated Israelite king, David (2.25-31, 34-35; cf. Ps. 16.8-11; 110.1). Secondly, in light of the familiar anthropomorphic symbol of God's right hand as the means through which he blesses and delivers Israel (Exod. 15.6; Ps. 18.35; 44.3; 60.5; 98.1), Jesus became the supreme *broker* of the Patron-Father's gifts to his client-people, culminating in that most powerful and salutary gift of the Holy Spirit: 'having received from the Father the promise of the Holy Spirit, *he* [Jesus] has poured out this that you both see and hear' (2.33).

Juxtaposing this high assessment of Jesus' honor and beneficence is Peter's pointed indictment of the crowd: 'Jesus of Nazareth, a man attested to *you* by God...this man...*you crucified and killed*' (2.23). 'God has made him both Lord and Messiah, this Jesus whom *you crucified*' (2.36). Ignoring the particular culpability of certain Jewish groups and individuals for the death of Jesus (chief priests, scribes, temple elite, Judas; cf. Lk. 19.47, 48; 22.1-6, 47-71) and treating the Romans as mere functionaries ('you crucified and killed [him] *by the hands of those outside the law*', Acts 2.23), Peter lays the blame indiscriminately on the entire audience (emphatic, plural 'you' [*hymeis*]) who in turn represent 'the entire house of Israel' (2.36). In Peter's view, reminiscent of Israel's prophets of old, the fate of the whole nation is in the balance because the people have rejected God's saving purpose.

But God's purpose still stands firm in the face of human obstinacy. Jesus' crucifixion, although a tragic and reprehensible watershed in Israel's history, has had its place in God's 'definite plan' from the beginning (2.23), providing the optimal context for vindicating God's sovereignty through Jesus' resurrection and exaltation. Moreover, Israel's resistance to God's will can still be overcome; God's saving call can still be heard and accepted. Indeed, Peter moves directly from indictment to invitation with dramatic results. Thousands are incorporated into the restored community of God's people through repentance, reception of the prophetic word, and baptism 'in the name of Jesus Christ' (2.37-41; cf. 'the name of the Lord', 2.21). The nature of this community is the focus of the concluding material in Acts 2.

Regrouping: 2.37-47

The dynamic effusion of the Spirit and expansion of the Jesus community on the day of Pentecost become paradigmatic of God's blessing of his people in subsequent days. The gift of the Spirit proffered to Peter's immediate audience ('you') will also be available to other generations at later *times* ('your children') and to other populations in more distant *places* ('all who are far away')—indeed, to 'everyone whom the Lord our God calls' (2.38-39). On top of the 3000 believers 'added' to the community on 'that day', the Lord continues 'add[ing]' new converts 'day by day' (2.41, 47).

The 'fellowship' (*koinōnia*) of the burgeoning congregation is characterized by a dedication to 'common' (*koinōn*) experiences and interests, including teaching, praying, worshipping, miracle-working, and almsgiving (2.42-47). Particular emphasis falls on the 'breaking of bread', the sharing of 'food' together 'day by day' (2.42, 46). While such table-fellowship no doubt includes eucharistic celebrations modelled on the Lord's Supper (cf. Lk. 22.14-20), it should not be limited to a purely liturgical setting. The lack of reference to the pouring/drinking of wine and the wider context of distributing basic goods to the needy (2.45) suggest a more mundane, material practice of breaking bread involving provision and consumption of food at a common table. The sharing of bread with a company of thousands receptive to the apostles' teaching and wonder-working more readily recalls Jesus' compassionate service to the multitude (5000) near the Sea of Galilee (Lk. 9.10-17) than his private, ceremonial meal with his disciples in the upper room.

Of course, with or without eucharistic overtones, patterns of *commensality*—what, how, where, when, why and with whom one eats—carry great social and cultural significance (see Crossan, pp. 66-70; Neyrey, 'Ceremonies'). On the long journey through Acts (as through Luke's Gospel), we can expect to dine with various hosts and guests on various occasions. Such table settings will represent much more than incidental breaks in the action; quite the contrary, they will provide critical maps of social interaction structuring the course of the expanding Christian mission. At this stage a general picture of open, inclusive commensality begins to develop:

> All who believed were together and had *all* things in common, they would...distribute the proceeds to all, as any had need...[they] ate their food with glad and generous hearts...having the goodwill of all the people (2.44-47).

However, such a brief, universal sketch of community life runs the risk of being superficial and idealistic. One minute the crowd is 'cut to the heart' by Peter's sharp incriminations (2.37); the next it has converted en masse and become a paragon of mutual charity. Are we really to believe, in light of their complicity in the death of Jesus, that *all* of the Israelites in Jerusalem now either unite with or rejoice over this community baptized in and bearing witness to the name of Jesus? Has the holy city finally 'recognized...the things that make for peace', despite Jesus' mournful judgment to the contrary (Lk. 19.41-44)?

Moreover, the localization of the early church's idyllic fellowship in both *temple* and *home* (2.46) seems hard to fathom in view of the mounting opposition between these two venues heretofore in the Lukan narrative (see above, p. 28). Has the 'den of robbers' marked for destruction been transformed into a true house of prayer and justice for all people?

Plots can, of course, reverse dramatically; tragic stories can have happy endings; antagonistic characters can be reconciled; readers' expectations can be adjusted as well as affirmed. But we still have a long way to go in Acts, long enough certainly for conflict to re-emerge between Jesus' home-based followers and the temple authorities. As it happens, certain tensions resume sooner rather than later in the narrative—much sooner, in fact, in the very next section! Sorting out the complex relationship between house-church and temple system—whether and to what extent it remains open or closed, congenial or conflictual—poses a major challenge in the interpretation of Acts 3-5.

Acts 3-5: Temple Tours

The statement in 2.46 situating the early church's 'daily' activity 'in the temple' (*en tō hierō*) and 'at home' (*kat' oikon*) is echoed in 5.42: 'And every day in the temple and at home (*en tō hierō kai kat' oikon*) they did not cease to teach and proclaim Jesus as the Messiah.' These references frame the material in Acts 3-5 and focus attention on the temple and house settings. As it happens, most of the action takes place in the temple area in two long, tightly-knit narratives at the beginning and the end of the section (3.1-4.22; 5.12-41).

Strategically placed in the middle is a shorter sequence of scenes dealing with private, internal church business away from the temple (4.23-5.11). The narrator leaves the specific venue of these scenes somewhat ambiguous, but the picture in 4.31 of the congregation's meetingplace as a site of fervent prayer, seismic Spirit-filling ('the place...was shaken') and bold proclamation of God's word mirrors the Pentecostal house scene in 2.1-5 (cf. 1.13-14). Also the disciplinary matter involving Ananias and Sapphira, who betray the community's trust through a shady land deal, recalls the Judas affair in 1.15-26 handled in some private locale, perhaps the upper-room headquarters of the early Jerusalem church (1.13). Thus the unit in 4.23-5.11 gives the impression of being a house-based interlude sandwiched between two major temple narratives or 'tours', as I am calling them, in keeping with the journey metaphor for the plot and readers' experience of Acts.

In sum, the broad structure of Acts 3-5 (actually reaching back to the 'hinge' statement in 2.46 which both concludes the Pentecostal narrative in ch. 2 and introduces the ensuing temple-house stories in chs. 3-5) may be sketched as follows:

> Temple-House Frame (2.46)
>> Public Temple Tour (3.1-4.22)
>>> Private House Interlude (4.23-5.11)
>> Public Temple Tour (5.12-41)
> Temple-House Frame (5.42)

The church's faithful observance of temple rituals (3.1) and its positive reception by fellow-worshippers (2.46-47; 3.9-11; 5.13-16, 26) in the early chapters of Acts hark back to similar presentations of temple involvement by the families of John and Jesus in the beginning Gospel stories (Lk. 1.5-23; 2.21-51) and signal a continuing commitment to reach out to Israel through her most sacred and central institution. But true success in this mission will require more than pleasant memories of

Jesus' childhood and persisting temple gathering by Jesus' disciples; it will also demand thoroughgoing repentance on the part of temple rulers and people for their ultimate rejection of Jesus as Lord and Messiah (3.17-26; 4.11-12; 5.29-32). Such a response is not forthcoming, however, and heated conflict between temple authorities and Jesus' followers—more reminiscent of the Lukan passion story than birth narrative—complicates and eventually dominates the plot of Acts 3-5.

In the midst of this period of conflict with the religious establishment in Jerusalem, the apostles find succour and fresh empowerment in a private, prayerful gathering with 'their own [friends]' (4.23). Although the temple continues to be a place of prayer for the early church (3.1), the true house of prayer—the dynamic center of messianic worship—remains the secluded *topos* (4.31) situated narratively in the center of Acts 3-5 between two temple conflict episodes. However, this haven of rest and renewal for the Spirit-filled community is not an entirely trouble-free zone. Conflict erupts here as well, this time from within the congregation over matters of property management (5.1-11).

Apart from the overarching *spatial* antithesis between public temple and private house and *social* conflict between temple authorites and church leaders, a number of redundant plot elements bind the narrative in Acts 3-5 into a coherent unit (the 'echo effect' of these chapters is discussed at length in Tannehill, *Narrative*, II, pp. 48-79).

(1) Both temple tours commence with apostolic miracles which attract an enthusiastic crowd to Solomon's Portico (3.1-11; 5.12-16).

(2) The apostles' wondrous deeds and persuasive teaching are repeatedly attributed to the continuing power of the *name* of the risen Jesus (3.6, 16; 4.10-12, 17-18, 30; 5.28, 40-41), God's holy and righteous servant-child (*pais*, 3.13, 26; 4.27), the author/source (*archēgos*, 3.15; 5.31) of life and liberation.

(3) Opposition to the apostles' mission consistently comes from designated temple elites: chief priests (including the high priest), rulers, elders, the captain of the temple and (other) Sadducees comprising the temple's judicial council (Sanhedrin) (4.1, 5-6, 8, 15, 23; 5.17, 21-27).

(4) Persecution of the apostles in both temple incidents involves imprisonment, interrogation, and explicit orders, backed by threats of further punishment, to cease proclaiming the name of Jesus in the holy city (4.1-3, 5-7, 15-21; 5.17-18, 27-28, 39-40). Such action proves ineffectual, however, as the apostles continue to witness boldly (4.8-20, 29; 5.19-32) and the church continues to grow exponentially (4.4; 5.14).

(5) The apostles' persistent commitment to minister in Jesus' name in the face of council prohibitions flows from their higher loyalty to the sovereign will of God ('we must obey God rather than any human authority', 4.19-20, 24-29; 5.29-32) and their inner strengthening by the Holy Spirit (4.8, 31; 5.32).

(6) Apostolic preaching in both temple episodes promises divine blessing to Israelites on condition that they repent of their violent rejection of God's messianic servant, Jesus (3.17-20; 5.30-32).

Another way of plotting the recurring pattern of conflict in Acts 3-5 utilizes the anthropological grid of an honor-shame contest. In ancient Mediterranean culture, social status depended in large measure on one's honor rating in the public arena. Nothing was more highly prized than gaining and maintaining a 'good name' in the community. However, as with other basic goods in this society, honor was viewed as a precious commodity in limited supply. This meant that one constantly competed for honor in a win-or-lose 'social tug of war'; in other words, one achieved or confirmed honor at the expense of another's shame. In the parallel temple scenes in Acts 3-5, the temple rulers and church leaders become embroiled in a classic honor-shame struggle, following a typical order of debate beginning with a provocative *claim* to honor which sparks a direct *challenge* from those threatened by the claim, then a counter *riposte* by the original claimant(s) and finally a public *verdict* determining the outcome of the contest (see Malina and Neyrey, 'Honor').

(1) *Claim*. The apostles advance a radical claim regarding the name (reputation) of Jesus. This one who had suffered the horrible and normally irrevocable shame of crucifixion has been raised from the dead and exalted to the position of highest honor at God's right hand (3.13-15, 26; 4.10; 5.30-31). The name of Jesus has thus been thoroughly vindicated. But more than that, the apostles both announce and demonstrate that this name has become the prime vehicle of God's saving grace: 'there is no other name under heaven given among mortals by which we must be saved' (4.12). In sum, the apostles put forward the good name of Jesus as the preeminent symbol of divine honor and power.

(2) *Challenge*. The temple hierarchs perceive the promotion of Jesus' name as a threat to their public image for two reasons. First, the idea of Jesus' continuing presence and healing power among his followers challenges their traditional Sadducean stance against belief in resurrection of the dead (4.1-2; Lk. 20.27-40). Second and most seriously, within a competitive limited honor culture the popularity of the apostles' ministry in Jesus' name ('all the people ran together to them', 3.11; 'the people held them in high esteem', 5.13; 'a great number of people would also gather', 5.16) inevitably diminishes the temple elites' base of support. Thus the latter are 'filled with jealousy' and seek to reclaim their community standing by censuring the apostles and forbidding any further speaking in Jesus' name among the Jerusalem people (4.17-18; 5.17, 27-28).

(3) *Riposte*. Undaunted by the council's resistance, the apostles boldly appeal to a higher authority, justifying their claims about Jesus as

nothing less than personal, God-revealed testimony: 'we cannot keep from speaking about what we have seen and heard [from God]'; 'we must obey God rather than any human authority' (4.19-20; 5.29).

(4) *Verdict*. Both temple contests end in favor of the apostles, signalled by the council's simple act of concession: 'they let them go' (*apelysan*, 4.21; 5.40). In each case, the temple authorities are forced to bow to weightier opinion. In the first episode they find themselves unable to withstand the will of *the people* who join in a massive chorus of approval for the crippled beggar's healing in Jesus' name (4.21; in the second incident, one of their own council members, the venerable Pharisee Gamaliel, gives them pause to consider that they 'may even be found fighting against *God*', just as the apostles' claimed (5.38-40).

In any event, irrespective of others' estimations, the apostles leave the tribunal 'rejoic[ing] that they were considered worthy to suffer dishonor for the sake of the name' (5.41). Ultimately, they play by different rules, transforming typically humiliating experiences of flogging, imprisonment and public censure into badges of honor acquired in the service of the one whose name is above all others, who himself attained the position of highest honor via the path of suffering and shame.

Up to this point we have taken a wide-angle look at Acts 3–5, noting large structural and thematic patterns holding the narrative together. We must now focus more closely on the sequence of individual episodes, observing how the plot develops in a cause-and-effect chain and maintains suspense through innovations and variations among otherwise parallel scenes.

First Public Temple Tour: 3.1-4.22

The opening incident in Acts 3 provides a concrete example of the typical activities of the early Jerusalem church summarized in 2.42-47. Having reported briefly and broadly that the entire congregation 'devoted themselves to...prayers', marvelled at the 'many wonders and signs' performed by the apostles, and 'day by day...spent much time together in the temple', the narrator now details a particular miraculous event (the healing of a lame beggar) wrought by particular apostolic characters (Peter and John) at a particular temple site (the Beautiful Gate) at a particular prayer time ('one day...at three o'clock in the afternoon') (3.1-10).

This event then leads directly to two closely related incidents involving wider audiences and the apostles' responses to them. In the first case, 'while he [the healed beggar] clung to Peter and John, *all the people* ran together to them...utterly astonished', prompting Peter to address the crowd and explain the christological significance of what they had witnessed (3.11-26; we encountered a similar alignment of provocative event and interpretive speech in 2.1-36). Then, 'while Peter and John were speaking to the people', another group burst on the scene with a different reaction to the proceedings. The *temple authorities* become 'much annoyed' rather than astonished, then duly arrest and question Peter and John, which in turn ignites the apostles' spirited defense of their ministry in Jesus' name (4.1-22).

Healing: 3.1-10

In this episode, our narrator-guide takes us to the threshold of the temple enclosure. We are 'about to go into the temple' through the Beautiful Gate along with Peter and John and a stream of other worshippers at the holy afternoon hour of prayer. But the main action centering on the two leading apostles stops momentarily at the gate just *outside* the temple. A lame man lying at this border station captures their attention, asks them for alms, and then receives both less and a good deal more than he bargained for. Peter offers no money but instead the ability to rise and walk in Jesus' name (3.3-6). As the man jumps to his feet, restored to health, the story of the apostles' entry into the temple resumes but with an important new twist: '*he* [the healed beggar] entered the temple *with them*, walking and leaping and praising God' (3.8). Ultimately the story appears more radical than conventional, focusing more on the beggar's miraculous leap over strict temple boundaries than the apostles' and other worshippers' customary visit to the sanctuary at the appointed hour of prayer.

A brief look at the social and religious status of the lame in the Jewish scriptures and Luke's Gospel will help us to appreciate further the radical nature of these proceedings. In keeping with the general symbolic connection between ritual holiness and physical wholeness in ancient Israel (Douglas, *Purity*, pp. 41-57), Mosaic law strictly prohibited the offering of lame (and other blemished) animals as sacrifices and the service of lame (and other disabled) priests in the sanctuary (Lev. 21.16-24; Deut. 15.21; cf. Mal. 1.8, 13). Such legislation laid the foundation for stereotyping crippled persons throughout Israelite society, not just in priestly circles, as 'dead dogs': that is, pathetic, impotent, despicable creatures (2 Sam. 9.8).

Not surprisingly, then, the Gospel of Luke groups the lame with blind and deaf persons, lepers, the deceased and the poor (7.22; 14.21)—in other words, typical social and religious outcasts. What is surprising, however, is the Lukan portrayal of these people as special objects of Jesus' compassion and honored partners with Jesus and his disciples in the fellowship of God's household (cf. 5.17-26; 7.21-23; 14.7-24). Thus, by reaching out in Jesus' name to the lame beggar at the temple gate and then entering the temple *with him*, Peter and John carry on Jesus' boundary-breaking, community-building ministry to the unfit and the unclean in Israelite society.

Other important links between the healing story in Acts 3 and the foregoing Lukan narrative include the lame man's extreme economic poverty on ironic display at the ostentatious ('beautiful') gateway to the temple during a period set apart for attentive communion with a just and merciful God. This cluster of socioeconomic (rich/poor), spatial (temple area) and temporal-liturgical (hour of prayer) elements emerges repeatedly in a sequence of scenes in Luke 18–21, exposing the corrupt tendency of the temple system in Jesus' day to exploit the poor and to masquerade as a center of prayer and channel of God's mercy.

(1) In his parable of the Pharisee and the tax collector (18.9-14), the Lukan Jesus recounts the contrasting *prayers* of the two characters in the *temple*. The Pharisee uses his prayer to trumpet both his *economic* support of the temple ('I give a tenth of all my income') and his social and moral distance from 'other people', such as the other figure in the story, the despised tax collector, who 'stand[s] far off' humbly pleading for God's mercy. By approving the tax collector's prayer and pronouncing him justified as he went *home*, Jesus takes his stand, in the classic tradition of prophetic critics, against self-aggrandizing temple personnel, represented by the Pharisee, whose piety and stewardship demonstrate blatant disregard for Israel's covenantal duty to care for needy 'others' in the community (cf. Elliott, pp. 213-15).

(2) At the end of the next chapter, Jesus more directly attacks the *economic* base of the *temple*, driving out the merchants who kept the temple business running (Lk. 19.45). His quarrel, however, is not so much with these particular sellers as with the temple system and its leadership as a whole. Appropriating two prophetic voices, Jesus laments that while the temple had been established by God to be 'a house of *prayer*' (Isaiah), the current institution has become 'a den of *robbers*' (Jeremiah), a haven for financial opportunists who milk the poor and defenseless ('oppress the alien, the orphan, and the widow, or shed innocent blood in this place', Jer. 7.6) rather than minister to their needs (19.46).

(3) The next chapter in Luke again ends with Jesus' denunciation of temple elites for defrauding the poor and making a mockery of prayer: 'they [the scribes] devour widows' houses and for the sake of appearance say *long prayers*' (20.47). A case in point immediately presents itself as the *temple treasury* swallows a poor widow's remaining two coins—'all she had to live on' (21.1-4). Tragically, in Jesus' estimation, the 'beautiful' temple structure (21.5) had been built at the expense of this and other victims' utter destitution (Spencer, 'Neglected Widows', pp. 726-28).

Against this narrative backdrop the story of the lame man in Acts 3 comes into sharper focus. Daily begging for alms at the foot of the temple's Beautiful Gate at the hour of prayer emerges as a tragic exercise in futility. From a Lukan standpoint, the temple economy takes from the poor more than it gives, and temple prayer ceremonies function more as pretentious shows of piety than genuine acts of fellowship with

God which motivate generous acts of ministry to destitute people. The lame man thus stands to gain little from his current mendicant enterprise *until* Peter and John come by as representatives of a renewed economic and religious system. They have no money to offer ('I have no silver and gold', 3.6), but not because they have hoarded their resources to advance their own wealth; rather they have relinquished their 'possessions and goods' to a community fund serving the needs of all members (2.44-45). They do offer prayers (1.14; 2.42), but not to call attention to themselves and partition themselves from undesirable neighbors; rather they seek God's blessing upon all people, near and far, who, with them, call on the name of Jesus (2.21, 38-39).

Such blessing comes to the lame beggar in Acts 3—as he is healed, 'saved', made 'whole' in Jesus' name and finally enabled to worship God *inside* the temple gates (3.6-8)—*inside* Israel's holy place controlled of late by an oppressive regime manifesting little more than contempt for marginalized persons like him. As he proceeds to bound about the temple courts, a key prophetic sign of Israel's restoration ('then the lame shall leap like a deer', Isa. 35.6) materializes before a wide-eyed temple assembly. Along with this sign comes an implicit call to repentance (soon to become explicit in Peter's speech) to the people at large and the temple hierarchy. Israel must acknowledge her crippling rejection of God's 'Holy and Righteous One' (3.14), change her course ('turning each of you from your wicked ways', 3.26), and begin to walk in the way of 'Jesus Christ of Nazareth'.

Preaching: 3.11-26

The miracle of the lame man's healing and cavorting about the temple elicits an overwhelming *visual* response from the crowd: they 'see' and 'stare' in wonder at both the former beggar and the attending apostles (3.9-12). Peter first meets their gaze ('When Peter *saw* it...', 3.12) and then provides incisive *verbal* commentary on the significance of what they have just witnessed.

The main thrust of Peter's homily is to redirect the people's attention away from the recipient and mediators (3.12) to the true *source* of the miracle: the name of Jesus (3.16). To be sure, the apostles' 'faith' in Jesus' name played an important facilitating role, but fundamentally, '*his name itself* has made this man strong'. (Note the chiastic arrangement—faith-name/ name-faith—in 3.16 with 'name' at the center.) The power of the divine name to deliver and protect God's people is a prominent theme in Israelite worship (Ps. 20.1-7; 44.4-8; 54.1-7), linked to the localization of this name in the Solomonic temple ('a house for the name of the Lord, the God of Israel', 1 Kgs 8.17; cf. 8.14-30). In Solomon's Portico, Peter now makes clear that the name of Jesus represents God's glory and strength revealed within ('in the presence of all of you', Acts 3.16), but not restricted to, the temple arena.

The name of Jesus thus emerges in Acts as more than a mere memory of Jesus' past ministry spurring the apostles to carry on his work. It is, in fact, a dynamic, personal symbol of Jesus' continuing presence and power on earth. Although ascended to heaven awaiting (we now learn) a return to earth at 'the time of universal restoration' (3.21), Jesus is not trapped within a fixed spatio-temporal system. Far from being an absentee landlord until his return, he remains in the interim an active friend and savior of God's people, channelling God's life-giving energy (cf. 3.15) to the poor and the lame just as he did before his departure.

In addition to setting the record straight about the cause of the lame man's healing, Peter's proclamation of Jesus' name inevitably exposes the shame of those who 'handed over [to crucifixion] and rejected' Jesus, who publicly disgraced his 'holy and righteous' name (3.13-14). Extending and sharpening a point from his Pentecost speech, Peter lays the blame for Jesus' death squarely at the feet of his fellow-Israelites. The role of the Roman governor, Pilate, is reduced to a reluctant administrator of a hostile Jewish plot against Jesus: 'he [Pilate] had decided to release him [Jesus], but *you* rejected [him] and asked to have a murderer [Barabbas, Lk. 23.18-19] given to you, and *you* killed the Author of life' (3.14-15).

Two factors, however, sustain the possibility that the Israelites' guilt may yet be 'wiped out' and engulfed by waves of 'refreshing...from the presence of the Lord' (3.19-20). First, Peter chalks up their violent rejection of Jesus to misguided 'ignorance' rather than cold-blooded perversity (3.17). Such a perspective recalls the unique assessment of the Lukan Jesus from the cross: 'they do not know what they are doing' (Lk. 23.34). The good news is that ignorance can be reversed and pardoned. As Peter enlightens the people regarding precisely what they did do, he confronts them with the opportunity to repent of their error and be restored to fellowship with God and his messiah. While Jesus simply petitioned God on behalf of his executioners ('Father forgive them'), Peter exhorts his audience to 'turn to God' for themselves (3.19-20).

Secondly, the Israelites' opposition to Jesus' mission may still be overcome because of the larger plan of God—'the God of Abraham, the God of Isaac, and the God of Jacob, the God of our ancestors' (3.13)—unfolding throughout Israel's history. As at Pentecost, Peter emphasizes once again that resisting Jesus even to the point of murder did not so much frustrate as fulfill God's saving purposes forecast in Israel's scriptures (3.18). Here, however, he broadens his base of support, looking beyond David (2.25-31, 34-35) to Isaiah, Moses and Abraham.

(1) The notion of a humiliated and rejected messianic *servant* (*pais*, 3.13, 26) finds its roots in the songs of Isaiah. The specific claim that God 'has glorified his [suffering] servant Jesus' closely echoes Isa. 52.13 (cf. 52.13-53.12).

(2) Peter also contends that Jesus fits the profile of the expected Moses-like *prophet* (3.22-23; Deut. 18.15-20). Such a vocation implies a measure of popular resistance such as that encountered by Moses throughout his leadership of the early Israelites. Little wonder, then, that Jesus faced stubborn antagonists 'who [did] not listen' to his message (3.23).

(3) Finally Peter suggests that Jesus also fulfills the Abrahamic covenant as the climactic *descendant* or 'seed' (*sperma*) of Abraham through whom God has chosen to bless Israel and 'all the families of the earth' (3.25; cf. Gen. 12.1-3; Gal. 3.16-18). As this ancient covenant has survived Israel's recurrent lapses into disobedience and faithlessness, so now with the coming of Jesus, God's blessed purpose remains firm in spite of his people's recalcitrance. Indeed, the primary ('first') design of God's sending his servant-messiah was to reclaim his people, 'to bless you [Israelites] by turning each of you from your wicked ways' (3.26).

While Peter once again offers hope for restoration to his compatriots, in the present speech (unlike at Pentecost) he also strikes a note of judgment: if they persist in rejecting God's prophetic word, they 'will be utterly rooted out of the people' (3.23). Moreover, the reference to the messiah's outreach 'first' to Israel hints at the prospect of turning to other people (Gentiles) who might prove to be more receptive. Israel may have priority, but she does not hold a monopoly on God's attention.

Defending: 4.1-22

In Peter's address to the crowd following the lame man's healing, the apostle made one passing reference to the Jewish authorities as a distinct group from the people: 'you acted in ignorance, *as did also your rulers*' (3.17). Although distinct, people and rulers acted in concert in turning their backs on Jesus. Now, however, as the authorities assert their presence, their response to the gospel becomes sharply divided from the people's. Many from the latter group, 'about five thousand [males, *andres*]' in number, repent and 'believe' Peter's message (4.4). This thousandfold expansion of the Jesus community continues the pattern of mass appeal evident at Pentecost (2.41) and in Jesus' ministry (Lk. 9.14). In contrast to and in large measure *because* of the people's enthusiastic response, the leaders, threatened by the potential loss of popular support, persist in opposing the Jesus movement, even to the point of arresting Peter and John (4.1-3; cf. v. 17).

The leaders are represented by temple hierarchs—the high priest (and family), captain of the temple guard (cf. 5.24, 26; Lk. 22.52), and legal experts (elders, scribes) included in the Jewish supreme court (council)—all closely aligned with the aristocratic party of the Sadducees which denied the reality of bodily resurrection (4.1-3, 5, 8, 15; cf. Lk. 20.27; *Ant.* 13.293-98; 18.16-17). As men of the highest standing in the highest institution in Israelite society, these rulers are predictably preoccupied with issues of power and reputation. And so they come right to the point in interrogating Peter and John: 'By what *power* or by what *name* did you do this [i.e. heal the lame man]?' (4.7).

Of course, Peter has already clearly answered this question (3.12-16), but true to form, the leaders have not been listening. So Peter repeats his basic argument regarding the beneficent power and name of Jesus Christ of Nazareth (4.8-10). But he also augments his case by introducing a fresh scriptural image of Jesus sure to hit home with the temple authorities in the present temple setting: 'the stone that was rejected by you, the builders; it has become the cornerstone' (4.11; Ps. 118.22).

Although presented for the first time by Peter in Acts, earlier in the Lukan narrative Jesus utilized this text in a similar situation. While 'he was teaching the people in the temple', the religious leaders intervened and began to question his authority (Lk. 20.1-2). After setting them back on their heels with a series of counter-questions (20.3-8), Jesus launched into a parable about wicked tenants in a vineyard who spurn the property owner by, first, mistreating his servants and, then, murdering his son. The owner is thus forced to take drastic measures: 'destroy those tenants and give the vineyard to others' (20.9-16). Upon concluding this judgment story, Jesus appended the Psalmist's statement about the rejected stone becoming the cornerstone and interpreted this stone, in keeping with the parable's tone, as a vehicle of judgment 'crushing' all who block its path (20.17-18). Directly the narrator makes clear that the targets of this tale had been the temple elites (20.19). In resisting Jesus they were rejecting God's chosen son/stone and risking severe retribution against themselves and their institution. In neighboring passages preceding and following Lk. 20.9-19, Jesus predicted in or near the temple area that 'not one *stone*' would be left intact in Jerusalem and its temple (19.44; 21.5-6). Combining these 'stones' creates a poignant picture of the fate of the temple builder-officials: in dislodging the true cornerstone of God's house, they trigger the collapse of the temple's beautiful stones around them.

The affiliation of the perverse builders in Ps. 118.22 with the current temple leadership is clarified and cemented by Peter's addition of 'by you' in his defense before the Jewish council in Acts 4.11: 'the stone that was rejected *by you*, the builders'. Their guilt cannot be sidestepped; what Jesus anticipated has already happened: Israel's religious rulers had him crucified (4.10). But there is now more to say on the matter in light of the fact of Jesus' resurrection. Instead of following the Psalm indictment with a sentence of judgment, as Jesus did before his death, Peter proclaims the necessity—and, by implication, the possibility—of *salvation* through the exalted Jesus: 'there is no other name under heaven...by which we must (*dei*) be saved' (4.12).

As the trial continues the temple authorities are by no means converted, but they are compelled to release the apostles without punishment. In the end, they cannot withstand the pressure of three sets of
persuasive witnesses.

(1) First, the council members find it difficult to reckon with the testimony of *Peter and John*, including *how* it is conveyed as much as its
content. They are particularly struck by the apostles' display of 'boldness' (*parrhēsia*), that is, their frank, confident, open manner of speaking 'in the presence of persons of high rank' (BAGD, p. 630). Such
outspokenness was normally not expected from common folk untrained
in rhetorical strategy. The fact that 'uneducated and ordinary men' like
Peter and John, companions of Jesus of Nazareth (cf. 4.10), speak with
extraordinary authority thus elicits 'amazement' from the temple
rulers—the same response, ironically, the crowd had earlier to the
apostles' miraculous healing of the lame man and to the Galilean disciples' glossolalia at Pentecost (*thaumazō*, 4.13; 3.12; 2.7; cf. 3.10; 2.12).
Being tongue-tied with wonder, unable to account for the apostles'
assertiveness, makes it hard for the council to prosecute their case
effectively.

(2) The religious leaders' plot to curtail the apostles' ministry is also
thwarted by the *people's* reaction, which ultimately moves beyond
amazement to 'prais[ing] God for what had happened' (4.21). By so
responding, the crowd affirms Peter and John's bold claim to be God's
messengers (4.19-20). Invoking God's authority shifts the case to a
higher court and puts the temple judges in an awkward position. As
reputed administrators of God's law and mediators of God's presence,
they could scarcely risk squelching the people's doxology and being
viewed as opposing God's work.

(3) The most powerful witness confronting the council is, in fact, a
silent one—*the restored lame man*. Simply standing at the apostles' side
without saying a word, this man leaves the authorities 'nothing to say in
opposition' (4.14). They are effectively silenced by his silent presence. A
new piece of information also comes to light about the healed man
which makes the supernatural origin of his transformation even harder
to refute: he 'was more than forty years old' (4.22). If no cure had been
forthcoming for that length of time (according to 3.2, he had been lame
from birth), it is most unlikely that any power but God's could bring it
to pass now.

Throughout the first temple tour, despite the prominence of the
apostles, the temple leaders, and the crowd, the narrative keeps drawing
all eyes (characters' and readers') back to the cured cripple; the fuss is
all about him! Throughout the proceedings he sticks close by Peter and
John 'in the presence of all' (3.11, 16; 4.10, 14). He becomes an integral
part of the Acts journey and an important sign of what kind of journey
this will be: a missionary journey of mercy in the name of Jesus where

those normally incapable of travel will be lifted up and brought into the Way. At every turn, we must be poised to seek out unfortunates lying paralyzed on the roadside, stop to render aid—rather than 'pass by on the other side' (cf. Lk. 10.30-37)—and embrace them as pilgrim companions.

Apart from providing a symbol of hope for the poor and disadvantaged in Israelite society, the healed lame man also represents an image of restoration for the entire nation. We have already noted the connection to Isa. 35.6 where the leaping lame typify Israel's glorious deliverance from exile through the desert (cf. 35.1-10). This scenario, of course, was modelled after the exodus and wilderness journey to the promised land in the days of Moses. The lame man's restoration after *forty years* of paralysis establishes a key temporal link to this same national tradition. As God's saving purpose for ancient Israel was finally realized after forty years of stumbling and meandering through the wilderness, so the moment of fresh renewal—signalled by the dance of a forty-year cripple—has dawned upon the present Israel. To join this joyous dance, however, Israel must now follow the lead not only of Moses, but also of the promised 'prophet like Moses', the crucified and risen Jesus of Nazareth, in whose name alone God brings full salvation to his people.

Private House Interlude: 4.23-5.11

After being publicly reprimanded and released from council custody, Peter and John leave the temple area for a more private, supportive environment where they can freely talk 'to their own (*tous idious*)' people about the authorities' threats to silence their witness (4.23). While providing no precise details about the size, composition, and location of this support group, the narrative creates a general impression of this group as a friendship-kinship network anchored in a holy place of prayer (4.24-31) and charity (4.32-37): in other words, the true household of God.

The two scenes in 4.23-5.11 (4.23-31; 4.32-5.11) depict similar facets of community life which in turn reflect a pattern already established in Acts. For example, the congregation again exhibits remarkable unity and piety in praying 'together' (*homothymadon*, 4.24; 1.14; 2.1, 46) in one voice and sharing 'one heart and soul' as they hold 'everything' they possess 'in common' (*hapanta koina*, 4.32; 2.44-45). Also, the community continues to experience the powerful presence of the Holy Spirit in its midst (4.25, 31; 5.3, 9; 2.1-13).

But this glowing report of community health does not tell the whole story. Certain complications begin to develop. For the first time since the defection of Judas, the early Jerusalem church faces serious *internal* conflict—in addition to its clash with outside authorities—which jeopardizes its unity and relationship with the Spirit. Two members, Ananias and Sapphira, conspire together to deceive the congregation over a financial matter and, in so doing, 'put the Spirit of the Lord to the test' (5.1-3, 9). While the friends united in prayer in 4.31 enjoy a fresh 'filling' with the Holy Spirit, enabling them to proclaim God's word, the fraudulent couple allow their hearts to be 'filled' by *Satan*, prompting them 'to lie to the Holy Spirit' (5.3).

The church thus finds itself embroiled in a spiritual battle with cosmic forces as well as a political struggle with earthly rulers. We turn now to examine how it manages these conflicts through prayer and discipline.

Praying: 4.23-31

We have already encountered various general reports of the Christian community's practice of prayer (1.14; 2.42; 3.1) and one terse account of a specific prayer: the request for divine guidance in selecting Judas' successor (1.24-25). Now a more extensive prayer is narrated dealing with the wider problem of both popular and official opposition to the messianic mission of Jesus and his followers.

Appropriating a Davidic tradition from Psalm 2, the prayer identifies the enemies of Jesus and lumps them together as co-conspirators. Corresponding to the Gentiles (*ethnē*), peoples (*laoi*), kings (*basileis*) and rulers (*archontes*) 'gathered together (*synagō*) against the Lord and his Messiah' (4.25-26; Ps. 2.1-2) are Herod (king), Pontius Pilate (governor), the Gentiles (*ethnē*) and the peoples (*laoi*) of Israel 'gathered together (*synagō*) against your [God's] holy servant Jesus, whom you anointed [christened, *chriō*]' ('anointed one' = Christ/Messiah, 4.27). This first mention in Acts of Herod Antipas, client-king of Galilee, recalls his interrogation and mocking of Jesus in Lk. 23.6-12, but not his willingness to set Jesus free (cf. 23.15); likewise, there is now no emphasis, as in Acts 3.13, on Pilate's decision to release Jesus. Furthermore, in comparison with 2.23, greater weight is placed on the culpability of the Roman soldiers (Gentiles), along with the Israelite mob, in crucifying Jesus. (Gentiles are cited before Israelites.) With its back against the wall, the persecuted community currently shows little concern with making fine distinctions among those who resist God's purpose in Christ.

And what about the Jewish religious authorities? With the reference to 'their threats' in 4.29 (cf. 4.17, 21), the prayer shifts its focus without skipping a beat to the recent action of the priestly council 'gathered together(*synagō*)' (4.5) against the apostles. By threatening the apostles' mission, the temple elites confirm their alliance with those rulers and people arrayed 'against the Lord and against his Messiah'. On the other side, the suffering church affirms its solidarity with the passion of Jesus. The journey of discipleship is the way of the cross (cf. Lk. 9.23-24).

But for all its hardship this way is not a way of weakness, since the praying church enjoys open access to none other than the 'Sovereign

Lord (*despotēs*)' of all creation (4.24). The title *despotēs* applied to the
God of Israel denoted his terrible, absolute authority over all earthly
nations and rulers, indeed, over the entire universe (Philo, *Who Is the
Heir of Divine Things?* 23). It was thus a particularly apt mode of
addressing God by victims of injustice pleading for the discomfiture of
their powerful oppressors (Sir. 36.1; *3 Macc.* 2.2). It was also well-suited
to first-century resistance movements like the 'Fourth Philosophy' led by
Judas the Galilean, which opposed paying taxes to Caesar on the
grounds that 'God alone is their leader and master' (*Ant.* 18.23; cf.
Horsley and Hanson, pp. 190-99).

As the threatened disciples in Acts acknowledge God's supreme,
'despotic' control over world events, they also recognize God's typical
pattern of managing his affairs through appointed agents. Specifically,
their prayer in 4.25-30 highlights four 'brokers' of God's will:

(1) God's assessment of the violent stand against his messianic purpose was announced long ago 'through the mouth' of the Psalmist
David (4.25). As Acts has already suggested, God's sovereign word is
mediated through prophets, poets, sages, priests, kings, apostles and
other anointed servants. Interestingly, the designation of David as God's
'servant' (*pais*) can also mean 'child'. A familial-patronal picture thus
emerges (note also David's appellation as Israel's 'father' [*patēr*]) alongside the more political-monarchal image of *despotēs*, affirming God as
the chief patriarch, guiding and blessing all families of the earth through
selected servant-children such as David.

(2) The anointing of monarchs like David to serve the people of Israel
as God's vice-regent (cf. 1 Sam. 16.1-13) has prepared the way for the
climactic anointing of *Jesus Messiah*, Israel's ideal servant-king (4.26-
27). The mention of 'Lord and Messiah' in 4.26 recalls the exalted label
applied to the crucified Jesus at the end of Peter's Pentecost sermon in
2.36. The double reference to Jesus as God's 'holy servant-child (*pais*)'
(4.27, 30) establishes a close kinship with both God (son) and David
(fellow *pais*) reminiscent of the angelic annunciation concerning Jesus
at the beginning of Luke's Gospel: 'He will be great, and will be called
the Son of the Most High, and the Lord God will give to him the throne
of his ancestor David' (2.32).

(3) The Sovereign Lord works not only through holy and honorable
servants such as David and Jesus. His 'hand' (*cheir*, cf. 4.30) is so powerful and his 'plan' (*boulē*, cf. 2.23) so determined that they can even turn
the evil of *opposing rulers and mobs* into good (4.27-28). Again the
community affirms that Jesus' attackers unwittingly played out their role
in fulfilling the messiah's predestined mission of healing and liberation
through suffering.

(4) Finally, the *praying disciples* continue to present themselves as
dynamic channels of God's blessing. In the face of official resistance,
they seek God's grace to persist in their ministry of speaking God's word

'with all boldness' and performing 'signs and wonders'—such as healing—in the name of Jesus (4.29-30; cf. 2.43; 3.6-10; 4.13, 16). They identify themselves as God's 'servants' but not with the same term (*pais*)
applied to David and Jesus. Rather they call themselves *douloi*, which
carries the connotation of 'slaves' (4.29). Addressing God as *despotēs*
(the only other Lukan use of this term outside of Acts 4), Simeon also
referred to himself as God's *doulos*: '*Master* (*despotēs*), now you are dismissing your *servant-slave* (*doulos*) in peace' (Lk. 2.29). The Sovereign
Lord of heaven and earth possesses his people and demands complete
loyalty and obedience from them. But he is a benevolent despot,
blessing his slaves and sharing his power with them. The picture of
God's outstretched hand performing signs and wonders through his
servants especially evokes memories of Yahweh's mighty actions
through Moses to redeem his people from oppressive slavery (cf. Exod.
3.19-20; 6.5-7; 7.4-5; Deut. 34.11-12; Acts 7.35-36).

In direct response to their supplication, the Holy Spirit again fills the
entire assembly and inspires them to proclaim God's word boldly (4.31).
The faithful community 'gathered together' in the dynamic presence of
the Holy Spirit, on the one side, proves to be much more than the political and religious rulers 'gathered together' against them, on the other
side, can constrain.

Disciplining: 4.32—5.11

As in 2.44-45, the narrative again stresses the characteristic unity of the
early Jerusalem church, evidenced in the pooling of all possessions for
the common good (4.32). The continued expansion of the community
(4.4) has not altered its basic commitment to meeting the needs of all
members (4.34). However alien this communitarian ethic might appear
to a modern, individualistic Western reader, in the ancient world it
echoed both classical Greek ideals of friendship ('Friends' goods are
common property'; 'Brothers have all things in common': Aristotle,
Nicomachean Ethics 8.9.1-2) and traditional Jewish notions of covenant
loyalty to neighbors ('There will be no one in need among you'; 'Open
your hand to the poor and needy neighbor in your land': Deut. 15.4, 11).

As this section recalls the summary of community life at the end of
Acts 2, it also provides much additional information, focusing on the
activities of three sets of characters, one already familiar to us and the
other two introduced for the first time: (1) the apostles, (2) Barnabas
and (3) Ananias and Sapphira.

(1) In addition to alluding again to the *apostles'* ministry of proclamation and miracle-working (4.33), the present narrative features their leadership roles in managing community funds. Three times we encounter
members' bringing their money and laying it at the *apostles' feet* (4.35,
37; 5.2). There is no hint that the apostles solicited or coerced these
donations, but they do appear to have complete control over their

distribution. In this capacity, however, the apostles direct their efforts exclusively to meeting the material needs of everyone in the community, in marked contrast to the exploitative practices of temple officials and other well-known 'lovers of money' (Lk. 16.14).

(2) Among those who bring proceeds from property sales is a disciple named Joseph, whom the apostles call *Barnabas* (4.36-37). This nickname distinguishes him from the Joseph introduced in 1.23 (the apostolic candidate also known as 'Barsabbas' and 'Justus') and highlights his important function as 'son of encouragement'. Here Barnabas encourages the community through his financial contribution. We can anticipate other encouraging ways he might live up to his name down the road.

The narrator fills out Barnabas's profile with information concerning his tribal and national identity: he was 'a Levite, a native of Cyprus' (4.36). The former term designates a member of the priestly tribe of Levi in ancient Israel, set apart for special service to God. Barnabas's reputation as a Levite devoted to helping the needy distinguishes him from the negligent Levite in Jesus' famous parable of the Good Samaritan (Lk. 10.32) as well as from the callous priestly aristocrats who recently opposed the healing of a lifelong cripple in Jesus' name. His Cypriot origins associate him with the host of Diaspora immigrants to Jerusalem present at Pentecost (although Cyprus is not included among the list of nations cited in 2.9-11). We are reminded of the church's mission to take the gospel beyond Jerusalem to all peoples (1.8) and alerted to the possibility that Barnabas might be instrumental in realizing that goal.

(3) As much as Barnabas's stewardship stands in contrast to the conduct of Jewish religious leaders outside the church, it is also antithetical to the ensuing action of a married couple within the congregation. *Ananias and Sapphira* do not directly exploit or cheat anyone, but they do *lie* to the community—they even lie to God and the Holy Spirit! (5.3, 4)—concerning the disposal of funds received from selling a piece of property. Apparently they bring 'only a part' of the money while pretending that it is the full amount (5.2). While surrendering one's possessions remains optional for community membership, honest communication is an absolute requirement.

As the Holy Spirit filled the company of praying believers, inspiring them boldly to speak God's word (4.31), so *Satan* fills the hearts of this land-owning pair, provoking them to bear false witness (5.3). It may seem surprising that Satan makes his first appearance in Acts not in the temple or some other territory hostile to the church, but actually within the church's own borders. Readers of the preceding Lukan volume, however, will recognize a pattern of diabolical efforts to infiltrate and sabotage the Jesus movement by appealing to human greed. At the beginning of Jesus' mission, the devil attempted—unsuccessfully —to lure Jesus away from God's service by offering him 'all the kingdoms of the world' (Lk. 4.5-8). In the last days of Jesus' earthly career, Satan wormed his way into the heart of Judas Iscariot, 'one of the twelve', prompting him to betray Jesus to the temple authorities for an undisclosed sum of money (22.3-6). As we have already seen, the narrator of Acts informs us that Judas eventually purchased 'a field with the reward of his wickedness' and met with a horrible disaster there (1.18-19). Judas bought land with tainted money at Satan's instigation; Ananias and Sapphira sell land and fraudulently withhold some of the proceeds under Satan's influence. Either way, Satan cleverly manipulates property and profit to ensnare Jesus' followers.

Jesus had already placed his disciples on alert, warning them that 'Satan has demanded to sift all of you like wheat' (Lk. 22.31). He also promised Peter special strength finally to overcome Satan's trials (after a period of weakness surrounding his denial of Jesus) and to protect the community (22.32-34). It is not surprising, then, to find Peter taking the lead in the disciplinary cases in Acts involving Judas and Ananias and Sapphira. Still, however much we may admire Peter's renewed courage and rectitude, as sensitive readers we are distressed by these three casualties of war with Satan. We have become painfully aware that amid all the joy and triumph of the Acts journey, there is also sorrow and tragedy along the way. The thousands which have joined us cannot fully compensate for the few we leave behind.

And how do we ever adequately make sense of the manner in which Ananias and Sapphira are taken away: suddenly struck dead by the hand of God (5.5-10)? Even granting the severity of their breach of community trust, does it warrant divine capital punishment? When the first human couple grasped for more than God allowed them and then sought to hide and cover up their crime, God expelled them from their garden home but did not exterminate them (even though the death sentence had been mandated in Gen. 2.17); moreover, in addition to judging them, God also provided clothing for the man and wife to conceal their shame (Gen. 3.20). In the strict, sectarian Jewish community at Qumran, willful 'lying in matters of property' was punishable by a year's ban from the 'pure Meal' and a quarter reduction in food allotments—but not the death penalty (1QS 6.24-25; Vermes, pp. 216-17). In comparison with these situations, the treatment of Ananias and Sapphira seems particularly harsh.

Other punishment cases in the ancient world, however, are more akin to the example in Acts 5. Robert Brawley notes important parallels involving both the Vaccaei and the Israelites (*Centering*, pp. 176-79). The Vaccaei, as reported by Diodorus of Sicily, were a collectivist society which executed any member who hoarded a portion of community land and crops for themselves (5.34.3). The book of Joshua tells of the ancient Israelites' stoning of Achan—and his family—because Achan 'kept back for himself' (*nosphizomai*, Josh. 7.1 LXX, the same verb used in Acts 5.3) some of the forbidden spoils of war. The community could not successfully move forward in battle until this covenant-breaker was exposed and eliminated (Josh. 7.1-26).

Acknowledging these precedents scarcely lessens the shock of the Ananias and Sapphira incident, not only for modern readers, but for ancient audiences as well. The story emphasizes in closing that 'great fear seized the whole church and all who heard of these things' (5.11; cf. v. 5). The threat of punishment from the Jewish council came as no surprise to the early Christians, given Jesus' prediction (Lk. 12.11-12) and experience, and did little to dampen their enthusiasm. (If anything it made them bolder.) The threat of punishment from *God*, however, is another matter. The same hand which stretches out to heal the diseased and disabled (4.30) might suddenly turn and strike down a pretentious disciple. Thrilling amazement over leaping feet miraculously energized by God's power (3.7-10) might give way to chilling dread of other feet which stand ready to carry out another victim of God's wrath (5.9: 'Look, the feet of those who have buried your husband are at the door, and they will carry you out.') The journey through Acts hits a new level of suspense subject to sudden outbreaks of God's vengeance as well as benevolence.

Also disconcerting are the implications for women's speaking roles in Acts. Since Peter via Joel forecast the emergence of women-proclaimers (2.17-18), Peter has still remained the chief spokes*man* of the church, addressing his message, as we have seen, primarily to males/brothers. The first woman's voice we hear in Acts is Sapphira's in 5.8. Unfortunately, what she says is a lie, supporting her husband's testimony ('Yes, that was the price'), and what results from her fraudulent utterance is her immediate death. The famous—or rather infamous—first words from a woman in Acts are her last!

Second Public Temple Tour: 5.12-41

We are scarcely allowed to catch our breath after the sudden deaths of Ananias and Sapphira, as the 'now' (*de*) in 5.12 marks an abrupt shift back to the Jerusalem temple, the public arena of conflict. We have already noted several parallels between the first and second temple tours. We are now poised to detect differences between the two chains of events and track new developments in the course of the journey.

Healing: 5.12-16

Although briefer and less detailed than previous accounts of community growth and the healing of the lame beggar, the progress report in 5.12-16 is in many respects broader in scope and more spectacular than anything encountered thus far in Acts. We learn that the apostles are now performing 'many signs and wonders' in the temple precincts and that 'more than ever…great numbers' are joining the community—including 'both men and women'—and enjoying dramatic experiences of deliverance—including 'those tormented by unclean spirits' as well as those debilitated by illness. An explosion of God's liberating power attends the ministry of the early church, answering the prayer of 4.29-30. The loss of Ananias and Sapphira, while a terrible tragegy, in no way deters the community from moving forward in its mission.

Although centered once again in Solomon's Portico at the temple's eastern side, the action now extends beyond this station as well. With so many sick folk needing attention, some are carried out on stretchers into the city's *streets* (*plateias*) in hopes of encountering Peter passing by (5.15). Such activity recalls Jesus' story of the banquet host reaching out 'into the *streets* (*plateias*) and lanes of the town and bring[ing] in the poor, the crippled, the blind, and the lame' (Lk. 14.21). The kingdom of God pushes outside the house and temple cloisters of city elites to embrace the poor and needy wherever they may be found.

Beyond the streets of Jerusalem, the influence of the Christian mission also begins to spread to 'the towns around Jerusalem', as large numbers of afflicted persons make their way into the holy city from outlying communities to be cured by the apostles (5.16). The movement is still *toward* Jerusalem rather than outward from it, but as with the influx of pilgrims from every region of the Diaspora at Pentecost, the attraction of residents from other Judean towns foreshadows the fulfillment of Jesus' missionary agenda in 1.8.

As the scope of the apostles' wonder-working ministry is enlarged, so is the means. Whereas before Peter ministered directly to the lame man through word and touch, now, in passing, he simply casts a healing *shadow* over the crowd (5.15). Such a powerful aura also attended the Lukan Jesus, as evidenced in the immediate cure of a hemorrhaging woman upon touching the fringe of his clothing (Lk. 8.44).

Defending: 5.17-42

Once again jealous temple officials attempt to quell the phenomenal success and popularity of the apostles' mission. On the whole, this second round of conflict between chief priests and church leaders is more dramatic and intense than the first, characterized by surprising interventions (from an angel and a Pharisee) and escalating hostilities ('they were enraged and wanted to kill them', 5.33).

More specifically, the present narrative gives more attention at the outset to temporal and spatial details of the apostles' detention. They are locked away for 'the *night*…in the *public prison*' (5.17-19), that is, quarantined in a marginal time and place outside the realm of normal, everyday life. Clearly the temple authorities want the apostles out of the spotlight, off the stage. But their strategy is completely overturned as 'during the night an angel of the Lord' breaks through the tight security system undetected (cf. 5.23) and breaks the apostles out of prison. 'At *daybreak*' they are back in the *temple* continuing their ministry. When the chief priests and temple captain are apprised of the situation, they become 'perplexed...wondering what might be going on' (5.24). The reader, however, knows what is going on. Night or day, prison or temple make little difference: the work of the Sovereign Lord and his servants goes on, uninhibited by conventional maps and schedules.

Upon finding the elusive apostles, the temple police take them into custody once again and bring them before the council for interrogation. Peter and his companions redirect the challenge back to the officials, accusing them of resisting God's purpose by killing Jesus, the divinely exalted 'Leader and Savior' of Israel (5.29-31). This basic point has already been well-established in the early chapters of Acts (2.22-24; 3.13-15; 4.10-11), but it is punctuated here by a fresh image of how Jesus was executed: 'you had [him] killed by *hanging him on a tree*' (5.30). This associates the Roman practice of crucifixion with a Jewish form of capital punishment—regarded as falling under 'God's curse'—levied against certain violators of the law within Israel as well as foreign rulers conquered in battle (Deut. 21.22-23; Josh. 8.29; 10.26-27). Peter thus charges the Jewish religious leaders of his day with a most egregious error: they have treated Israel's most glorious 'Leader and Savior' as an accursed criminal and enemy. Even so, through the risen and exalted Jesus, God still proffers 'repentance to Israel and forgiveness of sins' (5.31).

By this stage of the proceedings, however, the Jewish council is in no mood to repent or put up with the impudent apostles any longer. If the apostles persist in their preposterous claim (as the council sees it) that the crucified Jesus is Israel's messiah, then they can join him in death (5.33). But, suddenly, in the midst of this increasingly violent judicial scene, a member of the council named Gamaliel stands to intercede for the apostles.

Before reporting Gamaliel's conciliatory speech, the narrator distinguishes him from the rest of the council in terms of association and reputation (5.34). First, he is a *Pharisee* rather than a member of 'the sect of the Sadducees' to which the high priest and his associates belong (cf. 4.1; 5.17). While this is the first reference to the Pharisaic party in Acts, readers of the previous Lukan volume carry over multiple images of sharp conflict between Jesus and this group concerning table fellowship, sabbath observance, money management and other legal issues (Lk. 5.27-39; 6.1-11; 7.36-50; 11.37-54; 14.1-24; 15.1-2; 16.1-15; 18.9-14). It is thus quite surprising now to encounter a leading Pharisaic 'teacher of the law' functioning as an advocate for Jesus' followers. The perceptive reader will have also picked up other clues, however, which prevent Gamaliel's intervention from seeming utterly incredulous. Although resisting his teaching and practice of open commensality, Pharisees still gathered to hear Jesus and repeatedly invited him into their homes for dinner (5.17; 7.36; 11.37; 14.1); also, on one occasion some Pharisees warned Jesus of Herod Antipas's plot to kill him (13.31), and during the final days of conflict leading to Jesus's death, they dropped out of the picture while the spotlight fell on the murderous designs of the Sadducean chief priests, elders and scribes (19.47; 20.1-2, 19, 27-47; 22.1-6, 54-71).

Secondly, Gamaliel is characterized as a man of superior *honor*—'respected by all the people' (5.34). A similar high reputation among the citizens of Jerusalem had been forged recently by the Christian community and its leaders ('having the goodwill of all the people', 2.47; 'the people held them in high esteem', 5.13). A powerful, honorable alliance is thus established between Gamaliel and the apostles against the shameful temple authorities. Only the former are worthy of leading the people of God (cf. Gowler, *Host*, pp. 274-80).

To check the potential for misjudgment on the part of his volatile council partners, Gamaliel appeals the apostles' case directly to God, the Most Honorable Judge (ironically echoing the apostles' own appeal in 4.19; 5.29). As in recent years God allowed the misguided reform movements of Theudas and Judas the Galilean to be squashed by the Roman military, so God will ultimately determine the fate of the Christian mission (5.35-37; cf. *Ant.* 18.3-9, 23-25; 20.97-98; *War* 2.118). Any human 'plan (*boulē*)' not aligned with God's sovereign purpose for his people is doomed to fail; and, conversely, any movement consistent with God's purpose cannot help but succeed. Of course, the implied reader of Acts already knows that God's 'plan' for Israel and the world centers on Jesus Christ the Lord and operates in spite of; and even because of, violent opposition (cf. *boulē*, 2.23; 4.28). The Jewish council thus again risks putting itself in the untenable position of 'fighting against God' (5.39).

As it turns out, the judges heed Gamaliel's counsel and let the apostles go—but not before they call them back in (Gamaliel had dismissed them before his speech [5.34]) for a flogging and final mandate to desist from proclaiming Jesus' name (5.40). In short, the council maintains its belligerent stance. But, as Gamaliel had suggested, this proves to be a futile fight as the witness of the apostles continues unimpeded: 'And every day in the temple and at home they did not cease to teach and proclaim Jesus as the Messiah' (5.42).

Acts 6–12: Excursions outside Jerusalem

Summary texts strategically deployed at the beginning, middle and end of the next major segment of Acts mark the continued expansion of the early church (note the repeated use of the verbs, *auxanō* and *plēthynō*, both meaning 'spread' or 'increase'):

> Now during those days, when the disciples were increasing in number (*plēthynontōn*) …(6.1)

> The word of God continued to spread (*ēuxanen*); the number of the disciples increased greatly (*eplēthyneto*) (6.7).

> Meanwhile the church…had peace and was built up. Living in the fear of the Lord and in the comfort of the Holy Spirit, it increased in numbers (*eplēthyneto*) (9.31).

> But the word of God continued to advance (*ēuxanen*) and gain adherents (*eplēthyneto*) (12.24).

While this general growth pattern continues the trend established in Acts 1–5, it also branches out in a couple of new directions. First, we begin to see a marked *ministerial* increase, as personnel outside the circle of twelve apostles emerge alongside Peter and John (8.14-25; 9.32–11.18; 12.1-23) as co-leaders of the advancing mission. In the opening scene (6.1-7) we encounter a new task force of seven servants, two of whom—Stephen and Philip—become the major figures shaping the course of events over the next three chapters (6.8–8.40). In the closing unit (12.24-25) we find another pair singled out—Barnabas and Saul—reminiscent of their leading missionary roles in 9.1-31 and 11.19-30. Barnabas made a brief appearance earlier in Acts (4.36-37), but Stephen, Philip and Saul are introduced for the first time in chs. 6–12. Moreover, several other ministers make their debut in this section in more limited roles: Ananias (9.10), Tabitha (9.36), Agabus (11.28), John Mark and his mother Mary (12.12, 25), and James (12.17).

Secondly, Acts 6–12 charts the church's *territorial* progress beyond Jerusalem. Witnesses finally move outside the limits of the holy city instead of waiting for immigrants to come to them. The next stages of Jesus' plan in 1.8 begin to be realized. Outreach extends to Samaria and the Judeancoastal region around the cities of Gaza, Azotus, Lydda, Joppa and Caesarea (8.4-40; 9.32–10.48). Further still, beyond Israelite borders, the gospel stretches to Ethiopia (8.26-39), Phoenicia, Cyprus, Tarsus, and the Syrian centers of Antioch and Damascus (9.1-18; 11.19-30). The foundation for such expansion is laid earlier in Stephen's citation of several well-known biblical precedents of God's activity outside the land of Israel (7.2-53).

Amidst all of this movement, however, in Acts 6-12, the headquarters of the mission remain in Jerusalem. The section begins and ends in the Jewish capital (6.1-8.3; 12.1-25), and the various missionary excursions in between all start from and in some way loop back to this center. As new communities are established by pioneering missionaries in outlying areas, vital links are maintained with the mother church in Jerusalem and her apostolic leaders.

Along with the overriding emphasis on expansion, Acts 6-12 also coheres around recurrent patterns of *persecution* and *conversion*. Threats of severe persecution in the preceding chapters now become reality, as reports of the church's first martyrs in Jerusalem frame chs. 6-12: at the beginning, *Stephen* is stoned to death with council approval (6.8-8.1); and, at the end, *James* the apostle falls under Herod's sword (12.1-2). In between, other murderous plots against Jesus' disciples revolve around 'a young man named *Saul*', appearing first as the leading perpetrator of such 'havoc' (7.58-8.3; 9.1-2, 21) and then, after his remarkable conversion, as the target of the same hostility he had previously generated (9.23-25, 29-30).

However, despite the increased scope and intensity of the persecution, the church's mission continues to thrive. In fact, expansion and persecution ironically work together. As the terrorist campaign following the Stephen incident provokes a massive dispersion of disciples from Jerusalem, they scatter 'from place to place, *proclaiming the word*' (8.4; cf. 11.19-20). Far from stifling the gospel, persecution causes it to spread. Also, balancing the tragic executions of Stephen and James are the dramatic escapes of Saul and Peter from those who seek to kill them (9.23-25, 30; 12.6-11). Peter's release from prison on the eve of his scheduled execution is particularly notable, as 'an angel of the Lord' intervenes and escorts him to safety. The early Christians' alliance with higher, supernatural powers proves to be more than a match for malevolent authorities arrayed against them.

The theme of conversion clusters in Acts 8-11, focusing on two groups—Samaritans and Gentiles—and three individuals—the Ethiopian eunuch, Saul, and Cornelius—who become a part of the Christian community through faith and baptism. There is also a sense in which Peter undergoes a 'conversion' in his understanding of who qualifies for membership in the people of God. Common to these conversion experiences are dramatic mystical encounters, both aural and visual, with God, the exalted Jesus, the Holy Spirit, and angels of the Lord (8.17, 26, 39; 9.3-19; 10.1-20, 44-47; 11.5-16). The opening of the heavenly world (cf. 7.56) overwhelms all earthly attempts to obstruct ('prevent'/ 'hinder'—*kōlyō*—8.36; 11.17) the progress of God's inclusive kingdom. The timing of these conversion-visions varies, but they all occur during the day (as opposed to dreams or jail-breaks in the night), and two are specifically associated with the *noon* hour, the brightest time of the day (8.26; 10.9).

Stephen the Martyr in Jerusalem: 6.1–8.3

Although strictly speaking Stephen's entire ministry up to and including his death takes place in Jerusalem, at several points his story suggests a much wider setting. We have already hinted that Stephen surveys biblical history with a special eye to God's mobile presence with Israel outside the holy land and that Stephen's martyrdom touches off a wave of missionary activity into outlying areas. Other signs of broader horizons include Stephen's apparent affiliation with 'Hellenist' Jews from the Diaspora who congregate in their own synagogues as well as in the temple (6.1, 9) and his heavenly epiphany of 'Jesus standing at the right hand of God' ready to receive the dying martyr's spirit (7.55-56, 59). In short, the Stephen segment of the Acts journey dramatically propels the early church up and out from Jerusalem: up into the heights of heaven and out toward the ends of the earth.

Introduction: 6.1-7

The brief scene introducing Stephen as 'a man full of faith and the Holy Spirit' (6.5) associates him with several groups in the Jerusalem church mentioned rather abruptly for the first time in Acts: Hebrews, Hellenists, widows, priests, and a committee of seven table-servants. If not for the fact that this scene also features 'the Twelve' in a familiar leadership role, we might think we were meeting an entirely different community. In any case, we are kept on our toes as readers and travellers. As the band of disciples continues to expand (6.1, 7), new social and organizational challenges are bound to arise.

(1) *Hebrews and Hellenists.* As the idyllic church portraits of harmony and charity in 2.41-47 and 4.32-36 began to show signs of cracking in the Ananias and Sapphira incident, so now they break down even more with the sudden appearance of two factions—Hebrews and Hellenists—at odds with one another over the material neglect of a subgroup in the community—the Hellenist widows. The narrator introduces these 'Hebrews' and 'Hellenists' without explanatory comment, leaving readers to infer their meaning from linguistic and historical information outside the text. Most scholars start with a basic profile of 'Hellenists' as Greek-speaking Jews who migrated to Jerusalem from the Diaspora. The 'Hebrews', on the other hand, designate Aramaic-speaking Jews native to the land of Israel. Language and place of origin thus constitute the principal distinctives. (Some interpreters also suggest various differences in theology and social customs.)

Accepting these definitions, the Hellenist Christians would include people like Barnabas, the Levite from Cyprus (4.36), and the host of

Jewish immigrants 'from every nation under heaven' who became believers on the day of Pentecost (2.5-11, 41). On the other side, the Hebrew Christians are represented by disciples from Judea and Galilee (2.7, 14), including the twelve apostles and other early followers of Jesus. Although united in a common faith and mission, the Jewish Christians at Jerusalem do not all share a common language and background. Apparently, the glossolalia miracle at Pentecost was a singular phenomenon; thereafter, certain lines of communication between Aramaic- and Greek-speaking believers become crossed again. And when communication breaks down, some voices are not heard—for instance the distress calls of needy Hellenist widows.

(2) *Widows and Priests*. References framing 6.1-7 indicate the general growth pattern of the Jerusalem church (see above) and call attention to the special situations of particular groups—first, the negative experience of neglected *widows* (6.1) and then the positive case of obedient *priests* added to the community (6.7).

The poor folk singled out thus far in Acts as special beneficiaries of the Christian community's love and power have all suffered from some illness of body or spirit (lame, sick, demonized [3.1-10; 5.15-16]). In the widows' case, the focus of need shifts from curing disease to providing basic economic, social, practical and emotional support (see Spencer, 'Neglected Widows'). Without husbands and isolated from wider kinship support networks in their Diaspora homelands, the Hellenist widows are especially vulnerable and dependent on local 'Hebrew' assistance. Unfortunately, however, the Hebrew disciples fail to include these widows 'in the daily distribution of food', prompting the Hellenists to lodge a complaint (6.1).

With the phenomenal growth the early church has experienced thus far, we might regard the oversight of one group as understandable, excuseable, just a minor 'hiccup' along the path to success. But, in fact, against the backdrop of prior biblical and Lukan traditions, neglecting widows is a very serious offence. The Jewish scriptures repeatedly stress God's special role as 'father of orphans and protector of widows' in the vacuum created by absent or abusive males (Ps. 68.5; cf. Exod. 22.21-24; Deut. 10.17-19; 24.17-22; 1 Kgs 17.8-24; 2 Kgs 4.1-7; Ps. 146.9; Prov. 15.25; Jer. 49.11). And in Luke, Jesus emerges as a staunch supporter and defender of destitute widows against unjust judges (18.1-8), hypocritical scribes ('they devour widows' houses and...say long prayers', 20.45-47) and an exploitative temple system (21.1-6) (cf. Lk. 2.36-38; 4.25-26; 7.11-17; 20.27-40). Surprisingly, then, the apostle-led Hebrew Christians in Acts 6 now find themselves out of step with God and Jesus and in awkward alliance with widows' oppressors. Once this problem is exposed, the Twelve promptly devise a plan for meeting the widows' needs (6.2-6); however, their response still leaves something to be desired (see below).

After dealing with the widows' case, the church continues to expand its witness and receive new members—including 'a great many of the priests' (6.7). At first blush, this development may also seem surprising, given the strong priestly opposition to the Christian mission in Acts 4–5. But for the most part, as we have seen, this resistance stemmed from the *chief* priests controlling the ruling council. The cultic system also employed a large number of subordinate priests and Levites, some of whom—like the sectarians at Qumran—became disaffected with the temple hierarchy (cf. *Ant.* 20.181; *War* 2.409-410; Johnson, *Acts*, pp. 107-108). In Luke-Acts certain cultic servants are set apart from the corrupt aristocracy. The Gospel begins with the story of a devout priestly functionary, Zechariah, who becomes a prophet of the coming savior-messiah and father of John the baptizer, Jesus' precursor (1.5-25, 57-80); and in Acts, as we have seen, Barnabas the Levite becomes an exemplary member of the early messianic community (4.36-37). These individuals pave the way for the influx of numerous priests in 6.7 'obedient to the faith', obedient, that is, to God and the gospel of Jesus Messiah 'rather than any human authority' (5.29, 32), such as the high priest and his council.

(3) *The Twelve and the Seven.* To redress the grievance of the Hellenist widows, the twelve apostles lead the community to select a body of 'seven men of good standing, full of the Spirit and of wisdom' (6.3) to oversee the daily soup kitchen. Although the plan 'pleased the whole community' (6.5) and apparently proved to be effective (we hear no further complaints from the Hellenists), it reflects the Twelve's somewhat imbalanced view of ministry from the standpoint of the wider Lukan narrative. As the Twelve recommend appointing a new committee to manage the 'serving of tables (*diakonein trapezais*)', they make it very clear that they themselves want no part in this work lest it detract from their priority business of praying and 'serving the word (*diakonia tou logou*)':

> It is not right that *we* should neglect the word of God in order to wait on tables (6.2).

> [W]e, for *our* part, will devote *ourselves* to prayer and serving the word (6.4).

This narrow perspective marks a retreat from the apostles' recent blend of instructional and charitable service (including 'breaking of bread') to the needy in Acts (2.42-46; 4.32-37) and reversion back to old habits of resisting Jesus' comprehensive ministerial program. On several occasions in Luke, Jesus demonstrated to the apostles that 'menial' duties of table-service and charity went hand in hand with more 'spiritual' pursuits of prayer and proclamation. For example, after praying all evening on the mountain and selecting his apostles, Jesus descended 'with them' and began ministering to the assembled crowd, healing the infirm and pronouncing blessing on the poor, hungry and bereaved (6.12-21); later, while the Twelve wanted Jesus to dismiss the crowd after a long day of teaching and healing the sick, he insisted on feeding the people as well (9.10-17); and, at the last supper Jesus shared with the apostles, while they quibbled over which of them was the greatest, Jesus presented himself 'as one who serves (tables)', the measure of true greatness (22.14-27; cf. 11.1-13; 12.37-42; 17.7-10; 18.1-8). Therefore, in Acts 6, while the Twelve show genuine concern for helping the deprived widows, their reluctance to become personally involved in table-service suggests that they still have not fully accepted Jesus' holistic model of ministry.

The seven chosen table-waiters all appear to be Hellenists. Each has a Greek name, and one of them is explicitly identified as a Diaspora immigrant (Nicolaus from Antioch, 6.5). The well-established reputation of these seven men (6.3) implies a prior leadership role in the Hellenist community. The wisdom of appointing a committee of high-standing Hellenists to insure the Hellenists' welfare is obvious.

As for the Seven's relationship with the twelve apostles, the narrative sends some mixed signals. On the one hand, the Twelve appear to be in a position of authority over the Seven; they initiate and validate the selection process and speak as if they will officially appoint the Seven to their new task (6.3). On the other hand, by the end of the story an arrangement more collegial than hierarchical seems to prevail. As in the appointment of Judas' replacement in 1.23-26, the 'whole community' nominates the seven candidates and commissions them for service. (Following the most natural reading of 6.6, I view the congregation as the subject of all the verbs: after presenting their seven nominees to the apostles, they—the entire assembly—pray for the Seven and lay hands on them as a gesture of solidarity; cf. Spencer, *Portrait*, pp. 196-99.) Also, the Seven are no less 'full of the Spirit' than the Twelve (6.3), and as will soon become apparent, two of their group (Stephen and Philip) distinguish themselves as much as dynamic preachers and miracle-workers as table-servants. Whatever authority the apostles continue to possess within the expanding church, it is by no means exclusive and in no way extends to holding a monopoly over certain preferred forms of ministry.

Opposition: 6.8-7.1

Given the close integration of oratorical (preaching, teaching), therapeutic (healing, exorcism) and practical (food provision, table-service) types of service (*diakonia*) in Luke's Gospel, it is striking that once Stephen and Philip are introduced as table-servants, thereafter we hear nothing more about their pursuit of this vocation alongside the ministries of proclamation and miracle-working which they begin to perform. It is not the adding of these other tasks which is so unusual, but the dropping of the first one.

One effect of this abrupt shift is the impression that the problem surrounding table-service has been decisively tackled. Our narrator-guide is honest enough to mention internal church conflicts but does not dwell on them; after a brief report on basic issues and resolutions, the story swiftly moves on. Also, with or without problems, private church affairs receive comparatively little attention in the early chapters of Acts, relegated to succinct summaries and isolated incidents. Most of the action focuses on the disciples' expanding witness in the public arena, to which we now turn with Stephen.

Stephen's working of 'great signs and wonders among the people' and proclamation of Jesus of Nazareth land him, like Peter and the apostles earlier, before an angry temple council (6.8, 12-14). But Stephen's troubles start before this with another audience in another setting. He debates with a group of *Hellenist Jews* in *Jerusalem synagogues* (6.9). These Hellenists include 'Freedmen' (freed slaves, perhaps descendants of the Jewish captives taken to Rome by Pompey in 63 BCE; cf. Philo, *Embassy to Gaius* 155-57) and citizens from North Africa (Cyrene and Alexandria) and Asia Minor (Cilicia and Asia). Although revering the temple as the supreme 'holy place' (6.13), these groups also gather in their own local Greek-speaking synagogues in Jerusalem—like those in the Diaspora—for scripture study, prayer, and fellowship. The grammar of 6.9 suggests that Stephen confronts representatives from two separate synagogues, one comprised of Freedmen and North Africans, the other of immigrants from Asia Minor (Marshall, *Acts*, p. 129).

While many Hellenists since Pentecost have welcomed the gospel—perhaps including some among the Africans and Asians (cf. 2.9-10)—these at the end of Acts 6 react strongly against Stephen and his message. They mobilize others against him, both religious leaders and ordinary folk, haul him before the council and incite 'false witnesses' to accuse him of making incessant attacks against 'this holy place and the law' (6.12-13). More specifically, they charge Stephen with daring to claim that 'Jesus of Nazareth will destroy this place and will change the customs that Moses handed to us' (6.14). This is a new line of attack against Christian spokesmen in Acts. With Peter and John, official opposition was directed against their bold announcements concerning Jesus' resurrection and exaltation and the continued power of Jesus' name to heal and restore Israel. As we have seen, this apostolic message included an implicit critique of the temple establishment, but it never reached the level of blatantly forecasting Jesus' destruction of the holy sanctuary.

The labelling of Stephen's accusers as 'false witnesses' obviously devalues their testimony in some respect. The strict 'evidence' of the preceding Lukan volume shows that Jesus demonstrated against the temple (Lk. 19.45-46) and predicted its destruction (21.5-6) but stopped short of claiming that he would personally engineer the temple's razing. Moreover, no witnesses come forward at the Lukan Jesus' trial (as they do in Mk 14.58) suggesting that he had ever made such a claim. As for Jesus' attitude toward temple-based, Mosaic *customs*, whatever icono-clastic tendencies may have developed in his ministry are tempered by the thoroughly compliant scenario of the Lukan birth narrative (2.21-27, 39—'they had finished everything required by the law of the Lord') and the sweeping contention of the risen Jesus that 'everything spoken about me in the law of Moses...must be fulfilled' (24.44). Of course, however we assess the prior Lukan material, final judgments about the 'false' reports concerning Stephen's preaching about Jesus must be suspended until carefully attending to Stephen's own testimony in the next chapter.

Before recounting this witness, the narrator provides important clues as to the overall rhetorical effect of Stephen's speech. Not only *what* Stephen says is significant, but also *how* he *says* it and *shows* himself: his verbal and facial expressions both make a dramatic impression on his audience. In the first place, 'they could not withstand the *wisdom* and the *Spirit* with which he spoke' (6.10). This recognition of Stephen's wisdom-spirit endowment by synagogue-based Hellenists mirrors the recent judgment of the early church (6.3, 5) and the characterization of the young Lukan Jesus (Lk. 1.35; 2.40, 52). In certain streams of Hellenistic Jewish thought, wisdom was regarded not merely as an intellectual attribute but as a personal (feminine), spiritual force, indeed, the manifestation of the very presence of God communicating supernatural understanding, power and glory:

> I prayed, and understanding was given me; I called on God, and the spirit of wisdom came to me (Wis. 7.7).

> For she [wisdom] is a breath of the power of God, and a pure emanation of the glory of the Almighty (Wis. 7.25; cf. 6.22-8.1; 1 Cor. 1.18-2.16).

Secondly, the council members examining Stephen's case all 'saw that his face was *like the face of an angel*' (6.15). A romantic image of Stephen's sweet, cherubic innocence is scarcely in view here. Angels are dynamic, fearsome figures in Luke–Acts (and in the Bible generally), as demonstrated most recently in busting the apostles out of prison (5.19-21). As the high council could not control these angel-aided apostles, so now it cannot 'withstand' the angel-masked Stephen. Also, given the doubts about Stephen's commitment to 'the customs that Moses handed on to us' (6.14), his altered countenance may be associated with the transfigured Moses—aglow with the presence of God—descending Mt Sinai with restored covenant tablets in hand (Exod. 34.29-35; cf. Lk. 9.28-36). Whatever the 'false witnesses' might *say* about Stephen, any observers—including the council—who dare to *'look* closely' at this man will detect a true 'prophet like Moses' (cf. Acts 3.22; 7.37).

Proclamation: 7.1-53

The chief justice of the council, the high priest, sets the stage for Stephen's speech with a simple query: 'Are these things so?' (7.1). These few words encapsulate all that the chief priest contributes to the proceedings. By contrast Stephen takes the cue and launches into an extended discourse (the longest in the Lukan corpus). As we proceed through Acts, it becomes increasingly clear who speaks with authority and deserves a careful hearing and whose viewpoints can be dismissed.

Stephen addresses the council with the familiar 'males (*andres*), brothers (*adelphoi*)' designation (cf. 1.16; 2.29, 37) but also adds the term 'fathers (*pateres*)' (7.2). On the surface this new label seems to be a sign of respect for the council's leadership among the people (similar to 'rulers...and elders' in 4.8). But as the speech unfolds, a touch of ironic sarcasm may be detected in Stephen's lecturing these ostensible 'fathers' about the faithful founding 'fathers/patriarchs (*pateres/ patriarchai*)' of God's people (7.2, 8-9, 12, 14-15, 19, 32, 38, 44-45, 51-52).

The type of speech Stephen delivers is a selective and interpretive recital of key stages in Israel's biblical history, reminiscent of certain psalms and wisdom traditions (Psalm 78, 106, 135; Sirach 44-51; Wisdom 10-19). Through this historical review, Stephen presents various perspectives on Moses, the law and the temple, but for the most part he offers no formal, direct rebuttal of the charges levied against him in 6.13-14. A strong geographical interest related to the presence of God pervades the speech: Where has 'the God of glory appeared' (7.2)? Where does—and does *not*—'the Most High...dwell'? (7.48). In responding to these questions, Stephen sketches an innovative map of divine space extending above and beyond the holy land of Israel.

(1) *Abraham in Mesopotamia and Haran: 7.2-8.* Reports of Abraham's divine call to settle in 'this land (*gē*)' and to seal his covenantal relationship with God through circumcision (7.4, 8), along with the promise that Abraham's descendants would worship God in 'this place (*topos*)' (7.7), seem to affirm traditional estimates concerning the primacy of Israel's land, law and temple (cf. Gen. 12.1-3; 17.1-14). But a careful hearing of Stephen's complete testimony about Abraham will also pick up certain counterstrains. For all the apparent significance of the promised land as the locus of God's covenant with Abraham, Stephen underscores that in fact Israel's great forefather never owned as much as 'a foot's length' of this holy real estate (7.5). Abraham remained a wanderer, always on the move—and God moved with him; he did not so much find God in 'this land' as on the way to and through it. Abraham's initial encounters with God's glory in Mesopotamia—'the land (*gē*) of the Chaldeans' (7.4)—and Haran established important

precedents regarding the scope of divine revelation. Later, other well-known Israelites would encounter God in these same places outside the promised land, such as the patriarch Jacob (Abraham's grandson) in Haran (Gen. 27.43; 28.10; 29-31) and the prophet Ezekiel in the land of the Chaldeans (Ezek. 1.1-3).

What does this tutorial in historical geography have to do with Stephen's audience? At one brief but important moment, Stephen hooks the council's attention by shifting from third person narration about the past to second person direct address in the present: 'this land in which *you now* (*hymeis nyn*) are living' (7.4). The council is firmly entrenched in 'this land' where it seeks to delimit and protect God's interests. As Stephen sees it, however, God's interests range farther and wider. Thus, from their myopic vantage point, the current fathers of Israel run the risk of misconstruing or perhaps missing altogether the dynamic purpose of God for father Abraham's descendants.

A similar challenge is implied in Stephen's reference to 'this place'. In the present context such language readily evokes thoughts of the *Jerusalem temple* which Stephen has been accused of undermining ('this holy place'/'this place', 6.13-14). Now Stephen recalls God's intention—originally announced to Abraham—to bring his people out of a foreign land so that they might 'worship me in this place' (7.7). While such a statement may seem to support the centrality of the temple, in fact a check of Stephen's handling of scriptural sources reveals a different stance. For the most part, in 7.6-7 Stephen simply reproduces the text of Gen. 15.13-14, his primary source. At the end, however, he makes a significant alteration—actually, an interpolation from another text. Instead of emphasizing the bounty attending Israel's future liberation from slavery—'they shall come out with great possessions' (or 'much baggage', Gen. 15.14 LXX)—Stephen draws on Exod. 3.12 to stress the *goal* and *destination* of the exodus—'they shall come out *and worship me in this place*'. What was 'this place'? The original Exodus context leaves no room for doubt: 'this place' was 'this *mountain*', namely, Mt *Sinai*. Before the temple on Mt Zion came into existence and began to be venerated as *the* fixed holy place of Israel, the wandering children of Abraham found God perfectly well and re-established their covenant with him at a remote desert outpost. (This is a point which Stephen will develop at greater length later in the speech.)

Finally, we gain further insight into Stephen's views on the land and the law by attending to two specific time notes. First, he recalls God's forecast to Abraham 'that his descendants would be resident aliens in a country (*gē*) belonging to others' over an extended period of '*four hundred years*' (7.6). This protracted delay in actually possessing and settling into the promised land (Canaan) to some extent relativizes the importance of this territory. Although times were hard and oppressive, for centuries Abraham and his descendants managed to grow and survive on foreign soil. Secondly, the last thing Stephen recalls from Abraham's career is the covenantal act of circumcising his son Isaac 'on the *eighth day*' (7.8; cf. Gen. 21.4). However tenuous his attachment to the promised land, Abraham's commitment to follow God's revealed law remained firm and precise. His transience proved to be no obstacle to his obedience.

(2) *Joseph in Egypt and Shechem: 7.9-16*. Stephen quickly skips over generations to get to Abraham's great grandsons: Joseph and his brothers, the archetypal twelve heads of Israel (7.8). Their story, as Stephen tells it, illustrates even more dramatically than Abraham's the mobility of Israel's patriarchs beyond holy land limits. Within a brief narrative space, Stephen charts four separate treks from 'Canaan' (a term recalling the stubborn presence of non-Yahwistic peoples in the promised land) to Egypt by a progressively expanding number of Israelites—one (Joseph, 7.9) to seventy-five (the whole Jacobean clan, 7.14). In short, wandering became a way of life for the people of God.

The first journey, instigated by jealous brothers ('the patriarchs'), brought Joseph alone to Egypt as a slave destined to suffer many 'afflictions' (7.9-10). And so began the extended period of harsh exile predicted for Abraham's descendants (cf. 7.6). But alienation from household and homeland did not mean abandonment by God. Indeed, the headline for Stephen's story about Joseph's ordeal in Egypt reads simply: 'God was with him' (7.9). The main evidence supporting this statement concerns God's blessing of Joseph with remarkable favor (*charis*) and wisdom (*sophia*), prompting the Egyptian king not only to free him, but to put him in charge 'over Egypt and over all his household' (7.10). At this point Stephen's biblical report shades over into personal defense. He, too, is an outsider full of divine *charis* ('grace', 6.8) and *sophia* (6.10) in a hostile environment. Ironically, however, he faces opposition from *Jewish* authorities *within* the promised land. If the pagan Pharaoh came to realize Joseph's special gifts and calling, how much more should the priestly council acknowledge the validity and power of Stephen's prophetic mission?

The second and third journeys from Canaan to Egypt were undertaken by Joseph's eleven brothers for purposes of obtaining food during a season of famine (7.11) and ultimately restoring fraternal ties with the exalted Joseph (7.12). This reconstitution of the twelve patriarchs on Egyptian soil under Joseph's authority demonstrates to the Israelite officials in Stephen's day not only the mobility (once more) of God's appointed leaders but also a certain fluidity, even reversibility, of traditional leadership structures: elders may serve youths (Joseph was the second youngest brother); oppressors may be brought full circle to solicit aid from one of their victims. By the same token, Jerusalem high priests may find they have much to learn from a new corps of twelve leaders comprised of 'uneducated and ordinary' Galileans (cf. 4.13) or even from a lowly Hellenist table-servant outside the apostolic circle, such as Stephen.

The fourth journey brings the entire household of Israel ('Jacob and all his relatives...seventy-five in all', 7.14) to settle in Egypt for the rest of their lives (they 'died there', 7.15). Such a pervasive and permanent relocation creates a sense of stark separation from the promised land. But place of death does not necessarily determine one's final home, as bodies are often brought back for burial to cherished family plots, rich in social and cultural significance.

In the case of Jacob and the twelve patriarchs, Stephen reports that their remains were eventually transferred from Egypt northward to the ancestral tomb purchased by Abraham from the Hamorites at *Shechem* (7.15-16). Although it might appear that Stephen is turning the patriarchal story back to the promised land, a brief examination of comparative burial traditions uncovers a different territorial perspective. The dominant tradition lays the patriarchs to rest in the cave-tomb purchased by Abraham at *Hebron* from *Ephron the Hittite* (Gen. 23.1-20; 25.9-10; 50.13; *T. Reuben* 7.2; *T. Levi* 7.5; *T. Judah* 26.4-5; *Ant.* 2.199). Another tradition places Joseph's bones in the Hamorite plot at Shechem, as in Stephen's speech, but traces the purchase of this property back to *Jacob*, not Abraham (Josh. 24.32; cf. Gen. 33.19). Stephen thus conflates various elements from these burial legends into his own version linking all the patriarchs of Israel—including Abraham—to Shechem.

But why? Simple carelessness seems ruled out by the fact that Stephen mentions Shechem twice in 7.16 and otherwise picks his words carefully throughout his defense statement. If indeed he is trying to score a point with the Shechem reference, that point no doubt has something to do with Shechem's close proximity to Mt Gerizim, the sacred center of *Samaritan* society and bitter rival to the main Jewish cult based in Jerusalem/Mt Zion. Strong anti-Shechemite/Samaritan sentiments were commonplace among Jerusalem-honoring Jews in Stephen's day, as reflected in Sirach's reference to 'the foolish people that live in Shechem' whom 'my soul detests' (Sir. 50.25-26), the *Testament of Levi*'s labelling of Shechem as 'a city of imbeciles' (7.2), and Josephus' branding of the Samaritans as 'apostates from the Jewish nation' (*Ant.* 11.340-41). Three stories in the Lukan Gospel presume the background of hostile Samaritan-Jewish relations, but in each case the Samaritans are dealt with charitably; in fact, in the latter two cases, the Samaritans emerge as the heroes of the piece (Lk. 9.51-56; 10.25-37; 17.11-17)!

Stephen's rooting (interring) of Israel's patriarchs in Shechemite soil seems to continue the Lukan narrative's inclusion of the Samaritans among the favored people of God (which will be developed still further in Acts 8) and also to reinforce his polemic against those who attempt to restrict God's activity to select sacred zones. Although Stephen's judges may hold seats of power in Judaism's holiest city (Jerusalem) and institution (temple), that is no guarantee that they are currently in tune with God's purposes. Israel's forefathers, that is, *'our* fathers' (*hoi pateres hēmōn*)—as Stephen stresses three times to draw his audience into the discourse (7.11, 12, 15)—cry out from their graves in 'alien' Shechemite/Samaritan country that God calls his people to stay on the move, to journey with him beyond standard social and cultural boundaries to bless all families of the earth.

(3) *Moses in Egypt and Sinai: 7.17-44.* Following the canonical sequence, Stephen turns his attention from Joseph and his brothers to Moses and the developing Israelite community. After the terse accounts of the Genesis patriarchs, the tempo of the speech now slows, allowing for more extensive coverage of Moses' career structured around three forty-year phases (7.23, 30, 36, 42). Rhetorically, this drawn out, clearly ordered Moses-section functions as the centerpiece of Stephen's discourse, inviting careful deliberation on the part of his hearers. Within the larger Acts narrative, the forty-unit time span recalls the period of Jesus' post-resurrection appearances (1.3) and the age of the lame beggar healed at the temple gate (4.22).

In addition to continuing the speech's emphasis on God's oversight of his people outside the land of Israel (in Egypt and Sinai), this section brings to the fore a second theme, adumbrated in the Joseph account (7.9): the rejection of God's leader (Moses) by the household of Israel (7.21, 27-28, 35, 39-41). Amid this tragic, chaotic situation, however, God faithfully works across the generations (forty years is a standard generation) to vindicate his messenger and validate his purposes.

The first phase of Moses' life runs from his birth in Egypt during the harsh days of Pharaoh's infanticide to his forced flight—at age forty—to Midian/Sinai, where he settled and 'became the father of two sons' (7.17-29). Stephen's version of this period highlights two surprising rejections of Moses by his own people. Initially, against the terrible background of Pharaoh's coercing 'our fathers to abandon (*ektheta*) their infants so that they would die', Stephen reports succinctly that, after three months 'in his father's house', the baby Moses 'was abandoned (*ektethentos*)' and then adopted by Pharaoh's daughter who raised him as her own son (7.19-21). Conspicuously absent from this account is any mention of the persisting protective care of Moses' mother and sister (Exod. 2.1-10) or of any sense of grief Moses' parents might have felt (see Philo, *Life of Moses* 1.10-12) or indeed of possible motivation they might have had for abandoning their young son. (Josephus suggests that Moses' father [Amram] gave him up in order to entrust the child's safety fully to God rather than to frail human hands [*Ant.* 2.217-23]; cf. Ps.-Philo, *Bib. Ant.* 9.1-6; *Jub.* 47.1-9.) The implication is that Moses' father, acting like other Israelite fathers, simply turned his son out to die and that Moses' eventual salvation and cultivation of 'wisdom' and 'power' owed exclusively to God's favor ('he was beautiful before God', 7.20) manifested through Pharaoh's daughter, of all people, and in the Egyptian court, of all places (7.21-22).

Although rejected by his father and raised in Pharaoh's household, Moses later reached out to his 'brothers' (*adelphoi*, 7.23, 25-26), his fellow-Israelites, in an attempt to deliver them from their Egyptian oppressors. He even went so far as to kill one of the cruel Egyptian taskmasters, propelled by the conviction—which Stephen adds to the scriptural account—that his kinsfolk would appreciate his efforts and 'understand that God through him was rescuing them' (7.25). But, sadly, 'they did not understand'; moreover, they actively spurned his assistance, as exemplified by an Israelite who 'pushed Moses aside' (another added touch to the Exodus story) and brusquely dismissed Moses' pretensions to be 'a ruler and a judge over us' (7.27-28). Moses then fled to Midian as a fugitive from his own people as much as from the Egyptian authorities. In this place of refuge, he distanced himself further from the Israelites by settling down as a 'resident alien' and establishing kinship ties (fathering two sons) with the local population (7.29).

The second phase of Moses' career, encompassing a forty-year sojourn in this isolated environment, might appear to stretch the breach with his native kinsfolk beyond repair. But rather than dwelling on the development of this rift over a generation, Stephen hastens to report the dramatic denoument ('when forty years had passed') in which a theophany suddenly reversed Moses' course, sending him back to Egypt to deliver the beleaguered Israelites (7.30-35).

The reference to a fiery manifestation ('in the flame of a burning bush') of God's presence and power recalls the Pentecost spectacle earlier in Acts (2.3), but in a different setting. Moses' divine encounter took place 'in the *wilderness* (or desert, *erēmos*) of Mount *Sinai*' (7.30), far removed from the promised land and what would later become the religiopolitical center of Israelite society, namely, Mt *Zion* in the *city* of Jerusalem. As we have seen, the charges against Stephen focus on his alleged antagonism to this latter 'holy place' (6.13). By recounting Moses' awesome experience of 'the God of your fathers' in another 'place (*topos*)' which the divine voice identified as 'holy land' (*gē hagia*, 7.33), Stephen continues his scriptural line of defense relativizing the exclusive sanctity of his accusers' power base in Jerusalem.

Consistent with the implications of previous visionary experiences reported in Acts (Ascension, 1.8-11; Pentecost, 2.1-13), Moses' epiphany at Sinai led to a missionary journey. The Lord appeared to Moses not simply for his own edification, but for the purpose of commissioning him to return to Egypt to redeem the Israelites. In reporting this turn of events, Stephen particularly emphasizes the irony of God's choosing as the leader of his people 'this Moses whom they [had previously] rejected'. He also clarifies the nature of Moses' vocation envisioned by God in contrast with the people's expectations. Whereas the Israelites had mocked Moses' supposed pretensions to be their 'ruler (*archōn*) and judge (*dikastēs*)', the Lord affirmed Moses' appointment to be 'both ruler (*archōn*) and *liberator* (*lytrōtēs*)' (7.35). The final accent falls not on judgment, but on salvation. Although the Israelites had (unfairly) judged Moses, God sent him not to retaliate, but to redeem them. Such is the way of God with his people, as prophesied early in the Lukan narrative through the Spirit's voice: 'Blessed be the Lord God of Israel, for he has looked favorably on his people and redeemed (brought redemption [*lytrōsis*] to) them' (Lk. 1.68).

In the third and final forty-year block of his career, Moses fulfilled his divine calling to lead Israel's exodus from Egyptian bondage chiefly in the capacity of a *prophet* (7.37) 'mighty in deed and word' (cf. Lk. 24.19). His prophetic actions included 'wonders and signs' performed at strategic sites along the journey—'in Egypt, at the Red Sea, and in the wilderness' (7.36; cf. Deut. 34.10-12)—demonstrating God's dynamic guidance of his pilgrim people through hostile foreign territory and chaotic-liminal realms of sea and desert. In terms of proclamation, Moses' prophetic ministry focused on uttering 'living words' (*logia zōnta*) received via 'the angel who spoke to him at Mount Sinai' (7.38). The Sinai setting clearly associates these words with the law of Moses, which Stephen was accused of undermining (6.13-14). Here Stephen seems to counter this charge by affirming the supernatural origin of the law and its continuing validity for the people of Israel (notice the contemporizing shift to the first person plural pronoun—'he received living oracles to give to *us* [*hēmin*]'). Still, the use of the atypical phrase 'living words' rather than 'the law (*ho nomos*)' may suggest a degree of openness to new, updated ('living'), varied perspectives ('words') on the law in conflict with a more rigid, 'official' system of interpreting the law advocated by the chief priests and scribes.

Unfortunately, Moses' mediation of God's covenantal blessing through liberating miracles and life-giving oracles was not fully accepted by the ancient Israelites. Once again 'they pushed him aside' (7.39, cf. same verb, *apōtheomai*, in 7.27), although this time their frustration was over Moses' mysterious absence ('we do not know what has happened to him', 7.40) rather than his unwelcome assistance. Moreover, compounding their rebellion, the Israelites now pushed Yahweh aside as well as his prophet in favor of worshipping hand-made idols—like 'a calf'—in despicable, borrowed sanctuaries—like the Canaanite 'tent (*skēnē*) of Moloch' (later associated with ritual child sacrifice practiced by Israelite kings, Ahaz and Manasseh, in the Hinnom Valley below the temple mount; 2 Kgs 16.3; 23.10; Jer. 7.31; 32.35; cf. Lev. 20.2-5) (7.41-43). Such idolatrous 'images' (*typoi*) were antithetical to the true 'pattern' (*typos*) of worship revealed by God to Moses, which included not only the sacred stipulations of the law but also the blueprints for the proper place (*topos*) of worship: the portable 'tent (*skēnē*) of testimony in the wilderness' (7.43-44).

Before moving beyond the Moses story, Stephen makes explicit what he has already implied, namely, God's displeasure with Israel's disloyalty to the Sinai covenant and rejection of his appointed prophet. To drive this point home, Stephen echoes the denunciation of Israel's wilderness phase by another prophet from a later era, Amos (7.42-43; Amos 5.25-27). In the eighth century BCE, Amos identified the goal of God's judgment against the rebellious, wandering Israelites as banishment 'beyond Damascus' (i.e., to Assyria). Thus Amos collapsed Israel's history, jumping directly from the wilderness period to his own idolatrous age (as he perceived it) on the brink of foreign conquest and deportation. Put another way, Amos traced a direct line from exodus to exile, virtually effacing the intervening centuries of promised-land settlement in the process. Stephen's appropriation of Amos demonstrates not only a basic agreement with the prophet's radical view of Israel's history, but also an extension of this view reflected in a key geographical modification of the Amos text (LXX). At the very end of the cited passage, Stephen announces, 'I [the Lord] will remove you beyond *Babylon*', instead of 'beyond *Damascus*'. Thus Stephen broadens the focus of divine judgment to include the subsequent exile (sixth century BCE) of the house of Judah following Babylon's conquest of Jerusalem (including the razing of the temple) as well as the Assyrian captivity of the northern kingdom of Israel anticipated by Amos. This unexpected reminder of Judah's disastrous history delivers a jolting warning to Stephen's present audience of Second Temple officials: their social-and-spatial location is no more privileged or inviolable than that of their sixth-century forebears.

In forensic settings, defendants commonly appeal to higher authorities to neutralize charges of deviance mounted against them (Malina and Neyrey, 'Conflict'). Stephen's appeal to the great heroes of Israel's past—Abraham, Joseph, and especially Moses—seems to function precisely as a means of aligning his case with superior judges and witnesses than those represented by the current Jerusalem council. From the perspective of the wider Acts narrative, Stephen not only rehearses Moses' career; he also re-enacts it in several respects. Like Moses, Stephen is a man of 'wisdom' and 'power' in word and deed, a proclaimer of divinely-inspired revelation and a performer of 'great wonders and signs' (6.3, 8-10; 7.22, 36; note also the 'angel' connection in 6.15; 7.30, 38). Moreover, Stephen the Hellenist and Moses the Egyptian (by adoption) and Midianite (by marriage) are both Diaspora Jews, with social and cultural roots outside the land of Israel. Far from blaspheming 'against Moses', as his detractors contended (6.11), Stephen emerges as an exemplary 'prophet like Moses' (7.37). By the same token, Stephen's opponents find themselves precariously allied with the stubborn Israelites of the past who shoved Moses (and God!) aside in pursuit of their own ill-fated schemes.

(4) *God in Heaven and Earth: 7.45-50*. In the final section of his apologetic survey of Israel's history, Stephen appeals to the highest authority of all, the 'Most High' God (7.48), whom he had also been accused of speaking against ('Moses and God', 6.11). Actually, throughout the speech Stephen has invoked God's name numerous times in reporting the divinely directed activities of the Genesis patriarchs and Moses (*ho theos* appears twelve times in 7.2-44). Now, however, the human actors—namely, Joshua, David and Solomon—although notables in Israel's past, are reduced to bit players (their total contribution is compressed into three verses, 7.45-47), as the focus falls more fully on the cultic and cosmic dimensions of God's presence.

First, Stephen argues for God's preference of the wilderness tent (tabernacle) over the Jerusalem temple as the locus of true worship. The former sanctuary, fashioned according to divine specifications (7.44), originated in the wilderness era but was not confined to it. From the conquest of the promised land to the monarchy, from Joshua to David, the tent 'was there' too, brought into the land as a symbol of God's continuing, dynamic leadership (7.45-46). *But then (de)*, a change occurred with Solomon 'who built a house for [God]'—a fixed structure, the Jerusalem temple—displacing the mobile tabernacle (David inquired about such a project but never achieved it, thus retaining his 'favor [*charis*] with God') (7.46-47). While Stephen's high-priestly auditors would no doubt regard Solomon's magnificent temple-house as a crowning achievement in Israel's history, Stephen sharply counters such perceptions: '*But no (all' ouch)*; the Most High does not dwell in houses made with human hands' (7.48). The sting of this comment becomes most palpable in association with the earlier depiction of the golden calf, which the Israelites 'made (*emoschopoiēsan*)' at Sinai, as the product 'of their hands (*tōn cheirōn autōn*)' (7.41). Stephen comes very close to labelling the 'hand-made (*cheiropoiētos*)' Jerusalem temple an idol.

To buttress his polemic, Stephen turns once again to the biblical prophets. The passage he selects from Third Isaiah balances the negative judgment that God 'does *not* dwell in houses made with *human hands*' with a positive portrait concerning where God *does* dwell in relation to what *his own hand* has designed (7.49-50; Isa. 66.1-2). First, a simple, declarative couplet sketches a universal-cosmic image of God's (omni-) presence: 'Heaven is my throne, and the earth is my footstool'; in other words, God resides in and reigns over the entire created order. Next, a rhetorical, interrogative couplet challenges human attempts to delimit God's presence: 'What kind of house (*oikos*) will you build for me? What is the place (*topos*) of my rest?'; in other words, God's glory suffuses and stretches beyond the bounds of any particular cultic site (such as Solomon's temple-house [*oikos*], Jerusalem's holy place [*topos*]). Finally, a single rhetorical question logically links God's pervasive presence to creative omnipotence: 'Did not my hand make (*hē cheir mou epoiēsen*) all these things?'; in other words, nothing manufactured by human hands could ever adequately represent the cosmic splendor of the Divine Creator.

While the Isaiah citation clearly relativizes the importance of Solomon's temple in the narrative flow of Stephen's speech (7.47-50), in light of both its original setting and Stephen's present audience, the prophetic oracle also diminishes the cultic primacy of the *Second* temple. Third Isaiah's universal-cosmic theology was first advanced in the early post-exilic era as a counter-perspective to the 'hierocratic' stance of priests and prophets (such as Haggai and Zechariah), which promoted a rebuilt temple as the sacred center of Israel's restoration (see Hanson, pp. 253-90). Accordingly, Stephen's appeal to Third Isaiah before the current priestly heads of this second rebuilt temple seems strategically designed to undermine their authority.

(5) *Conclusion: 7.51-53.* Throughout his lengthy defense speech, Stephen has conducted a primarily *indirect* critique of his priestly judges. When relating Israel's history to the contemporary scene, his predominant narrative viewpoint has been first person plural (e.g. 'our ancestors'), including himself along with his hearers in the larger Israelite community (the lone exception is the brief second person aside in 7.4—'this country in which *you* are now living'—noted above). In his closing comments, however, Stephen sharpens both tone and perspective, launching into a *direct* 'condemnation of his condemners' (Malina and Neyrey, 'Conflict', p. 119), utilizing redundant, emphatic second person plural pronouns: '*you* (*hymeis*) are forever opposing the Holy Spirit, just as *your* (*hymōn*) ancestors used to do—so *you* (*hymeis*)!' (7.51; note also '*your* ancestors' and '*you* have become betrayers' in 7.52). Stephen thus distances himself ultimately from the present 'fathers' of Israel (cf. 7.2) who, in Stephen's judgment, are following in the wayward footsteps of their fore-'fathers'.

To punctuate his polemic, Stephen resorts to the familiar tack of name-calling (Malina and Neyrey, 'Conflict'), specifically attempting to pin five deviant labels on his accusers: (a) 'stiff-necked', (b) 'uncircumcised in heart and ears', (c) Spirit-resisters, (d) prophet-killers, and (e) law-breakers. The first three echo both scriptural language and various strains of Stephen's discourse.

(a) The image of a 'stiff-necked people' recalls Moses' angry assessment of the rebellious Israelites who worshiped the golden calf at Sinai (Exod. 33.3, 5; cf. Neh. 9.16-17; Soards, p. 151). Having previously outlined this tragic chapter in Israel's history (7.38-42), Stephen now accuses his present, 'stiff-necked' audience of repeating that history.

(b) The reference to 'uncircumcised ears' mirrors the prophet Jeremiah's indictment of the late sixth-century Judeans (just before the Babylonian conquest): 'their ears are closed (lit. uncircumcised), they cannot listen. The word of the Lord is to them an object of scorn' (Jer. 6.10). What they did heed, according to Jeremiah's sermon in the next chapter, were 'deceptive words' regarding the sanctity and security of the temple which had in fact become a 'den of robbers' destined for destruction (7.1-15). As we have seen, Stephen seems convinced that the current temple leadership is trapped in a similar deception (cf. Jesus' prophetic act and word in Lk. 19.45-46).

(c) The charge of 'forever opposing the Holy Spirit' may again reflect the influence of Third Isaiah who, looking back on Israel's apostasy both after the exodus and before the exile, lamented that the people 'rebelled and grieved his [the Lord's] holy spirit; therefore he became their enemy; he himself fought against them' (Isa. 63.10; cf. vv. 10-19). In addition to this possible prophetic background, the preceding Acts narrative depicts Spirit-resistance as both a serious offense—worthy of death for Ananias and Sapphira (5.3, 9)—and a futile enterprise—as Stephen's opponents should already know! ('they could not withstand...the Spirit with which he spoke', 6.10).

(d) After denouncing his hearers in prophetic style, Stephen proceeds to incriminate them for violently rejecting prophetic messengers, just as their ancestors had done. Implicitly, as he assumes the mantle of Moses, Jeremiah and Isaiah, Stephen himself emerges as the latest in this long line of persecuted prophets. Explicitly, Stephen also now includes in this company Jesus, 'the Righteous One' (*ho dikaios*) (the only clear reference to Jesus in the entire Stephen speech)—the object of ancient prophetic expectation who sadly became the victim of recent priestly opposition. Peter sounded a similar blast against Israel's rejection of this 'Righteous One' in 3.14; and, ironically, the Israelites were also put to shame by the affirmation of a Roman centurion, of all people, attending Jesus' crucifixion: 'Certainly this man was innocent' (or 'righteous', *dikaios*, Lk. 23.47).

(e) Stephen's parting shot addresses his audience's legal status. On the one hand, Stephen acknowledges that the present judicial heads of Israel have received the angel-mediated (cf. 7.30, 35, 38) Mosaic law as a holy legacy. On the other hand, however, Stephen bluntly asserts that they have shirked the solemn duty which accompanies this covenantal gift: in short, they 'have not kept' the law (7.53). Stephen leaves the matter with this sweeping charge of law-breaking without proceeding to cite any specific violations. He thus creates a final impression that Israel's current officials have led the people into wholesale abandonment of God's ways, reminiscent of ancient Israel's wilderness apostasy (cf. 7.38-43).

In sum, in response to the charges that Stephen habitually speaks against the venerable figures of God and Moses and the sacred institutions of temple and law, the Acts 7 speech challenges three of these points—repeatedly exalting God, honoring Moses, and affirming the law—but reinforces the remaining complaint concerning Stephen's anti-temple rhetoric. Simmering tensions between Jesus' followers and temple authorities, which we have sensed in chs. 1-5, have reached boiling point with Stephen in ch. 7. Stephen consistently highlights the dynamic presence of God with his people outside the holy place (temple), city (Jerusalem) and land (Israel) and ultimately casts the temple as a 'hand-made' human creation (on a par with the golden calf!) where the Most High God most certainly 'does not dwell'. These perspectives undergird Stephen's concluding diatribe against the present temple rulers who dare to sit as his judges.

In light of some interpreters' perceptions that Luke–Acts is riddled with anti-Jewish sentiment (e.g. J.T. Sanders), it must be appreciated that the harsh invective of Stephen's discourse is part of an essentially *inner-Jewish* polemic delivered by a Jew (the Hellenist Stephen) to a *particular* Jewish group (the priestly temple council) in the style of *Israel's* classical prophets (Amos, Jeremiah, Isaiah). Except for the reference to Jesus' unjust betrayal and crucifixion in v. 52, no uniquely 'Christian' elements appear anywhere else in the speech. Through an interpretive scriptural survey of Israel's history, Stephen drafts a prophetic blueprint for renewing God's covenant people.

Persecution: 7.54–8.3

Stephen's speech sparks a strong visceral and physical reaction from the audience: 'they became furious in their hearts and ground their teeth at Stephen' (7.54). The latter picture of teeth-gnashing recalls the bitter response which Jesus predicted by those 'evildoers' destined to be excluded from the community of Israel's patriarchs and prophets (i.e. the kingdom of God) (Lk. 13.27-28). Thus, from a Lukan perspective, in their rage against Stephen's interpretation of Israel's sacred history, the present Jewish authorities effectively position themselves outside the true people of God. This alienation is reinforced as hostile emotions soon erupt in violent mob action against Stephen. Israel's leaders tragically murder yet another of God's prophetic witnesses.

As Stephen comes under increasing attack, he offers no further riposte. He has had his say and now diverts his full attention to the heavenly arena. There he fixes on two magnificent sights: 'the glory of God and Jesus standing at the right hand of God' (7.55). Such visions signal a divine vindication of Stephen's ministry and testimony and associate him with other servants of God who had similiar experiences. The perception of God's glory links Stephen most directly with Abraham and Moses featured in the preceding speech (7.2, 30-32) and, more remotely, with other well-known biblical seers of theophanic glory, such as Solomon and the priests at the temple dedication (1 Kgs 8.10-13), Isaiah in the temple (Isa. 6.1-3), and Ezekiel in exile (Ezek. 1.4-28; 8.1-4; 10.1-22).

The glimpse of the exalted Jesus while 'gazing (*atenizō*) into heaven' recalls the apostles' observation of Jesus' ascension (Acts 1.9-11). In that scene, the apostles watched Jesus rise in cloudly splendor and depart into heaven out of sight. Now, for the first time since that momentous exit, Jesus becomes visible again from his heavenly station, reappearing not to one of the twelve apostles, however, but to Stephen the Hellenist, one of the seven table-servants. Of particular significance in this manifestation is the *posture* of Jesus' presence. Through a double reference—first by the omniscient narrator, then confirmed by Stephen's own testimony—the story accentuates that Stephen sees Jesus *standing* at God's right hand (7.55-56). The sudden variation from the customary *seated* position of authority (Lk. 22.69; Acts 2.34) suggests some new development in the plot. We might think that Jesus is standing in order to return to earth in power, as predicted (Lk. 21.37; Acts 1.11), to deliver his imperiled servant; but in fact Jesus makes no move to leave heaven or to liberate Stephen from death. Alternatively, since standing up typically cues the beginning of an important speech (cf. 1.15, 2.14; Soards, p. 32), we might anticipate some vital words from Jesus to help Stephen through the immediate crisis; but in fact Jesus says nothing at all.

We do, however, hear the dying Stephen utter two final prayer-statements—'Lord Jesus, receive my spirit' and 'Lord, do not hold this sin against them' (7.59-60)—which echo Jesus' own farewell pleas from the cross (Lk. 23.34, 46), and we soon learn that the wider persecution against the Jerusalem church following Stephen's stoning prompts many witnesses to disperse 'throughout the countryside of Judea and Samaria...proclaiming the word' (8.1, 4). Although Jesus himself does not move or speak, his followers do both in his name, carrying his message beyond Jerusalem, beginning to fulfill the next stages of his global missionary agenda announced just before his ascension (1.8). Jesus' standing, then, seems to reflect his affirmation of both Stephen's final witness (martyrdom) and the expanding witness of the early church. Although he does not return to earth in triumph, his cause is advanced amid suffering. Far from stifling the gospel, persecution ironically stimulates its growth.

Accompanying the scene of Stephen's execution and consequent outbreak 'that day' of official hostility against the Jerusalem church is a shuffling of characters. Appearing for the first time in the narrative is 'a young man named Saul'. The narrator provides only a brief introductory sketch at this point, but one that intimates a larger role to come. Notice the escalating significance of Saul's involvement: first, we learn simply of his *attendance* at the execution as valet to the stoning squad (they 'laid their coats at [his] feet', 7.58), then of his *approval* of the proceedings (8.1a), and finally of his aggressive *attacks* against early Christians, extending into their homes as well as public sites and encompassing women as well as men (8.3) (a hint of women's influence in the developing church: they are important enough to be arrested and imprisoned!).

As Saul enters the narrative, the apostles, somewhat surprisingly, exit (temporarily of course). They have actually been in the background since Stephen's ascendancy in 6.8, but now they are formally dismissed. The focus shifts to the entire—'*all*'—company of Christian exiles from Jerusalem—'*except the apostles*' (8.1b). Why do they stay behind while the action of 'proclaiming the word' is carried out by other missionaries (such as Philip, 8.5-13) scattered to other venues ('from place to place', 8.4)? Earlier in Acts the apostles had been the main targets of official persecution; why not now? Likewise, in 6.2, 4, the Twelve had been zealous to reaffirm their primary devotion to the ministry of the word; have they since changed their minds? And most curiously, perhaps, the apostles were the sole recipients of Jesus' final commission to bear witness beyond Jerusalem to the ends of the earth (1.8); have they suddenly abandoned this vocation? We can, of course, envisage more positive scenarios accounting for the apostles' 'except'-ional behavior in 8.1b. Possibly, while everyone else escapes, they stay to make one final courageous stand, to hold down the fort, so to speak, maybe even to join their brother Stephen in heroic martyrdom. Or maybe not. The narrative remains open to various judgments about the apostles at this stage, tantalizing us with the bare report of their distinctive location, but offering no explanation. We are thus spurred to continue the Acts journey, looking for clues to the apostles' whereabouts and activities.

Before moving on, however, it seems fitting to pay our respects one last time to the martyred Stephen. Marianne Sawicki has offered a particularly apt tribute encompassing the whole of Stephen's career in Acts 6–8, coordinating his dramatic Christophany as he faces death with his previous catering service to destitute widows. We must remember, she contends, that

> it is the soup-line worker Stephen…who, 'full of the Holy Spirit, was staring up into the sky and saw God's glory, and Jesus standing at the right hand'. No one in the New Testament understands resurrection better, or speaks of it more eloquently, than this man whose daily job was to distribute food to widows (pp. 90-91).

This characterization of Stephen supports, in Sawicki's reading, a basic Lukan conviction that 'recognition of the Risen Lord is possible only within a community that knows both how to be hungry and how to feed the hungry' (p. 91). Such a community accords special honor not only to men like Stephen (and Jesus), who assist women and perform typical women's work of food service, but also to women themselves distinguished as ministers to Jesus' needs and the *first* witnesses to his resurrection (Lk. 8.1-3; 24.1-10).

Philip the Evangelist in Samaria and Judea: 8.4-40

The focus on the wider ministries of the seven table-servants continues with the presentation of Philip's evangelistic endeavors. Philip takes up Stephen's mantle after his martyrdom and extends his work of gospel-preaching and miracle-working to 'the city of Samaria' and 'all the towns' along the Judean coast from Azotus to Caesarea (8.5, 40). Philip is thus distinguished as the first figure in Acts to bear witness to Christ beyond Jerusalem's borders, in fulfillment of Christ's commission in 1.8. In addition to spreading the gospel throughout 'all Judea and Samaria', Philip also launches its push to 'the ends of the earth' by evangelizing an Ethiopian official in transit from Jerusalem back to his distant homeland (8.26-39).

Although Philip is the leading character in ch. 8, he does not dominate the scene to the extent that Stephen did in the previous chapter. Other figures also play important roles. Two of the Jerusalem apostles, Peter and John, re-emerge as active participants in the narrative (8.14-25), and two of Philip's converts, Simon the magician and the Ethiopian eunuch, are not only passive objects of ministry but contributing subjects through direct speech as well (8.19, 24, 31, 34, 36).

This active role of religious seekers represents a notable new development in the plot of Acts. Up to this point most beneficiaries of the early church's mission have been summarily designated as a statistical mass (2.41-47; 4.4, 32-37; 6.7); others, like the lame beggar and hungry widows, received more individual attention but still remained quietly in the background. (There was a general reference to the Hellenists' complaint about their widows, but no record of any widows' specific pleas.) Now for the first time, needy characters take the initiative and speak out for themselves, expressing their *desires* for access to valuable spiritual resources. Simon desires the ability to impart the Spirit to others (8.19), and the Ethiopian eunuch desires assistance in interpreting the Jewish scriptures for himself (8.31). Such desires mark important junctures in the course of the story as they open up various possibilities for responsive action. How will these desires be addressed? Will they be frustrated, fulfilled, or modified in some way? (I owe this narrative-critical focus on 'desire' to David Gunn's analysis of the Lot story in Genesis 19.) As it happens, Acts 8 maintains a level of suspense through presenting very different responses to characters' desires: Simon's ambitions are thoroughly frustrated, even vilified, by Peter, while the eunuch's hopes are joyously fulfilled by Philip.

Such desires may also be explored in terms of their connection to core sociocultural codes structuring honor-shame and patron-client relations (see Moxnes). Both the magician and the eunuch are seeking to enhance their honor-standing (reputation) in the public arena among

particular communities, the former among the wonder-dazzled citizens
of Samaria, the latter among the scripture-grounded people of Israel.
And for both figures, the means to realizing their desires lies in tapping
the Heavenly Patron's rich storehouses of power and wisdom (Spirit/
Scripture) through authorized brokers (Peter and John the apostles/
Philip the evangelist).

Simon Magus and the Samaritans: 8.4-24

Philip's dynamic ministry of word and deed in Samaria follows the basic
agenda established by the apostles and Stephen while also adding
important new features. Familiar elements include performing wondrous signs and miracles (*semeia/dynameis*)—such as healing the
'lame' as Peter and John had done—proclaiming the name of Jesus
Christ, and baptizing believers into that name (8.5-8, 12-13). For the first
time in Acts, however, we encounter a minister who exorcises unclean
spirits and explicitly bears witness to 'the kingdom of God' (8.6, 12),
replicating the work of the Lukan Jesus (see Lk. 4.18-19, 31-44; 7.21-22;
8.1-2; 9.37-43; 11.14-26, especially Jesus' conjunction of exorcism and
kingdom in 11.22: 'If it is by the finger of God that I cast out the
demons, then the kingdom of God has come to you.'). The apostles, we
may recall, spoke earlier about the kingdom of God in Acts 1.6, but this
was in a query to the risen Jesus reflecting their narrow, nationalistic
conception of the kingdom and prompting Jesus' commission to reach
out to all peoples of the earth. Despite all their success in spreading the
word of God (6.7) and building the church at Jerusalem in Acts 2-6, the
apostles have yet actively to promote the inclusive kingdom of God
stretching beyond Jerusalem's and Israel's ethno-political borders. Philip
takes the lead here as a 'pioneering missionary' (Spencer, *Portrait*,
pp. 271-73), inviting non-Israelite citizens in non-Israelite territory into
the kingdom of God, while the apostles remain stationed quietly (for the
moment) in Jerusalem.

The particular 'city' (*polis*) and 'nation' (*ethnos*) of Samaria (8.5, 9)
evangelized by Philip is noteworthy in light of well-known hostilities
between Samaritans and Jerusalem-oriented Jews, discussed above
(p. 73) in connection with the Shechem references in Stephen's speech.
It was radical enough for Stephen, addressing leading Jewish authorities
in Jerusalem, to demarcate the Samaritans' cultic center (Shechem/
Gerizim) as the site of Abraham's only titled property in the promised
land, a tomb in which Israel's patriarchs were buried (7.16). But claims
of sacred Samaritan territory rooted in an isolated plot of ground housing dead heroes from Israel's archaic past leave ample space for questioning the status of present, living inhabitants throughout Samaritan
country. It is even more shocking, then, when a throng of residents ('all
of them, from the least to the greatest') in 'the [main] city of Samaria'
eagerly embrace Philip's message concerning Jesus Christ and enjoy

messianic blessings of healing, liberation, and fellowship in the kingdom of God.

The dividing wall of hostility between Samaritans and Jews has been officially broken down through Philip's mission. In Lukan terms, this watershed event not only updates Stephen's Shechem reference, but also reaches back to and dramatically inverts the initial Samaritan incident in Luke 9. Whereas the Jerusalem-bound Jesus was denied entry into a Samaritan village and then had to restrain two of his hotheaded apostles, James and John, from retaliating in incendiary, Elijianic fashion (Lk. 9.51-56), the Jerusalem-fleeing Philip receives an enthusiastic reception in the Samaritan capital for his Christ-centered gospel of blessing and salvation, instead of judgment and destruction.

As we journey with Philip into Samaria and notice the eager Samaritan crowds flocking to 'hear and see' this dynamic evangelist (8.6), our attention is also riveted more pointedly on a unique figure among the crowd, a magician named Simon. The narrator informs us that 'for a long time' prior to Philip's arrival, Simon had 'amazed' (*existēmi*) the whole town with his magical feats and gained a wide and welcome hearing (*prosechō*) for his personal claim to be the 'Great Power (*dynamis megalē*) of God' incarnate (8.9-11). A potentially tense situation thus arises: what will Simon do now that his supporters are thronging in mass to hear (*prosechō*) Philip's message, see his miracles, and ultimately join his Christian community through faith and baptism? Remarkably, Simon mounts neither a defense of his own reputation nor a challenge to Philip's, but instead he himself believes and is baptized and becomes Philip's constant companion, awestruck ('amazed', *existēmi*) by the 'signs and great miracles (*dynameis megalas*)' which the evangelist exhibits (8.13).

Obviously, then, Philip's power is quantitatively 'greater' than that of Simon, the reputed 'Great Power'. But the Christian missionary is also *qualitatively* superior to the Samaritan magician (Spencer, *Portrait*, pp. 92-103). In the narrative world of Luke–Acts, the performance of miraculous signs implies a channelling of authentic, divine power for altruistic ends in contrast to the demonic origin and fraudulent intent of the practice of magical arts. 'Miracle' is a positive term; 'magic' is pejorative. In the cases of Philip and Simon, the former utilizes his power to deliver 'many' Samaritans crippled by disease and demonization and conjoins this demonstration with good news about Jesus Messiah. In response, the Samaritan crowds are not so much mesmerized by Philip's personality or ability (*existēmi* is not used to describe their reaction) as by the Christ he proclaims ('they listened eagerly *to what was said* by Philip', 8.6), in whose name they believe and are baptized. Simon, on the other hand, seems only interested in advancing his own name, 'saying that he was someone great', utilizing his powers to bedazzle the people, not to benefit them, and garner their attention 'to him' (8.10). Although Simon appears to embrace the gospel, his continuing preoccupation with Philip's mighty works as amazing spectacles raises doubts about the sincerity of his conversion.

The nature of Philip's ministry and Simon's character are further clarified in relation to the visit of two apostolic representatives from Jerusalem. Peter and John's (re-) appearance on the scene demonstrates the apostles' continuing interest, albeit belated, in the missionary expansion of the church. While staying behind to maintain the belea-guered mother church in Jerusalem (8.1b), they also begin to reach out-side the city limits to new believers. The precise purpose of the apostles' visit to Samaria is not spelled out, but we may surmise some mixed intent both to inspect the fledgling congregation and to assist in its development, both to police and to pastor this new mission field. As it happens, they find a deficiency—'as yet the Spirit had not come upon any of them'—which they promptly remedy through prayer and the laying on of hands (8.14-17). Contemporary readers, steeped in Pauline and Johannine theology, are often puzzled by this time lag between believing-and-being-baptized-in-Christ (conversion-initiation) and receiv-ing the Spirit. However, this pattern is not so unusual for the Acts narra-tive up to this point. At Pentecost, Peter established a clear—but *not necessarily simultaneous*—link between repentance, baptism, and Spirit-reception (2.38). The apostles themselves were 'baptized with the Spirit' on Pentecost some time *after* they had received John's water-baptism of repentance (cf. 1.5, 22), and then they experienced yet another Spirit-filling *after* this while gathered in prayer with the Jerusalem church (4.31; was this the *first* infusion of the Spirit for those baptized and added to the congregation in 2.41?). In short, the Spirit seems bound to no rigid schedule in Acts.

More curious than the Spirit's 'late' arrival in Samaria is Philip's total lack of involvement in conveying the Spirit to his own Samaritan con-verts. The evangelist fades completely out of view while the apostles take center stage, raising possible doubts about Philip's competence as a Spirit-empowered witness. Again, however, an established Lukan pattern may help to explain the situation in more positive terms. The careers of John the Baptist and Jesus were correlated within a forerunner-culminator model particularly associated with the rituals of water-baptism and Spirit-baptism (Lk. 3.16-18; Acts 1.5; cf. 11.16):

Forerunner: John prepared the way by preaching the gospel and baptizing with water.

Culminator: Jesus came after to complete John's mission, culmi-nating in baptism with the Spirit (and fire).

Such a model accentuates the climactic greatness of Jesus' mission, but not in a way which denigrates John's preparatory work or diminishes his lifelong reputation (from the womb) as a Spirit-filled prophet, who in his own right was 'great in the sight of the Lord' (Lk. 1.15-16, 76-80). Overall, the Lukan John and Jesus are cast as cooperative partners, rather than competitive rivals, in building the kingdom of God in Israel. I suggest that the mission to Samaria in Acts 8 reflects a similar collaborative effort between Philip the forerunner who baptizes with water and Peter/John the culminators who impart the Spirit, in no way stigmatizing the 'great' evangelistic achievements of the former (see Spencer, *Portrait*, pp. 220-41). The apostles' laying on of hands may even betoken a gesture of solidarity (extending the hand of fellowship) toward Philip and his Samaritan converts, reminiscent of their earlier endorsement of Philip's table-service (6.6).

If the apostles can be viewed implicitly as supporting and complementing Philip's work in Samaria, it soon becomes clear that they react quite differently to Simon's activity and aspirations. Simon provokes Peter, in particular, into a heated debate over brokering the Spirit which may be structured along the lines of an honor-shame contest.

(1) *Claim*. By recounting the apostles' successful mediation of the Spirit to the Samaritans, the narrator effectively stakes a claim to their being authorized brokers of divine power. Simon's recognition of this claim is registered in the report that he 'saw' the apostles' dynamic action (8.18), just as previously 'he saw' Philip's miraculous feats (8.13). (Simon's perceptions and responses are triggered primarily by visual stimuli.)

(2) *Challenge*. While neither denying nor questioning the competence of the apostles to transmit the Spirit, Simon nevertheless challenges their honor rating in the Samaritan community by trying to buy a piece of the action (8.19-20). From a typical limited-goods perspective in Mediterranean antiquity, only a fixed amount of resources was available to go around, including the most valuable resource of all: public honor. Such a worldview promoted a precarious, competitive social system in which one inevitably gained honor at the expense of another's shame (a zero-sum, win-lose situation) (Malina, *NT World*, pp. 90-116). Thus, in Acts 8, the meteoric boost in the apostles' as well as Philip's reputation among the Samaritans may be linked causally with a corresponding precipitous decline in Simon's prestige; and, by the same logic, Simon's money-backed request (demand?—'give' is imperative in 8.19) for a share in Peter and John's Spirit-brokering business may be viewed as a calculated move to devalue the apostles' good name and thereby reclaim some of the honor which they had taken from him.

(3) *Riposte*. The sharp tone and lethal aim of Peter's retort ('May your silver perish with you!', 8.20) supports the idea that he regards Simon's offer as a serious honor challenge. What particularly offends Peter is the affront not merely to his own dignity but to the supreme honor of *his Divine Patron*: 'you thought you could obtain *God's gift* with money!' (8.20). Controlling the power of the Spirit is exclusively a

divine prerogative, beyond the scope of human manipulation. Anyone, then, who receives the benefits of the Spirit's power or the ability to channel these blessings to others is wholly indebted to God's sovereign grace; and, accordingly, all human honor derived from possessing or conferring the Spirit must be 'ascribed' by God, not 'acquired' from God or his agents (Malina and Neyrey, 'Honor', pp. 27-29). To pretend to acquire the Spirit as Simon has done marks the height of insolence against God on a level of abominable apostasy repeatedly denounced in Israel's deuteronomic-prophetic tradition ('your heart is not right before God'; 'you are in the gall of bitterness'; see Deut. 29.17-20). The only hope left for Simon is to 'repent' and 'pray (*deētheti*) to the Lord' for a chance at forgiveness ('if possible', *ei ara*—no guarantees!) (8.22).

(4) *Verdict*. Simon answers Peter's indictment with another plea which supercedes his previous request and represents a total capitulation to the superior honor of the apostles' Divine Patron: 'Pray (*deēthēte*) for me to the Lord, that nothing of what you have said may happen to me' (8.24). This prayer-centered response exactly matches Peter's admonition, but with a notable variation. Instead of daring to pray penitentially for himself, as Peter advises, Simon asks the apostolic pair ('pray' and 'you' are in the plural) to intercede on his behalf. Far from his former habit of proclaiming himself divine, this renowned Samaritan magician now shrinks back from approaching the God of Israel without a mediator.

What happens then to Simon? He obviously fears the execution of certain ominous penalties announced by the apostles. Precisely 'what they said' might befall him, however, is never specified in the narrative, except for the hint of excommunication in Peter's declaration that 'you have no part or share in this matter/word (*logos*)' (8.20). The notorious destructive force of divine retribution in the deuteronomic scheme (cf. Deut. 29.20-28) and the deadly fate, previously announced by Peter, of other apostates in Acts—namely, Judas and Ananias/Sapphira, whose greedy, acquisitive (*ktaomai*) acts of wickedness (*adikia*) and evil-hearted (*kardia*) testing of the Spirit echo Simon's offences (cp. 1.18-19, 24-25; 5.3, 9; 8.19-23)—suggest a similar threat of capital punishment hanging over Simon's head. But in fact no death sentence is carried out against Simon, leaving open some glimmer of opportunity for repentance and restoration not afforded to Judas or Ananias/ Sapphira. This open-ended scenario perhaps reflects a slight softening of discipline as the church expands into new areas (frontier communities often demand greater flexibility and toleration) or perhaps the historical awareness that Simon did not die immediately but continued to influence the development of Samaritan Christianity (perverting it, as later orthodox traditions would claim, by promoting heretical gnostic ideas).

The Ethiopian Eunuch and the Ends of the Earth: 8.25-40
After a fairly lengthy account of missionary activity in one locale, the narrative picks up the emphasis on scattered movement 'from place to place' (8.4) in the next section. Framing this unit are symmetrical reports of the two apostles' and Philip's evangelistic tours, fanning out from the city of Samaria through numerous intermediate stations en route to different destinations: back to Jerusalem, the religious capital of Judaism, for Peter and John, and out to Caesarea, the Roman provincial capital of Judea, for Philip.

> Peter and John…returned to Jerusalem, proclaiming the good news to many villages (*euēngelizonto pollas kōmas*) of the Samaritans (8.25).

> Philip…proclaimed the good news to all the towns (*euēngelizeto tas poleis pasas*) until he came to Caesarea (8.40).

In between these itinerary summaries, we find an extended report of a particular encounter on Philip's journey with a chariot-riding, scripture-reading official from Ethiopia. Befitting its sandwiched literary setting, the cultural significance of this episode may be related to its multi-faceted liminal location—temporally, spatially, and socially—'betwixt and between' conventional boundaries (Spencer, 'Ethiopian').

(1) *Temporal Location*. An angelic guide commands Philip to 'get up and go *kata mesēmbrian*' (8.26). While this may be a directional order, pointing Philip 'toward the south', it may also be a time note, scheduling his journey 'at noon'. Since *mesēmbria* clearly denotes 'noon, midday' in its only other usage in Acts (22.6) and throughout the LXX, I take this to be the most likely meaning in the present case as well. If it be objected that this dangerously hot hour of the day in the middle east ('at noon [the sun] parches the land, and who can withstand its burning heat?' [Sir. 43.3]), normally spent dining and resting indoors or in the shade (Gen. 18.1-8; 43.16, 25; 2 Sam. 4.5; Song 1.7), is an unusual, if not foolish, time for travel, I think that is precisely the point. Ordinary activity (travelling) at an extraordinary time (midday), out of 'synch' with regular natural and cultural rhythms, opens a window of opportunity for world-shattering knowledge and experience. And noon is a particularly auspicious time for piercing supernatural revelation because of its association with brilliant, blinding light from above. In the aura of such heavenly radiance, familiar sights may be eclipsed and fresh images may come into view, such as—'look!' (*idou*, 8.27)—a fellow-traveller who just happens to be reading scripture and needing illumination at the moment when Philip the evangelist-interpreter arrives on the scene and, again—'look' (*idou*, 8.36)—a body of water in the desert(!) at the moment when Philip's companion is ready to be baptized.

(2) *Spatial Location*. Philip meets the Ethiopian eunuch along a 'desert' or 'wilderness' (*erēmos*) road (8.26), once again a liminal zone

off the beaten path of regular traffic. Journeys through such desolate territory stripped of everyday distractions afford optimum settings for reorientation and transformation from one station in life to another. The classic biblical example, of course, recently recalled in the Stephen speech, is the formation of ancient Israelites into a covenant community on their way through the Sinai desert, putting behind them their identity as slaves in Egypt and pressing on to solidify their new status in the promised homeland (see 7.36-44, where *erēmos* appears four times).

By accepting the gospel and being baptized by Philip in the Gaza desert, the Ethiopian official undergoes a conversion and initiation into the scriptural-messianic community. But, significantly, the direction of his transforming trek through the desert is the reverse of the Israelites' wilderness course: he is heading *away from* Judaism's holy land *back to* his native African country (8.27-28). More specifically, he is returning from a worship pilgrimage to Jerusalem. The results of this visit are not detailed, but the thrust of the eunuch's questions to Philip suggest a prior experience in the Jewish capital of receiving inadequate assistance in understanding the Jewish scriptures ('How can I, unless someone guides me?', 8.31) and of being denied full access into the fellowship of God's people ('What is to prevent me from being baptized?', 8.36). Ultimately, it takes the desert ministrations of a fellow exile from Jerusalem, Philip the evangelist—not the temple authorities or even the twelve apostles (including Peter and John who had just returned to Jerusalem, 8.25)—to satisfy the eunuch's desires for insight and acceptance.

The movement of this transformed, exuberant chamberlain ('he went on his way rejoicing', 8.39) from the desert back home to Ethiopia propels the gospel mission even further out from its Pentecostal epicenter in Jerusalem. Indeed, since ancient Ethiopia—designating the Napata-Meroë kingdom located due south of Egypt between the first and sixth cataracts of the Nile—was renowned in Greco-Roman lore as the farthestoutpost of the known inhabitable world (*eschatoi andrōn, Odyssey* 1.22-24; cf. Strabo, *Geog.* 17.2.1-3), the eunuch's journey may be regardedasthe trailblazing expedition'to the ends of the earth (*eschatou tēs gēs*)' in Acts (1.8).

(3) *Social Location.* Comprehensive examination of the Ethiopian traveller's place in ancient society in relation to standard categories of race, class, and gender uncovers a fascinating, multifaceted character who defies easy classification. Ethnically, he appears to occupy some border position between Jew and Gentile. His employment in the service of an Ethiopian monarch might suggest a Gentile identity, but then again, Israelite tradition abounds with examples of well-placed Jews in foreign courts (Joseph, Ezra, Nehemiah, Esther, Daniel). The eunuch's deep interest in Judaism is certified by his pilgrimage to Jerusalem and personal study of the Isaiah scroll, but as noted above, his continuing

quest for understanding and his hint that something is obstructing his way into the covenant community point to some marginal status vis-à-vis the Jewish establishment in Jerusalem. Perhaps he best fits the category of 'God-fearer', as scholars have traditionally used the term, denoting a Jewish-sympathizing Gentile who has stopped short of (or been prevented from) becoming a full proselyte through rites of circumcision and baptism and commitment to strict observance of the Mosaic law.

While most academic interest in the Ethiopian eunuch's ethnic profile has revolved around the Jew-Gentile question, recently African-American scholars have called attention to this man's identity as a black-skinned, African official (Felder, pp. 182-86; Martin, pp. 791-94; Smith). In marked contrast to the tragic oppression and vilification of black Africans in modern Western history, Ethiopians in particular were idealized in ancient classical writings as people of great piety and beauty. Homer spoke of 'blameless Ethiopians' (*Iliad* 1.423-34); Herodotus extolled the 'burnt-skinned' Ethiopians as the tallest and most handsome of all humankind (*History* 3.20); and Diodorus of Sicily commented that 'it is generally held that the sacrifices practiced among the Ethiopians are those which are most pleasing to heaven' (3.3.1).

In the Jewish scriptures, admiration for the Ethiopians (Cushites) has more to do with their upper-class status as a powerful people economically and militarily, who would one day honor the God of Israel with their vast resources (2 Chron. 13.9-13; Job 28.19; Ps. 68.31-32; Isa. 45.14; Zeph. 3.9-10). The Ethiopian traveller in Acts 8 clearly fits this stereotype. He is portrayed as a prominent 'court official', indeed, the overseer of the 'entire treasury' of the queen-ruler, Candace (8.27). His long-distance journey by chariot (8.28), attended by servants (8.38), and possession of his own Isaiah scroll further attest to his personal wealth and prestige. Such high standing, however, does not prevent the Ethiopian eunuch from humbly seeking and accepting the instruction of divinely-directed prophets (Isaiah and Philip). In this respect, he provides an interesting counterpart to other prosperous, renowned non-Israelites—the Samaritan magician, Simon, in the preceding Acts episode, and the Syrian general, Naaman, in an analogous scriptural story (2 Kgs 5.1-15; cf. Lk. 4.27; Brodie, '2 Kgs 5')—who courted the favor of powerful messengers of God. Unlike their status-conscious, elitist responses involving the use of money—Simon's obsession with Philip's power followed by his attempt to buy his way back into power from Peter and John; and Naaman's initial refusal to wash in the lowly waters of the Jordan followed by his (futile) attempt to pay for Elisha's services—the Ethiopian finance minister sets aside his dignity and pocketbook to receive the gracious guidance of an intinerant evangelist leading to baptism in a wayside, desert pool. He offers only questions and openmindedness, no objections or bargains.

This humility on the chamberlain's part is further suggested by his special interest in the 'humiliation' of the Isaianic servant (8.33), motivated in large measure by a humiliating attribute of his own counterweighting, in certain settings, the honor he enjoyed as a prominent official. I am referring here to his peculiar gender-status as a *eunuch*. After describing the traveller in some detail at the outset of the story (8.27-28), the narrator refers to him exclusively thereafter as 'the eunuch' (*ho eunouchos*, four times). As for the social significance of this dominant, 'eunuch' label, some have thought that it merely reinforces the Ethiopian's status as a government official, irrespective of his physical-sexual condition. However, the use of another term for 'official' (*dynastēs*) immediately after *eunouchos* in 8.27 implies some distinction between the two labels, and the position of this official as close advisor to his nation's *queen* suggests, for obvious reasons, that he was a eunuch in the anatomical as well as administrative sense. (Many attendants of male regents in the ancient orient were also castrated.)

Although not an impediment to his social advancement in Ethiopia (indeed it was probably a requirement), this figure's identity as a castrated male would have placed him in a position of extreme, irrevocable dishonor and impurity in the eyes of the conservative Jewish religious establishment in Jerusalem. The Mosaic law was clear and final: 'No one whose testicles are crushed or whose penis is cut off shall be admitted to the assembly of the Lord' (Deut. 23.1). Such legislation was bolstered by first-century Jewish commentators, such as Josephus, who regarded eunuchs as unnatural 'monstrosities' who must be shunned on account of their gross effeminacy and generative impotence (*Ant.* 4.290-91), and Philo, who classed eunuchs with various 'worthless persons' banned from the sacred assembly because they 'debase the currency of nature and violate it by assuming the passions and the outward form of licentious women' (*Special Laws* 1.324-25). Unable to procreate or be circumcised (in the case of dismemberment) and thus carry on the covenant line, the eunuch had no place in the community (Malina, *NT World*, pp. 160-61). And being completely unable to gain or maintain public male honor by dominating women and protecting the reputation of one's wives and daughters—indeed, bearing in his 'feminized' body the marks of a violated male—the eunuch became the epitome of male shame (Gilmore). Whatever economic and political worth he possessed in some circles and whatever value he attached to the Jewish faith, the Ethiopian eunuch was regarded as socially and religiously 'worthless' in leading segments of Israelite society.

However, in addition to this standard hard-line perspective, the Jewish scriptures also present more hopeful prospects for devout eunuchs. The Isaianic prophet, in particular, foresees a day when pious eunuchs (and foreigners!) will be welcomed into the temple and given a permanent place ('everlasting name') in the household of God (Isa. 56.1-8). And in a similar vein a few chapters earlier, the same prophet speaks of a shorn and scorned figure 'cut off' from life and then seemingly (though not certainly) invigorated again to bring forth a new 'generation' (*genea*) (Isa. 53.7-8). It is this latter text that the eunuch examines while heading away from Jerusalem (Acts 8.32-33), pondering, we may surmise, the relevance of the mutilated, humiliated, ostracized servant of God to his own deviant social position.

Is there any good news here for him? Can he be included among the servant's 'indescribable' progeny, assuming that the query—'Who can describe his generation?'—means that there will be so many descendants that they can scarcely be tallied rather than so few as not to be worth mentioning? Can he participate in the rejected servant's final vindication, assuming that the 'taking' (*airō*) of his life from the earth refers to a 'taking up' in exaltation rather than a 'taking away' in extinction. Obviously, some ambiguity surrounds a positive reading of the selected passage from Isaiah 53. No wonder the eunuch seeks interpretive guidance from Philip. Fortunately, the evangelist clarifies that Isaiah's message is indeed 'good news' by announcing its connection to the person and work of Jesus Christ. Although the precise link is not specified in the Acts story, we may imagine that Philip identifies the rejected-vindicated, crucified-ascended Jesus as the humiliated-exalted Isaianic servant who sympathizes with the plight of social and religious outcasts and opens a way for them into the household of God. This would explain the eunuch's eagerness to embrace Philip's message and ask for baptism on the spot. In the inclusive messianic community founded by the suffering Jesus, the eunuch finds the understanding and acceptance he has been seeking.

Philip's boundary-breaking mission in Acts 8 is appropriately capped off by his sudden, miraculous removal from the scene, after baptizing the eunuch, and relocation at Azotus, from where he continues his evangelistic tour up the coast to Caesarea. The Spirit blows where it wills, sweeping the gospel across standard zones of time, space, and society.

Saul the Persecutor in Damascus and Jerusalem: 9.1-31

With Philip the evangelist dispatched up the Judean coast to Caesarea, the narrative shifts attention in ch. 9 ('meanwhile') to another character and itinerary: Saul the persecutor en route from Jerusalem to Damascus. The focus on Saul's violent action against the early Christians echoes and extends the previous report of his 'ravaging the church' which immediately preceded the account of Philip's mission (8.3): Saul is '*still* breathing threats and murder against the disciples of the Lord' (9.1). Thus Philip's evangelism is bracketed by Saul's terrorism. In one sense this envelope structure demonstrates that Christian witness continues to thrive even in the midst of opposition; in another sense, however, it also shows how persistent that opposition remains even when it appears to be thwarted. As the church's influence grows and spreads outside of Jerusalem, Saul, under the auspices of the 'high priest', takes his hostile campaign on the road, hunting down disciples as far away as Damascus in Syria with intent to haul them back to Jerusalem for judgment (9.1-2).

A funny thing happens, however, on 'the way' (*hē hodos*, 9.17, 27) to Damascus, forever altering the course of Saul's life. He encounters the risen Jesus in a blinding vision, submits to Jesus' Lordship, receives Christian baptism, and—most surprisingly—becomes a powerful proponent of the very 'Way' he had been trying to extirpate. ('The Way', *hē hodos*, is used as an epithet for the early disciples in 9.2, suggesting their commitment to follow God's 'way of salvation' paved by Jesus Messiah.)

The delicious irony of Saul's transformation is especially evident in the dramatic reversal of the protagonist's plan to 'bind' (*deō*) the detestable disciples and usher them back to the Jerusalem authorities. Three different voices confirm this plan:

> *Narrator:* 'Saul...went to the high priest and asked him for letters...so that if he found any who belonged to the Way, men or women, he might bring them *bound* to Jerusalem' (9.1-2).

> *Ananias:* 'Lord, I have heard from many about this man, how much evil he has done to your saints in Jerusalem; and here he has authority from the chief priests to *bind* all who invoke your name' (9.13-14).

> *Synagogue audience:* 'Is not this the man who made havoc in Jerusalem among those who invoked this name? And has he not come here for the purpose of bringing them *bound* before the chief priests?' (9.21).

This determined binder and director of the disciples' lives suddenly finds himself incapacitated and dependent on their gracious guidance. He who would lay destructive hands on others now finds himself in vulnerable positions, being led by various helping hands to health, safety and acceptance. Named individuals as well as undesignated groups get in on the act of assisting Saul:

> *Travelling companions:* 'He could see nothing; so they led him by the hand and brought him into Damascus' (9.8).

> *Ananias:* 'He laid his hands on Saul and said, "Brother Saul, the Lord Jesus...has sent me so that you may regain your sight and be filled with the Holy Spirit"' (9.17).

> *Damascus disciples:* 'The Jews plotted to kill him...but his disciples took him by night and let him down through an opening in the wall, lowering him in a basket' (9.23-25).

Barnabas: 'When he had come to Jerusalem, he attempted to join the disciples; and they were all afraid of him, for they did not believe that he was a disciple. But Barnabas took him, brought him to the apostles, and described for them how on the road he had seen the Lord' (9.26-27).

Jerusalem disciples: 'The Hellenists...were attempting to kill him. When the believers learned of it, they brought him down to Caesarea and sent him off to Tarsus' (9.29-30).

Whereas the Philip narrative is enveloped by parallel reports of Saul's perduring persecution (8.3; 9.1-2), the ensuing Saul narrative is framed by diametrically contrasting summaries of the church's fortunes (9.1-2, functioning as a 'hinge' between the Philip and Saul material; and 9.31). The sinister specter of Saul's 'threats' and 'murder' reaching beyond Jerusalem (9.1-2) is replaced, in the wake of Saul's conversion, by a joyous tide of 'peace' and 'comfort' spreading 'throughout Judea, Galilee, and Samaria' (9.31). Where before the church panicked in fear of Saul (cf. 9.13-14, 26), now it rests assured in the reverential 'fear of the Lord' (9.31). And finally, any prospects of losing members to imprisonment and execution under Saul's reign of terror give way in 9.31 to the reality of the church's being 'built up' and boosted in numbers.

The Persecutor Becomes the Proclaimer: 9.1-22

Saul's transforming journey from chief persecutor of the church to dynamic Christian witness may be divided into three segments associated with distinctive locations: the road to Damascus, the house on Straight Street, and the synagogue in Damascus.

(1) *The Road to Damascus: 9.1-9*. As Saul approaches Damascus on his Christian-hunting expedition, the risen Jesus 'suddenly' confronts him both visually, appearing in a brilliant flash of heavenly light, and vocally, addressing him directly and emphatically in the repeated vocative, 'Saul, Saul'. This event most readily invites comparison with the recent Christophany to Stephen just prior to his execution. At that time, Saul was associated with those who 'covered their ears' in horror when Stephen reported his heavenly vision (7.57–8.1); now Saul's ears are forcibly attuned to the words of Jesus himself and his eyes, though remaining physically open, become covered with darkness (9.4, 8). Whereas Stephen 'saw' the splendor of Jesus' glory at God's right hand before being struck by a barrage of rocky blows, Saul 'could see nothing' after being struck by a bolt of celestial lightning (9.8). Although Jesus does not speak directly to Stephen, he expresses to Saul a remarkable solidarity with martyrs like Stephen and others whom Saul has terrorized: 'I am Jesus whom you are persecuting' (9.5). Stephen's final words, flowing out of the experience of both vision and execution, were directed to the 'Lord', asking that his torturers be forgiven ('do not

hold this sin against them', 7.60). Saul's vision also prompts him to petition the 'Lord', but with a different aim: instead of intereceding for others, as Stephen did, Saul pleads for personal understanding ('Who are you, Lord?', 9.5). Moreover, Saul's encounter with the exalted Jesus on the Damascus road may be viewed, in a sense, as an answer to Stephen's merciful prayer. Although there is a punitive element in the Lord's striking Saul with blindness, he stops short of killing Saul (thus avenging Stephen's murder); and beyond that, the Lord even hints at some purposeful mission which the renewed Saul must carry out: 'Get up and enter the city, and you will be told what you are to do' (9.6). Stephen had been 'dragged out of the city' where his life and ministry were brought to a premature end. Now the church's chief opponent is ushered into the city where he will commence a radically new life and vocation.

The spatial significance of Saul's dramatic Christophany 'on the road/way (*hodos*)' may be related to this setting's liminal position between the headquarters of hostile action against the Christian 'Way' (Jerusalem) and the target of Saul's expanding tyranny (Damascus). This 'between-ness' marks the road as an apt place for initiating the seismic change in Saul's social and religious status: he is now 'between' roles, so to speak, clearly no longer the zealous persecutor of the church, but still uncertain regarding his future vocation. Other radical transformations reported in Acts were also triggered in liminal locations, such as those of Moses in the wilderness (*erēmos*) between Egypt and the promised land (also involving a luminous vision and commission, 7.30-34) and the Ethiopian eunuch on the desert road (*erēmos/hodos*) between Jerusalem and Gaza (8.26-39) (on status transformation, see McVann; Turner, pp. 94-130, 166-203).

(2) *The House on Straight Street: 9.10-19*. As the setting shifts to Damascus, new characters enter the picture whom the Lord enlists to assist Saul. A disciple named *Ananias* receives a vision instructing him to go and minister to Saul at the house of *Judas* (another disciple, presumably) on Straight Street (9.10-11). Although perhaps merely coincidental, it is intriguing that the names of these two disciples match those of the two apostates featured earlier in Acts, both of whom suffered fatal judgments (1.16-20; 5.1-6). Such associations illustrate that the work of the church goes on despite internal difficulties (as well as external opposition from Saul and the chief priests); other disciples are raised up to 'take the place' (cf. 1.25) of those who have fallen away.

Moreover, the sudden appearance of a Christian community in Damascus, with no reported details of how it was established, suggests how rapidly and pervasively the church is spreading. Disciples of the Lord and witnesses to the gospel are liable to pop up anywhere, it seems (a phenomenon already evident in the mission of Philip the evangelist, 8.38-40). The first-century city of Damascus was a major cosmopolitan center situated about 150 miles northeast of Jerusalem in the Roman province of Syria. It was part of a network of independent Hellenistic cities in the area, known as the Decapolis; in addition to its dominant Greco-Roman citizenry, it had a substantial Jewish population (*War* 2.559-61; 7.368) and, for a time at least, fell under some influence from the neighboring Arabian kingdom of Nabatea ruled by Aretas (cf. 2 Cor. 11.32).

We also learn of another prominent Greco-Roman city affected (albeit indirectly at this stage) by the Christian movement: Saul's hometown of *Tarsus* (9.11), the capital of the Roman province of Cilicia. This background opens up the interesting possibility of Saul's affiliation with 'those from Cilicia and Asia [who] stood up and argued with Stephen' in the Hellenist synagogue in Jerusalem (6.9). With the mention of Tarsus and Damascus along with Caesarea (Philip's final destination in 8.40), the narrative signals the beginnings of a shift in the church's mission further beyond Jerusalem to political and commercial hubs of the Roman empire.

From this wide urban setting, we telescope to the specific site of Saul's rehabilitation in Damascus: Judas' house on Straight Street (9.11). Here he receives the healing ministrations of Ananias, including baptism and the laying on of hands to restore his sight and infuse him with the Holy Spirit (9.17-18). It is fitting that such a transformation takes place in a local residence on the road called 'Straight' (*Eutheian*). In the early chapters of Acts, the church has repeatedly gathered in private dwellings for prayer, fellowship and decision-making in the fullness of the Spirit (1.12-26; 2.1-4, 42-47; 4.23-31). Now, ironically, the same Saul who had infiltrated 'house after house' to arrest Christian disciples (8.3) finds himself ushered into Judas' house as a fellow-disciple, a follower of the 'Way'. We might even say that his rough and crooked path of persecution has been 'made straight (*eutheian*)' (cf. Lk. 3.5-6). In contrast to Simon Magus who remained the enemy of the church because of a twisted heart 'not right/straight (*eutheia*) before God' (8.21), Saul is completely straightened out in his thinking about Jesus and his followers on an aptly named street in Damascus.

Beyond his experience of conversion, Saul also receives a commission to serve as the Lord's ambassador. As it happens, the details of this commission are not conveyed by the Lord directly to Saul, but rather in a vision to Ananias before his rendezvous with Saul. Specifically, Ananias learns that Saul is the chosen vessel to proclaim the Lord's name to a wide social spectrum, including 'Gentiles and kings and...the sons [*huiōn*] of Israel' (9.15). Outreach to the first two groups was recently adumbrated in Philip's mission to the Ethiopian eunuch, a Jewish-sympathizing Gentile and royal official. The stage is now set for Saul to witness more widely to Gentiles, including those without ties to Judaism, and more directly to government heads (all the way to Caesar?). The targeting of these new audiences, however, on the heels of increasing official Jewish opposition to the church, does not mean that the mission to Israel has been abandoned. Saul, who now knows better than anyone how hostile attitudes toward Jesus can change, will carry on the apostles' and Stephen's work of preaching to 'the sons of Israel' (the inclusive NRSV reading of 'people of Israel' goes beyond the Greek text; will Saul's mission extend to 'both men and women', as did his persecution campaign [8.3; 9.2], to both 'sons and daughters', in line with Joel's prophecy [2.17]?). A final dimension of Saul's destiny revealed to Ananias is the fact that 'he must suffer for the sake of my [Jesus'] name' ('must' [*dei*] connotes a strong sense of providential necessity) (9.15-16). The persecutor will become the persecuted.

The rhetorical effect of delineating Saul's future through Ananias's vision stresses Saul's limited knowledge (blindness) at this stage and dependency on the assistance of other believers. Before giving to others, including noble monarchs, Saul must receive from ordinary disciples like Ananias. (We know nothing of Ananias's status beyond his designation as 'a disciple' in 9.10.) Also the juxtaposing of Ananias's vision with Saul's vision on the Damascus road, directing them to meet at Judas' house, establishes a 'double vision', dual witness framework which confirms the Lord's sovereign orchestration of people and events to accomplish his purpose (see Tannehill, *Narrative*, II, pp. 115-17). This assurance is especially critical in the present case because of the high risk involved in dealing with the notorious arch-enemy of the church. Nothing short of supernatural intervention could allay Ananias's fears (cf. 9.13-14).

(3) *The Synagogue in Damascus: 9.19-22*. Following his disorienting encounter with the risen Lord on the Damascus road, leading to a liminal, reorienting period of three days without sight, food or drink (9.9) in Judas' house, Saul returns to normal physically (seeing and eating) but exhibits a whole new social identity (see Turner, pp. 94-97; McVann, pp. 338-41): first, as a fellow-congregant with the Damascene disciples 'for several days' in an unspecified locale (still Judas' house, perhaps?) and, then—'immediately' fulfilling the Lord's commission in 9.15—as a proclaimer of the Christian message in the Damascus synagogue (9.19-20). The brief narrative describing Saul's inaugural synagogue mission follows a chiastic pattern, centering on the audience's response to Saul's preaching (9.20-22):

> A   Saul proclaimed Jesus as the Son of God
> > B   All who heard him were amazed (*existēmi*)
> > B   The Jews were confounded (*sygchynnō*)
> A   Saul proved that Jesus was the Messiah

The responses of amazement and confusion exactly match those of the Pentecost crowd to the multilingual testimony of the early Jerusalem disciples in 2.6-7:

> [T]he crowd…was bewildered (*sygchynnō*), because each one heard them speaking in the native language of each. Amazed (*existēmi*)…they asked, 'Are not all these who are speaking Galileans?'

No less shocking a miracle, resulting from an overflow of the Spirit (2.4; 9.17), suddenly enables the determined harasser of the early church ('Is not this the man who made havoc in Jerusalem?' [9.21]) to declare publicly the honor of Jesus Messiah. Even more astonishing is Saul's enhancement of Jesus' glory by proclaiming him not only as Messiah, but also as 'Son of God' (the first usage of this title in Acts), recalling (a) the angel's announcement to Mary in the Lukan infancy narrative, linked to Jesus' destiny as the long-expected Davidic king ('He…will be called the Son of the Most High, and the Lord God will give to him the throne of his ancestor David', Lk. 1.32; cf. v. 35), and (b) the Psalmist's portrayal of the 'anointed' (messianic) ruler of Israel as Yahweh's adopted son ('You are my son; today I have begotten you', Ps. 2.2, 6-7).

The Persecutor Becomes the Persecuted: 9.23-31

Moving from initial puzzlement to final verdict, the crowd at Pentecost split into two juries: one mocking the Galileans' glossolalia (2.13) and the other embracing the gospel and joining the Christian community (2.41-42). The respondents to Saul's testimony, first in Damascus and then back in Jerusalem, likewise eventually divide into two camps: some approve of his message and either become '*his* disciples' (9.25; note progression from '*the* disciples in 9.19b) or accept him (eventually) as a true disciple (9.26-28), while others disapprove. This latter company of detractors, however, consisting first of 'the Jews' in Damascus and then 'the Hellenists' in Jerusalem, push way beyond verbal mocking to hatch vicious plots against Saul's life (9.23, 29; cf. the council's desire 'to kill' Peter and the apostles, 5.33). While Saul manages to escape on both occasions, abetted by fellow-believers, his troubles are far from over. He is just beginning to learn, as the Lord disclosed to Ananias in 9.15, 'how much he [Saul] must suffer' for Christ's sake.

(1) *The Jews' in Damascus: 9.23-25*. Peter's speech at Pentecost and the reported prayer of the threatened Jerusalem community both emphasized that Jesus' death at the combined hands of Israelites and Romans took place according to the predetermined 'plan' (*boulē*) of God (2.23; 4.25-28). When the priestly-led Jerusalem council became 'enraged and wanted to kill' the insolent apostles, the Pharisee Gamaliel intervened and suggested that cooler heads prevail, allowing the mission 'plan' (*boulē*) of the apostles to run its course in accordance with God's will (5.33-39). Now, when it comes to attacking Saul, we learn only of the murderous 'plot' (*epiboulē*) of a company of Israelites generically labelled 'the Jews' for the first time in Acts (9.22-24). No Gentile

accomplices are mentioned this time, and no distinction is made between specific Jewish opponents (Sadducean chief priests) and Jewish sympathizers (Pharisee Gamaliel). A parallel text from Saul's (Paul's) own hand hints at Nabatean responsibility for his early troubles in Damascus (2 Cor. 11.32-33). Acts knows nothing of this, however, placing full blame on 'the Jews'. A critical tension thus develops in the narrative: Is Saul's forecasted mission to 'the people of Israel' doomed to fail because of 'the Jews'' recalcitrance? Will 'the Jews' in fact be the major contributors to 'how much Saul must suffer'? Or will subsequent accounts of Paul's ministry sketch a more differentiated pattern of Jewish response?

(2) *The Hellenists in Jerusalem: 9.26-30.* Fleeing from persecution back *to* Jerusalem (contrast the escape *from* Jerusalem in 8.1), Saul seeks refuge among the local community of disciples. Suddenly, a congregation larger than the twelve apostles appears again in Jerusalem, leading us either to suspect exaggeration in 8.1 or to suppose new evangelization on the part of the apostles and/or a return of some disciples who earlier fled the holy city. In any case, Saul is initially shunned by the wary Jerusalem believers (cf. Ananias's first reaction in 9.13-14) until Barnabas takes him under wing and confirms before the apostles the validity of Saul's recent Christophany on the way to Damascus and subsequent proclamation of Jesus' name within the city (9.26-27). Unlike Ananias, Barnabas receives no visionary assurance of Saul's transformation. Presumably, he takes Saul's word for it, willing to give Saul the benefit of the doubt. Barnabas thus lives up to his billing as 'son of encouragement', bringing his advocacy of a beleaguered brother to the apostles as he had previously brought his money to help the needy (4.36-36).

While Saul is eventually accepted by the believers in Jerusalem, he does not fare so well among the non-believing *Hellenists*. He 'spoke and argued' with them (9.29), just as Stephen had done earlier in the local synagogues (6.9-10; note the same two verbs—'speak [*laleō*]' and 'argue [*syzēteō*]'); and Saul now encounters the same bloodthirsty reaction which he and other Hellenists, in league with temple authorities, had previously mounted against Stephen (9.29). Ultimately, however, the Stephen-Saul parallel pulls apart: whereas Stephen fell prey to his attackers, Saul escapes (once again) with the assistance of fellow disciples (9.30). At this point, we may recall a more apt Lukan parallel with an interesting twist surrounding the first reported incident of Jesus' public ministry. Like Saul, Jesus managed to escape a hostile audience of his own people who sought to kill him; Jesus, however, fled *from* his Galilean hometown of Nazareth, where all the trouble had erupted, while Saul was dispatched *to* his Cilician hometown of Tarsus (Lk. 4.28-30; Acts 9.30).

Peter the Apostle in Sharon and Caesarea: 9.32-11.18

As the Jerusalem apostles, Peter and John, followed up and expanded on Philip's missionary efforts in Samaria (8.14-25), so Peter, now working alone, complements Philip's ministry along the coastal plain of Sharon up to Caesarea before returning, as before, to his home base in Jerusalem. Philip's evangelistic itinerary covering 'all the towns' from Azotus to Caesarea (8.40) would have included the cities of Lydda and Joppa, where we now find Peter ministering. We may thus infer that the believing communities which Peter encounters in these places (9.32, 36-38, 41) had been founded or built up by the forerunning Philip. In Caesarea, however, where Philip was last stationed, Peter meets exclusively with prospective (not established) disciples (Cornelius and household), staking his own claim to be a community founder as well as developer.

Apart from focusing on specific cities in Judea, Samaria and Syria, the mission narrative also targets other locales, both more general and more particular. Generally, the opening statement of this Peter cycle reports that the apostle 'went here and there among all the believers' or, more literally—'passed through all of them', that is, through all of the areas in the region where believers resided. More particularly, within the designated cities Peter's work takes him, as we have come to expect by now, to individual *houses* (*oikos* or *oikia* appear ten times in this section) and, in Joppa, to specific elevated parts of those houses: a room upstairs (9.37, 39) and a rooftop (10.9).

In these various settings, Peter's ministry focuses on three individuals presented in an alternating male-female-male sequence: Aeneas, Tabitha/Dorcas, and Cornelius. The pairing of male and female characters in related episodes is a common Lukan technique (e.g. Lk. 1.5-20, 26-38; 2.25-38; 7.1.17; Seim, pp. 11-24; D'Angelo, pp. 41-48); here, within a triadic network, the female story in the middle is strategically linked to both flanking male narratives. Apart from the gender pattern, the sequence of Peter scenes in Acts 9-10 also exhibits a progressive increase in length and dramatic force, accompanied by notable changes in Peter's character:

(1) The cycle commences with a brief snippet (9.32-35) featuring Peter's restoration of a man named *Aeneas* who had been paralyzed for eight years. Such a miracle is impressive but not overwhelming at this juncture, given Peter's earlier healing of another lame man who had been disabled from birth for forty years.

(2) The second episode runs about two-and-a-half times longer than the first (9.36-43) and features a new 'sign' of apostolic power in Acts: bringing the deceased *Tabitha* back to life. In addition to noting this heightening of Peter's potency, we may also appreciate a widening of

his compassion, as he now becomes more personally involved in helping needy widows by restoring—through prayer (9.40)—their beloved
benefactress (9.39, 41). In 6.2-4, we may recall, Peter and his fellow
apostles distanced their priority vocations of prayer and proclamation
from practical service to widows, which they delegated to the seven
table-servants; now Peter himself conjoins these contemplative (prayer)
and active (providing for widows) forms of ministry (see Spencer,
'Neglected Widows', pp. 731-33).

(3) Spanning the entire tenth chapter of Acts (10.1-48), the story of
Peter's outreach to the centurion *Cornelius*, while not displaying any
healing miracles, revolves around a variety of other supernatural events:
a dazzling angelic visitation (10.1-6, 30-32), a shocking heavenly vision
(10.9-16), and a surprising Spirit manifestation (10.44-48). These events
work together to effect and legitimate the most radical socio-religious
breakthrough thus far in Acts, involving the (table-) fellowship of a
Jewish Christian and Gentile God-fearer in the latter's home and the participation of believing, uncircumcised Gentiles in the Pentecostal blessing of the Spirit (the household setting and outpouring of the Spirit
mark dramatic advances over the forerunning incident of Philip's outreach to the God-fearing Ethiopian eunuch in 8.26-39). Ironically, the
one most resistant to this progressive mission is the apostle Peter. He
thus requires persuasion and conversion as much, if not more so, than
Cornelius.

Another character singled out in chs. 9–10 is a man called *Simon*.
Throughout the story he remains a background figure with no lines to
speak or part to act out; he is merely identified as a tanner who hosts
Peter in his seaside home in Joppa. But in this capacity he is referred to
no fewer than four times by a variety of voices: narrator (9.43), angel
(10.5-6), narrator (10.17-18), and Cornelius (10.32). Such redundancy
suggests some significance behind Peter's association with this tanner
and his beachfront residence beyond adding local color to the story.

While highlighting Peter's encounters with named individuals, these
narratives also trace the wider effects of the apostle's ministry: as testimony of Aeneas' wondrous recovery spread, 'all the residents of Lydda
and Sharon...turned to the Lord' (9.35); likewise, as Tabitha's resuscitation 'became known throughout Joppa...many believed in the Lord'
(9.42); and, finally, the auditors of Peter's preaching and recipients of
the Spirit's outpouring in Caesarea included not only Cornelius but also
all 'his relatives and close friends' whom he had gathered together
(10.24, 27, 44). Clearly, miraculous manifestations (healings, visions) in
these chapters (as throughout Acts) function not as ends but as means to
bringing many to faith and discipleship.

The character of Peter developed in this section ultimately pivots
around the legitimacy of his status as *apostle* and, to a lesser degree, as
prophet. The climactic episode situates Peter back in Jerusalem, where

he gives account of his recent fraternizing with Gentiles before a concerned assembly of 'apostles and brothers', including some most distressed 'circumcised believers' (11.1-2). Effectively, Peter is on trial
again, only this time before his own community rather than the
Jerusalem council. The major point of contention is why Peter deliberately went to associate and 'eat with' uncircumcised men (11.3). Put
another way, can he legitimately claim to have been 'sent' (*apostellō*) by
God on such a mission, which is the mark of a true apostle (*apostolos*,
'sent one')?

As Peter mounts his defense, he stresses the Spirit's direct guidance
('the Spirit told me to go', 11.12) and God's sovereign control ('who
was I that could hinder God?', 11.7) of his recent activities, and twice
explicitly testifies that he acted in response to 'sent' messengers who
'sent for' (*apostellō*) him to come to Cornelius' house (11.11, 13).
This emphasis echoes several previous references to Peter's 'sending'
(utilizing *apostellō* and other common 'send'-verbs, *pempō* and *meta-
pempomai*) uttered by multiple characters, both human and divine, to
multiple audiences in strong confirmation of Peter's apostolic status.

> *Angel to Cornelius*: 'Now *send* (*pempson*) men to Joppa for a cer-
> tain Simon who is called Peter' (10.5).
>
> *Spirit to Peter*: 'Look, three men are searching for you. Now get up,
> go down, and go with them without hesitation; for I have *sent*
> (*apestalka*) them' (10.19-20).
>
> *Cornelius' men to Peter*: 'Cornelius...was directed by a holy angel
> to *send for* (*metapempsasthai*) you to come to his house and to
> hear what you have to say' (10.22).
>
> *Peter to Cornelius*: 'So when I was *sent for* (*metapemphtheis*), I
> came without objection. Now may I ask why you *sent for*
> (*metepempsasthe*) me?' (10.29).
>
> *Cornelius to Peter rehearsing angel's commission*: '*Send* (*pempson*)
> therefore to Joppa and ask for Simon, who is called Peter... There-
> fore, I *sent* (*epempsa*) for you immediately' (10.32-33).
>
> *Peter to Jerusalem assembly*: 'Three men, *sent* (*apestalmenoi*) to
> me from Caesarea, arrived at the house where we were' (11.11).
> (*Apestalmenoi* is passive with an unspecified subject, implying per-
> haps a collaborative sending by both divine [God, Spirit, angel] and
> human [Cornelius and men] agents.)
>
> *Peter rehearsing angel's message to Cornelius*: *Send* (*aposteilon*)
> to Joppa and *send for* (*metapempsai*) Simon, who is called Peter
> (11.13).

As Peter comes to understand it, he is not the first one sent to proclaim God's good purpose of accepting 'in every nation anyone who

fears him and does what is right' (10.34-35). Such good news has its foundation in the reconciling word which God 'sent (*apesteilen*) to the people of Israel...by Jesus Christ...Lord of *all*' (10.36). Jesus was God's preeminent apostle sent to bring healing and salvation (cf. Lk. 4.18—'He has *sent* [*apestalken*] me to proclaim release') to 'all flesh' (3.6), including bedridden paralytics and bereaved widows, among the people of Israel (5.17-26; 7.11-17), and God-fearing centurions among the Gentiles (7.1-10). Thus, in Acts 9–11, Peter follows precisely in Jesus' apostolic footsteps.

The identity of the Lukan Jesus as 'sent one' is closely related to his role as *prophet* ('A great prophet has risen among us!' [Lk. 7.16]). In working healing miracles, restoring the dead to destitute widows, and ministering to foreign officials, Jesus particularly fits the classic prophetic mold of Elijah and Elisha ('Elijah *was sent* [*epemphthē*]', Lk. 4.26; cf. vv. 25-27; Brodie, 'Luke–Acts'; Evans). By association, then, Peter fits the same pattern in Acts. But Peter also follows a very different prophetic model represented by *Jonah* in his notorious reluctance to bring God's message to non-Israelites—in particular, to powerful enemies of Israel (Assyrians) in their capital city (Nineveh). This connection becomes especially intriguing in light of the fact that Peter's struggle with God's radical purity standards—culminating in his summons to preach to a Roman soldier in the provincial capital—takes place *by the sea in Joppa*, precisely the spot where Jonah ventures his daring escape from the Lord's assignment (Jon. 1.3; see Wall, 'Peter').

'Here and There' in Sharon: 9.32-35

Moving 'here and there among all of them' suggests the image of Peter as a circuit-riding preacher-pastor among several congregations throughout the region (Johnson, *Acts*, pp. 177-80). The focal territory is 'the Sharon' (9.35), referring to a swath of coastal land (the Plain of Sharon) running from Lydda and Joppa in the south to Caesarea in the north. Known in earlier Israelite history largely as a bucolic area with lush pastures for grazing (e.g. 1 Chron. 27.29; Isa. 65.10), with the development of Caesarea Maritima as a major commercial and political center in the Roman period, Sharon became 'the most densely populated area of the coastal plain' (Weeks, p. 1162). The double emphasis on Peter's mission to 'all' (*pas*) the inhabitants of the region implies a substantial population (9.32, 35).

On this tour throughout Sharon, Peter visits the 'holy ones' ('saints', *hagioi*) in Lydda, a place, according to Josephus, 'in size not inferior to a city' (*Ant.* 20.130). The attribute of 'holiness' has been ascribed numerous times in Acts to the Spirit (*hagion pneuma*) and to Jesus (*ho hagios*, 'the holy one' [3.14]; *hagios pais*, 'holy servant' [4.27, 30]). The designation of Christian disciples as 'holy ones', first in 9.13 (referring to the Jerusalem community) and now in 9.32, thus closely identifies them with both the Spirit and Jesus: as partakers of the former and partners with the latter.

Peter's continuing partnership with Jesus becomes evident in his healing ministry to Aeneas, not only because the *act* of rehabilitating a paralytic mirrors one of Jesus' mighty works (Lk. 5.17-26), but also because of the actual therapeutic *words* which Peter speaks: 'Jesus Christ heals you' (9.34). As in his earlier dealings with a lame man, Peter makes it clear that he is simply a broker for Jesus, the true enabler (cf. 3.6, 16). It is not so much that Peter heals in imitation of Jesus as that *Jesus himself* continues to heal through Peter. Though absent in body, the exalted Jesus remains a force to be reckoned with on the mission field. Just how powerful Jesus remains is conveyed through temporal contrast: after a protracted 'eight years' of paralysis, Aeneas gets up 'immediately' (*eutheōs*, 9.34; the same term describes Saul's recovery of sight in 9.18).

In a Matron's Upstairs Room in Joppa: 9.36-43

While in Lydda, Peter receives messengers from 'nearby' Joppa (about ten miles northwest) summoning him to come 'without delay' on behalf of their suffering sister-disciple, Tabitha (9.38). Beyond these close spatial ('nearby') and temporal ('without delay') links, the Aeneas and Tabitha incidents are paired together in terms of *character* (the male-female sequence noted above), *audience* (wider congregation of 'saints', 9.32, 41), and, most importantly, *event*: both figures *rise* when Peter calls their names and commands them to 'get up' (*anastēthi*, 9.34, 40). Several times before, we have heard Peter use this same verb (*anistēmi*) to refer to God's raising of Jesus from the dead (2.24, 30, 32; 3.26). The same resurrection power, operative through Jesus and his apostle, was experienced, figuratively, by the disabled Aeneas and now, literally, by the deceased Tabitha.

Peter's function as an agent of resurrection to Aeneas and Tabitha dramatically counterpoints his role in precipitating the death penalty for Ananias and Sapphira. As the sudden appearance of Judas and Ananias earlier in ch. 9 may compensate for the tragic apostasy of two disciples with the same names (see p. 98), so perhaps at the end of the chapter the restoration of the male Aeneas and female Tabitha may redeem in some measure the loss of the married couple, Ananias and Sapphira. May we even detect here a kind of repentance and restitution on Peter's part for earlier rash behavior, in line with other 'conversions' he experiences in this incident and the next (with respect to aiding widows and eating with Gentiles)?

While appreciating the close ties between the Aeneas and Tabitha stories, we must not ignore a number of differences, particularly pertaining to Tabitha's considerably more developed profile.

(1) Whereas Aeneas was referred to simply as 'a man' (or 'person', *anthrōpos*, 9.33), Tabitha is dubbed 'a disciple' (*mathētria*, 9.36). This

latter term catches the eye as the only use of a *feminine* form of 'disciple' in Luke–Acts (indeed, in the entire New Testament). It thus resists the tendency to efface the presence of women within a male-oriented generic group, illustrated, for example, in Peter's Pentecostal address to 'males, brothers' (references to 'both men and women' in 5.14 and 8.3 represent similar inclusive countermoves).

(2) Whereas Aeneas is designated by a single name, the next character is identified twice by equivalent Aramaic ('Tabitha') and Greek ('Dorcas') appellations, meaning 'gazelle' (9.36, 39-40). This double name fits the mixed Jewish-Gentile demographics of Joppa (Barrett, *Acts*, I, pp. 482-83) and acts as a bridge between Aeneas (Jew) in Lydda and Cornelius (Gentile) in Caesarea.

(3) While we are told nothing about Aeneas beyond his infirmity, we learn of Tabitha's honorable reputation as a benefactress (matron), 'devoted to good works and acts of charity', particularly providing 'tunics (*chitōnas*) and other clothing' for needy widows (9.36, 39). As such she fulfills the earliest public requirement for discipleship in Luke's Gospel, announced by John the baptizer, that 'whoever has two coats (*chitōnas*) must share with anyone who has none' (3.10; she actually exceeds this requirement by *making* multiple tunics for a group of widows; Tannehill, '"Cornelius" and "Tabitha"', p. 352). Tabitha also distinguishes herself as the first active female minister in Acts. Like the seven male table-servants in ch. 6, she engages in noble, charitable service to widows. But *unlike* them, it must be noted, Tabitha does not also preach the word and work wonders. As seamstress and caretaker of widows she remains wholly within the bounds of traditional 'women's work' and acceptable patroness activity in both Jewish and Greco-Roman worlds (see Anderson, pp. 120, 128-39; O'Day, pp. 309-10). The great prospect of Spirit-inspired women prophets, promulgated by Peter through Joel at Pentecost, has yet to be realized in Acts.

(4) But despite the absence of oracular and miraculous ministry (a serious omission by Lukan standards), there are some signs of Tabitha's higher status as a community leader. The fact that the larger company of 'disciples' (*mathētai*—back to the generic masculine term) urgently dispatches 'two men (*andres*)' to Lydda to bring back Peter on behalf of the deceased Tabitha implies enormous community sympathy and respect for this woman—by men as well as women—as does Peter's presentation of the revived Tabitha not only to a band of weeping widows but also to 'the saints' as a whole (9.38, 41). Furthermore, we may logically infer from the text that Tabitha is a single, independent woman (there is no man of the house) of some means (witness her philanthropy), likely the owner of the home where, in an upper chamber, she is laid to rest, raised up, and reunited with the Joppa congregation. Recalling that the early church in Acts typically gathered in private homes, even in upstairs rooms (1.13; 2.46; 5.42; 8.3), we may posit that

Tabitha regularly hosted the Joppa assembly for occasions of worship and fellowship—other than her own funeral! The example of Martha—an apparently autonomous, well-to-do woman who hosted Jesus in her own home in Lk. 10.38-42—lends some support to this hypothesis (cf. Seim, pp. 97-112). Of course, in Tabitha's case, being community *host* does not guarantee her position as community *head*, but within a patronage society it certainly points in that direction.

The focus on a private upstairs room (*hyperōon*) as the locus of pious action and spiritual power continues the contrast with the corrupt and impotent public temple drawn at the end of Luke and beginning of Acts. While the Jerusalem temple, in Jesus' judgment, was a failed 'house of prayer' (Lk. 19.46), Tabitha's upper room in Joppa, like the upper room in Jerusalem, is a fertile place of prayer ('Peter...knelt down and prayed', Acts 9.40; cf. 1.13-14, 24). Likewise, while Jesus denounced the temple as an exploitative 'den of thieves' for those who 'devour widows' houses' and milk widows of their last pennies (Lk. 19.46; 20.46-21.4), Tabitha's upper room becomes a benevolent haven for destitute widows (Acts 9.39, 41). And, finally, while the temple establishment became a death trap, intent on killing Jesus and itself destined for demolition (Lk. 19.47; 21.6), Tabitha's upper room, like the gathering place at Pentecost, erupts as a center of Jesus' resurrection power sparking an influx of new believers (Acts 2.37-47; 9.40-42). The fact that Tabitha's upper room serves as a functionally 'holy place' of prayer and ministry in Joppa—*outside* the limits of the holy city—further relativizes the centrality of the Jerusalem temple along the lines of Stephen's speech.

On a Tanner's Rooftop in Joppa: 9.43-10.23

A transitional verse between the Tabitha and Cornelius incidents informs us that Peter tarries in Joppa 'for some time', quartering in the home of a tanner named Simon (9.43). Why he does not stay at Tabitha's house we can only speculate (the impropriety of lodging in a single woman's home or a need for retreat from the spotlight?). In any event, as the Joppa segment of Peter's story continues, the focus of the plot shifts from what Peter accomplishes for others to what happens to Peter himself. He becomes the target rather than catalyst of change.

The medium of supernatural intervention also shifts from healing miracle to heavenly vision. In another 'double vision' framework, like that which brought Ananias and Saul together in the previous chapter, Cornelius and Peter both receive special divine revelations which pave the way for their rendezvous. Again, extraordinary vision leads to expanding mission; the heavens open up (10.11) to stimulate the church to move out toward the ends of the earth (cf. 1.8-11; 7.55-8.4; 9.3-16). More specifically, the coordinated visions of Cornelius and Peter prompt a major missionary advance to *Gentiles*, realizing preemptively the goal of *Saul's* mission disclosed in Ananias's vision (a curious complication of

Saul's status as the Lord's 'chosen instrument' of witness to the Gentiles, 9.15).

Framing the two visions is a fairly developed profile of Cornelius, first described by the third-person narrator (10.1-2) and then focalized through Cornelius' emissaries to Peter (10.22). Yet another voice—that of the 'angel of God'—reinforces certain aspects of the narrator's characterization (10.4).

First and foremost, in both 10.1 and 10.22, Cornelius is identified as a *centurion*. This marks our first encounter with Roman military personnel in Acts, apart from two passing references to Pilate's involvement in Jesus' death (3.13; 4.27; cf. also the oblique reference to the crucifixion squad in 2.23). The principal authorities have been the temple hierarchs, not imperial officers. In the preceding Lukan volume, however, two centurions appeared in quite a favorable light (unlike the villainous temple elites), first, as a bold-yet-humble supplicant of Jesus' power on behalf of a dying servant (Lk. 7.1-10) and, then, as a surprising proclaimer of Jesus' innocence at the foot of the cross (23.47).

Cornelius is also cast in positive terms, though as yet with no reference to Jesus. He is 'devout' (*eusebēs*, 10.2; cf. his 'devout' soldier-servant, 10.7) and 'upright' (*dikaios*, 10.22; the centurion at the cross announced that Jesus was *dikaios*), a twice-attested 'God-fearing man' (10.2, 22). As evidence of Cornelius' piety, the narrator and angel of God offer the familiar combination of active and contemplative service: generous almsgiving 'to the people' (*laos*, typically referring to Israelites in Acts) and constant praying to God (10.2, 4). The former activity recalls Tabitha's charitable works (9.36, 39) and answers John's demand that soldiers should not use their position to intimidate and defraud others financially (Lk. 3.14). A centurion—typically earning 16 times a basic soldier's wage and possessing 'both considerable military and social status and wealth' (Kennedy, pp. 790-91; Tannehill, '"Cornelius"', p. 349)—may have been more or less susceptible to such greedy practices, depending on whether he used his superior rank and resources to exploit or assist the poor and lowly. Cornelius chose the latter path. His other exemplary habit—vigilance at prayer—apparently includes the observance of standard Jewish hours of prayer, such as 'three o'clock' in the afternoon when the angel visits him (Acts 10.3). Such devotion parallels that of the early disciples, especially Peter and John's coming to the temple to pray at the same hour, which, interestingly, resulted in their aiding a poor, *alms-begging* lame man (thus combining prayer and charity in the same way as Cornelius) (3.1-7).

On the whole, the noble character of Cornelius is presented in terms of traditional *Jewish* piety. Indeed, the final component of Cornelius' reputation which his servants report to Peter is that he 'is well spoken of by the whole Jewish nation' (10.22). Similar claims were made for the centurion in Luke 7 by Jewish elders in Capernaum (7.3-5). While Luke-

Acts is obviously pro-Roman to a certain degree, this stance must not be facilely polarized over against an anti-Jewish sentiment. It may be true that 'Josephus regularly depicts troops in the [Judean] province displaying a general insensitivity towards the Jewish religion, indeed, often an open partiality for the non-Jew' (Kennedy, p. 796), but that would not be true of the Lukan writer who extols Roman officers precisely because of their sympathy with the Jewish people and religion. The emphasis on the remarkable faith and piety of centurions in Luke–Acts certainly functions to shame those Israelites—particularly the priestly leaders—who fail to exhibit such qualities ('I tell you, not even in Israel have I found such faith', Lk. 7.9). But the flip side of this shaming is honoring Israel and her traditions on a global scale: they are worthy of faithful attention by powerful Romans as well as dedicated Israelites.

While Cornelius enjoys the favor of 'the whole Jewish nation', he is never identified as a *proselyte* or full convert to Judaism. Since Acts has twice designated certain persons as 'proselytes' (Roman visitors at Pentecost [2.10], and Nicolaus of Antioch, one of the seven servants [6.5]), the absence of the term with respect to Cornelius is noteworthy. We may assume at this stage that Cornelius occupies the same marginal 'God-fearer' status vis-à-vis Judaism that we assigned to the Ethiopian eunuch, who also otherwise parallels the Roman centurion as a wealthy, foreign official. While Cornelius, unlike the eunuch, possesses no obvious defect to bar him from Israel's covenant, he has apparently chosen not to submit to circumcision or baptism (requirements for proselytes) and thus remains, for all his piety, an unclean Gentile according to conservative Jewish legal standards. Raising this purity question leads us to consider Peter's vision, which is all about clarifying boundaries between clean and unclean, holy and profane.

After a period of prayer, while waiting for lunch to be prepared, Peter sees descending from heaven something like a large, rectangular sheet on which are displayed 'all kinds' of animals (10.9-12). A three-part dialogue then ensues with two declarations from 'a voice' (presumably a divine voice from heaven, cf. Lk. 3.18) enveloping a single response from Peter:

(1) The heavenly voice commands Peter by name to 'get up, kill and eat' (10.13). The first mandate (*anastas*) echoes Peter's call to both Aeneas and Tabitha. Now the apostle himself must 'rise' to a new level of experience.

(2) Peter then retorts in no uncertain terms: 'By no means, Lord (*kyrie*); for I have never eaten anything that is profane (*koinon*) or unclean (*akatharton*)' (10.14). Unlike the general queries to the 'Lord' by either Saul or Cornelius in their bewildered visionary states—'Who are you, Lord (*kyrie*)?' (9.5); 'What is it, Lord (*kyrie*)'? (10.4)—Peter's declarative rather than interrogative reply exudes confidence rather than confusion and reflects, we may assume from his earlier speeches, a more

personalized understanding of 'Lord' with reference to Jesus Christ (cf. 1.21; 2.36). This is not the first time Peter talks back to Jesus (cf. Lk. 5.5; 22.33). Here the issue concerns dietary regulations. Peter staunchly affirms his kosher commitment in the grand tradition of Daniel (Dan. 1.8), Tobit (Tob. 1.10-11), Judith (Jdt. 10.5; 12.1-2), Judas Maccabeus (2 Macc. 5.27), Eleazar (2 Macc. 6.18-31) and other faithful Israelites who refused to defile themselves with foreign foods (cf. 1 Macc. 1.62-63). Culinary controversies over clean and unclean food have not surfaced in Acts until this point and play no major role in Luke's Gospel (e.g., Mk 7.1-20//Mt. 15.10-20 have no Lukan parallel). But the Lukan Jesus had a great deal to say and demonstrate concerning the closely related matter of table-fellowship (purity systems concerned with food typically circumscribe *who* one eats with as much as *what* one eats). Time and again Jesus pushed the boundaries of conventional etiquette, thoroughly meriting the Pharisees' opprobrious charge: 'This fellow welcomes sinners and eats with them' (Lk. 15.2; cf. 5.27-32; 7.36-50; 14.7-24; 15.11-32; 19.1-10). Peter seems to have missed the point.

(3) The dominical voice overrules Peter's objection sharply, but somewhat indirectly. It does not insist that Peter goes ahead and consumes unclean meat on this occasion, but it does demand that Peter acknowledges God's sovereignty in determining purity boundaries and, by implication, adjusting those boundaries if he so chooses: 'What God has made clean (*ekatharisen*), you must not call profane (*koinou*)' (10.15). The counterforce of this answer to Peter is punctuated by chiastic inversion:

> Peter: profane...unclean (10.14)
> God: clean...not profane (10.15)

For all the vividness of this audio-visual experience and despite the fact that it is repeated three times (10.16), Peter remains 'greatly puzzled' by the whole ordeal until the Spirit directs him to accompany three visitors—who 'suddenly' arrive on the scene—to Cornelius' house 'without hesitation' (10.17-23; cf. Peter's previous call to go with the Joppa messengers 'without delay', 9.38). It is still not spelled out, however, precisely what Peter's recent animal vision and food lesson have to do with meeting a centurion. But the connection is not difficult to imagine if we recall the close nexus, suggested above, between what one eats and with whom one eats or associates. What one takes into the physical body is a mirror of who one permits into the social body; the individual mouth through which food is consumed and the corporate table around which food is shared represent analogous social-symbolic borders or checkpoints (Douglas, *Natural Symbols*, pp. 65-81; Neyrey, 'Symbolic Universe'). Thus the implied significance of Peter's vision extends beyond zoological and gastronomical matters to more broadly anthropological and cultural concerns. Killing and eating unclean reptiles and birds is not the major advance Peter needs to make here; staying and eating with an unclean (Gentile) centurion and household is. More than that, Peter is being called to drop the 'unclean' label for Gentiles altogether.

In conjunction with these social factors, various temporal and spatial dimensions also shed light on the significance of Peter's vision.

(1) *Noon*. The midday hour (10.9), while providing an apt occasion for Peter's hunger and tutelage concerning food and eating, also, at the brightest point of the day, suits the disclosure of an illuminating vision. It also coincides, we may recall, with the schedule of Philip's rendezvous with the Ethiopian eunuch arranged by an angel of the Lord and the Spirit (8.26, 29). In Peter's case, his noon-time vision gives way to the sudden appearance of Cornelius' men—directed to Peter by 'a holy angel' (10.22)—with whom the Spirit charges Peter to 'get up and go' immediately (10.20). Normally a time of repose and conserving energy, the noon hour marks a busy and urgent moment of breakthrough for the Gentile mission in Acts.

(2) *Rooftop*. After shocking his Pharisee host by not washing for dinner and then using the occasion to blast the Pharisees for betraying their outward commitment to purity by their uncleanness of heart and unjust dealings with others, the Lukan Jesus announced to the crowd that such hypocrisy will ultimately be unmasked publicly 'on the *rooftops*' (Lk. 11.37–12.3). In Acts 10, the risen Jesus indeed exposes hypocrisy on a *rooftop*, not of the Pharisees, however, but of his own leading apostle! Peter has spoken eloquently about God's gracious promise of salvation 'for all who are far away' (2.39) and covenantal purpose of blessing 'all the families of the earth' (3.25); but he has failed to bolster this rhetoric with active outreach around the dinner table (as Jesus had modelled) to outcasts and 'sinners', irrespective of traditional purity boundaries.

(3) *Seaside*. Stationed at the coastal border in the port of Joppa, resisting God's call to foreign mission, Peter finds himself, as noted above, in the same position as the prophet Jonah. In the well-known biblical story, Jonah attempts to flee by ship but is soon brought down by the Lord to the belly of a great fish for three days and nights, where he is finally convinced to heed the divine commission to 'get up and go' (*anastēthi kai poreuthēti*, Jon. 3.2 LXX) to Nineveh. Peter never sets sail from Joppa, but he may well have seen a ship's sail (a logical explanation for 'something like a large, four-cornered sheet'; see Barrett, *Acts*, I, p. 506); and while he himself does not supplement a giant sea creature's diet for three days, he is commanded by God—three times—to supplement his own diet with a variety of land creatures. However rearranged the details, the result is the same: Peter answers the Spirit's charge to 'get up and go' (*anastas...kai poreuou*, 10.20) to Caesarea to minister to a Gentile household. The church's expanding Gentile

mission is thus duly authorized not by some alien power but by the same Spirit, the same Word, the same God who guided Jonah—Yahweh, the God of Israel, witnessed to in Israel's scriptures (see Wall, 'Peter'). (That the implied Lukan author knows the Jonah story is evident from Lk. 11.29-32, which associates the 'sign of Jonah' with the prophet's mission to receptive foreigners in contrast to Matt. 12.39-40, which links Jonah's ordeal in the fish's belly with Jesus' forecasted resurrection after three days and nights.)

(4) *Tanner*. The repeated identification of Peter's host as 'Simon, a *tanner*' (9.43; 10.6, 32) suggests a certain significance surrounding this occupation beyond simply distinguishing him from Simon (Peter) the apostle. A check of rabbinic materials reveals a consistent disdain for tanners and tanneries as unclean people and places. The former, for example, were classified with anyone 'who is afflicted with boils, or who has a polypus, or who collects [dog excrement]', or other blemished men required to divorce their wives (*m. Ketub.* 7.10); the latter were zoned with cemeteries and dumping grounds for carrion 'at least fifty cubits away from a town' (*m. B. Bat.* 2.9; cf. *m. Shabb.* 1.2; *m. Meg.* 3.2). Among the factors contributing to tanners' generally despised status were a malodorous working environment and a reputation for immorality (Jeremias, pp. 5-6, 309-310).

Given this stigma associated with tanners and Peter's openness to board in such a laborer's home 'for some time' (9.43), it is puzzling why Peter would firmly maintain—on the rooftop of this house—conventional scruples about eating unclean food and mixing with unclean persons. Some commentators think it so strange that they regard Simon's vocation as an incidental detail without import in Acts' mission narrative (Haenchen, p. 340 n. 1; Barrett, *Acts*, I, pp. 486-87). But another interpretive approach may prefer to appreciate and negotiate, rather than mitigate and obviate, apparent incongruities in the text. One possible reading imagines more of a complex developmental *process* in Peter's socio-religious orientation, pushing certain radical boundaries here while toeing the party line there. It may indeed be illogical, even hypocritical, to defend kosher laws on a tanner's roof, but realizing fallacy and hypocrisy is often a necessary step to transformation. One has come part of the way to accepting a new idea or new kind of community: why not complete the operation? Also major changes in worldview are as likely (if not more so) to come in fits and starts rather than once-for-all bolts of lightning. Even the classic lightning conversion—that of Saul in Acts 9—takes time to work itself out. Although commissioned to go to the Gentiles, Saul starts preaching in the synagogues of Damascus and Jerusalem and, as far as we know at this stage, still has not evangelized a single foreigner. We might suspect that the chastened Saul of Acts would be somewhat more charitable regarding Peter's ambivalence on the Gentile question than the strident Paul of Galatians (cf. Gal. 2.11-14).

In a Soldier's House in Caesarea: 10.23-48

The anticipated meeting between God-fearing Roman centurion and
Jewish Christian apostle now takes place in the former's Caesarean residence. This marks the first episode in Acts set in a Gentile's home and
a dramatic climax of the mission to Caesarea intimated in 8.40. As
Jerusalem was the center of Jewish religio-political interests in first-
century Judea, Caesarea Maritima (on the Mediterranean coast, distinguished from inland Caesarea Philippi) was the seat of Roman military
and commercial power administered by provincial governors such as
Pontius Pilate, Antonius Felix and Porcius Festus (4.27; 23.24; 24.27). Its
prominence in the empire dates back to the second decade BCE, when
Herod the Great rebuilt the city (formerly Strato's Tower), complete
with a magnificent new harbor and extensive plumbing system, in
honor of Caesar Augustus (Rousseau and Arav, pp. 30-33).

The encounter between Cornelius and Peter occurs not only in the
presence of Cornelius' household but also in the presence of 'certain
brothers' who accompanied Peter from Joppa (10.23-24). Thus we sense
an occasion pregnant with social as well as personal significance,
confirmed by multiple witnesses. The plot unfolds in three stages surrounding the central element of Peter's proclamation:

(1)   So now all of us are here...to listen to all that the Lord has
      commanded you [Peter] to say (10.33).
(2)   Then Peter began to speak to them... (10.34).
(3)   While Peter was still speaking... (10.44).

(1) *Introduction: 10.23-33.* Peter first addresses Cornelius with the
familiar order, 'Get up (*anastēthi*)' (10.26); precisely what he had
said earlier to both Aeneas and Tabitha (9.34, 40). In this case, however,
the apostle's command does not trigger any physical healing or
resuscitation, but only an elevation of Cornelius' socio-religious status.
Cornelius had greeted Peter by falling at his feet in worship, but Peter
will have none of such hierarchical deference. He raises the centurion to
his level, the level of a common 'mortal' (human being, *anthrōpos*),
as Peter describes himself (10.26; cf. Peter's similar response in 3.12-13).
Such a confession of finitude follows appropriately on the heels of
Peter's reluctance to obey the heavenly vision.

As Peter continues his opening remarks, he elaborates in two respects
on recent events which have propelled him to this meeting. First, he
makes explicit what we have already suggested regarding the *social*
significance of the sheet vision. Notice the direct move from impersonal
matters of diet involving clean and unclean animals to personal issues of
fellowship among clean and unclean people, specifically, Jews and
Gentiles:

> I have never eaten *anything* (*pan*) that is profane or unclean...
> What [things] God has made clean, you must not call profane
> (10.14-15).

> You yourselves know that it is unlawful for a Jew to associate with
> or to visit a Gentile; but God has shown me that I should not call
> *anyone* (*anthrōpon*) profane or unclean (10.28).

Secondly, Peter announces that once the reality of this new, inclusive
social order had sunk in, he came to Cornelius' house 'without objection' (10.29). Ironically, however, and perhaps somewhat disingenu-
ously, he glosses over the strong objections he had in the first place.

Although Peter has come a long way in grasping the import of this
visit with Cornelius, he still inquires of his host, 'Why [have] you sent
for me?' (10.29). Tension is thus maintained in the narrative as we await
Cornelius' response. The centurion begins by offering his own rehearsal
of recent preparatory events, stressing first the synchrony—and, by
implication, divine coordination—between the time of his vision and
the present three o'clock hour ('four days ago at this very hour', 10.30).
On the whole, he echoes the narrator's account in 10.3-5, albeit with a
somewhat different perception of the angelic intermediary. Cornelius
describes this figure as 'a man in dazzling clothes [who] stood before
me' (10.30; cp. 'angel of God' in 10.3), recalling most closely the portrait of the messengers who appeared to the women at the empty tomb
(Lk. 24.4). Finally, Cornelius answers Peter's question about why he was
summoned in terms which create further suspense by invoking the
solemn presence of the Lord and putting the onus back on to Peter: 'So
now all of us are here in the presence of God to listen to all that...ou
[have] to say' (10.34). We are poised on the edge of our seats to attend
to Peter's message.

(2) *Proclamation: 10.34-43*. As with previous speeches in Acts, this
one is thoroughly theocentric, stressing the salvific action of 'God'
(*theos*, cited six times) through Jesus Christ and his apostolic witnesses
on behalf of 'the children of Israel' and 'every nation'. Fitting the occasion, Peter especially underscores the universal scope of God's favor at
the beginning and end of the speech:

> God shows no partiality, but in every (*pas*) nation anyone who fears
> him and does what is right is acceptable to him (10.34-35).

> Everyone (*pas*) who believes in him receives forgiveness of sins
> through his name (10.43).

At Pentecost, Peter had preached to Jewish settlers in Jerusalem from
'every nation under heaven' and announced, via Joel, that 'everyone'
will be saved who calls on the Lord (2.5, 21). Now, outside Jerusalem,
he launches a more inclusive and aggressive mission to 'every nation' by
witnessing to a group of Gentiles in Gentile territory. Of course, his

profile of the 'acceptable' foreigner as one who fears God and does good is tailor-made for Cornelius (cf. 10.1-2).

In the body of his speech, Peter emphasizes the mediation of God's global plan of redemption through the ministry, death, and resurrection of Jesus Christ proclaimed by divinely appointed eyewitnesses. This Messiah to Israel has become 'Lord of all (*pas*)' (10.36). In relating his credentials to serve as Christ's witness, Peter recalls that he and the other apostles saw Christ and 'ate and drank with him after he rose from the dead' (10.41). This information harks back to the penultimate Gospel episode, in which the risen Jesus consumed a piece of broiled fish in the company of the apostles (Lk. 24.41-43; cf. also Acts 1.1-4). The link to the present scene in Cornelius' house may relate to what Jesus said while eating with his disciples, namely, that they must proclaim 'repentance and forgiveness of sins...*to all nations*' (Lk. 24.44-48). Moreover, Peter's recollection of dining with the risen Jesus may evoke wider reflection on the controversial eating habits of the earthly Jesus relevant to Peter's recent struggle with proprieties of diet and table-fellowship.

(3) *Interruption: 10.44-48.* In a surprising twist in the narrative, the Holy Spirit abruptly falls on the Gentile audience in the middle of Peter's speech, causing them to break out in glossolalia and praise to God (10.44-46). Peter takes this as a cue to baptize the household in Jesus' name and thus incorporate them into the messianic community (10.47-48). Apart from its obvious effect on the Gentile assembly, this momentous incident also shapes the development of three other characters: the Spirit (on the Spirit as a character in Luke–Acts, see Shepherd), Peter, and Peter's companion-witnesses from Joppa.

The *Spirit* once again acts freely and dynamically on its own timetable. At Pentecost, the Spirit 'suddenly' filled the Jerusalem congregation *before* any sermonizing or baptizing took place; in Samaria, it came on the believers through apostolic hands some time *after* Philip's evangelistic mission; here, the Spirit energizes Cornelius and company *while* Peter is preaching, but *before* they are baptized. Amid this temporal variety, however, the outpouring of the Spirit creates remarkable social unity. Whenever it happened, the fact that Samaritans and now Gentiles 'have received the Holy Spirit *just as we [Jews] have*' binds these different groups together in the community of God's people (10.47).

As for *Peter*, the interruption of his speech suggests that he is still partly out of step with God's agenda (cf. a prattling Peter—'not knowing what he said'—being cut off by the heavenly cloud and voice at the transfiguration, Lk. 9.33-35). The situation calls not for extended, interpretive speech, as at Pentecost, but for prompt, decisive action in embracing devout Gentiles as brothers and sisters in the household of God. Put another way, the inclusive gospel which Peter has amply enunciated in the opening chapters of Acts must now be enforced.

Finally, we learn of the astonishment of Peter's *circumcised companions* over the Spirit's outpouring on the Gentiles (10.45). This is the first time in the Cornelius narrative that circumcision has been explicitly mentioned as an identity marker. Of course, it represents a distinctive badge of membership in Israel's covenant community dating back to Abraham (cf. 7.8). By calling attention to the Joppa disciples' circumcised status at this point in the story, the narrator suggests that their shock over the recent conferral of the Spirit is due to the fact that Cornelius and household remain *un*circumcised. Whatever the attachment of these Gentiles to Israel's religion, they are marginalized from the social body by Peter's Jewish attendants because they lack the proper genital-kinship brand in the physical body, much like the Ethiopian eunuch was banned from the temple community because he had the wrong kind of genital scar. But the Spirit has broken through such barriers in forceful, undeniable fashion, prompting Peter to ask his companions rhetorically, 'Can anyone withhold [prevent, *kōlyō*] water for baptizing these people?' (10.47), just as the eunuch asked Philip, 'Look, here is water! What is to prevent (*kōlyō*) me from being baptized'? (8.36).

Before the Circumcised Assembly in Jerusalem: 11.1-18

Once introduced, circumcision joins table-fellowship as the major points of contention surrounding the Cornelius incident when Peter returns to his home base in Jerusalem. A contingent of 'circumcised brothers' in the Jerusalem church critically interrogate Peter: 'Why did you go to *uncircumcised* men and *eat with them?*' (11.3). (Peter's eating with Cornelius' household was never spelled out as such in the preceding narrative but is clearly assumed throughout and all but stated in the last verse: 'they invited him [Peter] to stay for several days' [10.48].) Peter is back on trial again, only this time before fellow believers rather than temple authorities. He responds by taking his accusers 'step by step' (in order, *kathexēs*, cf. Lk. 1.3) through the events of recent days. Of course, all of this has already been *shown* to us readers in panoramic scale by the omniscient, third-person narrator. Now, however, there is an interesting shift in narrative perspective, as a character within the story, Peter himself, *tells* us his version of the story from his limited point of view (see Kurz, *Reading*, pp. 87-89, 125-31). Peter's report naturally repeats a great deal but also provides a number of new details, a few key omissions, and a different order of presentation. In other words, his 'steps' follow the same general trail but not the exact footprints of the preceding narrative.

The most glaring change in sequence is that Peter starts with his own vision and then subsequently describes Cornelius' vision as told to him in Cornelius' house. This, of course, reflects the order of experience for

Peter and the order of importance for Peter's audience (they are examining Peter, not Cornelius). As Peter recounts his vision he first supplements the narrator's version by emphasizing how 'close' the sheet came to him and how 'closely' he examined it (11.5-6). These items reinforce the overwhelming impact of the vision: he could not avoid it and did not take it lightly. Then he gives a fuller catalogue of the displayed animals, adding 'beasts of prey' (carrion-eaters) which intensifies the image of uncleanness (cf. Lev. 11.13-40; Deut. 14.11-8). Finally, when Peter rehearses his objection to the Lord's kill-and-eat mandate, he tightens the image of purity from 'I have never eaten anything profane or unclean' (10.14) to 'nothing profane or unclean *has ever entered my mouth*' (11.8). Peter's scrupulosity was beyond question; his circumcised brothers would have been proud of him. (Conveniently, he never discloses that he was lodging with Simon the tanner: that would have been too much to explain.)

After describing the vision, Peter glosses over his quandary about its meaning (cf. 10.17) and quickly moves to the meeting in Cornelius' house. Here he informs us for the first time that he was accompanied by 'six brothers' from Joppa (11.12). This quantification serves to strengthen the support of these witnesses; it also makes for a total company of seven (six plus Peter) dealing with a dietary crisis, reminiscent of an earlier group of table-servants in the Jerusalem church (6.1-6). Peter then relays Cornelius' introductory remarks, focusing on the angel's earlier command that the centurion send for Peter who 'will give you a message by which you [Cornelius] and your entire household will be saved' (11.14). This first explicit use of 'save'-language (*sōzō*) in Acts 10–11 closely links the Cornelius incident to Peter's preaching at Pentecost ('everyone who calls on the name of the Lord will be saved', 2.21; cf. 2.40, 47), which was so foundational for the Jerusalem church. Indeed, Peter clinches his defense by further binding the recent experience of the Caesarean Gentiles with that of the Jerusalem Jewish Christians 'at the beginning': both groups—'them' and 'us'—received the descending Spirit just as the ascending Christ had forecast (11.15-16; cf. 1.4-5, 8).

Given this divinely-sanctioned solidarity between believing Jews and Gentiles evidenced in the common dynamic 'gift of the Spirit' and prophetic 'word of the Lord', Peter concludes that any continued resistance to accepting uncircumcised Gentiles into the covenant community is tantamount to resisting *God* ('Who was I that I could hinder [*kōlyō*] God?' [11.17]). Like Gamaliel, Peter's present jury wants no part in obstructing God's plan; beyond Gamaliel, they positively affirm God's plan with their final verdict: 'Then God has given even to the Gentiles the repentance that leads to life' (11.18).

Barnabas the Encourager in Antioch and Judea: 11.19-30

While the church's mission has finally stretched into Gentile territory, the extent of this outreach is still quite modest. Two evangelists, Philip and Peter, have each instructed and baptized a single Jewish-sympathizing foreign official. In the latter case (Cornelius), ministry also extended to the official's household but no further among the Gentiles of Caesarea, as far as we are told. The gospel road has been paved to the Gentiles, but the traffic remains sparse. All of that is about to change, however, in the next scene, as the new congregation in Syrian Antioch is flooded by a multitude of *Greek* as well as Jewish believers. (The reading *Hellēnas* ['Greeks'] in 11.20 seems preferable to the variant *Hellēnistas* ['Hellenists', i.e. Greek-speaking Jews], given the clear contrast with *Ioudaiois* ['Jews/ Judeans'] in 11.19). Three times the narrator stresses the 'great number' or 'large crowd' of disciples at Antioch (11.21, 24, 26), including Gentiles as well as Jews, perhaps even Gentiles without prior attachments to Judaism. (We learn of no 'God-fearing' piety, like that of Cornelius or the Ethiopian eunuch.)

The plot of the Antioch story is propelled by a combination of divine and human action. The mighty 'hand of the Lord' is instrumental once again in bringing many to faith and repentance (11.21; cf. 4.28, 30; 7.25). But the 'hand of Barnabas and Saul' also plays an important role, for example, in carrying an offering from the Antioch congregation to the needy communities back in Judea (11.30). On the human side, Barnabas emerges as the main character, nurturing the young church in Antioch as well as conveying its charitable contributions to the Judean disciples. Saul assists Barnabas in both tasks but remains a subordinate figure at this stage (11.25-26). Other supporting actors also enter the picture:

(1) Anonymous *fugitives* from the persecution in Jerusalem sparked by Stephen (cf. 8.1) first introduce the gospel *to* Cyprus, Phoenicia and Antioch; among these are certain men originally *from* Cyprus and Cyrene who witness to the Gentiles as well as Jews of Antioch (11.19-20). The double Cyprus-reference recalls Barnabas' own native roots (4.36), and the Cyrenian company may be linked back to the Pentecost audience (2.10) and to the synagogue assembly who disputed with Stephen (apparently some Cyrenians took Stephen's side; 6.9).

(2) Once the Antioch church is established and thriving, it receives a group of itinerant *prophets* from Jerusalem; among these is one named Agabus who forecasts a disastrous famine which, in turn, prompts the relief mission back to Judea (11.27-30). Although ministers such as Stephen, Philip, Saul, and Peter have been functioning as prophets, this marks the first explicit designation of prophetic activity in Acts in fulfillment of the Joel promise (2.17-18).

(3) Through their messengers, Barnabas and Saul, the Antioch Christians send their collection to ruling *elders* in Judea (11.30). On several occasions we have encountered the leading 'elders' (*presbyteroi*) of Israel associated with the hostile temple authorities in Jerusalem. This marks the first time that the Jerusalem *church* is said to be governed by elders, implying both a vital link to traditional Jewish social structures and a developing rift with the current hierarchs of Israel. (Appointing their own elders amounts to a repudiation of the incumbent elders.)

Pastoral Support in Antioch: 11.19-26

The only mention of Antioch thus far in Acts was in connection with the list of seven table-servants in ch. 6. One of them, named Nicolaus, was identified as 'a proselyte of Antioch' (6.5), that is, a Gentile convert to Judaism who had migrated to Jerusalem and eventually joined the developing Christian party in that city. Now the flow of movement is reversed, as Hellenist (Cypriot and Cyrenian) missionaries *from* Jerusalem proclaim the gospel to a receptive audience of both Jews and Gentiles *in* Antioch. In this metropolis, the disciples have reached one of the leading cities of the Roman empire, ranking third in population and prosperity, according to Josephus, behind only Rome and Alexandria (*War* 3.29). Moreover, in attracting a mixed congregation of Jews and Gentiles, the new church begins its own intriguing chapter in a checkered story of Jew-Gentile relations in the Syrian capital. On the one hand, Josephus informs us, after the villainous reign of Antiochus Epiphanes, a sizeable Jewish colony mushroomed in Antioch which included numerous Greek proselytes. On the other hand, Jewish fortunes could also plummet, as during the first Jewish War when one of their own number (ironically named Antiochus) spurned his native religion and incited a brutal repression of the Jewish people by the Roman authorities in Antioch (*War* 7.41-53) (see Brown and Meier, pp. 30-32).

When the Jerusalem church gets wind of the burgeoning new congregation, they dispatch Barnabas to Antioch. Why he is chosen rather than Peter or John, who were sent to Samaria under similar circumstances (cf. 8.14), is not specified; perhaps it has to do with the Cypriot connection (noted above). In any event, we observe once again that the episcopal authority of the Jerusalem apostles is by no means absolute in Acts. New churches are springing up and growing too rapidly and in too many places for any one administrative body to keep up with, much less control them.

When Barnabas encounters the Antioch believers, his ministry to them is different than that exercised by Peter and John toward the Samaritans and Peter toward Cornelius' household. Here we find no conferral of the Spirit (the only mention of the Spirit is in connection with Barnabas' character: 'he was a good man, full of the Holy Spirit', 11.24), no evangelistic preaching, and no baptizing—in other words, no activities targeted explictly toward conversion and initiation. Presumably those activities had been carried out by the first wave of missionaries. Barnabas' main work is *pastoral* in orientation, 'exhorting' ('encouraging' [*parakaleō*], true to his name as 'son of encouragment [*paraklēsis*]' [4.36]) the Antiochenes 'to remain faithful to the Lord' and instructing them in the faith 'for an entire year' (11.24, 26). Such prolonged nurturing creates an impression that the church at Antioch will be around for a while and will play a key role in further advancing and shaping the global Christian mission.

In the course of strengthening the young believers at Antioch, Barnabas also encourages Saul by enlisting him as a fellow-teacher. We last encountered Saul fleeing for his life from Jerusalem to Tarsus; while the wary Jerusalem apostles finally accepted the radically changed Saul—because of Barnabas' advocacy!—the Hellenistic Jews sought only to kill him (9.26-30). On the run, Saul's prospects for effective ministry seemed limited. But now Barnabas intervenes once more, providing him with a fresh opportunity for service in a new place. This is not a case where Saul just 'happens' to be in the neighborhood, ready at hand to assist Barnabas; on the contrary, Barnabas takes the full initiative, seeking Saul out in Tarsus (over a hundred miles away overland) and bringing him to Antioch. Teaching a receptive, mixed community, comprised of Gentile as well as Jewish disciples, marks a pioneering step for Saul in fulfilling the commission of 9.15. (Witnessing before 'kings' still awaits a future occasion.)

As well as being the first community in Acts to include a substantial number of Gentiles and to receive extended instruction from Saul, the Antioch disciples are also the first to be explicitly dubbed 'Christians' (11.26). The term simply refers to 'followers or associates of one called Christ' (somewhat analogous to 'Herodians' in relation to 'Herod'; cf. Mk 3.6; 12.13). Thus far in Acts, it has been appropriate to speak descriptively of the 'Christian' orientation of the early disciples as 'followers of *the* Christ', that is, within a fully Jewish context, as believers in Jesus 'the Messiah/Anointed One', the longed-for royal restorer of Israel (cf. 2.36; 3.18-20). Now, however, the use of 'Christian' as a distinctive group label appears to generate outside the Jewish sphere, reflecting a more limited perception of 'Christ' by the wider Gentile citizenry in Antioch as an individual name rather than an official title. By pinning a new, personalized tag on the believers in (the) Christ, the Antiochenes effectively separate the upstart 'Christian' faction from the established people known as 'Jews'. The logic behind this demarcation probably has to do with the mass acceptance of Gentiles within the community. But note well: such Christian exclusivism vis-à-vis Judaism is more of an outsider's than an insider's assessment at this stage in Acts. From the church's (and implied author's) own point of view, Gentiles are still being incorporated into a renewed kingdom of Israel, the messianic people of God.

Material Support in Jerusalem: 11.27-30

Although the believers at Antioch developed into a strong, independent community under the tutelage of Barnabas and Saul, they continue to maintain close ties with the mother church in Jerusalem. This link is particularly demonstrated in the Antioch disciples' benevolent response to the predicted outbreak of devastating famine by a Jerusalem prophet named Agabus. The Jerusalem church, of course, had earlier set the standard of sharing resources to sustain those in need (2.44-46; 4.32-37; 6.1-6). Apparently, however, after the hardships of persecution resulting in the dispersal of many members, the Jerusalem and Judean communities became hard pressed economically and particularly vulnerable to the ravages of famine. Although Agabus makes the rather melodramatic claim that famine will engulf 'all the world' (11.28), his hearers would know from experience that food shortages hit some areas and people (namely, the poor) harder than others (Hemer, pp. 164-65). The Antioch disciples are better off financially and thus able to assist their less fortunate Judean brothers and sisters. More importantly, they are *willing* to help, 'each according to their own ability' (11.29).

This Antiochene relief mission to Jerusalem 'during the reign of Claudius' (11.28) parallels the efforts of Queen Helena of Adiabene and her son Izates, both dedicated converts to the Jewish faith who, as reported by Josephus, sent abundant quantities of food (corn and figs) and funds to the famine-stricken residents of the holy city (*Ant.* 20.51-53, 101). On a narrative level, the famine scenario also recalls the well-known scriptural story of Joseph, previously alluded to in Acts 7.9-14 (Stephen's speech). After being forcibly driven out of his homeland to Egypt, Joseph predicted an upcoming season of famine (as with Agabus, Joseph's foresight was Spirit-inspired; cf. Gen. 41.37; Acts 11.28) and then rose to a position where he was able to provide food for his hungry brothers. In Joseph's case, of course, this relief effort was also an act of reconciliation, since these brothers had been the agents of Joseph's expulsion (7.9, 11-13). In Acts 11, the famine-relief mission of the Antioch church to Judean 'brothers' (*adelphoi*, 11.29) is not conciliatory per se (since the persecutors of the original witnesses to Antioch were *un*believing Hellenistic Jews), but it nonetheless marks an important expression of solidarity defying conventional sociocultural boundaries: a maverick, mixed Jewish-Gentile church in a major cosmopolitan Greco-Roman city generously reaches out to assist more established Jewish communities in the heart of Judea. Although the two groups do not physically sit down to eat together, the sharing of food symbolically betokens an experience of table-fellowship in line with the recent breakthrough in Cornelius' house. There is, in any event, no hint of divisiveness between Jerusalem Jews and Antioch Gentiles over dining habits, such as that exposed by Paul in Gal. 2.14-17. (Certainly Acts knows nothing of *Barnabas's* 'hypocrisy' in this matter; cf. Gal. 2.13.)

Peter the Prisoner in Jerusalem: 12.1-25

Amidst the joyous account of the thriving mission in Antioch, a flash-back to the persecution campaign against Stephen and his associates (11.19) and a forecast of harsh famine (11.27-30) remind us of the more vulnerable situation back in Jerusalem and prepare us to face a new crisis in ch. 12. Once again, violence breaks out against the Jerusalem believers in the form of execution and imprisonment. Like Stephen, James the brother of John dies as a martyr, and once more, the apostle Peter lands in jail. While the acts of persecution are familiar, however, the authorizing agent is different. 'King Herod' is now the villain of the piece, rather than the high priest and temple authorities, operating with the approval of 'the Jews' at large, not just a group of religious leaders (12.1-3; we previously encountered this generalizing of 'the Jews'' hostility in relation to Saul's ministry in 9.23, but this has not prevented Jewish-Christian missionaries, including Saul, from continuing to witness to Jewish audiences).

Historically, this Herod may be distinguished as Agrippa I, client-king (by edict of Claudius Caesar) of all Jews throughout the territory of Israel from 41 to 44 CE (*Ant*. 19.274). Literarily, however, this figure is closely fused with other Herod-titled rulers in Luke–Acts to form a composite Herodian profile. Up to this point in the narrative, this profile has been predominantly shaped by accumulated reports of malevolent dealings with John the baptizer and Jesus, on the part of Herod the tetrarch of Galilee. He is credited with incarcerating and finally beheading John for denouncing 'all the evil things that Herod had done' (Lk. 3.19-20; 9.7-9) and with seeking (unsuccessfully) to kill Jesus at one stage in Galilee (13.31) and then treating him with disdain later at his trial in Jerusalem (23.11). Although appearing to favor Jesus' release, Herod ultimately shares responsibility with his 'friend' Pilate—egged on by the chief priests and an angry mob—for Jesus' crucifixion (23.10-25; Acts 4.25-28). Well he deserved to be called 'that fox (*alōpēx*)' by Jesus (Lk. 13.32), an image which John Darr associates in its Lukan and Septuagintal contexts not so much with cleverness or slyness as with 'malicious destructiveness', casting Herod as 'a varmint in the Lord's field, a murderer of God's agents, a would-be disrupter of the divine economy' (p. 144) (cf. Song 2.15; Ezek. 13.4-5; Lam. 5.17-18; Neh. 3.35 LXX; Darr also links the Lukan Herods with classic royal enemies of Israelite prophets and Greco-Roman philosophers).

On the surface, the envelope structure of the narrative in Acts 12 rein-forces Herod's evil plan to bind and confine Peter. The apostle's central story in 12.5-19 is embedded or 'bound' within two snippets featuring King Herod on either side (12.1-4; 12.20-23). But the unfolding plot of these incidents ironically shatters their restrictive frame in dramatic fashion, as Peter miraculously breaks out of Herod's maximum security prison and then, at the end, Herod himself meets a violent death.

While the conflict between antagonist Herod and protagonist Peter dominates the action in ch. 12, a variety of other characters play interesting auxiliary roles. The angel of the Lord palpably 'strikes' (*patassō*) both Peter and Herod—but to notably different effects (12.7, 23). Two figures named 'James' make brief entrances (12.2, 17): for one (the martyr) it is his last appearance; for the other, it is a proleptic hint of a more significant role to come. Finally, we are introduced to another household, headed this time by a new character named Mary, distinguished from other Marys in Luke–Acts as the mother of John Mark and mistress to a servant called Rhoda (12.12-13).

Key temporal and spatial markers continue to inform our journey through Acts. Early on in ch. 12, the narrator parenthetically provides the critical calendar note: 'This was during the festival of Unleavened Bread' (12.3). Spatially, the action locates in the familiar zones of prison (12.4-11), private home (12.12-17), and public arena (12.20-23), with a particular emphasis on *gates* as boundary points between areas (12.10, 14).

Herod Kills: 12.1-4

In contrast to missionaries who have laid benevolent hands on various people to impart healing and the gift of the Spirit (8.17; 9.17), Herod 'laid violent hands' on certain church leaders (12.1). Such attack extends even to murdering the apostle James (cf. 1.13) 'with the sword' (12.2). This particular means of execution varies from the stoning barrage which felled Stephen but recalls the beheading of John the bapitzer by another Herodian tyrant (Lk. 9.9). Mention of the sword also brings to mind the words and conduct of the Lukan Jesus just before and during his arrest. With a keen sense of impending danger, Jesus initially seemed to encourage his disciples to arm themselves with swords for protection (22.35-36). But then he quickly changed tack as the disciples' seized on Jesus' suggestion with rather too much zeal. Their prompt display of two swords already at their disposal was first met with a dismissive—'It is enough'—from Jesus (22.38); then, when they decided to wield this weaponry against the temple party who came to arrest Jesus, he retorted with a more emphatic—'No more of this!'—and even went so far as to restore a priestly servant's ear which one of his followers had hacked off (22.49-51). The Lukan perspective is clear: enemies will come out against Jesus and his followers with 'swords and clubs' (22.52) (and crosses and stones), but they will neither deserve such treatment nor retaliate with physical violence. Vindication against sword-striking high priests and Herodian kings will ultimately come from the hand of God, not zealous vigilantes.

The popularity of James' execution spurs Herod to go after Peter, the ringleader of the new Christian sect, during the Passover festival when throngs of visitors would flood into Jerusalem. Peter had created quite a stir at a previous pilgrimage festival (Pentecost), garnering the support of thousands of new disciples (2.41-42). Herod seems determined to ensure that Peter will not disrupt the present proceedings (or any other occasion, for that matter, assuming that Herod intends 'to bring him [Peter] out' after Passover not for trial but for public execution [Barrett, *Acts*, I, p. 577]). He has the apostle arrested and imprisoned under the blanket oversight of 'four squads of soldiers'—a fresh company for each watch of the night (Gaventa, p. 2081). Peter's notoriety for nocturnal jail-breaks has obviously preceded him (5.17-21).

The Passover setting for seizing and binding God's people with intent to kill evokes memories of both Jesus' arrest, during the same season (Lk. 22.1, 7), and the ancient Israelites' bitter enslavement in Egypt, associated with the festival's origins (Exodus 12–13). Within this framework, Herod is affiliated with 'the chief priests and scribes who were looking for a way to put Jesus to death' (Lk. 22.2) and especially, by virtue of his royal status, with the villainous Pharaoh of Egypt who sought to annihilate his Israelite subjects. Of course, these analogies are bad omens for Herod, portending the backfire of his evil scheme, even his own violent demise.

Peter Escapes: 12.5-19

The opening verse of this section sets up a conflict between two parties and environments wrestling over the fate of the apostle Peter: 'While Peter was kept in prison, the church prayed fervently to God for him' (12.5). On the one side, the king exercises his own political authority to bind and humiliate Peter in a public prison; on the other side, the church, still based in a private home (cf. 12.12), appeals—through prayer—to superior divine authority for Peter's release and vindication. Such recourse to prayer has been typical of the church's response to persecution in Acts (cf. 4.23-31). In the present story, the church's petition proves effectual. Peter is indeed released from Herod's den of bondage (12.6-11) and then reunited with fellow believers in Mary's house of prayer (12.12-17).

More specifically, the narrative maps this march to freedom through a series of inside-outside moves (1) from a sequestered dungeon (Herod's prison), (2) out into the open city (Jerusalem), (3) through a public street and, finally, (4) into a private sanctuary (Mary's house)—proceeding en route (5) through a pair of *gateways* (*pylē/pylōn*) at key checkpoints.

> Herod's Prison (12.5-9)
> Prison Gate (*pylē*)—leading into the city' (12.10)
> City Street (12.10)
> Private Gate (*pylōn*)—leading into the house (12.13-14)
> Mary's House (12.16)

This course also reflects movement in Peter's social position from marginal deviant (prisoner) outside the bounds of 'normal' society to esteemed leader (apostle) within the fellowship of a sectarian community.

At the two gateways, ironic twists and turns complicate Peter's journey and heighten dramatic tension. The first gate, made of iron and meant to keep Peter securely locked up, amazingly opens for the apostle 'of its own accord' (12.10). Conversely, at the second gate, likely a simple wicket-door (Barrett, *Acts,* I, p. 584) marking the entry to a supportive household of prayer, Peter is left standing and knocking for some time while the bewildered believers deliberate over whether he is even there (12.13-16)!

(1) *Release from Herod's Prison: 12.5-11.* Beyond the basic scene of a night-time, angel-directed escape from prison presented in 5.17-20, the current story features a more elaborate security system which Peter breaks through, as well as interesting intertextual links with the Exodus-Passover plot. We have already learned that four military squads have been assigned to guard Peter throughout the night (12.4); now we find out how they are deployed. Out of a detachment of four soldiers (quaternion, *tetradion*; see Bruce, pp. 245, 248), two flank the sleeping prisoner—who is 'bound with two chains'—while the other pair stand watch at the cell door (12.6). Adding to this picture the iron gate at the perimeter of the prison compound, Peter seems well and truly clamped within Herod's powerful vice with little hope of escape. But even the king's most extreme efforts are no match for the Lord's angel who watches over his ministers. Gliding through barricades of gates, doors, guards, and chains, the angel 'taps' (or 'strikes', *pataxas*) Peter on the side, wakes him and leads him to safety (12.7). God's purposes cannot be blocked or bound by human machinations.

The particular strategy for thwarting Herod's evil plan against Peter remarkably parallels God's action on behalf of his afflicted people at the first Passover (see Tannehill, *Narrative*, II, pp. 151-58; Wall, 'Successors': 637). On that occasion, the Lord instructed the Israelite slaves in Egypt to eat their passover meal at night with 'your loins girded, your sandals on your feet, and your staff in your hand; and you shall eat it hurriedly' in preparation for an urgent flight to freedom (Exod. 12.11). Although the events of Acts 12 are not set at meal-time, it is during the Passover season that the angel commands the shackled Peter to 'get up quickly...fasten your belt and put on your sandals...wrap your cloak around you and follow me' out of bondage to freedom (Acts 12.8-10). It takes a while for the reality of these proceedings to dawn on Peter (12.9), but when it does, he clearly acknowledges his deliverance as the Lord's doing: 'Now I am sure that the Lord has sent his angel and rescued me from the hands of Herod' (12.11). Not quite the high poetry of Moses' song by the sea ('The Lord has triumphed gloriously; horse and rider he has thrown into the sea...' [Exod. 15.1-18]), but it makes the same point.

(2) *Reunion at Mary's House: 12.12-17.* While the narrator has previously noted the regular gathering of the Jerusalem church in local homes (2.46; 5.42), until now no particular home has been singled out. The present meetinghouse where Peter heads straightaway after his release belongs to a woman named Mary, the mother of John Mark. Since this introduction to Mary and her son comes after the mass dispersal of the congregation in 8.1, we might regard them as recent immigrants to the holy city and/or new adherents to the Christian faith. Like Tabitha, upon whom Peter earlier came to call in Joppa, Mary seems to represent an independent (no husband is mentioned), wealthy (she has a maid-servant and a gate; cf. Lk. 16.20), female host of a local house church. Whether she also functions as a leader and teacher in this community, as we might assume, is left open in the narrative. Mary plays no role at all in the encounter with Peter. Moreover, it may be that her main claim to fame in Acts is as the mother of John Mark, who emerges again at the end of the chapter in a potentially important partnership with Barnabas and Saul (12.25). (Mary never appears again in Acts.)

Interestingly, a larger role is given to Mary's maid-servant, *Rhoda*. She comes to greet the visitor at the gate, recognizes his voice as Peter's and then returns to the assembly to announce her discovery (12.13-14). She is thus both perceptive and prophetic (as well as a little overwrought—who can blame her?—leaving Peter standing at the gate). We may be confronted here with a modest fulfillment of Peter's Pentecost prediction that women in general—and *female servants* in particular—would prophesy in the new order established by the Spirit (2.18). Curiously, outside of the lying Sapphira, no women's voices have been heard in the church thus far in Acts. Now, finally, a slave-girl (*paidiskē* in 12.13 and *doulē* in 2.18 are close synonyms) has something to proclaim—not a great theological sermon, to be sure, though still a vital bit of news for the church—Peter is alive, well and here! But in fact the group is not at all receptive to Rhoda's message, at first ridiculing her for even suggesting it—'You are out of your mind!'—and then correcting her judgment when she sticks by her story—'It is his angel' (not Peter himself) (12.15). Only when they see Peter for themselves do they accept Rhoda's word. Apparently, the Jerusalem disciples are not yet ready to adopt the Pentecost agenda fully, particularly when it comes to heeding the voice of women and lower-class servants. In this pattern, of course, they more mirror than challenge wider Jewish and Greco-Roman society and make little progress beyond the Lukan apostles who dismiss the women's report about Jesus' empty tomb as an 'idle tale' until they confirm it with their own eyes (Lk. 24.10-12; see O'Day, p. 310).

Once the prayer-group recognizes Peter, welcomes him inside, and hears the account of his recent exodus experience, the apostle shifts attention to another group—'Tell this to James and to the brothers (*adelphoi*)'—and then departs for 'another place' (12.17). Ultimately, the significance of Mary's house church is reduced to a kind of messenger service and halfway house for the apostle Peter, subordinate to the more eminent brotherhood headed by James.

The reference to James by name only assumes readers' knowledge of his prominent status in the Jerusalem church and hints at a larger role to come in the story of Acts. As Robert Wall ('Successors') has persuasively demonstrated, the significance of James' sudden introduction into the narrative at this juncture relates to preceding events in both the present and first chapters of Acts surrounding Jesus, Peter and the twelve apostles. With the martyrdom of one of the apostles—also named James as it happens—in 12.2, a vacancy was created in the circle of the Twelve. We recall that in ch. 1, following the appearance and ascension of the crucified-risen Jesus, Peter promptly moved to replace the deceased apostle Judas, thus restoring the Twelve as the leading body of messianic witnesses to Israel and the world. Now in ch. 12, rather than restoring the Twelve after losing one of its members, Peter seems to be *transferring* the authority and responsibility of this body to another cohort of (male) ministers in Jerusalem under the leadership of (another) James. In other words, Peter appears to be shifting roles in the narrative, away from one commissioned by Jesus to spearhead the apostolic mission to one who, like Jesus, *commissions others* to carry on his work. Peter has just followed the basic typology of Jesus' (a) execution, (b) resurrection, and (c) manifestation to disciples with his own (a) death row imprisonment, (b) miraculous release, and (c) appearance to anxious supporters. Now he continues the pattern by (d) recognizing apostolic successors before (e) departing ('going' [*eporeuthē*], 12.17; cf. 'while he was going' [*poreuomenou*], 1.10) to another place. Peter's stint as chief apostle within the Jerusalem community and the Acts narrative appears to be ending, as he passes the reins over to James and makes room for others—like Barnabas and Saul (cf. 12.25)—to take on greater roles.

Herod Dies: 12.18-25

After Peter's release and departure from the scene, the story returns to Herod, picking up where it left off with an emphasis on the king's brutal volatility. He first vents his frustration over losing Peter by having the hapless guards executed (12.18-19); then he becomes 'angry' with the

Phoenicians (from Tyre and Sidon) for an unspecifed reason, prompting him apparently to withhold, or at least threaten to withhold, food supplies which the Phoenicians required (12.20). Perhaps the famine which Agabus predicted has hit the region; in any event, Herod displays nothing of the charitable spirit modelled by the church at Antioch or the patriarch Joseph.

Herod's tyrannical reign, however, is about to come to its just end. He appears before the desperate Phoenician contingent bedecked in his splendid royal robes, which, according to Josephus, were made entirely of silver, causing them to glisten in the sun in mesmerizing fashion (*Ant.* 19.343-44). In Lukan perspective, such robes typify the cruel, exploitative practices of the rich and powerful, as in the mock-investiture of Jesus by a previous Herod (Lk. 23.11) and the callous neglect of poor Lazarus by a purple-clad nobleman in Jesus' parable (16.19-21). As the rich man in Jesus' story is punished with a tormenting death, so Herod now meets a horrible fate. While basking in the crowd's attributions of divine status ('The voice of a god, and not of a mortal!') rather than giving glory to the true God, as Peter had previously done (cf. Acts 3.12-13; 10.25-26), Herod is fatally smitten by the Lord's angel and brought down from his royal seat where he refused to feed the needy, to a lowly grave where he himself becomes food for 'worms' (12.21-23). And so, the angel 'strikes' (*epataxen*) again, not gently this time to liberate a captive apostle, but violently to eliminate a powerful enemy of the church, just as the Lord had 'struck' out against another royal terrorizer of his people on the first Passover night (cf. *patassō* in Exod. 12.12, 23, 29 LXX).

Following the report of Herod's death, a brief paragraph provides both a summary to the preceding section and a transition to the next:

(1) *Summary*: 'But the word of God continued to advance and gain adherents' (12.24). The church not only survives but actually thrives in the face of persisting opposition from cruel rulers, like Herod.

(2) *Transition*: 'Then Barnabas and Saul returned [to Antioch], after they had completed their mission in Jerusalem', accompanied by John Mark (12.25). (This translation obviously fits the narrative logic of Acts 11-12 better than the enigmatic, 'Barnabas and Saul returned *to Jerusalem*', preferred in the NRSV; see Metzger, pp. 398-400; Gaventa, p. 2082). This mission refers to the provision of famine relief in 11.27-30, an effort in marked contrast (as noted above) to Herod's apparent restriction of food supply to Tyre and Sidon. The re-emergence of Barnabas and Saul (along with John Mark) after Peter's departure from the story (12.17) prepares us, like the introduction of James in 12.17, for their expanding missionary roles in the chapters to come.

Acts 13.1-21.26:
Expeditions into Gentile Territory

> When they arrived, they called the church together and related all
> that God had done with them, and how he had opened a door of
> faith for the Gentiles (14.27).

> He [Paul] related one by one the things that God had done among
> the Gentiles through his ministry (21.19).

The 'door of faith for the Gentiles' cracked by Philip the evangelist
(Ethiopian eunuch) and the apostle Peter (Cornelius' household) and
pushed further ajar by missionaries in Antioch, is now flung wide open
by Saul and a variety of associates. This changing role for Saul as the
dominant protagonist in the narrative and chief engineer of the Gentile
mission (intimated in 9.15) is signalled by the switch in name in 13.9
from the Jewish 'Saul' to his Greco-Roman cognomen, 'Paul', and the
subsequent reversal in order of presentation, now listing Paul before
Barnabas and other travelling companions (13.13). Of course, Paul's
emerging prominence, like that of all human figures in Acts, remains
tempered by the affirmation that the Gentile mission, as, indeed, all
redemptive work, is supremely *God's doing* ('all/the things that God
had done', 14.27; 21.19).

Although it is common to demarcate three missionary journeys of Paul
in this portion of Acts, I think that the narrative more naturally coheres
around *two* expeditions in territory proximate to two seas ([eastern]
Mediterranean and Aegean), each commencing with a divine commission (in Antioch/Troas) and concluding with a nurturing review of
churches established along the journey and a final evaluation, conducted
in Jerusalem by James and other Jewish-Christian leaders, of Paul's mission strategy pertaining to Gentiles. Paul does make another return trip
to Jerusalem and Antioch in 18.22-23, but this appears to be more of a
brief interlude in the second expedition than a clear-cut break between
a second and third journey. After this interlude, Paul does not embark
on a new mission but returns to complete the work which he had previously started in Ephesus and left under the management of Priscilla
and Aquila in his absence (18.18-19.1).

I. *MEDITERRANEAN EXPEDITION: 13.1-16.5*
  1.   Commission in Antioch: 13.1-3
  2.   Contending in Cyprus: 13.4-12
  3.   Preaching in Pisidia: 13.13-52
  4.   Miracle-Working in Lycaonia: 14.1-20
  5.   Nurturing the Churches: 14.21-28
  6.   Evaluation in Jerusalem: 15.1-16.5

II. *AEGEAN EXPEDITION: 16.6-21.36*
  1.   Commission in Troas: 16.6-10
  2.   Imprisoned in Philippi: 16.11-40
  3.   Hunted in Thessalonica; Welcomed in Beroea: 17.1-15
  4.   Questioned in Athens: 17.16-34
  5.   Reviled in Corinth: 18.1-17
  6.   Mobbed in Ephesus: 18.18-19.41
  7.   Nurturing the Churches: 20.1-21.14
  8.   Evaluation in Jerusalem: 21.15-36

(1) The *commissions* which inaugurate both expeditions come through supernatural means and thus convey a strong sense of divine legitimation. In the first, the Holy Spirit dispatches Saul and Barnabas on a personal mission ('for me', 13.2-3); in the second, while the Spirit blocks certain paths that Paul wants to pursue, a visionary figure summons him to Macedonia to 'help us' (16.6-10). The Spirit and visions also periodically convey additional guidance along the course of the expeditions (15.28; 18.9-10; 19.21; 21.4, 11-14). In sum, the Lord both starts and sustains the Pauline missions.

(2) Although the outline above specifically associates *contending* (with magic), *preaching* (the gospel), and *miracle-working* (signs and wonders) only with the first expedition, such activities, as we might expect, also occupy Paul in the second mission (as indeed they have occupied missionaries heretofore in Acts). Likewise, the numerous hardships (*imprisoned, hunted,* etc.) catalogued above in relation to the second expedition are also typical of the first (for example, headings could be changed to '*Expelled* in Pisidia' or '*Stoned* in Lycaonia'). In sum, Paul's missionary actions regularly spark hostile reactions from a variety of audiences.

(3) But such is not the whole story. Amid persisting persecution, Paul is still *welcomed* wholeheartedly in Beroea and sufficiently elsewhere to plant an extensive network of new churches in the eastern Mediterranean world. Moreover, despite the risk involved, Paul retraces his steps at the close of each expedition to *nurture* the young congregations, 'encouraging' them to press on in the face of difficulty and appointing and instructing local 'elders' to carry on his ministry (14.21-23; 20.1-2, 17-38).

(4) The final *evaluations* by James and the Jerusalem church both focus on Paul's law-free mission to the Gentiles, but from different vantage points. At the council following the first expedition, the issue concerns the propriety of Paul's approach to the *Gentiles: must Gentiles become Jews*, that is, submit to circumcision and keep the Mosaic law, to be part of God's people (15.5)? Following the second expedition, however, the leaders of the Jerusalem church are more concerned with Paul's dealings with Diaspora *Jews* living in the Gentile world: is he teaching that *Jews must become Gentiles*, that is, 'forsake Moses and...not circumcise their children or observe the customs' (21.21), to remain in God's household? The answer to both questions proves to be 'no'. Put positively, the first council affirms Paul's practice of accepting Gentiles solely 'by faith...through the grace of the Lord Jesus' (15.9, 11), while at the second Paul agrees to demonstrate both his personal practice of the Jewish law and support of others' observance (21.23-26; cf. similar demonstrations in 16.1-3; 18.18; 20.16). As a further concession to Jewish concerns, both evaluative councils stress the need for Gentile believers at least to abstain from a few 'essential' taboos pertaining to idolatry, impurity, and immorality (15.19-21, 28-29; 21.25).

Beyond the basic plot structure sketched in the outline above, the travel narratives in Acts 13-21 may be mapped along spatial, temporal, and social lines. From a panoramic view, these expeditions carry us further than we have ventured thus far toward the ends of the earth, moving progressively northwestward from Israel (Jerusalem) and Syria (Antioch) into the great urban centers of Asia Minor and Greece. (I use the term 'expedition' rather than 'journey' or 'excursion' [as in the previous section, chs. 6–12] to connote a greater sense of extensive exploration of remote territory.) On a smaller scale, the action localizes in a variety of places in and around the cities: synagogues (in almost every city), temples—both Greco-Roman (14.13; 19.27) and Jewish (21.27)—waterfront prayer stations (16.13, 16; 21.5), marketplaces (*agora*, 16.19; 17.5, 17), private homes (16.15, 32, 40; 17.5; 18.7; 21.8, 16), a prison (16.23), a hilltop court (*Areopagus*, 17.19, 22), a judicial bench (*bēma*, 18.12), a lecture hall (19.9), a theater (19.29), and an upper room (20.8). Finally, while Paul sets out on predominantly overland expeditions, he travels by ship on occasions across the Mediterranean and Aegean Seas and stops at various *islands* along the way (13.6; 16.11; 20.14-15; 21.1).

As for temporal settings, the narrator provides regular reports, as we might expect in travelogues, of how long Paul and company remain in various locations, ranging from brief stopovers of one day (21.7) or week (20.6; 21.4) to protracted stays of eighteen months (Corinth, 18.11) or three years (Ephesus, 20.31). As for special days, Paul faithfully continues to follow a standard Jewish schedule revolving around the weekly sabbath (13.14, 42, 44; 16.13; 17.2; 18.4) and annual pilgrimage festivals, Passover (20.6) and Pentecost (20.16). Within a given twenty-four hour period, night-time, particularly *midnight*, emerges as the occasion for several significant events in the second expedition (16.9-10, 25-34; 18.9-10; 20.7-12).

The most pervasive and radical dimension of Paul's Diaspora missions concerns the disruption of conventional social-symbolic systems, epitomized in the vivid complaint of Thessalonian officials: 'These people who have been turning the world upside down have come here also' (17.6; cf. Neyrey, 'Symbolic Universe', pp. 271-73). We may gain an initial sense of these world-flipping effects by briefly charting Paul's dealings with several social groups which may be classified for discussion into four categories (acknowledging overlap between them):

I. *JEWISH*
    A. *Religious leaders; synagogue rulers; 'the Jews'*: 13.5, 15, 45-52; 14.2-7, 19; 16.3; 17.5-7, 10-13; 18.6-8 (Crispus); 18.17 (Sosthenes); 20.18-19; 21.11, 20, 27-36
    B. *'God-fearers' (phoboumenoi/sebomenoi ton theon) and Proselytes*: 13.16, 26, 43; 13.50; 16.14 (Lydia); 17.4, 17; 18.4, 7 (Titius Justus)
    C. *'Devout women of high standing'*: 13.50; 16.14 (Lydia); 17.4, 12, 34 (Damaris); 18.2-3, 18-26 (Priscilla)

II. *GRECO-ROMAN*
    A. *Religious and philosophical leaders*: 14.13 (priest of Zeus); 17.18-21 (Epicurean and Stoic philosophers)
    B. *Economic leaders; businessmen*: 16.19-21 (owners of fortune-teller); 19.23-27 (Demetrius and silversmiths)
    C. *Political officials; administrators*: 13.7-12 (Sergius Paulus); 13.50; 16.20-24, 35-39 (magistrates, *stratēgoi*); 17.6-8 (politarchs); 17.34 (Dionysius the Areopagite); 19.31 (Asiarchs); 18.12-17 (Gallio); 19.38 (proconsuls); 21.31-33 (tribune)

III. *CHRISTIAN*
    A. *Church leaders*: 14.23; 15.4-29 (Peter, James); 18.24–19.7 (Apollos and baptist disciples); 20.17-38 (Ephesian elders); 21.17-26 (James)
    B. *Missionary hosts and partners*: 13.1-5, 13; 15.36-40 (Barnabas and John Mark); 15.40–16.3 (Silas and Timothy); 16.15, 40 (Lydia); 17.6-7 (Jason); 18.1-3, 18-26 (Priscilla and Aquila); 18.7 (Titius Justus); 19.22 (Erastus); 20.4 (Sopater, Aristarchus, Gaius, Tychicus, Trophimus); 21.1-18 ('we'-party); 21.8 (Philip); 21.16 (Mnason)

IV. *CHARISMATIC*
   A.   *Practitioners of magic*: 13.6-12 (Elymas); 16.16-18 (slave-
         girl); 19.13-16 (sons of Sceva); 19.18-19
   B.   *Beneficiaries of miracles*: 14.8-10 (lame man); 16.16-18
         (slave-girl); 19.11-12; 20.9-12 (Eutychus)

(1) *Jewish*. As 'the Jews' in Damascus were offended by Saul's early preaching to the point of plotting to kill him (9.22-24), so 'the Jews' throughout the cities of Asia Minor and Greece repeatedly stir up violent opposition against Paul and his missionary companions. In chs. 13–21, however, these antagonistic 'Jews' are, for the most part, limited to religious leaders—synagogue officials in particular—in clear distinction from the Jewish people at large (e.g., 'when the Jews saw the crowds...' [13.45]). And even with respect to synagogue rulers, there is a notable exception to this hostile pattern in the case of Crispus, who 'bec[omes] a believer in the Lord, together with all his household' in Corinth (18.8).

Not only are the Jewish religious elites distinguished from the crowds in general; they are also set apart in these expedition accounts from particular Jewish audiences that prove more responsive to Paul. Chief among these are groups on the ethnic-religious border between Jews and Gentiles: Greeks who have become proselytes to the Jewish faith ('many Jews and *devout converts*', 13.43) and, further out on the periphery of Jewish society, Greeks who 'fear' the God of Israel (hence the label 'God-fearer' coined by modern scholars) and worship in Jewish synagogues but for various reasons stop short of full conversion ('you descendants of Abraham's family and *others who fear God*', 13.26). 'Not a few Greek women and men of high standing' (17.12) attending the synagogue constitute an important subset of 'God-fearers' receptive to Paul's ministry (among the many supportive Greek women, only the Athenian Damaris has no reported Jewish sympathies or ties to the local synagogue [17.34]). While Gentile sympathizers with Judaism generally prove to be more open to Paul's mission than the synagogue leaders, there are a few counterexamples preventing us again from making blanket, stereotypical judgments regarding various social groups (13.50; 14.2, 5).

(2) *Greco-Roman*. In the present discussion, this category is reserved for thoroughly 'pagan', polytheistic Gentiles with no attachments to Judaism. Again, we detect a mixture of responses to Paul's mission. The businessmen whose livelihood is tied either to popular magical superstition (fortune-tellers in Philippi) or to institutional goddess worship (silversmiths in Ephesus) are consistently aggravated with Paul for threatening their profits. By contrast, government officials typically protect Paul's interests as a Roman citizen and defuse mob violence against him; in the case of Sergius Paulus, a proconsul even goes so far as to 'believe' Paul's gospel (13.12). Once more, however, the pattern is not

perfect, as the politarchs in Thessalonica join the crowd in being 'disturbed' by Paul's subversive activity (17.8).

Falling somewhere between sympathy and hostility would be the reactions of Greco-Roman religious and philosophical leaders. The priest of Zeus in Lystra is certainly enamored with Paul and Barnabas, but his insistence on offering sacrifices to them as if they were Greek gods totally misses the point of their message (14.14-18). The Epicurean and Stoic philosophers in Athens happily engage Paul in religious debate, but mostly as frivolous curiosity seekers who 'spend their time in nothing but telling or hearing something new' (17.21). This is not to say, however, that some Athenians do not take Paul seriously, either scorning him as a fool, on the one hand, or accepting his word and uniting with his cause, on the other hand (e.g. Dionysius the Areopagite [17.32-34]).

(3) *Christian*. We shift the focus here away from the unbelieving world, both Jewish and Greek, which Paul seeks to evangelize to the community of disciples, both Jewish and Greek, which watches over and works with the itinerant missionary. First, there are other Christian leaders either who are threatened in some way by Paul, like James and the elders of the Jerusalem church, or who themselves pose a threat to Paul, such as the eloquent but slightly misguided Apollos and the believing but Spirit-less baptist 'apostolate' ('about *twelve* of them', 19.7) in Ephesus. For the most part, these potential conflicts are dealt with decisively in the interest of Christian unity; but at Ephesus at least, the specter of internecine opposition continues to hang over Paul's mission, as he warns the elders that 'some even from your own group will come distorting the truth' and marauding as 'savage wolves...not sparing the flock' (20.29-30).

Secondly, the extensive Pauline expeditions require the assistance of a large company of hosts and partners, many more than attended the earlier excursions of Philip and Peter. Philip actually emerges again, not as itinerant evangelist, however, but as resident host (21.8-9). Priscilla and Aquila serve a dual role, as both Paul's hosts in Corinth and his missionary deputies in Ephesus (18.1-3, 18-26). The presentation of a vast network of associates, most of whom are identified by name, creates an overall impression of harmonious support for Paul and his work. But yet again a significant divergence from this pattern must not be ignored, involving as it does Paul's principal partner at a strategic and ironic point in the narrative: *Barnabas*, of all people, falls out of favor and parts company with Paul between the two expeditions—right after they had worked together in Jerusalem to secure a unanimous endorsement of their Gentile mission (15.36-41)!

(4) *Charismatic*. This category focuses on brokers and beneficiaries of supernatural power within a competitive, dualistic universe. On the one side in the Lukan world view, there are agents of the devil, like

Elymas ('son of the devil', 13.10), who perform 'magic' for evil ends; on the other side, there are instruments of the Holy Spirit, like Paul, who work 'miracles' for good purposes. As these opposing forces clash in chs. 13-19, the magicians/sorcerers typically make the first strike against Paul, attempting to thwart (Elymas) or co-opt (sons of Sceva) his dynamic ministry or simply irritating him (slave-girl) as he goes about his work. Each of these attacks draws swift and sharp counterfire which throttles the magicians' power. The two Jewish charismatics—a pseudo-prophet (Elymas) and a band of priestly exorcists (sons of Sceva)—suffer physical punishment (blinding and beating), while Paul frees the Philippian slave-girl from her evil soothsaying spirit. This latter case, in which magic is overwhelmed by miracle, illustrates Paul's contrasting, salutary use of divine power. Here he liberates the possessed; on other occasions, he heals the crippled (unnamed man in Lystra) and raises the dead (Eutychus in Troas).

On the whole, Paul's missionary expeditions in Acts 13–21 elicit a *divided* response from a *variety* of social groups. Paul creates quite a stir wherever he goes, but not always in the same way among the same people. General patterns of support or opposition built up over the course of the expedition accounts are periodically deconstructed by glaring exceptions. Such 'loose threads' make for a more interesting, suspenseful narrative and invite closer attention to the distinctive elements of individual episodes.

Mediterranean Expedition: 13.1-16.5

This expedition sets out by sea from Syrian Antioch to an island in the Mediterrean (Cyprus) and then on to the south-central mainland of Asia Minor. A three-member party begins the trek—Paul, Barnabas and John Mark—but the latter deserts the expedition early on (13.13), only to re-emerge at the end as the focus of controversy between the other two missionaries (15.36-41). While Paul engages in a full range of apostle-style activities (he and Barnabas are even called 'apostles' in 14.4, 14), proclamation emerges as the most dominant ministry, occurring in some form at every stop and particularly featured in a lengthy speech at Pisidian Antioch (by far the longest segment of this travel report) in the center of the expedition (13.16-47).

Commission in Antioch: 13.1-3

The earlier material recounting the beginnings of the church at Antioch featured the formative *teaching* ministry of Barnabas and Saul and the predictive insight of itinerant *prophets* from Jerusalem (11.25-28). Now we learn that five resident 'prophets and teachers'—Barnabas and Saul plus three others—direct the congregation. We might speculate that these three new ministers represent certain of the visiting Jerusalem prophets who elected to settle in Antioch. In any event, the added leadership fits the pattern of continued church growth suggested in 12.24.

The particular list of leaders in 13.1 is noteworthy both for its diverse character and surprising order.

> Barnabas
> Simeon called Niger
> Lucius of Cyrene
> Manean, court companion (*syntrophos*) of Herod
> Saul

Gerhard Krodel (p. 226) vividly captures the 'remarkable diversity of backgrounds and origins' of these leaders, appropriate to the cosmopolitan context of Antioch:

> A Levite from Cyprus [Barnabas], a black man [Niger], a North African from Cyrene [Lucius], a boyhood friend of Herod Antipas [Manean] and a Pharisee educated under Gamaliel [Saul] were acknowledged to be spiritual dynamos [the profile of Saul is gleaned from later in Acts—22.3; 23.6].

The apparent African roots of both Simeon and Lucius remind us of some of the Pentecost pilgrims in 2.10 and the Ethiopian eunuch in 8.27. The specific connection of Lucius with *Cyrene* suggests that he may have been among the original founders of the church (11.20). Manean's close association with Herod the tetrarch (*syntrophos* suggests the relationship of 'foster-brother' or 'intimate friend' from childhood; BAGD, p. 793) recalls an earlier link to Herod's household through Joanna, a supporter of the Jesus movement and wife of Herod's steward, Chuza (Lk. 8.3). Moreover, the emergence of an Herodian courtier into a leader of the Christian community at Antioch proves to be another embarrassment for the recently stricken Herod who sought (unsuccessfully) to exterminate the apostle Peter.

In terms of order, previous leadership lists in Acts have reserved the top slots for the chief heads of the group who play a major role in subsequent narratives: Peter and John among the twelve apostles (1.13; 3.1-4.22) and Stephen and Philip among the seven table-servants (6.5; 6.8-8.40). In the present case, however, the ministerial pair which has worked together before and is being set apart by the Spirit for a new expedition (13.2) appears in the first (Barnabas) and *last* (Saul) position. Perhaps this arrangement reflects abiding suspicion regarding Saul's commitment. Whatever the explanation, the stage is set for a dramatic reversal of roles for Saul: the last shall be first.

The commission to send Barnabas and Saul on special assignment comes *from* the Holy Spirit *through* the worshipping and fasting congregation (I take the ambiguous 'they' in 13.2 to refer to the entire church [*ekklēsia*, v. 1] rather than strictly the five leaders gathered in closed session; cf. Marshall, *Acts*, p. 215)—another telling sign of the partnership between Spirit and community (God's purpose is realized in and through God's people) and between contemplative and active service (worship inspires mission) (cf. 1.8; 2.1-47; 4.23-31). The emphasis on communal 'fasting' (*nēsteuōn*)—repeated in the center of a chiasm, 'worshipping and fasting' (13.2)/'fasting and praying' (13.3)—is a first for Acts. Saul's three-day stint without food or drink in Damascus was a private affair, as was Cornelius' four-day fast reported in the Textus Receptus of 10.30 but dropped in modern Greek editions. While Jesus was physically among his disciples providing immediate access to God's will, they did not need to fast as did the Pharisees and followers of John. But now in Antioch, at a time and place far removed from the occasion of Jesus' departure to heaven, the early Christians resume fasting, as Jesus predicted they would (Lk. 5.33-35), as a means of seeking divine guidance. The connection seems to be that fasting both expresses and produces a humble attitude conducive to receiving special revelation. As the *Shepherd of Hermas* puts it toward the end of the first century CE: 'Every request needs humility: fast therefore and you shall receive what you ask from the Lord' (*Vis.* 3.10.6; cf. 2.2.1; 3.1.2; *Sim.* 5.1.2; Meeks, *Origins*, pp. 99-100).

Contending in Cyprus: 13.4-12

The island of Cyprus, where the expedition party first stops, is more than just a way station en route to the mainland of Asia Minor. It marks the initial center of ministry as the missionaries proceed 'through the whole island' in a southwesterly diagonal from Salamis to Paphos, 'proclaim[ing] the word of God in the synagogues of the Jews' (13.5-6). Strategically placed at the beginning of an extended travel narrative, the Cyprus episode, though relatively brief, establishes foundational patterns for the rest of the account through what some literary critics call the 'primacy effect' (cf. Tannehill, 'Gospels', p. 69). Particularly important in this regard is Saul's sudden emergence as captain of the expedition, a remarkable elevation of status from his subordinate role in 13.1-2. This new identity is signified by the introduction of another name—Paul—and by the report of his discomfiting a powerful magician in a contest of honor, validated by none less than the island's chief political official (13.9-12). In the hierarchic and dyadic culture of Mediterranean antiquity, character and reputation were strongly determined in relation to others on the social ladder (see Malina and Neyrey, 'First-Century Personality'). In addition to charting Paul's rise in honor in a relation to Bar-Jesus/Elymas (magician) and Sergius Paulus (proconsul), we may also note his altered status vis-à-vis the venerable Lukan figures of Barnabas and Jesus.

(1) *Bar-Jesus/Elymas*. The mission to Cypriot Jews is summarily reported in 13.5 without disclosing their reaction. The present story places the focus not so much on 'the Jews' at large as on an individual

Jewish wonder-working prophet named Bar-Jesus—a transliteration from Aramaic, denoting 'son of Jesus or Joshua'. 'Elymas' does not really translate Bar-Jesus, as the narrator claims (13.8), but the use of an alternative Greek name signals the Jewish magician's syncretistic link to the pagan world and perhaps the narrator's desire to remove any hint of kinship tie to another *Jesus* (the Christ, as discussed below).

Bar-Jesus clearly regards the presence of the two missionaries on the island and especially their appeal to the proconsul as invasions of his territory, threats to his favored status under the patronage of the island's honorable governor (we should probably think of Bar-Jesus as a 'court magician' [Garrett, p. 81]). Judging the missionaries' proclamation of the 'word of God' as a *claim* of superior authority, Bar-Jesus mounts a counter-*challenge* by 'oppos[ing]' their work and attempting 'to turn the proconsul away from the faith' (13.7-8). In turn, 'Saul, also known as Paul' (here is the name change)—acting alone (see more below)—follows with a direct *riposte*, hurling a string of insulting epithets and ultimately imposing a curse of blindness on Bar-Jesus.

This punitive sign—Paul's first miracle in Acts—shows how difficult it is to distinguish between magic and miracle. As Arthur Nock suggests, blinding hexes are just what one would expect from someone like Bar-Jesus; Paul's retaliating in this way thus presents him beating 'the magician at his own game' (pp. 185-86). Still, elements of benefaction also attend Paul's curse, as it is set to last only 'for a while' (contrast the more severe and permanent death threat against Simon Magus [8.20]), and is designed not simply to stifle the magician but also to facilitate the proconsul's hearing of the gospel. Indeed, the proconsul effectively pronounces the final *verdict* on this honor contest when he 'believes' Paul's message after 's[eeing] what had happened' to Bar-Jesus (13.12). Paul wins the match and solidifies his new missionary authority.

Other elements in the Bar-Jesus incident enhance this position. Labelling Paul's opponent a *false* prophet (*pseudoprophētēs*) as well as an occultic specialist (*magos*) associates him with the Canaanite mediums opposed to the true 'prophet like Moses' in Deuteronomy (18.9-22) and, before that, with the Egyptian wizards pitted against Moses himself in Exodus (7.9-12, 22; 8.7, 19). Moreover, the charge that Bar-Jesus persists in 'making crooked the straight paths of the Lord' sets him in diametric opposition to the prophetic script outlined by Isaiah and fulfilled by John the baptizer (Lk. 3.4-5). By beating such a false prophet, Paul thus establishes himself as an authentic 'prophet like Moses' and messenger like John, speaking the true 'word of God' (13.5, 7), inflicting a plague of darkness/blindness on Bar-Jesus (13.11; cf. Exod. 10.21-29; Deut. 28.28-29), and blocking his crooked path.

The blinding of Bar-Jesus by the Lord's hand—operating through Paul—and his being led around by the hand of others (13.11-12) also remind us of Paul's own experience on the Damascus road (9.3-8). Even after he regained his sight and began proclaiming the Christian message, Paul continued to need others' helping hands to guide him out of danger and into mission opportunities (9.23-25, 27-30; 11.25-26). Now for the first time he takes charge of his own ministry, reversing, as it were, his former blindness and helplessness by imposing such a state on Bar-Jesus. In sum, Paul's 'triumph', as Susan Garrett comments, 'confirms the change that has taken place in his own life, and brings him a new external status to match the new internal one: he departs from Paphos as the leader of the mission' (84-85). (From Bar-Jesus' perspective, the parallel with Paul's experience also leaves open the possibility of future conversion and useful service. Perhaps he too will be led to a 'straight' way [cf. 9.11]).

(2) *Sergius Paulus*. Paul does not yet fulfill his destiny of witnessing before 'kings' (9.15), but he comes close in preaching to and ultimately persuading the highest ranking official on Cyprus, the provincial governor, Sergius Paulus (13.7, 12). In addition to his political and military power as proconsul, he is also known for his mental prowess as 'an intelligent (*synetō*) man' (13.7). Previously, as a police agent of the chief priests in Jerusalem, Saul functioned as a 'retainer' to 'the governing Jewish elite classes' (Neyrey, 'Luke's Social Location', pp. 260-61). Now, by impressing such a noble figure as the sagacious governor of Cyprus, Paul evinces his honorable standing in the Greco-Roman world: he can hold his own before prominent politicians and philosophers. The coincidence of the missionary's new name—Saulus *Paulus*—matching the governor's—Sergius *Paulus*—may offer subtle confirmation that Paul is a worthy retainer, if not the social equal, of a Roman dignitary (see Nobbs, pp. 287-89).

Notably, this accent on Christian respectability among the aristocracy and intelligentsia tilts away from the preference toward the weak and simple in Luke's Gospel—'you have hidden these things from the wise and the intelligent (*synetōn*)' (10.21, see more below)—and in the historical Paul's own writings: 'I will destroy the wisdom of the wise, and the discernment of the discerning (*synetōn*) I will thwart... Not many of you were wise by human standards, not many were powerful, not many were of noble birth' (1 Cor. 1.19, 26).

(3) *Barnabas*. While the narrator reports in 13.7 that Sergius Paulus 'summoned Barnabas and Saul' to learn of their teaching, when it comes to dealing with Bar-Jesus in word and deed in the proconsul's presence, Saul-Paul acts alone without any apparent assistance from Barnabas. That this episode marks the rise of Paul and fading of Barnabas becomes clear in the narrator's next identification of the expedition party as simply, 'Paul and his companions' (13.13). In ironic fashion, the measure of Paul's elevated status is heightened by the fact that he surpasses his chief missionary patron, Barnabas (9.27; 11.26), on the latter's *home turf* of Cyprus (cf. 4.36).

(4) *Jesus and the Devil*. While the Jewish magician styles himself as 'son of (*bar*) Jesus (savior, deliverer)', Paul strips away this mask and exposes him as a completely deviant 'son of the devil...full of all deceit' (13.9-10). Beyond the reference to Philip's encounter with 'unclean spirits' in Samaria (8.6)—where he also confronted another powerful magician (Simon)—this is the first mention of demonic interference in Acts. By challenging a magician-agent of the devil in the power of the Holy Spirit, Paul engages in a cosmic battle on Cyprus, reminiscent not only of Philip's Samaritan mission, but more fundamentally, of Jesus' work in Galilee. As the Lukan Jesus, 'filled with the Spirit', proved his mettle at the outset of his public ministry in a desert clash with the devil (Lk. 4.1-13), so Paul, 'filled with the Spirit', passes his first missionary test in an island showdown with the son of the devil (Acts 13.9-11).

Paul also both fulfills and goes beyond Jesus' message to the 70 returning missionaries on a later occasion (Lk. 10.17-24):

(a) *Jesus* said: 'I watched Satan fall from heaven like a flash of lightning. See I have given you authority...over all the power of the enemy (*echthrou*)' (Lk. 10.18-19). *Paul* demonstrates his Christ-given authority over the 'son of the devil, [the] enemy (*echthre*) of all righteousness', by enshrouding him in darkness (Acts 13.10-11).

(b) *Jesus* said, 'rejoic[ing] in the Holy Spirit': 'I thank you, Father, Lord of heaven and earth, because you have hidden these things from the wise and the intelligent (*syneton*) and revealed them to infants' (Lk. 10.21). *Paul*, 'filled with the Spirit', enacts a prophetic demonstration in the presence of 'an intelligent (*syneto*) man' which sparks his faith and amazement 'at the teaching of the Lord' (Acts 13.7, 12). What had been hidden in the ministry of Jesus is now revealed through Paul.

(c) *Jesus* said to the disciples: 'Blessed are the eyes that see what you see! For I tell you that many [Israelite] prophets and kings desired to see what you see, but did not see it, and to hear what you hear, but did not hear it' (Lk. 10.23-24). *Paul*, by blinding Bar-Jesus, reinforces the pattern of Jewish prophets who 'do not see'; however, he also subverts the pattern of ignorant Israelite rulers by enabling a *Roman* official to both 'see' and 'hear the word of God' (Acts 13.7-12).

We may explore the elevation of Paul's status in 13.4-12 not only in relation to other characters, but also in the context of its *island setting*. My interest here is not with the geographical island of Cyprus in particular, but with the broad social-symbolic concept of 'island' (*nēsos*) in the Hellenistic-Jewish world.

(1) Mediterranean islands represented two opposite points of reference in dealing with the dangers and misfortunes of first-century life. On the one hand, they afforded welcome *refuge* from the turbulent storms of the sea (e.g. Aristobulus on Crete, *Ant.* 17.335; Paul on Malta, Acts 27.22-28.1); on the other hand, they served as ideal, out-of-the-way places of *exile* for enemies of the state (e.g. John on Patmos, Rev. 1.9).

Since his conversion to 'the Way' of Jesus, Paul has been on the run from hostile Jewish opponents (Acts 9.23-30). He has found some refuge in Antioch but is now on the move again. As he arrives at the island of Cyprus, we wonder: will this be a place of further acceptance or alienation for Paul? As it happens, he meets Jewish resistance once again, but this time he stands his ground and successfully fights back. Moreover, far from being treated as an enemy, Paul is honored by the local imperial governor. This island marks a safe zone for Paul where his fortunes change for the better.

(2) In presenting the debate between Theophrastus and Stoic philosophers over 'the eternity of the cosmos', Philo conveyed a common geological perception of islands in the ancient world. Islands were typically compared with mountains as irregular protrusions from the earth's surface, having emerged above rather than been engulfed or eroded by the 'the great rains pouring down from everlasting each year' (*Eternity of the World* 118; cf. 117-23, 132-42). From his island perch, John the Seer reflected a similar geology in portraying the cataclysmic transition between the old and new world as a *levelling* of islands and mountains: 'And every island fled away, and no mountains were to be found' (Rev. 16.20; cf. 6.14). We are familiar with mountains as isolated, liminal peaks, separated from and rising above mainstream society, closer to the divine, heavenly realm, propitious sites for religious conversion and status transformation—particularly status *elevation*—as in the case of Moses on Mt Sinai, Elijah on Mt Carmel and Jesus on the Mount of Transfiguration. I suggest that the *Isle* of Cyprus functions in a similar way for Paul in Acts—marking his inauguration as a channel of divine power and his elevation as a leader of the Christian mission. From this point we expect Paul to return to the mainland to spearhead a new phase of missionary expansion.

(3) The ancient landlocked Israelites reflected in the Jewish scriptures viewed the islands of the sea as the habitat of the distant Gentile nations. Genesis 10 refers to the 70 (MT) or 72 (LXX) peoples spread throughout the earth after the flood as 'the islands of the Gentiles/nations' (*nēsoi tōn ethnōn*, 10.5, 32 LXX). Deutero-Isaiah appropriates this same worldview in relation to the mission of the Lord's servant, Israel:

> Listen to me, you islands (*nēsoi*), pay attention, you nations (*ethnē*)! The Lord called me before I was born...
> And he said to me, 'You are my servant, Israel, in whom I will be glorified...
> It is too light a thing that you should be my servant to raise up the tribes of Jacob and to restore the survivors of Israel; I will give you as a *light to the nations* (*ethnōn*), that my salvation may reach to *the end of the earth*' (Isa. 49.1-6; cf. 51.5; 60.9; 66.19-20).

In Acts Paul appears destined to fulfill the mission of the Isaianic servant, bearing witness to his own fellow-Israelites and extending the light of salvation to Gentiles at the earth's outer limits (9.15). How fitting, in view of Isa. 49.1, that he begins this pioneering expedition on an *island* in the sea, calling both Jews and Gentiles far away to pay attention to the Lord's message. (In the next episode Paul will actually cite Isa. 49.6 as the blueprint for his mission; Acts 13.47 [see below].)

Preaching in Pisidia: 13.13-52

The expedition party which disembarks on the mainland of Asia Minor (modern day Turkey) at Perga and heads from there to Antioch in Pisidia is not only now led by Paul rather than Barnabas, as noted above, but is also minus the company of John Mark who 'left them and returned to Jerusalem' (13.13). Although the narrative supplies no specific motive for or evaluation of John's departure, the term used for 'leaving' (*apochōreō*) can connote the idea of 'deserting' or 'abandoning' a cause, as in the case of renegade Jews in Alexandria who, according to the tale in 3 Maccabees, 'separated themselves' (*apochōrountas*) from the faithful during the oppressive reign of the Egyptian king, Philopator (Ptolemy IV; 3 Macc. 2.33). This raises the possibility of unresolved conflict between John and Paul which will erupt again somewhere down the road (cf. 15.36-41).

Paul's ministry in Pisidian Antioch centers around a lengthy 'exhortation' he gives to 'Israelites and others who fear God' assembled in the synagogue on the sabbath day (13.14-16). The sermon and surrounding context echo many of the same emphases heard in earlier speeches, but more explicitly than before, the present episode underscores the conviction that Jesus' death and resurrection mark the 'necessary' (13.46) fulfillment of Israel's *entire* scriptural canon—'the law and the prophets' (13.15, 27, 39-40) together with the psalms (13.33, 35). The same fulfillment motif appears in the report of Jesus' final words to his disciples in Luke's Gospel:

> Then he said to them, 'These are my words that I spoke to you while I was still with you—that *everything written about me* in the *law* of Moses, the *prophets*, and the *psalms* must be fulfilled'. Then he opened their minds to understand the scriptures (Lk. 24.44-45; for a similar tripartite division of the biblical canon, see the prologue to Sirach by the author's grandson).

Following Jesus' lead and carrying it further, Paul seeks to 'open the minds' of Diaspora Jews and other God-fearers in Antioch to comprehend that 'everything that was written about him [Jesus]' (13.9) in the law, prophets and psalms has come to pass, preparing the way to 'forgiveness of sins' (13.38; cf. Lk. 24.47). We now turn to explore some of the details of this scripture-centered mission as they unfold in the narrative.

(1) *Synagogue/Sabbath Setting: 13.13-16a*. Following the terse report that Paul and Barnabas had proclaimed the gospel in the Jewish synagogues of Cyprus (13.5), we now encounter a description of a particular synagogue service in which the missionaries participate. It takes place on the sabbath and focuses on exposition of 'the law and the prophets'. After the reading of unspecified texts, the synagogue officials invite the visiting missionaries—whom they address collegially as 'brothers'—to exhort the congregation, presumably in the form of commentary on the day's lections (13.14-15). Paul seizes the opportunity and, with standard Greek oratorical posture (standing) and gesture (hand motion), begins to speak (13.16).

We noted above the parallel between the scripture-based mission of Paul in Antioch and the end of Jesus' ministry in Jerusalem. In this opening synagogue scene we can also detect a patent connection to the *beginning* of Jesus' public career. After overcoming the devil in the wilderness, the Lukan Jesus came to the synagogue on the sabbath day in his home village of Nazareth (Lk. 4.16), just as Paul does in Antioch following his victorious clash with the devil's agent on the island. (Antioch, to be sure, is not Paul's home town of Tarsus, but it is located in the same general area, in a neighboring province of Asia Minor.) Jesus then proceeded to explicate the prophetic scripture reading of the day, just as Paul does, except that he *sat down* rather than stood, in line with local Jewish custom (he had previously stood to *read* the text) (4.16-21). Jesus' message focused on his self-fulfillment of Israel's messianic hopes and on his people's characteristic rejection of prophetic ministry leading to outreach beyond the homeland to receptive Gentiles. After some initial enthusiasm over Jesus' comments, the audience turned against him and drove him away (4.22-30). This scenario provides suggestive points of comparison with Paul's sermon in Antioch and the assembly's reponses, as they develop.

(2) *Scriptural Message: 13.16b-41*. As in Stephen's speech before the Jerusalem council, Paul prefaces his address with a survey of Israel's history (13.16b-22). Only in this case, Paul offers a much abbreviated version, rushing past the patriarchal and Mosaic periods, so central to Stephen's discourse, with barely a mention. Moreover, when Paul mentions the sojourn in Egypt, rather than stressing the hardships which the Israelites suffered prior to the exodus (cf. 7.6, 9-11, 19-24, 34), he only reports that 'the God of this people Israel...*made the people great*' before leading them out (13.17). Clearly, Paul is playing here before a Diaspora audience seeking to thrive as a distinctive people under benevolent Roman rule, as opposed to Stephen who sought to indict corrupt temple hierarchs by associating them with oppressive foreign rulers.

Paul quickly moves to the climax of his historical survey: Israel's early monarchic era surrounding the figures of the prophet Samuel and the first two kings, Saul and David (13.20-22). Samuel and David have both been featured before in Peter's previous speeches in Acts and in the Lukan birth narratives (Luke 1.5-15, 46-55 [allusion to Samuel's birth]; 1.32, 69; 2.11; Acts 2.25-34; 3.24; Stephen also mentions David in 7.45-46), but this is the only occasion in Luke–Acts where King Saul appears. It is intriguing to speculate that the narrator is exploiting some kind of connection between the Saul of Israel's national history, mentioned by Paul in the present Antioch speech, and the Saul of Paul's personal history, featured until the name switch in the previous Cyprus incident.

King Saul, though initially 'given' by God to the people and allowed to reign for 'forty years' (a typical generation; cf. 7.23, 30, 36, 42), was ultimately 'removed' by God in favor of a new monarch-designate, David (13.21-22). The cause of Saul's downfall, according to the biblical source, was a propensity to overstep his authority, to take religious matters into his own hands rather than obey the strict regulations of God's law ('your kingdom will not continue...because you have not kept what the Lord commanded you', 1 Sam. 13.14; cf. 13.1-15; 15.10-33). Thus God turned to one who 'will do (*poiēsei*) all my will' (Acts 13.22). Where Saul had his external human ties to God's people—'son of Kish, a man of the tribe of Benjamin'—his successor will also enjoy a special internal bond with God himself—'I have found David, son of Jesse, to be a man after my heart' (Acts 13.21-22; cf. 1 Sam. 13.14; 16.1-13). The resonance with Saul-Paul's own career may be his divinely wrought transformation from one, like his biblical namesake, who pursued his own misguided agenda to one, like David, who now 'must do' (*dei poiein*, Acts 9.6) the Lord's bidding. Another possible link may be made between King Saul's maniacal hunt for David and his supporters, once David became successful and popular with the people (see 1 Sam. 18–31), and the terrorist crusade by the Saul of Acts against the followers of Jesus, the son of David.

Whatever the implications for Paul's own characterization in Acts, his concentration on David's key role in carrying out God's plan for Israel is primarily a prelude to setting forth *Jesus* as the promised heir of David (13.23) who has not merely fulfilled but surpassed his forefather's destiny. David, to be sure, 'served the purpose of God in his own generation', but after that, he died and decayed; by contrast, God has raised up David's descendant, the Holy One Jesus, 'no more to return to corruption', as even David himself had predicted in Psalm 16 (13.30-37). All of this is familiar from earlier Acts speeches, but Paul adds some new scriptural justification and condemnation for those Israelites who miss the point.

Paul affirms generally that 'the words of *the prophets* that are read every sabbath' (as at the present synagogue service [13.15]) clearly disclose the salvific work of Jesus accomplished through his death and resurrection. Ironically, however, these words were fulfilled by Jewish citizens and leaders in Jerusalem who 'did *not* recognize...or understand' the prophetic message and thus condemned Jesus to death (13.27-28). At first Paul rhetorically distinguishes those ignorant Israelites ('*they*'), on the one side, from his present audience ('*you* sons of Abraham's family...') and himself and other messianic messengers ('to *us* the message of this salvation has been sent'), on the other side, joined together as 'brothers' in God's household (13.26-27; Paul's 'men, brothers' [*andres adelphoi*] address in 13.26 exactly reciprocates the officials' address to the Pauline party in 13.15). At the close of the sermon, however, though still reaching out to them as 'brothers' (13.38), Paul also isolates his hearers and, through a specific prophetic text (Hab. 1.5), alerts them to the possibility of missing the significance of God's 'work' of deliverance through Jesus (Acts 13.40-41). In effect they must choose which side of the prophetic cause they will embrace: that of scornful opponents of Jesus, like those in Jerusalem, or that of believing disciples, like Paul and associates.

While stressing Jesus' fulfillment of the prophets throughout the Antioch speech, at the end Paul sounds a somewhat different note concerning Jesus' relationship to the Mosaic *law*. Here the idea is not so much fulfillment of the law as it is *freedom from the law*, or more properly, 'free[dom] from all those sins from which you could not be freed by the law of Moses' (13.39). We have heard repeatedly in Acts the announcement of 'forgiveness of sins' through Jesus' death and resurrection, but not until now has this been juxtaposed against the tyranny of the law. When the law has been considered, it has either been treated positively or partially modified. Stephen may have blasted the temple institution, but he only extolled the Mosaic law as 'living oracles...ordained by angels' (7.38, 53). Peter came to regard adherence to the law as unnecessary for Gentiles' inclusion among the people of God, but he did not gainsay its efficacy for native Israelites. Paul's emphasis on salvation apart from the law for '*everyone* who believes' in Jesus (13.39) thus introduces a potential source of conflict not only in Jewish synagogues on the mission field but also in established Christian communities. Paul's letters contain ample evidence for such tension; if and how this tension will be played out in Acts remains to be seen.

(3) *Mixed Response: 13.42-52*. Paul's speech sparks varied reactions, alternating between positive and negative poles, from a variety of groups: Jewish crowds (including many proselytes), Jewish leaders, Gentiles, and high society folk (women and men).

First, the *crowd* exhibits enthusiastic interest in an encore performance on the following sabbath:

> The people urged them to speak about these things again the next
> sabbath (13.42).
>> Many Jews and devout converts to Judaism followed Paul and
>> Barnabas (13.43).
> The next sabbath almost the whole city gathered to hear the word
> of the Lord (13.44).

Paul's popularity actually spreads throughout the week from his original
audience to 'almost the whole city'. Although some of the masses doubtless respond out of mere curiosity, we learn in the central statement
above that *'many Jews and devout converts (prosēlytōn)'* exhibit a
deeper commitment, 'following' (*akoloutheō*) Paul and Barnabas in the
fashion of disciples (cf. Lk. 5.11, 27-28; 9.11, 23, 57-61; 18.22, 28, 43).

In contrast to and as a consequence of the general excitement of the
multitude, *'the Jews'*—apparently denoting the *synagogue officials* in
distinction from 'the crowds'—are 'filled with jealousy' (13.45). Their
honor is being diminished by Paul's mass appeal. We have encountered
this jealous attitude before on the part of the temple aristocracy toward
Peter and the apostles (5.17). The retaliatory action of denigrating Paul's
message to the point of 'blaspheming', as the narrator dubs it, is new for
Acts, but recalls the slanderous attacks against Jesus by temple police
and one of the criminals crucified with him (*blasphēmeō*, Lk. 22.65;
23.39).

Paul and Barnabas defend their honor not by further explicating their
message or answering any specific charges, but by switching to a judicial role, 'boldly' pronouncing the divine verdict on the present contest.
'The Jews' have had their 'necessary' (*dei*) opportunity to receive God's
message of salvation spoken through his authorized witnesses. Since
they have spurned this offer, however, 'the Lord has commanded' Paul
and Barnabas to 'turn to the *Gentiles*', extending the light of the gospel
'to the ends of the earth' in accordance with the divine plan disclosed in
Isa. 49.6 (and confirmed by Jesus in Acts 1.8) (13.46-47). Of course,
Gentiles in both Syrian and Pisidian Antioch have already heard Paul's
teaching (assuming that the 'others who fear God' in 13.16, 26 refer to
non-Israelites), but they have done so alongside Jews, whether in new
congregations or established synagogues. Now Paul seems to signal the
beginning of a separate Gentile mission, a strategy to disseminate the
gospel not only in local Jewish assemblies but 'throughout the region'
where Gentiles reside (13.48-49).

In the face of this shameful snubbing by upstart Christian missionaries, the synagogue rulers ('the Jews') enlist the support of *prominent
citizens* in driving Paul and Barnabas out of their area (13.50). These
'high standing' allies include 'devout' (*sebomenas*, cf. 13.43) noble-
women and 'leading men of the city' (listing the women first, before the
'first-ranking men' [*prōtous*], accentuates their prominence). Previously,
the Christian movement has fared well among such figures, like the

Ethiopian eunuch, Tabitha, Cornelius and Sergius Publius. But Paul cannot take this response for granted; he will have to fight to gain the respect of urban elites.

In the present situation, however, Paul and Barnabas choose flight over fight, 'shak[ing] the dust off their feet' and moving on to Iconium (13.51). This parting gesture signals that the missionaries are not retreating in fear but rather turning away 'in protest' and advancing in freedom to new opportunities. They refuse to be bogged down in hostile territory. A similar radical itinerancy, including dramatic dust-shaking exits, typified the missions of Jesus' disciples in Luke's Gospel (the Twelve: 9.5; the Seventy: 10.11).

Miracle-Working in Lycaonia: 14.1-20

Paul and Barnabas head southeast from Antioch to three neighboring cities—Iconium, Lystra and Derbe—in Lycaonia (14.1, 6, 11), a southern district in the Roman province of Galatia. At the first stop (Iconium), we learn that 'the same thing occurred' here as just before in Antioch. The missionaries start preaching in the local synagogue and again meet with divided reactions from *both* Jews and Gentiles, together 'with their rulers'. 'A great number' of this mixed audience become believers, while others conspire to persecute Paul and Barnabas, forcing them to flee (14.1-6). Notable in this redundant pattern is a tempering of the brusque break with the Jews and turn to the Gentiles announced in the preceding episode. The Jewish synagogue still represents a fruitful mission field (as well as a hotbed of opposition), and not all Gentiles welcome the Christian message as good news (although many do). The Acts narrative continues to resist sweeping stereotypes.

Although the experience in Iconium mirrors that in Antioch to a great extent, we should not think that all is business as usual in Lycaonia. Some interesting new developments emerge: (1) Rather than focusing on Paul's ministry of the word detailed in a lengthy speech (13.16-41), the present section accentuates the performance of corroborative 'signs and wonders', first in a general summary of activity in Iconium (14.3) and then by reporting a particular miraculous deed and its effects in Lystra (14.8-18). (2) The goal of persecution now intensifies beyond expulsion to extermination in the form of stoning, attempted in Iconium (14.5) and executed in Lystra (14.19). (3) The mission in Lystra (after Iconium) marks the first occasion in Acts of outreach to an exclusively pagan (non-Jewish) audience with no apparent ties to the synagogue, causing us to wonder if this is the watershed shift from Jews to Gentiles anticipated in 13.46. In place of Jewish religious leaders, Paul and Barnabas now deal with 'the priest of Zeus' (14.13). Hostile Jews eventually enter the picture, but they are not from Lystra; they represent the same opponents encountered before, chasing Paul down from Antioch and Iconium (14.19).

Beyond an obvious mapping of Paul's associations with Jews and Gentiles, in more subtle ways the present narrative also positions Paul in relation to key Christian ministers in Acts: Peter, Barnabas, and Stephen.

(1) The fact that Paul's first restorative sign (distinguished from his punitive miracle against Bar-Jesus) involves a *lame man* naturally recalls the earlier mission of the apostle *Peter* in ch. 3. Both disabled men are described in identical terms as 'a cripple from birth' (*chōlos ek koilias mētros autou*, 3.2; 14.8). Both Paul and Peter 'look intently' (*atenizō*) at the lame men before raising them up (3.5; 14.9); both cripples demonstrate their healing by 'leaping/springing and walking' (*exallomenos...kai periepatei*, 3.8; *hēlato kai periepatei*, 14.10). Both miracles take place in the vicinity of temple 'gates' (3.2; 14.13—Gill [p. 85] suggests that these are gates to the sacred precincts of Zeus rather than the city gates of Lystra); both are accomplished through 'faith' (3.16; 14.9); and both elicit extreme adulation of human ministers on the part of the crowds which Peter and Paul decisively repudiate, insisting that they are but humble instruments of divine power (3.11-16; 14.11-18).

The connection with Peter is confirmed by the sudden labelling of Paul (along with Barnabas) as an 'apostle' (twice: 14.4, 14). Although Paul does not fit the strict apostolic qualifications which Peter set forth in 1.21-22, he has become a bona fide witness to the living Christ and begun to perform signs and wonders, just like Peter and fellow Jerusalem apostles (cf. 2.43; 4.33; 5.12). In its own more impressionistic way, the Acts narrative is supporting the blunt Pauline claim in 2 Cor. 12.11-12: 'I am not at all inferior to these super-apostles... The signs of a true apostle were performed among you... signs and wonders and mighty works.'

While appreciating the patent parallel which Acts establishes between Peter and Paul as dynamic healers of the lame, we must not ignore important *differences* in method, context, and response. For example, whereas Peter made clear that the crippled man was restored 'by faith *in his [Jesus'] name*... and the faith that is *through Jesus*' (3.16), in the Lystra incident the object of the lame man's faith is not specified and, in fact, no reference is made to Jesus at all. We learn nothing of the content of Paul's opening message in Lystra (14.9), and when he addresses the crowd after the miracle, he focuses exclusively on 'the living God', the sole Creator of the universe to whom his creatures owe all praise and allegiance (14.15-17). Such a word is appropriate in the polytheistic environment of Lystra where Paul and Barnabas are being mistaken for Hermes and Zeus—as opposed to the sacred center of Jewish monotheism in Jerusalem where Peter and John ministered. Christology builds on theology in Acts; Christianity flows out of Judaism. Apart from bedrock belief in the one true God, the gospel of Jesus Christ has no meaning.

Although the awe-struck crowds in Jerusalem and Lystra react to the apostolic miracle-workers in similar fashion, the local religious authorities manifest divergent responses. The Jewish chief priests in Jerusalem, bitter over the popularity of Peter and John, sought to impede their ministry through threats and imprisonment (chs. 4–5). In stark contrast, however, the high priest of Zeus in Lystra (or perhaps a coterie of 'priests', as the Western text has it; cf. Hemer, pp. 195-96) *joins the crowd* in heaping praise on Paul and Barnabas and offering them sacrifices (14.13, 18). Although he is misguided in these efforts, he at least honors the apostles and welcomes their ministry. The Jewish temple leaders thus receive another satirical slap: even an ignorant pagan priest sees more than they do.

(2) After fading into the background and playing second fiddle to Paul in Cyprus and Antioch, *Barnabas* emerges briefly again in the spotlight. In the report of the missionaries' deification by the Lycaonians, Barnabas is mentioned first and identified with Zeus, the chief god of the Greek pantheon, while Paul is identified with Zeus' messenger, Hermes ('because he was the chief speaker', 14.12). And when introducing the apostles' reaction to this idolization, the narrator continues to give Barnabas top billing ('When the apostles Barnabas and Paul heard of it, they tore their clothes...', 14.14). Nevertheless, in surrounding material, only Paul is credited with raising the lame man, and only Paul is targeted for stoning when the crowd turns angry. His dominance of the first missionary expedition continues, but despite Paul's ascendancy, Barnabas also remains an important figure to be reckoned with, a worthy partner of Paul's, capable of holding his own should conflict arise (cf. 15.36-41; Gal. 2.13).

(3) Paul's fate at the end of the Lystra episode signals another dramatic, ironic reversal of his former role as persecutor of *Stephen* and colleagues. Before his encounter with Christ, Paul (Saul) had superintended the Jerusalem mob which 'dragged him [Stephen] out of the city and began to stone him' and then terrorized Christian households by 'dragging off (*syrōn*) both men and women' to prison (7.58–8.3). Now, in Lystra, it is Paul himself who is 'stoned' and 'dragged (*esyron*)' outside the city by crowds whom visiting Jews had incited against him (perhaps the crowds had been offended by Paul's rejection of their accolades) (14.19). Although closely matching Stephen's ordeal, Paul's ultimate destiny is different: he 'gets up' (*anastas*—resurrection? revival?), returns to the city, and then moves on to Derbe to continue his mission (14.20).

Finally, apart from depicting Paul's ministry in Lycaonia in relation to various human characters in Acts, the current narrative also stresses the connection with the gracious work of *the Lord*, particularly as dynamic *witness*. Throughout Acts, the apostles have been cast as persuasive verbal witnesses (*martyres*) to God's mighty act of raising Jesus from the dead (1.8, 22; 2.32; 3.15; 4.33; 5.32; 10.39, 41; 13.31). Now Jesus himself, the exalted Lord (cf. 2.36), 'testifie[s] (*martyreō*) to the word of his grace by granting signs and wonders to be done through them [apostles Paul and Barnabas]' (14.3). This witness is still mediated, of course, through human channels but in a personal way which stresses the Lord's continuing immediate presence with his messengers. Addressing the Lystran crowd which had just seen (and misinterpreted) a miraculous sign demonstrated by the Lord through Paul, the apostles speak of another avenue of personal divine witness accessible to all humankind. By creating heaven and earth and providing rain and harvest to sustain human life, God 'has not left himself without witness (*amartyron*)' (14.15-17). Through wondrous operations performed throughout the natural world and on the physical body (as in the case of the crippled man), 'the living God' manifests his sovereignty over all creatures and 'worthless things' (14.15)—worthless, that is, in comparison with the Creator's supreme honor.

Nurturing the Churches: 14.21-28

Following pioneering missions to Samaria and Syrian Antioch by Philip the evangelist and others scattered from Jerusalem after Stephen's death, the church in Jerusalem dispatched *additional* emissaries (Peter/John and Barnabas) to inspect and strengthen the new congregations (8.4-17; 11.19-26). This pattern continues with the communities established on Paul's first expedition, except for the fact that now the founding missionaries, Paul and Barnabas, make *their own* follow-up visits to Lystra, Iconium, and Antioch (14.21-22). The expedition thus appears to be independent of the Jerusalem church at this stage.

The type of nurture which Paul and Barnabas provide the fledgling disciples centers around two elements: (1) an announcement concerning participation in the kingdom of God and (2) an appointment of local leaders in each church.

(1) *Announcement*. 'It is through many persecutions that we must (*dei*) enter the kingdom of God' (14.22). We know that the plan of God disclosed in the Jewish scriptures and Lukan narrative mandated that Jesus Messiah '*had* (*dei*) to suffer' before rising from the dead and offering salvation 'in his name to all nations' (Lk. 24.46-47) and that Paul '*must* (*dei*) suffer' much to carry the Lord's name before Gentiles and Israelites (Acts 9.15-16). Now for the first time in Acts the believers at large, including Gentiles, are required to endure hardship in solidarity with Christ and his messengers as a means of securing their place in the kingdom of God. Such a vocation echoes the Lukan Jesus' earlier insistence that true disciples must 'deny themselves, take up their cross daily and follow me' (Lk. 9.23-27) and reinforces his claim that those who forsake earthly riches and family ties 'for the sake of the kingdom of God' will enjoy 'very much more in this age, and in the age to come eternal

life' (18.24-30). The Pauline mission may reach out to elite imperial authorities, like Sergius Paulus, but it does not cut any easy deals with them. It is still exceedingly 'hard...for those who have wealth to enter the kingdom of God' (Lk. 18.24-25). The lowly path of suffering remains the best way.

(2) *Appointment*. 'And after they had appointed elders for them in each church, with prayer and fasting they entrusted them to the Lord' (14.23). The ordaining of ministers with *prayer and fasting* recalls Paul and Barnabas' own commissioning by the church in Antioch (13.1-3). In this case, however, the ministers are appointed to stay and oversee local community affairs rather than sent out to spread the gospel further. Also it is interesting that the resident leaders are called *elders* (*presbyteroi*) rather than 'prophets' or 'teachers', as in Antioch (13.1). In Luke–Acts, this term has been applied exclusively to *Jewish* authorities, mostly with reference to rulers of the Jerusalem Council (along with chief priests and scribes, Lk. 9.22; 20.1; 22.52; Acts 4.5, 8, 23; 6.12), once with reference to leaders of the Jerusalem church (11.30). Thus, even in the Diaspora among developing, mixed communities of Jews and Gentiles, the Pauline mission maintains certain structural associations, if not official ties, with the Jewish capital in Jerusalem.

Evaluation in Jerusalem: 15.1-16.5

After Paul and Barnabas return to their home base of Antioch (14.24-28), the Judean/Jerusalem church enters the picture again to evaluate the Mediterranean expedition, particularly regarding the status of Gentile believers in the new congregations. First, a group of Judean brothers come to Antioch and insist that, in addition to exercising faith, all Gentiles must be circumcised in order to be 'saved'. This judgment triggers 'no small dissension and debate' with Paul and Barnabas (15.1-2). The seriousness of the issue prompts the Antioch church to send Paul and Barnabas to Jerusalem for further discussion with the apostles and elders (15.2-4). The circumcision party—now identified as a group of Christian Pharisees—reiterates its position (15.5). Then Peter and James speak in support of Paul and Barnabas (15.6-18). A compromise decision is proposed by James and approved by the apostles and elders, 'with the consent of the whole church': the Gentiles do not have to be circumcised nor must they observe the entire law of Moses, but they should abstain from a few 'essential' moral and religious taboos (15.19-29). This decision is codified in a letter and disseminated back to Antioch and throughout the region evangelized by Paul and Barnabas (15.30–16.4). The new churches all joyfully accept the decision and, as a result, they are 'strengthened in the faith and increased in numbers daily' (16.5).

On the whole these proceedings unfold in a smooth and orderly fashion through four acts or stages: from *dissension* to *discussion* to *decision* to *dissemination*. Within each act, we may identify a simple *A-B-A* envelope structure, in which characters at the beginning and end (*A/A'*) make closely related assertions (first three acts) or engage in similar actions (fourth act) surrounding the middle component (*B*) which consistently features some narrated information about the activity of Paul and Barnabas. Such a tidy circular pattern befits the prevailing emphasis on Christian unity throughout this section.

Act I: DISSENSION (Antioch and Jerusalem): 15.1-5

A. *Some (tines) individuals from Judea*: 'Unless you [Gentiles] are circumcised according to the custom of Moses, you cannot be saved' (15.1).

> B. *Paul and Barnabas* debate with the circumcision party over the Gentile question and come to Jerusalem for further discussion, where they are 'welcomed by the church and the apostles and the elders' (15.2-4).

A'. *Some (tines) Pharisaic believers in Jerusalem*: 'It is necessary for them [Gentiles] to be circumcised and ordered to keep the law of Moses' (15.5).

Act II: DISCUSSION (Jerusalem): 15.6-18

A. *Peter*: 'God made a choice among you that I should be the one through whom the Gentiles would hear the message of the good news and become believers' (15.7).

> B. *Barnabas and Paul* recount 'all the signs and wonders that God had done through them among the Gentiles' (15.12).

A'. *James*: 'Simeon has related how God first looked favorably on the Gentiles, to take from among them a people for his name. This agrees with the words of the prophets' (15.15).

Act III: DECISION (Jerusalem): 15.19-29

A. *James*: 'I have reached the decision that we should not trouble those Gentiles who are turning to God, but we should write to them to abstain only from things polluted by idols and from fornication and from whatever has been strangled and from blood' (15.19-20).

> B. *Barnabas and Paul* are endorsed by the Jerusalem assembly as 'beloved' brothers, 'who have risked their lives for the sake of our Lord Jesus Christ' (15.25-26).

A'. *The apostles, elders, and entire church*: 'It has seemed good to the Holy Spirit and to us to impose on you no further burden than these essentials: that you abstain from what has been sacrificed to idols and from blood and from what is strangled and from fornication' (15.28-29).

Act IV: DISSEMINATION (Antioch and Southern Asia Minor): 15.30-16.5

A. *Paul, Barnabas, Judas, and Silas* 'were sent off and went down to Antioch. When they gathered the congregation together, they delivered the letter. When its members read it, they rejoiced at the exhortation' (15.30-31).

B. *Paul and Barnabas* 'part company' with one another after a bitter dispute over the next missionary expedition (15.36-41).

A'. *Paul, Silas, and Timothy* 'went from town to town [and] they delivered to them for observance the decisions that had been reached by the apostles and elders who were in Jerusalem. So the churches were strengthened in the faith and increased in numbers daily' (16.4-5).

Taking a closer look at each of the four acts, we pay particular attention to the contributions and development of key characters.

(1) *Dissension (Christian Pharisees): 15.1-5.* In Acts 11, we encountered the assembly of 'circumcised believers' in the Jerusalem church objecting to Peter's table-fellowship with 'uncircumcised men' in Cornelius' house. They were eventually won over by Peter's testimony and came to rejoice in God's gracious dealings with the Gentiles (11.1-18). Now a particular faction within the believing Jerusalem community again raises the issue of circumcision and observing the law of Moses (which would include dietary regulations), this time concerning the more extensive Gentile mission of Paul and Barnabas. This group does not impugn the faith of these Gentile converts but insists that they must also accept traditional socio-ethnic badges of Jewish identity to maintain 'saved' status among the people of God. According to this view, the boundaries of the people of God (or kingdom of God) are co-extensive with the nation (*ethnos*) of Israel.

The association of the church's 'Judaizing' party with a group of *Pharisees* (15.5) is both predictable and surprising within the Lukan narrative. As we have already noted, the Pharisees in Luke repeatedly complain about Jesus' careless disregard for conventional social and religious boundaries, particularly his penchant for eating with unclean 'sinners'. It comes as no surprise, then, that Pharisees in Acts now object to Paul's open acceptance of uncircumcised, un-kosher Gentiles. What is surprising, however, is that these Pharisees are regarded as 'believing' (*pepisteukotes*) members of the Jesus community in Jerusalem. While maintaining their purity standards, they nonetheless embrace Jesus as Messiah. The tolerance advocated by the Pharisaic member of the Jerusalem council, Gamaliel, in Acts 5, has mushroomed into a full-blown Christian faith on the part of some of his co-religionists.

The opposing position of Paul and Barnabas on the Gentile question is not spelled out in this unit, but we may infer from prior material its basic conviction that the saving work of God transcends nationalistic barriers. The fact that God has sent his messengers 'to be a light for the Gentiles/nations' and 'opened a door of faith for the Gentiles/nations' (13.47; 14.27) is all that is 'necessary' for their salvation. This view will be articulated more fully by Peter and James in the following segment.

(2) *Discussion (Peter and James): 15.6-18.* Our last encounter with Peter and James suggested a transition in leadership within the Jerusalem community from the former to the latter. After instructing the assembly in Mary's house to report recent events 'to James and the brothers', Peter abruptly 'left and went to another place' (12.17). At that point in our journey, we wondered whether we would hear from Peter again. As it happens, after a long hiatus Peter does emerge again, speaking at the Jerusalem conference on behalf of Paul's law-free mission to the Gentiles. Still, the final word belongs to James, who now clearly assumes the role of the principal overseer of the Jerusalem church.

Peter's argument rests on another review of his divinely-orchestrated encounter with Gentiles in Caesarea, and the conclusions he now draws from this experience are similar to those advanced in ch. 11 before the assembly of circumcised believers in Jerusalem. Since God gave the Holy Spirit to these uncircumcised Gentiles—'just as he did to us [Jews]'— then clearly God 'has made no distinction between them [Gentiles] and us [Jews]' within the community of God's people (15.8-9; cf. 11.12, 15, 17). To resist this inclusive principle by imposing legal restrictions on the Gentiles, as the Pharisees wish, is tantamount to 'hindering' God himself (11.17) or 'putting God to the test' (*peirazete*, 15.10)—precisely what Ananias and Sapphira did to their peril (*peirasai*, 5.9; Johnson, *Acts*, p. 272) and similar to what Gamaliel warned the council against ('you may even be found fighting against God!', 5.39).

Apart from these parallels between Peter's speeches in Acts 11 and 15, certain distinctive emphases emerge in the present context. For one, Peter now lays greater stress on the Gentiles' 'faithful' response to God's gracious bestowal of salvation ('the Gentiles... become believers [*pisteusai*]'; 'cleansing their hearts by faith [*pistei*]', 15.7, 9). For another, Peter buttresses his claim that Gentiles should not be required to keep the law by portraying the law as an oppressive 'yoke that neither our ancestors nor we have been able to bear' (15.10). This is a puzzling development. The yoke as an image of the law was common in Jewish tradition, but typically it was viewed in positive terms as a joyous blessing rather than an onerous burden (cf. *m. Abot* 3.5; *m. Ber.* 2.2; Sir. 51.26). Peter himself earlier voiced a robust commitment to the law ('I have never eaten anything that is profane or unclean', 10.14), and while he eventually came, under the Lord's guidance, to view certain purity laws as irrelevant, he never regarded them as *unbearable* (cf. Barrett, *Freedom*, pp. 94-96). Has he suddenly changed his mind in 15.10? Perhaps he is recalling Jeremiah's indictment of Israel's law/yoke-breaking ('Surely they know the way of the Lord, the law of their God. But they all alike had *broken the yoke*, they had burst the bonds', Jer. 5.5) or Jesus' rebuke of the hypocritical and unreasonable application of the law by Pharisees and lawyers for their own benefit ('You load people with burdens *hard to bear*, and you yourselves do not lift a finger to ease them. Woe to you!', Lk. 11.46-47; cf. Johnson, *Acts*, p. 263). In light of these ideas, Peter may be arguing something like: We Jews can and should keep the law as a covenantal privilege and duty, but given our history of repeated violation and exploitation of the law, what right do we have to impose it on non-Jews?

The speech of James, which follows a brief report of God's legitimation of the Gentile mission through 'signs and wonders' (cf. Paul's healing of the lame man in Lystra) (15.12), affirms Peter's testimony and adds further support from the prophetic scriptures (15.14-17; Amos 9.11-12 LXX). In each case, James emphasizes God's purpose to incorporate Gentiles into the family of people bearing God's 'name' (*onoma*, 15.14, 17). The immediate juxtaposition of 'Gentiles/nations' and 'people' in 15.14 as *intersecting* entities ('out of the Gentiles/nations a people', *ex ethnōn laon*) is striking, given the common biblical pattern of *separating* God's chosen people (*laos*) from the nations (*ethnē*) (e.g.: 'the Lord your God chose you to be a special people [*laon*] for himself out of all the nations [*ethnōn*] on the face of the earth', Deut. 14.2 LXX; cf. Bruce, p. 293).

Apart from the content of James' speech, the form of his rhetoric demonstrates both authority and diplomacy. In addition to addressing the assembly with the familiar, 'Men, brothers', as Peter did (15.7), James commands extra attention with the mandate, 'listen to me' (15.13). He then displays an interesting linguistic technique, referring to Peter by the *Aramaic* form of his name ('Simeon', 15.14) and citing the Amos text in its *Greek* version. (The Hebrew text makes a rather different point about the Gentiles' destiny.) If we assume some continuing distinction between Hebraist (Aramaic-speaking) and Hellenist (Greek-speaking) branches of the Jerusalem church (cf. 6.1), then James' bilingual references may reflect an inclusive strategy. His authority and diplomacy become more evident in the next unit.

(3) *Decision (James): 15.19-29*. James declares his authority within the present council in emphatic fashion: 'I (*egō*) have reached the decision' or 'make the judgment' (*krinō*) concerning what we should and should not do with respect to the Gentile converts. Other 'apostles and elders' together with 'the whole church' also contribute to the decision, suggesting a more collegial conference, but basically they accept the content of James' proposal by acclamation ('we have decided *unanimously*', 15.25; note the close parallel between 15.19-20 and 15.28-29). The only new business generated after James' speech is the selection of delegates (Judas Barsabbas and Silas) to bear the missive containing the church's decision (15.22, 25-27).

James first determines that 'we should not trouble (*parenochlein*) those Gentiles who are turning to God' (15.19). Interestingly, the same verb was used in the Maccabean period in a letter from the Seleucid king, Demetrius, promising the Jews that 'no one shall have authority to exact anything from them or annoy (*parenochlein*) any of them' by restricting their observance of festivals and holy days (1 Macc. 10.34-35; Johnson, *Acts*, p. 266). Just as the Jews did not want to be harassed into giving up their laws by pagan authorities, so, James contends, Gentiles should not be pressurized into keeping Jewish laws.

Still, the diplomatic James encourages the Gentile disciples to make a few basic concessions to their Jewish neighbors—not with respect to circumcision and national identity—but pertaining to certain matters of moral and religious conduct. The goal of these requirements seems to be the maintenance of fellowship among Jewish and Gentile believers in the mixed congregations of the Diaspora. One version of the 'decree' proscribes four items: anything contaminated by idols (such as sacrificial food), illicit sexual relations, anything that has been strangled, and blood. The last two probably should be grouped together as a prohibition against eating meat from which the blood has not been fully drained. In biblical thought, such a rule had long applied to all humanity in the Noachan covenant (Gen. 9.4) and to resident aliens as well as native Israelites in the Levitical holiness code (Lev. 17.10-16; Deut. 12.23), based on the fundamental premise that 'the life of the flesh is in the blood'.

Another version of the Gentile regulations in Acts 15 eliminates the 'strangling' veto and dietary emphasis, reducing the list of vices to idolatry, fornication and murder (taking 'blood' in the sense of 'bloodshed'). Prohibitions against this evil triad have deep roots in the Decalogue (Exod. 20.1-6, 13-14, 17) and function during the Bar Kokhba period (132–135 CE) as a litmus test of Jewish faithfulness: while other compromises may be permissible, the righteous man must choose martyrdom rather than commit any of these three cardinal offences (cf. *b. Sanh.* 74a; Cohen, pp. 76-77).

(4) *Dissemination (Paul, Barnabas and Timothy): 15.30-16.5.* The recurring circular (*A-B-A*) structure delineated above creates an overall impression of rallying around Paul and Barnabas in supportive fellowship. The unfolding linear plot of the first three acts confirms this impression. The Jerusalem church—leaders and congregation—welcome, hear, and honor the two missionaries and ultimately accept their new Gentile converts with only minor modifications. Even the troublesome Pharisees apparently capitulate and endorse the 'unanimous' decision. This story of harmony and goodwill now culminates in the fourth act, as the mixed congregations in Antioch and Asia Minor embrace the messengers and endorse the message from the Jerusalem conference.

However, a startling breach suddenly appears within this spiralling portrait of unity—not between the Jerusalem church and any of the communities affiliated with Paul and Barnabas—but between Paul and Barnabas themselves! Enveloped by affirming partners in mission, they incredibly turn against *one another* and 'part company' over whether to take John Mark with them on another return visit to the Asian churches. Barnabas wants to take Mark along; Paul wants nothing more to do with the erstwhile deserter. Barnabas takes Mark on a separate mission back to Cyprus; Paul takes on Silas as his new partner (15.36-41). Ironically, closely related verbs are used to describe Mark's departure in 13.13 (*apochōreō*) and the separation of Paul and Barnabas in 15.39 (*apochōrizomai*, Johnson, *Acts*, p. 282).

Why does this split occur? On a redaction-historical level, we might surmise that the squabble over Mark masks a deeper, more substantial rift between Paul and Barnabas than the author of Acts wanted to expose. Paul's Galatian letter suggests a falling out with Barnabas over the critical issue of *table-fellowship*. Barnabas (as well as Peter), Paul claims, refused to eat with Gentile believers at Antioch when members of Jerusalem's circumcision party came to visit (Gal. 2.11-14). Such a scenario is obviously antithetical to the inclusive purpose of the Jerusalem council in Acts 15.

On a narrative level, the conflict between Paul and Barnabas is best interpreted in light of the cumulative characterization of these two figures and their relationship within the Acts story. Recently we have noted the shift in mission leadership from Barnabas to Paul, with no apparent objection from Barnabas. However, a hint of Barnabas' continuing importance re-surfaced in the Lystra incident where he was associated with Zeus (14.12) and named before Paul ('the apostles Barnabas and Paul', 14.14) and emerges once again in the order of presentation in the second and third acts of the current drama in Jerusalem ('the whole assembly...listened to Barnabas and Paul', 15.12; 'our beloved Barnabas and Paul', 15.25). Barnabas has not completely given way to living in Paul's shadow, particularly in Jerusalem where his influence had been established. We may recall that Barnabas was the one who first persuaded the skeptical Jerusalem apostles to accept Paul (Saul), the former persecutor, as a fellow disciple (9.26-27). We may also recall that this action was paradigmatic of Barnabas' dominant reputation as an *encourager* of young, needy believers (cf. 4.36; 11.22-25). This ministry of encouragement is precisely what Barnabas demonstrates again by affording John Mark a second chance on the mission field. Barnabas plays true to form by standing up to Paul on Mark's behalf. The one who steps out of line, so to speak, is *Paul*, who is not willing to give Mark the same benefit of the doubt as a reformed deserter that he himself received earlier (from Barnabas) as a reformed persecutor. While he may continue to outshine Barnabas as a dynamic missionary to the Gentiles, Paul still has a thing or two to learn from the venerable son of encouragement.

Although alienating Barnabas and John Mark, Paul goes out of his way in the next and last scene of the fourth act to *conciliate* scrupulous Diaspora Jews and restore the pattern of unity (see Brawley, *Luke-Acts*, pp. 151-52). While delivering the decision of the Jerusalem council to the churches of Lycaonia, he picks up a new travelling companion in Lystra named Timothy—the son of a believing Jewish mother and a Greek father—and 'ha[s] him *circumcised* because of the Jews who were in those places, for they all knew that his father was a Greek' (16.1-3). This action, though conciliatory, is almost as surprising as the conflict with Barnabas. From the beginning of ch. 15, the whole thrust of the narrative has been directed toward freeing the Gentile disciples from the demands of the circumcision party. Now Paul appears to cave in to those demands in his treatment of Timothy. But as the product of both Jewish and Greek parents, Timothy is a special case requiring special handling. Having a Jewish mother legally makes Timothy a *Jew*, even though his father is Greek. Being uncircumcised, then, brands him as a renegade or apostate in the eyes of the Jewish community rather than merely a pagan outsider, like his father (Hengel, p. 64). By having the Jewish Timothy circumcised, Paul thus demonstrates his continuing solidarity with his own people and clarifies the limits of the recent ecclesiastical ruling. The representatives at the Jerusalem conference— including Paul—agreed only to release *Gentile* believers from the obligation of circumcision; the possibility of nullifying this covenantal duty for Jewish disciples was never considered.

Aegean Expedition: 16.6-21.36

Paul's second expedition takes him further west to several major urban centers around the Aegean Sea. From Troas in northwest Asia, where he receives a special commission, Paul and his companions head counterclockwise around the coast through Macedonia and Greece, stopping at Philippi, Beroea, Athens, and Corinth, and then return across the sea to the metropolis of Ephesus in west-central Asia. Apart from lasting longer and being further removed from Jerusalem and Antioch than the first journey, this second trek poses both more widespread and more particular opposition to Paul's mission. Earlier, Paul had been harassed primarily by jealous Jewish religious leaders who attempted to undercut his popular appeal but never (as far as we were told) pressed any specific legal charges against him. Now, however, attacks come from a variety of quarters, both Jewish and Gentile, secular and religious, in the form of clear and pointed calumnies.

Drawing on Robert Alter's (pp. 47-62) analysis of the use of 'type-scenes' in biblical narratives, Robert Tannehill (*Narrative*, II, pp. 201-203) has detected a recurring 'public accusation type-scene' in Acts 16–19 following a pat sequence of events:

(1)   hostile seizure of missionaries and/or associates and 'dragging' them before a public tribunal
(2)   explicit declaration of charges

(3)   violent reaction of protest and punishment from crowds and authorities

The direct accusations uttered by various prosecutors at the heart of each scene merit full citation, anticipating careful examination in due course.

SCENE ONE: Philippi
Greco-Roman Fortune Peddlers:
These men are disturbing our city; they are Jews and are advocating customs that are not lawful for us as Romans to adopt or observe (16.20-21).

SCENE TWO: Thessalonica
'The Jews':
These people who have been turning the world upside down have come here also...They are all acting contrary to the decrees of the emperor, saying that there is another king named Jesus (17.6-7).

SCENE THREE: Corinth
'The Jews':
This man is persuading people to worship God in ways that are contrary to the law (18.13).

SCENE FOUR: Ephesus
Greco-Roman Silver Shrine-Traders:
Paul has persuaded and drawn away a considerable number of people by saying that gods made with hands are not gods. And there is danger not only that this trade of ours may come into disrepute but also that the temple of the great goddess Artemis will be scorned... (19.25-27).

We may expand this pattern to the scene in Acts 21 where a final, climactic charge is issued against Paul.

SCENE FIVE: Jerusalem
Asian Jews:
This is the man who is teaching everyone everywhere against our people, our law, and this place; more than that, he has actually brought Greeks into the temple and has defiled this holy place (21.28).

Given the obvious polemical, forensic setting of these scenes, we may profitably supplement Tannehill's narrative-critical perspective with applications of the social-scientific model sketched by Malina and Neyrey pertaining to sociocultural practices of deviant labelling ('Conflict'). In Acts 16–21, various legislative authorities and interest groups team up as 'agents of censure' to brand Paul officially as a law-breaker, disturber of the peace, even traitor. Particular interest within this scenario focuses on *precisely how* the process of denunciation works. How do the agents of censure define deviant behavior? How do they go about making the deviant tag stick? How do they attempt to 'broaden the respectability' of their accusation and thus garner public support? What established 'rituals of status degradation' do they employ to enforce their scheme? Of course, given the strong apologetic cast of the narrative at this point, ever concerned with defending the reputation of Paul and his missionary cohorts, we must also pay special attention to how the process of deviant labelling is 'interrupted' or 'neutralized'. How does Paul answer or otherwise circumvent the accusations arrayed against him? On the whole, then, the present stories reflect a persisting struggle for 'moral clarity of meaning' regarding the claims of the Pauline gospel vis-à-vis first-century Jewish and Greco-Roman society.

Finally, a cursory survey of Paul's repeated escapes from angry mobs and magistrates in Acts 16–21 discloses a curious pattern in which other figures are periodically put forward to 'take the rap' for Paul. Three cases stand out in particular:

(1) In Thessalonica, Paul's host, Jason, and other local believers are hauled before the authorities and eventually forced to post bail (17.6-7).

(2) In Corinth, after Paul is dismissed without penalty from Gallio's court, the Jewish prosecutors take out their frustration, strangely enough, on the synagogue ruler, Sosthenes, 'beat[ing] him in front of the tribunal' (18.12-17).

(3) In Ephesus, the riotous throng, agitated over Paul's threat to the honor of their renowned goddess, Artemis, seizes two of Paul's companions, Gaius and Aristarchus; although Paul wants to join the fray, he is dissuaded by both disciples and officials concerned about his welfare (19.23-31).

On the one hand, we may admire these victims as heroic protectors of Paul. On the other hand, however, we may be puzzled and even disturbed by the heavy toll exacted upon others to secure Paul's freedom. The Lukan Jesus certainly did not have any stand-ins for his trials; he suffered and died alone and was remarkably known for his continuing benevolence (e.g. healing the slave's ear at his arrest and ushering the thief into paradise at his death [Lk. 22.49-51; 23.39-43]). The imperiled Paul of Acts, by contrast, allows others to suffer in his place; ironically, he remains a cause of Christians' persecution even after his conversion.

Commission in Troas: 16.6-10

As we have come to expect, the Holy Spirit continues to plot the missionary agenda of Acts through revelatory visions and other means of divine communication. Notable on this occasion is the Spirit's intially *negative* guidance, twice blocking the Pauline party's plans to evangelize certain areas in Asia Minor: first, the province of Asia to the south and west, then the region of Bithynia to the north (16.6-7). While no one can 'hinder' (*kōlyō*) God's purpose in mission (11.17; cf. 10.47,

8.36), God can and does frustrate ('prevent', *kōlyō*, 16.6) others' schemes. No explanation is given for the closed doors other than the sovereign will of the 'Holy Spirit'/'Spirit of Jesus' (notice the abiding sense of Jesus' involvement with his emissaries). Paul is certainly no stranger to sudden changes in itinerary, as attested by his revolutionary experience on the Damascus road. Now, even after his conversion, he continues to take wrong paths which the Lord must redirect. The journey remains both a challenge and an adventure with unexpected twists and turns.

Skirting the forbidden zones, Paul and company arrive at the Aegean port of Troas on the northwestern tip of Asia Minor closest to Greece. Here, during the night, Paul's uncertainty about where to head next is overcome by a clear vision of 'a man' (*anēr*) begging him to 'come to Macedonia and help us' (16.9). Although the aura of divine authority surrounds this epiphany, the vision itself features an unmistakeably *human* figure—a Macedonian male—requesting aid, not an angel or the Lord himself mandating ministry. This phenomenon highlights the importance of human receptivity to the gospel in charting the church's mission. Despite its expansionist goals and dynamic backing from the sovereign Lord of all, the church is not an imperial juggernaut steamrolling its way to the ends of the earth. Christian missionaries seek out those who most welcome their work; when they are not welcome they shake the dust from their feet and move on (cf. 13.51). Of course, it is especially prudent to stress this responsive rather than invasive approach toward Roman officers like Cornelius (note his God-directed inviting and receiving of Peter in 10.4-8, 30-33) and Roman colonies like Macedonia. By going only where invited, answering pleas for help, Christian messengers can scarcely be regarded as threats to the empire.

Upon receiving the visionary call, the missionary team waste no time in making their way to Macedonia. They set sail 'immediately' across the Aegean, thoroughly 'convinced' they are fulfilling God's purpose (16.10-11). Apart from the geographical shift to Europe, this commissioning scene also signals a perspectival shift to first person narration. The party of Paul, Silas and Timothy (15.40; 16.1-4), collectively designated in third person as 'they' (16.6-8), abruptly become 'we' in 16.10. The narrator—the 'I' identified in the opening statement of Acts as the presenter of the two-volume story of Jesus and the early church (cf. Lk. 1.1-4)—now intrudes for the first time not only as a reporter but as a personal participant in the journey. Why this sudden appearance at this time? Historical explanations suggest the narrator-author's 'real', firsthand partnership with the Pauline mission beginning in Troas or perhaps a direct appropriation of another's eyewitness account, such as a travel diary. Whatever the historical cause of introducing 'we' at this juncture (which in the absence of synoptic sources remains indeterminable), the rhetorical effect injects a fresh sense of both intimacy and legitimacy into the narrative. While we have attempted to follow the Acts journey-story as involved traveller-readers, the third person viewpoint has allowed ample space for us to remain detached observers. Now this gap is closed; the storyteller has joined the story and pulled us in with him. We are now part of 'we', living and experiencing this second missionary expedition first hand. Thus we are poised to 'feel' the mission more keenly and 'know' its truth more assuredly (cf. Lk. 1.4).

Why such intensification at this point? Perhaps it represents a strategy to relieve some suspicion about the Pauline mission which the narrative itself recently created in reporting the bitter parting of Barnabas and Paul at the end of ch. 15. As discussed above, Paul's role in this break-up is open to criticism, and in any case, his abandonment by Barnabas leaves him in a vulnerable position within the wider Christian community and the overall Acts story. All along the unequivocally good and noble Barnabas has vouched for the radical and controversial Saul-Paul. What do we now make of Paul without Barnabas beside him? Is he ready to stand on his own? Apparently, not quite. In place of Barnabas, the narrator inserts not only Silas and Timothy—relative unknowns in the story (cf. 15.32; 16.1-3)—but also himself, the reliable 'I' from the story's beginning. Together 'we' may validate the authority of Paul's mission. 'We' become 'convinced that God ha[s] called *us* to proclaim good news' (16.10).

Imprisoned in Philippi: 16.11-40

Across the Aegean, the missionary party disembarks at Neapolis in the northeastern corner of Macedonia. From there they head overland to nearby Philippi, 'a leading city' (though not the capital) within the first of four Macedonian districts, where they labor 'for some days' (16.12). Socially and politically, Philippi is distinguished as 'a Roman colony' (16.12), dating back to the conquests of Antony and Octavian and their resettlement of the city with war veterans in the last half of the first century BCE. This official Roman setting provides an apt place for clarifying Paul's support of Roman law (16.21) and status as a Roman citizen (16.37-38). Economic and commercial interests in the form of cloth dealing (16.14) and fortune peddling (16.16-19) are also featured in the present narrative, consonant with Philippi's location along the Via Egnatia, a major east–west trade route stretching across Macedonia.

Paul's experiences in Philippi revolve around two groups of people and two sets of contrasting places. First, Paul encounters a *receptive assembly of women* at a riverside '*place of prayer*' outside the city gate. One woman in particular, a purple dealer named Lydia, stands out as a model of faith and devotion, opening both her heart to the gospel and her *home* to the visiting missionaries (16.13-15). Paul then meets another working woman, a fortune-telling slave, whose response is more ambiguous (16.16-18). She functions as a bridge to another group of characters whose reaction to Paul is diametrically opposed to that of Lydia's prayer group: a *hostile coalition* of commercial (owners of the slave-girl), political (magistrates), popular (crowds) and penal (jailer) personnel who harass Paul in the *marketplace* and ultimately consign him to *prison* (16.19-24). However, a remarkable break in this pattern occurs in the middle of the night as the jailer suddenly becomes a believer and host to the freed prisoners in *his own home* (16.25-34)—thus matching the action of Lydia (cf. 16.15, 40). The antithesis between the private house and prayer sanctuary, on the one hand, as safe quarters for mission, and the public square and prison, on the other hand, as danger zones, recalls similar scenarios in the first half of Acts, with the marketplace in Roman Philippi now taking the place of the temple compound in Jerusalem.

People:	Receptive Women	vs	Hostile Coalition
Places:	Place of Prayer		Marketplace
		vs	
	Private House		Prison Cell

Taking a closer look at Paul's dealings with these various Philippian characters, we must first appreciate the significance of the initial outreach to women in general and Lydia in particular. In his prevous expedition, Paul typically began his work in a new city by preaching in the local synagogue on the sabbath day. In Philippi, by contrast, Paul sojourns in the city for a few days and then inaugurates his sabbath mission 'outside the [city] gate by the river' with a group of female God-fearers. In terms of its focus on sabbath-day prayer and worship, this assembly functions as a synagogue; however, its physical location—twice removed from the city limits by architectural (gate) and natural (river) boundaries—and socioreligous composition—women devoted to the Jewish faith—betray its restricted, marginal status within the Roman colony. We might imagine that Paul seeks out such a group because he cannot find within the city a quorum of ten Jewish males necessary to form a traditional synagogue (Bruce, pp. 310-11). Still, Paul and associates seem to have no qualms about approaching these women 'outsiders'. A Macedonian male may have been the first to call for Paul's gospel (16.9), but Macedonian women are the first to hear and receive it.

Spotlighting the response of one woman, Lydia, provides an interesting counterpoint not only to the man in the Troas vision but also to Cornelius (10.1-48). Like Cornelius, Lydia is 'a worshipper of God', devoted to prayer, who eagerly accepts the gospel through faith and baptism, leads her household to follow suit, and entertains missionaries in her home (16.13-15). As Cornelius was the first Roman-Gentile convert in Acts, so Lydia is the first European convert. (Whether she is a Jew or Jewish-sympathizing Gentile is not specified, however.) As household head and trader in expensive purple textiles (cf. 16.19), she also parallels the Caesarean centurion as a person of some wealth and influence. Moreover, she recalls other single, independent women of means in Acts, such as Tabitha and Mary (Mark's mother), whose homes become bases for Christian communities (9.36-42; 12.12-17). Tabitha represents a further link as a 'woman of the cloth', although she supplied garments as a charitable ministry (9.36, 39) whereas Lydia distributes fabrics as a commercial enterprise.

While suggesting a degree of wealth and independence, Lydia's occupation also intimates a more marginal social position than that held by military officers (like Cornelius) or other merchants. The fact that Lydia provides fine purple material to bedeck kings and other elites does not mean that she shares their status. Textile work—traditionally a woman's domain—might bring a measure of profit but was not typically regarded as a prestigious profession in the ancient world. Purple dyeing was particularly stigmatized as a smelly, 'dirty' process involving the use of animal urine. Accordingly, dye-houses were normally situated in remote zones outside the city (Plutarch, *Pericles* 1; Pliny the Elder, *Natural History* 9.60, 64; Martial 1.49; 4.4; 9.62). As a handler (probably manufacturer as well as seller) of purple goods who likely lives and works as well as worships outside the city gate, Lydia would seem to fit among the lower, despised classes of Philippian society, whatever her financial standing (Schottroff, pp. 131-37; Reimer, pp. 102-109). Again, we emphasize that her marginal status seems to be of no concern to Paul. He appears as comfortable in the riverside home of Lydia the purple-dyer as Peter was in the seaside residence of Simon the tanner (a similarly scorned profession; see discussion of 9.43, p. 113).

Regardless of her lowly professional rank, Lydia holds an honored place in Acts as host to the developing community of disciples, which by the end of ch. 16 includes men ('brothers') as well as women (16.40). We might assume that this scenario also suggests Lydia's leadership (headship) role within the local house-church. However, unlike the clear endorsement of women ministers as 'co-workers' in Paul's Philippian letter (Phil. 4.2-3), the story in Acts leaves Lydia's ministerial status somewhat in doubt. As recent feminist commentators have noted, Lydia appears more as a *passive hearer and helper* of Paul than a dynamic co-worker (O'Day, pp. 310-11; Martin, p. 784). The story stresses her aural response to Paul's message through a double reference, the second of which intensifies her passivity by crediting 'the Lord' as the one who 'open[s] her heart to listen eagerly to what was said by Paul' (16.14). Lydia also has a brief speaking part, but the words she utters are suppliant rather than prophetic (we still await the fulfillment of Joel's promise), thoroughly subject to Paul's authority ('if you have judged me faithful to the Lord') and wholly within the bounds of standard domestic duty ('come and stay at my home') (16.15).

The next woman Paul encounters fares even worse. In contrast to Lydia's affirmed role as passive hearer and helper, this woman appears as an *active announcer and annoyer* of Paul, who within the space of a few verses is silenced, put out of work, and completely dropped from the story (16.16-18). Of course, from her portrayal as a pathetic slave-girl (*paidiskē*) possessed by a 'spirit of divination' who irks Paul with her repeated pronouncements, we can easily conclude that she deserves such harsh treatment. This mantic spirit which overtakes her is characterized as 'pythian', related to the serpent (python)-slaying Apollo, thought to inspire the famous oracles at Delphi. By overcoming such a force 'in the name of Jesus', Paul again demonstrates Christian superiority over magical-pagan religion (cf. 13.6-12).

Whatever victory may be won, however, the story shows no concern for the effects of Paul's power display on the slave girl. All we know is that she has been rendered useless to her greedy employers (16.19). What becomes of her then? Does she become a believer? Is she 'saved' (as the jailer will be, 16.30-31)? Is she taken in by the local Christian community? We might like to think so, but we are never told. The story becomes wholly preoccupied with the troubles of Paul and Silas, leaving us to guess and worry about the fate of the girl (see O'Day, pp. 310-11).

Another curious feature of the slave-girl's treatment in the narrative is that Paul silences her for *speaking the truth* about him and his fellow missionaries. She announces, 'These men are slaves of the Most High God, who proclaim to you a way of salvation' (16.17)—a seemingly accurate and noble description which Paul himself might have uttered. Why then does he squash it? No doubt Paul is most upset by the nagging interference of the alien spirit controlling the girl's speech. We know from Luke that unclean spirits typically acknowledged the truth about Jesus ('you are the Son/Holy One of God') before he cast them out (Lk. 4.33-34, 41; 8.28). But often in these cases the demons also remonstrated with Jesus: 'Let us alone! What have you to do with us?' (4.34; 8.28). Nothing like that comes from the lips of the pytheness in Acts 16, however. Indeed, by tagging along with the missionaries 'for many days' and repeating her announcement, she seems at some level to be interested in the 'way of salvation' which they proclaim. Moreover, apart from the link with the exorcism stories in Luke, the pytheness ironically fits the Pentecostal mold of Acts 2.18. Here we find, just as Peter and Joel predicted, a spirit-inspired slave-girl who prophesies concerning the good news of salvation. Nonetheless, her message is flatly rejected. Is this only because she speaks through an unholy spirit, or perhaps is it also due to her dubious status as a *female* witness? We may recall the case of another slave-girl (*paidiskē*), Rhoda, whose truthful word was dismissed and mocked by a Christian audience (12.13-15; cf. also Lk. 22.56-58; 24.9-11). Despite the Pentecostal promise, women's voices continue to be more suppressed than celebrated in Acts; however much it may support the ideal of women prophets, the narrative has done little to mitigate the very real difficulties such women face in gaining a hearing.

The remaining Philippian story, focusing on Paul and Silas' legal battles arising from their disruption of the fortune-telling business, unfolds in three scenes both *chronologically*, from the missionaries' accusation and beating one day to their imprisonment and supernatural release around midnight that evening and finally to their official release and vindication the next morning; and *cyclically*, featuring two public confrontations with antagonistic city magistrates—the first displaying the missionaries as passive criminals, the second as aggressive citizens—surrounding a private encounter with a sympathetic jailer.

> A   Public Accusation and Beating before City Magistrates (16.19-24)
>
>> B   Midnight Imprisonment and Supernatural Release before Jailer (16.25-34)
>
> A′   Official Release and Vindication by City Magistrates (16.35-40)

The attack against Paul and Silas is initiated by the owners of the slave girl for economic reasons: with her powers stripped, 'their hope of making money was gone' (16.19). However, since their authority is limited and their financial grievance somewhat shaky (Paul and Silas had not stolen money directly from them or damaged their property in a violent sense), these businessmen seek to 'broaden the respectablity' of their claim by enlisting the support of other 'agents of censure', both legal (magistrates) and popular (crowds), and expanding the charges to 'disturbing our city' and 'advocating customs that are not lawful for us as Romans' (16.20-21)—completely glossing over their personal economic interest. The slaveowners do not cite any specific violations of Roman law by Paul and Silas, but they do label them as 'these Jews'. Although officially a licit religion within the empire, Judaism—with its strange, exclusive practices (such as sabbath observance, 16.30) and belief in one God ('the Most High', 16.17)—while appealing to some Gentiles ('God-fearers'), alienated many others in the ancient world (see Ferguson, pp. 403-405). A Roman colony like Philippi could be expected to be rife with anti-Judaic sentiment, indeed, with prejudice against all 'others' who threaten the dominant interests of 'us Romans' (cf. Johnson, *Acts*, pp. 295, 298).

Given no opportunity for defense, Paul and Silas receive a 'severe flogging' and are then thrown into 'the innermost cell' of the prison and bound with stocks (16.22-24). From all appearances, they are in dire straits, helpless and hopeless. But we know better by now. Prisons, however secure, do not hold dynamic witnesses in Acts. And, lo and behold, just like the Jerusalem apostles and Peter (5.17-21; 12.1-11); Paul and Silas find themselves miraculously freed from prison in the middle of the night. Actually, the cases are not exactly alike; some interesting innovations in the present story maintain dramatic interest and contribute to a distinctive characterization of Paul and his mission:

(1) Compared to the apostles' rather passive role in their prison breaks, particularly exemplified in Peter's slumber until awakened by the angel (12.6-7), Paul and Silas are busy praying and singing to God at the midnight hour (16.25). Other believers had been seeking God during Peter's incarceration (12.5, 12), but these prisoners joyfully raise their own voices to heaven, anticipating divine intervention.

(2) In addition to the miraculously loosened chains and opened doors in the previous escapes, the present case also features a dramatic, prison-shaking earthquake (16.26). The effects of such a cataclysm are such that 'all' prison doors fling open and 'everyone's' shackles come loose—not just those of the missionaries. This pervasive 'shaking' (*saleuō*) in response to prayer recalls the energizing infusion with the Spirit experienced by the persecuted Jerusalem church (4.31).

(3) The inhabitants of the Philippian prison are affected not only by the violent shifting of the earth but also by the persuasive witness of Paul and Silas. While Peter and the apostles went out from their prison cells to resume preaching in the temple courts, much to the chagrin of the temple police (5.19-26), Paul and Silas bear witness within the prison compound, first to their fellow-prisoners who hear their praying and singing (16.25), and then, surprisingly, to the attending jailer who inquires after the quake about the path to salvation (16.29-30). Ultimately, the missionaries proclaim the good news to the 'entire family' of this unlikely seeker, all of whom believe and are baptized 'without delay', and seal the bond of fellowship by sharing a meal in the jailer's home (16.32-34). These events vividly illustrate Paul's own claim in his Philippian letter that imprisonment, far from being an obstacle to his mission, poses a unique opportunity to spread the gospel boldly to Roman guards and others who come his way (Phil. 1.12-14).

(4) Another element of the jailer's response affords a suggestive contrast with the prison story in Acts 12. Seeing the open doors following the earthquake, the jailer 'drew his sword...to kill himself' (16.27), knowing that death was the penalty for failing to secure his post. Earlier, King Herod, intent on executing Peter with the sword, had the guards put to death instead for allowing Peter to escape (12.1-6, 18-19). In the case of the distraught jailer in ch. 16, however, Paul intervenes to stop the suicide and goes on to lead the man to salvation. Such compassion and resistance of violence are reminiscent of Jesus' rebuking the sword-play of his disciples at the scene of his arrest and restoring the severed ear of a member of the arrest party (Lk. 22.49-51).

After charting the eventful evening in the prison chambers and jailer's residence, the story picks up the response of the city magistrates the next morning. They begin by sending orders to release Paul and Silas, allowing them to 'go in peace' (16.35-36). We detect a clear case of sarcastic irony at this point, since we know that Paul and Silas are already free, no thanks to the magistrates, and doing quite well. The embarrassment of the authorities becomes even more acute when Paul refuses to go quietly and demands that they make amends for violating his and Silas' rights *as Roman citizens* (16.37). Long-standing Roman legal tradition protected citizens from beatings and imprisonment without a trial (cf. Livy, *History* 10.9; Cicero, *The Republic* 2.31.54). Thus, fearing reprisals from Rome, the Philippian judges promptly apologize to the mistreated missionaries and escort them from the city (16.38-39). As for Paul, while not repudiating his ethnic-religious identity as a faithful Jew, this sudden introduction of citizen status does effectively neutralize the slaveowners' charge that he opposes the legal conventions governing 'us Romans'; in a sense, Paul's citizenship makes him one of 'us'. It also opens up greater potential for extending Paul's ministry to Roman officials and other leading citizens, adumbrated in his persuasive encounter with the Cypriot proconsul, Sergius Paulus, on his first expedition (13.4-12).

Hunted in Thessalonica; Welcomed in Beroea: 17.1-15

Further west along the Via Egnatia, the missionary party comes to Thessalonica, the most populated, cosmopolitan city in Macedonia and the seat of Roman provincial government. The account of the Thessalonian mission is narrated once again from a third-person point of view, concentrating on the activities of Paul and Silas (17.1 ['they'], 4, 5). Actually, the 'we'-group faded into the background early in the Philippian story (16.18). Only Paul and Silas were reportedly involved in the imbroglio over the slave-girl, and only Paul was attributed any direct speech (three times: 16.18, 28, 37). While serving a key legitimating function for the new Aegean mission, the 'we'-retinue works mostly behind the scenes, as the spotlight stays trained on Paul and his principal partners. (Timothy resurfaces along with Silas in 17.14-15.) Further insight into the significance of 'we' awaits the point when this first-person perspective suddenly reasserts itself in the narrative (cf. 20.5-12).

The present campaign in Thessalonica (17.1-9) is closely connected with the succeeding mission in Beroea (17.10-15) in terms of *space* and *time*, as Paul and Silas commence their work in the neighboring Macedonian town of Beroea on the 'very night' they leave Thessalonica (17.10), and in terms of various comparative and contrastive elements pertaining to *character* and *plot*:

(1) The ministries of Paul and Silas in both Thessalonica and Beroea center around the exposition of the Jewish 'scriptures' in the local

synagogue (17.1-3, 10-11). The specific Christological aim of this preaching—to show the necessity (*dei*) of the death and resurrection of Jesus Messiah—although spelled out only in the Thessalonian setting (17.3; cf. Lk. 24.45-46; Acts 3.18; 13.26-33) may be assumed to characterize the Beroean message as well.

(2) In both places, 'many' respond favorably to the Pauline message, including 'not a few' (*ouk oligai/oligoi*) socially prominent, God-fearing Greek women and men (17.4, 12). This reaction stands in contrast to the hostility of high-ranking Gentile women and men toward Paul in Pisidian Antioch (13.50). Paul's stock among the Greco-Roman aristocracy seems to be rising in Macedonia. Particular stress is given to female support, as believing elite women are singled out for mention in Thessalonica and identified before the leading men in Beroea.

(3) Counterbalancing the gracious reception of many synagogue worshippers in Thessalonica is the bitter resistance of synagogue leaders ('the Jews', 17.5). These 'Jews' not only stir up trouble for Paul in their home city but pursue him in Beroea and seek to turn the population there against him (17.13). At this point, however, the parallel between the two cities pulls apart, for 'the Jews' at Beroea prove to be 'more receptive than those in Thessalonica' (17.11). Instead of dismissing the gospel and searching through the city to arrest Paul and Silas, the Beroeans 'welcome the message very eagerly' and search through the scriptures to confirm the validity of the missionaries' claims (17.5, 11).

Regarding the Thessalonian Jewish officials, we consider further both the *motive* and the *method* of their opposition to Paul and Silas. Once again 'the Jews' are driven to attack God's messengers on account of 'jealousy' (*zēlos/zēloō*, 17.5), the same impulse that turned the patriarchs of old against their brother Joseph (7.9), the temple leaders against Peter and the apostles in Jerusalem (5.17), and synogogue rulers against Paul and Barnabas in Pisidian Antioch (13.45). The issue is not so much a doctrinal dispute over Paul's handling of Scripture as it is a social conflict arising from Paul's popularity in the community. With honor and social standing inextricably tied to finite public opinion, Paul's sudden jump in the polls—especially among high society folk—means a slump in rank for the synagogue elites. And so they fight to restore their honor, not by arguing against Paul's biblical exegesis, but by aiming to downgrade his social reputation.

To this end, 'the Jews' broaden their base of support by moving outside the synagogue to the 'marketplace' (*agora*), where they enlist a group of 'marketfolk' (*agoraioi*) in their cause. Together they form a riotous mob hunting down Paul and Silas with intent to expose them to public ridicule (17.5). Abraham Malherbe notes that in the ancient world *agoraioi* designated common laborers, artisans, and small businesspeople who plied their trades in the city square. In terms of social status, these workers were regarded as 'people of low

birth...contrasted with the nobility or upper classes' (*Paul*, p. 16). This
market 'rabble' (RSV) or group of 'ruffians' (NRSV) thus appear in rather
surprising roles in Acts 17, both as allies of the Jewish religious leaders,
who are endeavoring to win back the esteem of God-fearing elites, and
as enemies of Paul, who previously reached out to lowly people like the
lame man at Lystra (14.8-9) and found acceptance among marginal merchants such as Lydia (16.14-15, 40). Even more striking is the contrast
with Paul's testimony outside of Acts that, during his stay in
Thessalonica, he himself toiled around the clock as a manual laborer to
make ends meet (1 Thess. 2.5-9; 2 Thess. 3.7-10). At present Acts seems
more concerned with building a prestigious rather than proletarian
image of Paul.

Attempting to broaden their case further, the mixed mob come before
the city officials ('politarchs'), accusing Paul and Silas of disrupting the
peace and transgressing imperial law (17.6-7). Generally speaking, this
matches the previous trial scene in Philippi, but on closer analysis, the
scope of the charges has been both expanded and sharpened in the
Thessalonian incident. Now the complaint concerns the missionaries'
drastic overturning of the entire 'world-order' (*oikoumenē*), not merely
their 'disturbing our city' (17.6; 16.20); and now, instead of leaving
open the nature of Paul and Silas' anti-Roman conduct, a very specific
and serious allegation is made: they promote 'another king [than Caesar]
named Jesus' (17.7). Multiple ironies swirl around these accusations. In
one sense, they are right. As a Spirit-empowered witness driven to bring
God's salvation to the ends of earth (13.47), Paul can be said to advance
a truly world-changing mission; moreover, his core claim in the
Thessalonian synagogue that 'this is the Messiah, Jesus whom I am proclaiming to you' (17.3) is tantamount to heralding the kingship of Jesus
Christ. In another sense, however, the accusations miss the mark, as
Paul has never aligned his messianic mission with plots to overthrow
Roman rule or incite public disturbances. In fact, in the present story, it
is the violent gang of *accusers*, not the accused, who 'set the city in an
uproar' (17.6, 13).

The methods of prosecution in the Philippian and Thessalonian
episodes diverge even further in their physical handling of Paul and
Silas. Unlike the personal assault which they faced at Philippi, including
beating and binding, the two missionaries are attacked only *indirectly* at
Thessalonica. A local resident named Jason and other members of the
new Christian community are dragged before the city officials and
forced to post bail on account of their association with the seditious
missionaries. Jason in particular is implicated for harboring such fellows
in his home. Meanwhile, Paul and Silas are whisked away to Bereoa
during the night (17.5-10). This sudden shielding of Paul from physical
suffering, unlike his treatment at Philippi and even before that at Lystra
(14.5, 19), coordinates with his developing profile as a Roman citizen of

some standing. The protective patronage of Jason, apparently a Gentile of some means and influence in the city who assumes financial and legal responsibility for the visiting preachers, further enhances Paul's position (Meeks, *First Urban*, pp. 62-63; Malherbe, *Paul*, p. 15).

Questioned in Athens: 17.16-34

When the Thessalonian Jews come to Beroea and begin to foment further opposition to the Pauline mission, the local believers promptly send Paul away again, this time down the eastern coast of the Greek peninsula. Silas and Timothy stay behind in Macedonia—perhaps to nurture the diligent Beroean converts—but anticipate rejoining Paul as soon as they can (17.14-15). Paul stops for a while and waits for his partners in Athens, the cradle of classical Greek learning and culture and still a vital intellectual and religious center in the Roman era. He does more than simply wait, however, in this provocative place. 'Deeply distressed' over the city's rampant idolatry, Paul cannot resist engaging in public debate (17.16-17). At the heart of his mission in Athens is a formal address in the Areopagus (17.22-31), preceded and followed by responses from various audiences (17.17-21, 32-34).

> A   Audience Responses from Epicureans, Stoics and Others (17.17-21)
>
> B   Paul's Address in the Areopagus (17.22-31)
>
> A′ Audience Responses from Dionysius, Damaris and Others (17.32-33)

(1) *Audience Responses.* As usual Paul preaches to the Jews and God-worshipping (*sebomai*) Gentiles in the local synagogue. Surprisingly, however, we learn nothing of this assembly's reaction to Paul's message. The present narrative focuses instead on Paul's exchange with various passersby in the lively Athenian marketplace or city square (*agora*). Neither dragged into the marketplace against his will, as in Philippi, nor driven away, as in Thessalonica, for the first time in Acts Paul deliberately and regularly ('every day') directs his mission to the hub of Greco-Roman urban life (17.17).

Also for the first time Paul discusses the nature of divine reality with professional Greek philosophers. In Lystra, we may recall, after healing a lame man, Paul had to deal with a zealous priest who wanted to worship him and Barnabas as Greek gods (14.8-18). Paul works no miracles in Athens, however, and is offered no sacrifices. In this more sophisticated setting, Paul confronts intellectual speculation concerning his own ideas about God rather than superstitious deification.

Paul particularly rouses the interest of some Epicurean and Stoic thinkers. Epicureans were known for their pursuit of happiness and contentment through detachment from social competition and denial of divine interference in human affairs, especially the threat of retribution. The Stoics, whose name derived from the Stoa or portico in the

Athenian *agora* where their founder Zeno (340–265 BCE) expounded his philosophy, sought through logic and discipline to live in harmony with the natural order which they believed was permeated by a rational divine principle or *Logos* (see Malherbe, 'Cultural Context', pp. 18-20). Overall Paul's teaching strikes these philosophers as something 'new' (*kainos*) and 'strange' (*xenos*) (17.19-20); in particular, some interpret his message about 'Jesus and the resurrection' as promoting the claims of 'strange/foreign (*xenōn*) divinities' (17.18), perhaps taking the term for 'resurrection' as the name of some new goddess, 'Anastasia' (Longenecker, pp. 473-74). Such a presentation of novel and exotic ideas is not necessarily a bad thing in an academic center like Athens. As the narrator accurately, if somewhat derisively, puts it: 'Now all the Athenians and the *strangers/foreigners* (*xenoi*) living there would spend their time in nothing but telling or hearing something *new* (*kainoteron*)' (17.21). Whatever problems Athens might have had, xenophobia was not one of them.

Although certain Epicureans and Stoics dismiss Paul as a senseless 'babbler' (17.18), others are more intrigued by his perplexing words, curious to learn 'what it all means' (*tina thelei tauta einai*, 17.20), much like the response of some Pentecost pilgrims to the glossolalia of the early Jerusalem church ('What does this mean?', *ti thelei touto einai*, 2.12). And so they invite Paul to explain his views more fully before the Areopagus, the highest governmental council in the city named after its original headquarters at the 'hill of Ares/Mars'. The scenario of 'taking (*epilabomenoi*) and bringing (*ēgagon*)' (17.19) Paul before the city authorities matches the terminology of the Philippian episode ('they seized [*epilabomenoi*] Paul and Silas and...brought [*prosagagontes*] them before the magistrates', 16.19-20), but not the tone. The Athenian scene has more the appearance of an open inquiry than a hostile inquisition; there is no flogging or sentencing, only asking and hearing. A closer parallel is suggested in Barnabas' earlier presentation of Paul before the leaders of the Jerusalem church ('But Barnabas took [*epilabomenos*] him and brought [*ēgagen*] him to the apostles', 9.27).

After Paul delivers his address before the Areopagus, he receives mixed reviews. Some 'scoff' (*echleuazon*) at his belief in bodily resurrection, again reminiscent of the Pentecost episode ('But others sneered [*diachleuazontes*]...', 2.13). Others, however, continue in a more open-minded, though noncommital mode, willing to give Paul another hearing on the matter (17.32). Still others take a decisive step of faith and join the Pauline movement, including a male member of the Areopagus council named Dionysius and a woman named Damaris (17.34). Her close association with Dionysius may imply that Damaris is also a distinguished Areopagite. While there was no shortage of prejudice against women scholars in the ancient world, some philosophical communities remained more open to female members on egalitarian principles. Epicureans and Stoics, singled out above, were among these more inclusive groups, especially the Epicureans who accepted women as both students and teachers in their societies of 'friends' (Reimer, pp. 246-48).

Within the churches recently established by Paul at Thessalonica and Beroea, we noted the presence of high-ranking Greek women, though not expressly as intellectual leaders (17.4, 12). Needless to say, such an accent on women's involvement in the Acts communities has not been appreciated by all readers. In the present Athenian narrative in fact, one early 'Western' editor (Codex D) *deleted* 'a woman named Damaris' from the record altogether, substituting another flattering descriptive term for *Dionysius*—'high-standing' (*euschēmōn*)—which was unnecessary, since 'Areopagite' already implied his lofty status. An alternative explanation is that another scribe had first added *euschēmōn* to clarify *Damaris'* ranking, in keeping with this term's application to elite women in each of its two other uses in Acts (13.50; 17.12). The 'Western' reviser then came along and simply shifted the *euschēmōn* reference to Dionysius by eliminating Damaris (see Metzger, pp. 459-60; Reimer, pp. 246-48).

(2) *Paul's Address*. Paul's overriding concern in his oration before the Areopagus is to reveal true knowledge about God, redressing both the Athenians' basic theological ignorance, symbolized in the altar dedicated 'to an unknown deity' (17.23), and their gross perversion of God's nature through the worship of manufactured images (17.29-30; cf. 17.16,22). At the core of Paul's theology is his belief in one God as the sovereign creator and sustainer of everything in the universe, including human beings. Repeated emphasis falls on the *totality* of this cosmic role: God is the *all* (*pan*)-encompassing 'Lord of heaven and earth' (17.24).

> God who made the world and *everything* (*panta*) in it... He himself
> gives to *all* (*pasi*) mortals life and breath and *all things* (*panta*)...
> He made *all* (*pan*) nations to inhabit the *whole* (*pantos*) earth
> (17.24-26).

In a shrewd rhetorical move appropriate to his present situation, Paul cites the Greeks' own philosopher-poets in support of his position: '"In him we live and move and have our being"' (probably from Epiminides of Crete in the sixth century BCE); and '"For we too are his offspring"' (applied to Zeus by Aratus of Cilicia in the third century BCE). Of course, Paul uses these sources and other resonances with Greek philosophy selectively and critically. While affirming God's presence in the world all around us, Paul also declares God's self-sufficiency and independence from the world he created; Paul is no Stoic pantheist. And he certainly is no Greek polytheist either, advocating Zeus' supreme creative power among the gods (Longenecker, p. 476). Although he does not quote the

Jewish scriptures, Paul's theology remains firmly anchored in them.

This biblical foundation becomes most evident in the conclusions which Paul draws from the premise of God's creatorship against the Athenians' practice of idolatry. His logic runs as follows:

(a) Because God creates and sustains everything in the natural world, he cannot be adequately represented by any particular element within that world.

(b) Because God creates and sustains every human being in the world, he cannot be adequately represented by anything that 'human hands' fashion from the world (17.24-25).

(c) Because living, breathing human beings are God's 'offspring' and thus reflect God's likeness, inanimate objects of 'gold, or silver, or stone' which human beings manufacture cannot adequately represent the dynamic image of God (17.28-29).

Paul develops his argument further around the conviction that God not only generates all human life but also dictates *when* and *where* each life will be lived out: God 'allotted the *times* of their existence and the boundaries of the *places* where they would live' (17.26). This divine control over space and time imposes additional limits on human access to God.

(a) Because the omnipresent God 'in whom we live and move and have our being' determines the boundaries of all human dwelling, God cannot be localized 'in shrines made by human hands (*cheiropoiētois*)' (17.24). As Paul establishes this principle to undermine the pagan temples in Athens, he echoes Stephen's earlier critique of the 'handmade' (*cheiropoiētois*) Solomonic temple in Jerusalem (7.47-48).

(b) Because the eternal God determines the schedule for all human existence, he has the authority to set a time of reckoning for human conduct. For a season, God has let 'times of human ignorance' unfold, in which idolatry has persisted; but 'now' he insists that 'all people every-where' turn to righteous worship and living in preparation for a 'fixed day' of judgment on the divine calendar (17.30-31).

Despite the parenthetical note in 17.18 that Paul 'was telling the good news about Jesus and the resurrection', in addressing the Areopagus, Paul focuses on proclaiming the truth about God with little reference to the Christian gospel. He took a similar approach with the idolatrous Gentile audience in Lystra, where he did not mention Jesus at all (14.15-17). At the very end of the Areopagus speech in Athens, Paul finally does allude to the risen Jesus as the one who will preside over the day of judgment; but he does not disclose Jesus' name and is careful to main-tain God's sole sovereignty over the proceedings. The world's judge will be '*a man* whom he [God!] has *appointed* (*hōrisen*)' (17.31), just as surely as God appointed ('allotted', *horisas*) the spatio-temporal perime-ters of human life (17.26). Christology remains subordinated to theology through the Areopagus discourse.

Reviled in Corinth: 18.1-17

After leaving Athens, Paul proceeds west across a narrow isthmus to the city of Corinth, the administrative capital of the southern Greek province of Achaia and a major commercial hub between the Adriatic and Aegean seas. Here he reunites with Silas and Timothy, who arrive from Macedonia (18.5), and also recruits another pair of missionary partners, Priscilla and Aquila (18.1-3, 18).

On the whole Paul's mission in Corinth follows a predictable course: (1) He starts by debating in the synagogue every sabbath with Jews and Gentile God-fearers (18.4). (2) He eventually encounters heated opposition from 'the Jews', forcing him to leave the synagogue and reach out more widely to the Gentiles. The details of this conflict, featuring the Jews' 'reviling' or 'blaspheming' (*blasphēmeō*) Paul and his retaliatory action of shaking the dust from his clothing and announcing his turn to the Gentiles (18.6), especially mirror the earlier hostilities in Pisidian Antioch (13.45-51). (3) Finally, Paul is once again brought before a Roman tribunal and accused of illegal activity (18.12-16).

Not all, however, is business as usual for Paul in Corinth. Key spatial and temporal variations disrupt the stereotypical plot. Whereas we have come to expect Paul to leave not only the synagogue but also the city as soon as possible after becoming a target of persecution, in Corinth, after being attacked by 'the Jews', he moves only a short distance from the synagogue—right *'next door'* in fact—and ends up staying a long time— a full *'year and six months'*—proclaiming God's message to *'many'* receptive Jews as well as Gentiles who believe the word and are baptized (18.7, 11). All of this occurs before the public accusation scene. But even after Paul appears before the tribunal, he continues to remain 'many days' longer (18.18). The Corinthian mission thus flourishes in spite of Jewish opposition.

The impetus for Paul's perseverance comes from another nocturnal vision like that which inaugurated the expedition to Greece (cf. 16.6-10). In the present epiphany, the Lord speaks directly to Paul (not through a man or an angel), exhorting him to resist fear and persist in preaching to the Corinthians under the assurance that 'I am with you, and no one will lay a hand on you to harm you' (18.9-10). Similar commissions, backed by the promise of divine presence and protection, were issued to anxious Israelite prophets of old, such as Moses (Exod. 3.10-15; 4.10-12), Joshua (Josh. 1.1-9) and Jeremiah (Jer. 1.4-10). As with other visions in Acts, this one signals a notable expansion of mission. Paul is fortified to settle in Corinth for several months in order to bring 'many people (*laos*)' to the Lord (18.10). As in James' report of Peter's testimony before the Jerusalem council in 15.14, the customary Lukan term for the 'people (*laos*)' of Israel now includes Gentiles (Greeks) as well as Jews within the one people of God.

The Corinthian segment further enriches the plot of Acts by introducing a number of new characters which may be grouped into three pairs associated with different movements in the story.

(1)   Aquila and Priscilla: Entry to and Departure from the City (18.1-3, 18)

(2)   Titius Justus and Crispus: Exit from the Synagogue (18.7-8)

(3)   Gallio and Sosthenes: Trial before the *Bēma* (18.12-17)

(1) *Aquila and Priscilla*. Upon entering the city, Paul lodges and labors with a married couple named Aquila and Priscilla who have recently migrated to Corinth from Rome (18.1-3). And when he finally leaves the city after an extended ministry, he takes only this pair with him, as far as we are told (18.18). They seem to take the place of Silas and Timothy as Paul's primary travel companions, assuming that Silas and Timothy are left behind once again, as at Thessalonica, to nurture the new Corinthian believers in Paul's absence.

Interesting facets pertaining to race, gender, and class characterize Aquila and Priscilla and their relationship to Paul.

(a) The narrative first defines Aquila as 'a Jew' who, along with his wife Priscilla, had been forced out of Rome because of Emperor Claudius' edict against 'all Jews' in the capital (18.2). This emphasis on the *Jewish* identity of these friends of Paul is significant in light of the recent build-up of Jewish antagonism to Paul in Macedonia and the main interest in relating Paul's gospel to Greek philosophers in the immediately preceding episode in Athens. Not all Diaspora Jews persecute Paul and drive him away; indeed, some Jews themselves, like Aquila and Priscilla, know what it is to be expelled by angry authorities and are happy to share their home and trade with Paul. For his part, Paul takes the initiative in seeking out the fellowship of kindred Jews: 'he found a Jew named Aquila...he went to see them' (18.2). He might be able to hold his own before the Athenian Areopagus, but his primary social and cultural ties remain with his own people. Apart from living and working in Aquila and Priscilla's home in Corinth, Paul's Jewish identity is reinforced when he leaves the city with this couple and enacts a traditional Jewish (Nazirite) rite of dedication in the neighboring port of Cenchrea (18.18; cf. Num. 6.1-21).

Whether or not Aquila and Priscilla are already Jewish-*Christian* believers when they encounter Paul is not specified. However, the fact that nothing is reported concerning their conversion and baptism in Corinth suggests their prior acquaintance with the gospel in Rome (Marshall, *Acts*, p. 293). Support for this conjecture may come from testimony outside of Acts that Claudius banished the Jews from Rome because they 'constantly made disturbances at the instigation of *Chrestus* [Christ?]' (Seutonius, *Life of Claudius* 24.5).

(b) In terms of gender issues, we are concerned primarily with the role of Priscilla in relation to both her husband and Paul. Consistently, Priscilla and Aquila are presented *together*, either through proper names or pronouns, as cooperative partners in marriage, occupation, and association with Paul and his mission.

> There he found a Jew named *Aquila*...with his wife *Priscilla* (18.2).
>
> Paul went to see *them*...he stayed with *them*, and *they* worked together—by trade *they* were tentmakers (18.2-3).
>
> Paul said farewell to the believers and sailed for Syria, accompanied by *Priscilla and Aquila* (18.18).

The spousal sharing of business matters recalls the earlier portrayal of Ananias and Sapphira (5.1-11), albeit in a much more positive context. The alternating order of names in the first and last references above may be viewed in two ways. Taken as a whole, it simply reinforces the mutuality of the couple's relationship: they are interchangeable, collegial partners. On the other hand, taken as a progression, reversing the customary husband-and-wife sequence may signal Priscilla's rising importance in the Pauline mission. In the Pauline letters outside of Acts, two of the three references to this beloved pair of missionary associates list Priscilla first (Rom. 16.3-5; 2 Tim. 4.19; cf. 1 Cor. 16.19). Actually the name mentioned in all three places is 'Prisca'. 'Priscilla' in Acts represents a diminutive form ('little Prisca') and perhaps a closer level of familiarity and affection.

(c) To determine the position of Priscilla, Aquila and Paul in Corinthian society, we must understand the nature and status of their 'tentmaking' trade. The main skills associated with the craft involved the cutting and stitching of leather material with specially designed knives and awls. It was hard work, demanding long hours hunched over a workbench to make ends meet. As for their social position, Ronald Hock has demonstrated that tentmakers belonged to a class of humble artisans clustered in the marketplace who were looked down upon by aristocrats and some leisured intellectuals.

> Stigmatized as slavish, uneducated, and often useless, artisans [like tentmakers], to judge from scattered references, were frequently reviled or abused, often victimized, seldom if ever invited to dinner, never accorded status, and even excluded from one Stoic utopia (Hock, p. 36).

By lodging with an artisan couple and, beyond that, actually joining in their trade, Paul suddenly appears no longer as the rising star among noble ladies and gentlemen and lofty academicians. Rather, he restores his links with lowly cloth-handlers, like Lydia (cf. 16.13-15), and builds new ties with the rabble of market laborers (*agoraioi*) who previously were turned against him (cf. 17.4-5).

It is thus becoming increasingly difficult to construct a consistent portrait of Paul's social identity in Acts. We seem to be facing a more idealistic than realistic image of the great missionary as a kind of 'everyman', able to span the spectrum of human society. It is, nonetheless, an image in keeping with one who himself claimed in correspondence with the Corinthians: 'I have become all things to all people, that I might by all means save some' (1 Cor. 9.22; cf. 9.19-23).

(2) *Titius Justus and Crispus.* After leaving the hostile synagogue, Paul finds refuge in the home of a Gentile (apparently) 'worshiper of God' named Titius Justus (18.6-7). We are not told whether this is a temporary visit or a permanent change of residence from Priscilla and Aquila's house. In any case, what is significant here, as noted above, is that Titius Justus lives right *next door* to the synagogue. For all his bluster about going away from the Jews to the Gentiles (18.6), Paul does not go very far. Moreover, he continues to evangelize members of the local Jewish synagogue, including one rather special member named *Crispus*: the *archisynagōgos*, 'the synagogue president'!

Yet another stereotype is deconstructed. Up to this point in Acts, temple and synagogue authorities, with the exception of Gamaliel, have been firmly entrenched in their opposition to the gospel. Now one such official not merely tolerates (like Gamaliel) but actually accepts this word and leads 'all his household' to follow suit (18.8). This household conversion links Crispus with Cornelius (10.44-48; 11.14), Lydia (16.14-15), and the Philippian jailer (16.31-34). Remarkably, the messianic mission brings together people as diverse as synagogue rulers, Roman centurions, female purple-merchants, and prison wardens within the one household of God.

(3) *Gallio and Sosthenes.* While Paul enjoys the favor of Crispus' household and presumably other Corinthian Jews over an eighteen-month span, opposition from 'the Jews' persists and eventually follows the familiar tack of accusing Paul before the local magistrate (18.12). Perhaps we should imagine these 'Jews' as other synagogue leaders particularly upset over Crispus' defection. In any event, in the present setting Paul's prosecutors bring him before the elevated judicial bench (*bēma*) of the Achaian proconsul, Gallio, and charge him with promoting a form of worship which is 'contrary to the law' (18.13).

In the two previous trial scenes, the focus was clearly on Paul's alleged transgression of *Roman* law (16.21; 17.7); now, however, it is initially ambiguous whether 'the law' refers to Roman and/or Jewish regulations. Just as Paul is about to offer his perspective, governor Gallio steps in to clarify the situation. First he stresses that this case is really none of his concern since it has nothing to do with serious crimes against the state (18.14); thus an important voice of authority from the Roman side validates Paul's compliance with Roman law. Then Gallio limits the issue to a controversy about *Jewish* law: 'it is a matter of questions about words and names and your own law' for the Jews to handle on their own (18.15). Gallio says more than he realizes here. More than quibbles about trivial 'words (*logou*) and names', the debate centers on the legitimacy of Paul's 'teaching *the word (ton logon) of God*' (18.11) and proclaiming *the name of Jesus* as the only means of messianic deliverance (18.5; cf. 4.12). As for Paul's respect for Jewish law, the jury is still out. His openness to Gentiles continues to challenge traditional social customs, but his hair-cutting demonstration of a vow of consecration (18.18), like his previous insistence on Timothy's circumcision, exhibits an abiding respect for Jewish practice.

The relationship between Paul and the Corinthian Jews is further complicated by the strange denoument to the trial. Once Gallio dismisses the case, the entire audience pounces on *Sosthenes*, another synagogue ruler (*archisynagōgos*), and pummels him in front of Gallio's bench (18.17). While some manuscripts identify the attackers as 'all the Greeks', preferred texts simply read 'all', implying the same group of Jews which had brought Paul to the tribunal. But why would these Jews suddenly take out their frustrations over Paul's case against one of their own religious leaders? We might speculate that Sosthenes had not supported their cause vigorously enough or was even siding with Crispus in support of Paul (Paul mentions 'our brother Sosthenes' in greeting the Corinthians [1 Cor. 1.1]). The narrative, however, offers no such explanations, and we must not rush too quickly to resolve messy situations which the narrative itself creates. As it stands, the story mocks its own assertion that 'the Jews made a *united (homothymadon)* attack on Paul' (18.12). If they lose one of their leaders to Paul's sect and lash out at another when things do not go their way, 'the Jews' scarcely represent a model of unity and stability. Quite the contrary, they seem to be self-destructing while Paul calmly presses on with his work. As it happens, Paul says and does nothing to defend himself. A dispassionate Roman judge and volatile Jewish assembly collaborate unintentionally to vindicate Paul and his mission.

Mobbed in Ephesus: 18.18-19.41

After his extended stay in Corinth, Paul proceeds eastward back across the Aegean Sea to Ephesus, the administrative capital of the province of Asia, the commercial center of the region, and the fourth largest city of the Roman Empire in the first century CE after Rome, Alexandria, and Antioch. The report of the Ephesian mission is the longest and most complex account in Acts 16-21, including several scenes set in various times and places within Ephesus interspersed with reports of both actual and proposed travel beyond Ephesus. The basic itinerary may be sketched as follows.

Within Ephesus: Paul, accompanied by Priscilla and Aquila, makes a brief initial visit to the *synagogue* (18.18-19).

Beyond Ephesus: Promising to return to the Ephesians 'if God wills', Paul leaves Priscilla and Aquila behind while he heads to *Jerusalem*, *Antioch*, and the areas of *Galatia* and *Phrygia* (18.20-23).

Within Ephesus: Paul returns to the *synagogue*, preaching and debating for *three months* (19.8). In the face of stubborn resistance, he then leaves the synagogue along with his followers and proclaims his message *daily* in the *hall of Tyrannus* over a period of *two years* (19.9-10).

Beyond Ephesus: Paul dispatches two of his associates, Timothy and Erastus, to *Macedonia*, while he remains in Ephesus *'for some time longer'*. At the same time he himself makes plans 'in the Spirit' to travel through *Macedonia* and *Achaia*, then on to *Jerusalem*, and finally all the way to *Rome* (19.21-22).

Within Ephesus: An angry mob, incited by pagan artisans, assembles in the *theater* in protest against the Pauline mission, seizing two of Paul's partners, Gaius and Aristarchus, and shouting their allegiance to the 'great goddess Artemis' for *two hours* (19.28-34).

   (1) *Times*. The range of time notes from two hours to two years conveys a sense of intense activity—every hour counts—sustained over an extended period. The 'Western' text further accentuates the hourly focus by setting Paul's daily lecture schedule in the hall of Tyrannus 'from the fifth hour to the tenth', that is, 'from eleven o'clock in the morning to four in the afternoon' (19.9). Comparing 'narrative time'—the time devoted to recounting an incident—with clock/calendar time, we detect an inverted pattern: the longest narrative (19.23-41) revolves around the shortest time frame, the two hours of public protest against Paul; conversely, his two-year teaching stint is reported summarily in a brief two-verse statement (19.9-10).

   (2) *Places within Ephesus*. In addition to the familiar synagogue setting, two new venues stand out: the *scholē* of Tyrannus and the city theater. Both are public centers attracting large numbers of people from the area, thus indicating the wide scope of Paul's ministry in Ephesus. (There is no mention of Paul's staying or working in a private home, as in Philippi, Thessalonica, and Corinth.) The *scholē* probably represents a guildhall or instructional center ('lecture hall' or 'schoolhouse'); Tyrannus may have been a local philosopher who held classes here, or simply the owner of the building. The Ephesian theater, with a seating capacity of close to 25,000 people, was the site of the tri-monthly meeting of the civic assembly (see Bruce, p. 376; Trebilco, pp. 348-50). Thus, in synagogue, *scholē*, and theater, Paul's Ephesian mission touches religious, intellectual, and political sectors of Asian society, both Jewish and Gentile, professional and popular.

(3) *Places beyond Ephesus*. In intermittent journeys outside the city, Paul either goes himself or sends his associates to the two principal fountainheads of the early Christian mission (Jerusalem and Antioch) and to areas already visited on his previous expeditions (Galatia and Macedonia). Moreover, he makes plans to go again to the Jewish capital of Jerusalem and then on from there to the imperial capital of Rome. Macedonia and Rome are located west of Ephesus; the other places are to the east and south. Thus, just as Ephesus functioned as a major social and commercial hub in the first-century Greco-Roman world, so in the narrative world of Acts, Ephesus marks a pivotal site for reviewing and previewing major stages in the church's missionary saga. Stationed centrally at Ephesus and spanning east and west from Jerusalem to Rome, this section allows us to glimpse the global horizon of the Acts story. Also, the introduction of Alexandria, the second largest city in the empire, in 18.24 as the home of an impressive visiting missionary (Apollos) stretches the vista even further.

Rome, Italy		Antioch, Syria
	Ephesus, Asia	
Alexandria, Egypt		Jerusalem, Judea

(4) *Characters*. The travel texts cited above continue to portray the Pauline mission as a team effort. While Paul clearly remains the leading figure, he receives vital support from three pairs of workers: Priscilla and Aquila, Timothy and Erastus, and Gaius and Aristarchus. The last three men appear for the first time in Acts, notably expanding the company of Paul's associates. The final pair, we are told, are 'Macedonians' (19.29); thus in the course of extending help in Macedonia as requested (16.9), Paul also enlisted fellow-helpers. As for the function of Paul's co-workers in Ephesus, it is striking that all three pairs act with a measure of independence, standing in for an absent Paul in some situation. Priscilla and Aquila oversee the new mission in Ephesus while Paul is away; Timothy and Erastus check the progress of the Macedonian churches while Paul stays in Ephesus; and Gaius and Aristarchus bear the brunt of the mob's agitation against Paul's mission while the disciples restrain Paul from entering the crowd. For all his heroic stature in Acts, Paul does not stand alone.

In addition to these characters who assist Paul, other characters emerge in the Ephesian narrative who are affected by the Pauline mission in various ways. They appear in a progressive sequence based on their proximity to the Jewish-Christian gospel promoted by Paul, ranging:

(1) from a Spirit-inspired Jewish-Christian teacher very close to Paul except for a need to receive 'more accurate' instruction about Jesus (18.24-28);

(2) to a group of twelve Jewish (presumably) followers of John the baptizer who 'became believers' in Jesus but still need to be (re-) baptized in Jesus' name and blessed with the gift of the Holy Spirit (19.1-7);

(3) to a band of seven Jewish exorcists who use the name of Jesus proclaimed by Paul in their work but do so in complete ignorance (not as committed believers) with disastrous results (19.11-20);

(4) to a guild of pagan shrinemakers of the goddess Artemis far removed from the Jewish-Christian Paul and his thoroughgoing opposition to the idolatrous worship of Greco-Roman gods (19.23-41).

Having briefly described these escalating crises surrounding various characters, we now turn to explore more fully how these conflicts are resolved. Interestingly, the scenes become progressively longer as the distance from Paul's position widens; put another way: the greater the conflict with Paul, the greater the attention given to resolving it.

(1) *Apollos*. The story of Apollos quickly runs through four movements: (a) from Alexandria (b) to the synagogue in Ephesus (c) to a private meeting with Priscilla and Aquila (d) to Achaia. His Alexandrian origin fits his profile as 'a Jew...an eloquent man, well-versed in the scriptures' (18.24). Since the conquests of Alexander the Great after whom the city was named, Alexandria emerged as the leading intellectual and cultural center of the Hellenistic world (as Athens had been of the classical world), built around a massive museum and 400,000-volume library. A large Jewish community developed here, including a group of scholars who produced the Greek version of the Hebrew scriptures, known as the Septuagint (LXX). It is these scriptures which Apollos knows so well and now communicates so effectively to the Jews of Ephesus. He is also, we are told, acquainted with the baptismal mission of John and 'the things concerning Jesus', which he proclaims 'fervently in the Spirit' (*zeōn tō pneumati*), 'boldly' and 'accurately' (*akribōs*) in the Ephesian synagogue (18.25-26).

What more could we readers of Acts ask for? Apollos' connection to both John and Jesus and his Spirit-ignited boldness associate him with the early Jerusalem apostles; his intelligent and dynamic proclamation of the Christian message further links him with Stephen who previously spoke with 'wisdom and the Spirit' before an assembly of Diaspora Jews, including both Alexandrians and Asians (6.9-10); and his accurate, scripture-based teaching of 'the Way of the Lord' (18.25) in the local synagogue recalls the ministry of Paul.

Nevertheless, however impressive Apollos' credentials appear to be, there is room for improvement. At this point, Priscilla and Aquila re-enter the picture; after hearing Apollos in the synagogue, they 'take him aside' (perhaps outside the synagogue to their home, as Seim [p. 130] suggests) and 'explain the Way of God to him *more accurately* (*akribesteron*)' (18.26). Since Apollos had already been credited with teaching 'accurately', we should probably regard this new education not as correcting false ideas but as clarifying fine points. Priscilla continues to be presented before her husband (except in the patriarchal 'Western' revision), suggesting her primary role as Apollos' tutor. This is the closest we have come to encountering a woman as a minister of the Word, not a hearer only. Even here, however, we hear no direct speech from Priscilla and learn nothing specific about the content of her message.

As a newcomer to the region, Apollos also needs assistance when he decides to cross over the Aegean to minister among the Pauline congregations of Achaia. This he receives in the form of letters of recommendation from the 'brothers' (*adelphoi*—why not Priscilla?) of Ephesus. Upon arriving in Achaia, he 'greatly' bolsters the faith of the local disciples (18.27-28). This marks the first occasion that someone other than Paul or his close missionary partners nurtures a church which Paul has founded. Whatever dissension within the church or rivalry between Apollos and Paul might be created by this situation is downplayed in Acts. The overall picture of harmony and mutual support remarkably matches Paul's own perspective in 1 Corinthians:

> What then is Apollos? What is Paul? Servants through whom you came to believe, as the Lord assigned to each. I planted, Apollos watered, but God gave the growth... The one who plants and the one who waters have a common purpose, and each will receive wages according to the labor of each. For we are God's servants, working together (1 Cor. 3.5-9).

(2) *Twelve baptist disciples*. Upon returning to Ephesus, Paul first encounters 'about twelve' disciples who, like Apollos, know the baptism of John and in some sense 'believe' in Jesus whom John heralded, but unlike Apollos, know nothing of the Holy Spirit. This is a puzzling deficiency since John had clearly announced that the powerful coming Jesus Messiah would baptize his followers with the Spirit (Lk. 3.16; cf. Acts 1.4-5; 11.16). Somehow this company had missed that promise. Of course, another group of twelve disciples, Jesus' own apostles, did not always apprehend their master's teaching; in fact, they were preoccupied with other things (Israel's national interests) precisely when Jesus was declaring that the promised outpouring of the Spirit would occur 'not many days from now' (1.4-8).

While some ignorance may be overlooked, that regarding the Spirit must be remedied. As the Jerusalem apostles could not hope to continue the prophetic mission of John and Jesus without the Spirit's power, neither can the twelve Ephesian disciples. So Paul proceeds to impart the Spirit to them, whereupon they bear witness to God's grace through speaking in tongues and prophesying (19.6), as did the early disciples at Pentecost (2.1-42). As a gesture of conveyance and fellowship, Paul lays his hands on the Ephesians, as Peter and John did for the Samaritan believers who had also not received the Spirit at the moment they believed (8.14-17). In the present case, Paul also insists on (re-)baptizing the disciples in Jesus' name (they had already received John's baptism) before laying hands on them (19.3-5). This further conforms to the Samaritans' experience, except that their baptism in Jesus' name took place when they believed rather than just before they received the Spirit. Such differences in timing reinforce a sense of freedom regarding the Spirit's activity. (Remember that Cornelius and household were baptized *after* they received the Spirit! [10.44-48].) Still, on the whole, the nexus of believing in Jesus, being baptized in Jesus' name, and receiving the gift of the Spirit remain foundational for salvation and witness in Acts (cf. 2.38).

As for Paul's role in this incident, he functions as a culminator or perfecter of others' work. As Jesus came after the forerunner John (19.4) and supplemented his ministry by baptizing the twelve Jerusalem apostles with the Spirit at Pentecost (the apostles' previous knowledge of John's baptism is certified in 1.22), so Paul completes John's work by conveying the Spirit to twelve Ephesian baptist disciples. Perhaps we should also view Paul as following up on the ministry of Apollos in Ephesus. The link between Apollos and John in the foregoing scene, accentuated by the comment that Apollos 'knew *only* (*monon*) the baptism of John' (18.25), may imply Apollos' involvement with the twelve disciples, perhaps as their teacher. If so, 'while Apollos [is] in Corinth' (19.1) strengthening Paul's converts, Paul is in Ephesus advancing Apollos' students. Again it appears that, although they never meet, Apollos and Paul mutually support each other's efforts (see Spencer, *Portrait*, pp. 232-40).

(3) *Seven Jewish exorcists*. As the dynamic Jewish rhetorician, Apollos, had come to Ephesus for a time to teach about Jesus, so a company of 'itinerant Jewish exorcists', the seven sons of a high priest named Sceva, appear in the city attempting to cast out demons in Jesus' name (19.13-14). But while Apollos spoke 'accurately' about Jesus in substantial harmony with Paul's gospel, these exorcists use Jesus' name fraudulently and antithetically to Paul's purpose. In a vivid tragicomic twist, their judgment comes from one of the evil spirits they try to expel who first rebuffs them—'Jesus I know, and Paul I know; but who are you?'—and then pounces on them and *drives them out* 'naked and wounded' (19.15-16). At this point, a contrast also develops with the recent experience of the twelve baptist disciples. While they, as discussed above, submitted to the authority of Jesus' name through baptism and thereby received the outpouring of the *Holy Spirit* ('the Holy Spirit came upon them', 19.6), these exorcists misappropriate the name of Jesus and become overwhelmed by the *evil spirit* they seek to conquer ('the man with the evil spirit leaped on them', 19.16).

While counterposing the sons of Sceva with both Apollos and the disciples of John at various points, the narrative sets up a more direct and drastic contrast between the seven exorcists and Paul over their use of supernatural power. Once again the scenario pits *miracle* (Paul) against *magic* (exorcists), authentic transmission of divine power against counterfeit manipulation. Of course, the miracle-working Paul clearly emerges as the winner in this contest, as demonstrated in several ways. First and foremost, he is successful in driving out evil spirits and also curing diseases (19.11-12), whereas the seven exorcists are completely ineffectual. Moreover, the miracles are accomplished in particularly 'extraordinary' fashion by bringing garments to the afflicted which had merely touched Paul's skin. (The situation evokes memory of restoring infirm Judeans through contact with Peter's shadow [5.14-16].) Paul need not say a word or lift a finger himself to produce mighty works, while the sons of Sceva speak and act to no avail.

This passive approach to miracle-working is significant for other reasons. It certifies, most importantly, the divine source of the miracles: they are acts which '*God did...*through Paul' (19.11). It also indicates that Paul does not aggressively promote himself as a powerful figure, as magicians are prone to do (cf. Simon Magus, 8.9-10). We have heard nothing of Paul's miracle-working on his second missionary expedition until now, and here he does not initiate such activity. Such hesitancy no doubt relates to the unwelcome worship he received as a supposed god the last time he initiated a miraculous deed (healing the cripple at Lystra, 14.8-14).

Paul's passivity also extends to exposing the magician-exorcists as charlatans. As noted above, the evil spirit effectively challenges the exorcists' usurpation of Paul's authority to broker the mighty name of Jesus; Paul himself never confronts these men. Evidently his reputation is so well-established in the spirit world ('Paul I know') that he need not be present to defend it. Also Paul is not responsible in this case for the violent retaliation against the false exorcists, unlike an earlier incident in which he cursed another Jewish magician (Elymas) and inflicted him with blindness (13.10-11).

The extraordinary impact of God's dynamic work through Paul in Ephesus culminates in the public reaction to the discomfiture of the seven exorcists. News spread 'to *all (pasin)* residents of Ephesus, *both Jews and Greeks*, and fear came upon *all (pantas)* of them; and the name of the Lord Jesus [which the exorcists had profaned] was praised' (19.17). Paul's two-year teaching ministry in the hall of Tyrannus also had such a universal effect on the region: '*all (pantas)* the residents of Asia, *both Jews and Greeks*, heard the word of the Lord' (19.10). Despite typical opposition from some Jews in the synagogue (19.8-9) and the ignorance of the sons of a Jewish high priest, there is no hint in Ephesus, as in previous stations, of turning away from the Jews to the

Gentiles. For the first time in Acts the potential of global witness to *both Jews and Gentiles* is realized; 'the climax of universalism' among the people of God is reached (see Pereira).

Hearing the news of the exorcists' humiliation provokes active as well as affective responses, as many believers divulge their secret interest in the magical arts and willingly destroy their magic manuals in a public bonfire (19.18-19). Such a religious sacrifice comes at a high economic price: an estimated 'fifty thousand silver coins' worth of business based on these magic books. Earlier Simon the magician sought to invest his silver in the lucrative trick (as he perceived it) of imparting the Spirit, thereby drawing Peter's lethal judgment: 'May your silver perish with you' (8.20). The Ephesian magicians make the better choice from a Lukan perspective, giving up their profitable trade to save their lives and secure their place in the kingdom of God (cf. Lk. 9.23-24; 18.18-30).

(4) *Demetrius and the silversmiths*. Paul's disruption of the Ephesian economy, related once again to silver, continues in the case involving Demetrius and fellow artisans. Unlike the magicians, however, who willingly abandoned their enterprise to become Christian disciples, these workers create 'no little disturbance...concerning the Way' advocated by Paul on account of the 'no little business' which this Way was threatening to cut off (19.23-24). The business in question deals with the manufacture and sale of silver replicas of the temple of Artemis. One silversmith named Demetrius leads the opposition against Paul. Realizing Paul's mounting popularity in the region, Demetrius seeks both to broaden his base of support and to heighten the importance of his case. He gathers together not only other shrinemakers but also additional craftsmen from related guilds and addresses not only their financial dilemma but also the serious religious crisis confronting the worship of 'the great goddess Artemis' throughout 'all Asia' as a consequence of Paul's anti-idolatry campaign (19.25-27). Specifically, Demetrius presents his grievance as a *loss of honor* in an ascending hierarchy of values (a) from the *trade* of fashioning miniature temples of Artemis for use as votive offerings in the temple (Trebilco, pp. 336-38), (b) to the actual *temple* of Artemis itself, (c) to the supreme *goddess* Artemis herself.

(a) this *trade* of ours may come into *disrepute*...
(b) *the temple* of the great goddess Artemis will be *scorned*, and
(c) *she* will be *deprived of her majesty* that brought all Asia and the world to worship her (19.27).

By positioning himself and his co-workers as clients of the great Asian goddess Artemis and patrons of her holy sanctuary, such that their reputation is wrapped up with hers, Demetrius makes an effective 'appeal to higher loyalty', a common tactic in legal argument (see Malina and Neyrey: 'Conflict', pp. 109, 119-20). Demetrius is so persuasive that he whips his fellow tradesmen into a frenzy of rage against Paul and an outburst of praise for 'Great Artemis of the Ephesians'. In turn this commotion incites a larger mob of Ephesian citizens to rush into the public theater, dragging with them two of Paul's assistants, presumably for questioning, or even lynching (19.28-29).

Turning to consider Paul's side of the story, we notice first that neither Paul nor any other character including the narrator offers any rebuttal of Demetrius' accusation. Why should they? Although aiming to discredit Paul, Demetrius nonetheless gives a perfectly reliable report of Paul's activity. His complaint that Paul denies the reality of 'gods made with hands' (19.26) echoes Paul's own testimony before the Athenian council (17.24-29), and his calculation that 'almost the whole of Asia' has been attracted to Paul's message (19.26-27) coincides with the narrator's prior stress on the universal impact of Paul's mission (19.10, 17).

While allowing Demetrius' witness about Paul to stand without objection, the narrator cannot condone the mob action taken against Paul. One way in which he undermines such action is by a double emphasis on the crowd's 'confusion' (*sygchysis*/ *sygcheō*, 19.29, 32); these proceedings can hardly be taken seriously when most participants 'did not know why they had come together' in the first place (19.32). Beyond this external critique of the mob scene, the narrator enlists the support of two important voices within the story: the *Asiarchs*, who send a private message to Paul, and the *town clerk*, who issues a public announcement. The first group, representing 'the foremost men of the province of Asia, chosen from the wealthiest and the most aristocratic inhabitants of the province' (Taylor, p. 256), show that they are Paul's 'friends' (*philoi*) by urging him to stay away from the riotous assembly he wishes to address (his 'disciples' also hold him back) (19.30-31). Having such friends in high places further validates Paul's rising reputation in the region.

The town clerk or scribe (*grammateus*) in ancient cities like Ephesus functioned not only in a secretarial role as keeper of public records, but also in a political capacity as convener and chief spokesman of the civic assembly (Trebilco, p. 351). In the present story this official finally intervenes to control the crowd after their clamorous two-hour demonstration. Commanding their attention, he cautions the assembly against rash action against 'these men here who are neither temple robbers nor blasphemers of our goddess' and advises Demetrius and his cohorts to pursue proper judicial channels rather than the illegal course of mob violence. In short, the city clerk decrees that 'there is no cause' for the current disturbance (19.35-40). While the crowd disperses after this pronouncement and Paul appears to be vindicated (19.41), it is hard to believe that Demetrius and the silversmiths would be much satisfied with the clerk's opinion. From their perspective, by diminishing their market of miniature temples of Artemis and denouncing idol worship, Paul *was* a kind of temple robber and blasphemer of the great Asian goddess. Although the narrative comes to an end, it leaves the door open for the affronted artisans to take their case before the proconsuls in the 'open courts', as the town scribe suggests (19.38).

Before leaving the Ephesian story, we have one additional character to consider, one whose role is rather ambiguous within a portion of the riot account 'nearly as confused as the crowd's state of mind', as one commentator quips (Johnson, *Acts*, p. 349). Amid the boisterous throng in the theater, the Jews 'pushed forward' a man named *Alexander*, hitherto unknown in Acts. The crowd's initial reaction to this figure is unclear, as evidenced in the vagueness and variety of a sample of modern translations: 'some of the crowd *prompted* (RSV, NAB)//*gave/ shouted instructions to* (NRSV, NIV)//*explained the trouble to* (REB)// pressed together against* (Johnson, *Acts*, p. 345) Alexander' (19.33). In any case, Alexander proceeds to signal for the assembly to be quiet as he attempts to speak. But when they notice that he is '*a Jew*', their response becomes unequivocal: they shout him down in a united chant of praise to Artemis (19.33-34). While the anti-Jewish sentiment of the pagan mob is plain enough, the question of why the Jews suddenly enter the fray and put forward one of their own spokesmen remains unsettled. Is Alexander rising to speak in Paul's defense, representing the many Asian Jews who have heard and embraced his gospel (19.10, 17-18), or is he endeavoring to distance himself from Paul's disruptive brand of messianic Judaism (cf. 19.9)? The intriguing openness of the narrative to either possibility reminds us of the complex balance of relations between Paul and fellow Jews in the Diaspora.

Nurturing the Churches: 20.1-21.14

As Paul had 'resolved in the Spirit' in 19.21, he now sets off on a return journey through previously evangelized regions, ending up in Jerusalem. Specifically, he makes his way through Greece (Macedonia and Achaia), along the western coast of Asia Minor, across the Mediterranean to Phoenicia, down to Caesarea and finally, Jerusalem. For the most part Paul travels by sea at a steady clip, stopping only at various ports for brief visits with disciples lasting no more than a week or so (20.6; 21.4, 10). He urgently presses toward his goal, 'eager to be in Jerusalem, if possible, on the day of Pentecost' (20.16).

The very first verse of this section establishes a typical pattern of Paul's nurturing visits: he (1) sends for the disciples, (2) offers them encouragement, and finally (3) bids them farewell (20.1; cf. 20.17, 36-38; 21.4-6). Although Paul does not stay long, he packs 'much encouragement' into each visit (20.2). He converses with the believers in Troas throughout the night until dawn (20.7, 11) and delivers a lengthy parting address to Ephesian elders at Miletus in which he recalls his pattern of ceaseless 'night and day' watchcare over his followers (20.31) (see Tannehill, *Narrative*, II, p. 246). The farewell element especially colors these nurturing scenes with a somber shade, as Paul takes *final* leave of his disciples, anticipating that 'they would never see his face again' (20.25, 38). This ominous outlook arises from the sense of foreboding that 'the plots of the Jews' against Paul would thicken along the way and ultimately triumph in Jerusalem, leading to Paul's imprisonment and perhaps death (20.3, 19, 22-24; 21.11-13).

The type of advice Paul gives to the congregations and their response to it are particularly suited to the farewell scenario. In the face of impending danger and separation, Paul does not worry about himself—he is ready to be a martyr for 'the Lord Jesus' (20.24; 21.13)—but he is concerned about the security of these disciples he leaves behind. And so he urges keen vigilance through direct exhortation to the Ephesian elders ('keep watch'/ 'be alert', 20.28-31) and symbolic demonstration before the assembly in Troas (awakening Eutychus from a fatal fall caused by 'deep sleep', 20.9-12). Paul also presents important final reviews of his career for both apologetic and pastoral purposes, affirming his clear conscience and providing a character model for his followers to imitate (20.18-21, 26-27, 33-35). In return, Paul's hearers typically weep with sorrow, plead with him not to go, and join him in a farewell prayer of benediction (20.36-38; 21.5-6, 12-14). These and other common characteristics of biblical farewell scenes will be further discussed below chiefly in relation to Paul's address to the Ephesian elders (20.17-38), which functions as the centerpiece of this section.

Chronologically, Paul's farewell trek to Jerusalem is framed by two significant Jewish holy-days: 'the days of Unleavened Bread' culminating in Passover, occurring near the beginning of the journey while Paul is in Philippi (20.6), and 'the day of Pentecost' which Paul hopes to celebrate at the end of the course in Jerusalem (20.16). Apart from generally reminding us of Paul's loyalty to Jewish traditions as a means of under-cutting the Jewish opposition against him, these festival references evoke particular memories from the larger Lukan narrative. *Passover* recalls the setting of Jesus' tumultuous last week in Jerusalem leading to his arrest by Jewish authorities and eventual crucifixion (Lk. 22.1-2, 7, 15). Now during the same season, Paul, already the target of Jewish plots (Acts 20.3), heads to Jerusalem expecting to encounter increased persecution, even death. The 'passions' of Jesus and Paul are thus correlated in the closing chapters of Luke and Acts. *Pentecost*, of course, recalls the provision of the Spirit in Acts 2 to direct and empower the witness of the early church. Multiple references to the Spirit's oversight of Paul's mission appear in the present section of Acts (20.22-23, 28; 21.4, 11). Of particular interest in this material is the blatant *contradiction* of Spirit-inspired opinion concerning Paul's itinerary. Paul himself and a prophet named Agabus assume that the Spirit is driving Paul to Jerusalem (20.22; 21.11), whereas the Tyrian disciples, speaking 'through the Spirit', flatly exhort Paul 'not to go to Jerusalem' (21.4).

Complementing Paul's nurturing mission in Acts 20-21 are a number of sympathetic supporting characters, including travelling companions (seven named associates and 'we', 20.4-6), pastoral deputies (the Ephesian elders. 20.17-35), and residential hosts (Philip and daughters, 21.8-9). Two figures especially stand out as actors in dramatic demonstrations: *Eutychus*, taken up in Paul's arms after falling from a third-story window—a scene of relief and comfort (20.12); and *Agabus*, tying up his hands and feet as a sign of Paul's impending peril in Jerusalem—a scene of distress and heartbreak (21.12-13).

(1) *Back to Troas (20.1-12)*. From Ephesus, Paul heads first to Greece and then loops back across the Aegean Sea to Asia Minor for a week's sojourn in Troas. An advance party of seven named associates prepares for Paul's arrival in Troas. We have previously met three of these companions (Gaius, Aristarchus, and Timothy); the other four—Sopater, Secundus, Tychichus and Trophimus—appear for the first time. Paul's entourage continues to grow. The associates' designated places of origin—Beroea, Thessalonica, Derbe, and Asia—are all sites of Paul's earlier missionary work (20.4-5). They are obviously willing to leave their homes to follow Paul (as did Jesus' disciples, Lk. 18.28).

After the festival of Unleavened Bread and a five-day sea voyage from Philippi to Troas, Paul rejoins these seven co-workers. He is not alone on this journey, however. The anonymous 'we'-party suddenly enters the picture again at Philippi—the spot where this group was last mentioned (16.16)—and sails with Paul to Troas (20.6-7). This first-person plural narrative perspective again brings 'us' readers closer to Paul's experiences. Such intimacy will compel us to feel the emotional pangs of the forthcoming farewell scenes all the more keenly.

Also, the re-introduction of 'we' on a return trip from Philippi to Troas takes us back to this group's debut at the beginning of the second missionary expedition and invites a comparison between the two Troas incidents in 16.6-10 and 20.7-12. In the first scene, a standing man appeared in a night vision and summoned Paul to Macedonia, thus clearing up Paul's confusion about where to direct his mission. The current Troas episode also features night-time illumination, suggested by the midnight meeting lighted by 'many lamps' (20.8). On this occasion, however, Paul is the source of revelation to 'a young man named Eutychus' (among others) rather than the recipient of a call from an unnamed man from Macedonia. But far from standing to command Paul's attention, as did the Macedonian, this young man 'sits' in a upstairs window during Paul's talk, drifts off to sleep, and then tumbles out the window to the ground below (20.9). He is a model of dullness rather than perception. But Paul gives Eutychus a second chance. He comes down, revives the young man's lifeless body, and then returns upstairs to resume his discussion 'until dawn' (20.10-11). We can be assured that in these final evening hours Paul now has the full attention of Eutychus and the entire assembly.

Apart from reminding us of the previous Troas episode, this vignette also recalls earlier 'upper room' incidents. As Paul comes downstairs to resuscitate Eutychus, Peter went upstairs to raise Tabitha from the dead (9.36-43). Paul thus joins Peter as a life-giving prophet of God in the line of Jesus (Lk. 7.11-17; 8.49-56), Elijah and Elisha (1 Kgs 17.17-24; 2 Kgs 4.8-37). The Passover background (Acts 20.6) and double reference to 'breaking bread' at the opening and conclusion of the Troas scene (20.7, 11) evokes even stronger memory of Jesus' farewell meal with his disciples in 'a large room upstairs' (Lk. 22.7-23). This meal became the occasion of Jesus' final instructions to his followers before his death, exhorting them to 'remember' him in his absence (22.19) and alerting them to trials and temptations they will soon face (22.22-23, 31-38). These concerns carry over into the next scene at the Mount of Olives in which Jesus admonished his disciples to overcome impending tribulation through vigilant prayer. Unfortunately, however, while Jesus proceeded to agonize in prayer over his own fate, his disciples fell asleep. When Jesus later found them in this condition, he roused them and repeated his challenge: 'Why are you sleeping? Get up and pray that you may not come into the time of trial' (22.39-46). In Acts 20 the content of Paul's parting table talk with the Troas assembly in an upper room is not recorded, but we might well imagine similar calls to thoughtful remembrance and watchful prayer. But again sleep 'overcomes' a weak disciple, this time with fatal consequences. While the Troas community is 'not a little comforted' when Paul 'awakens' the comatose Eutychus (20.12), they must also be not a little shocked into special alertness. What will happen to them when Paul leaves? Who will be there to pick them up when they fall? They themselves must stay on guard, keeping their windows closed to outside threats and their eyes opened to the light of God's protective word.

(2) *Farewell to the Ephesians: 20.13-38.* Sailing southward around various Aegean islands off the coast of Asia Minor, Paul soon arrives at the mainland port of Miletus, where he summons the Ephesian elders for a farewell meeting (20.13-17). He deliberately stages this rendezvous outside of Ephesus for the sake of time: he cannot allow the bustling Asian capital to bog down his urgent journey to Jerusalem (20.16).

Paul's farewell address to the Ephesian leaders has a pivotal function as both *review* and *preview*, both looking back on Paul's completed work in and around Ephesus and looking ahead to the fate of Paul himself and the Ephesian church he leaves behind. The *review* dimension is most prominent in the speech, especially in the opening and closing segments (20.18-21, 33-35). In this material Paul offers a fresh, highly personal perspective on the Ephesian mission described in Acts 18-19. There the omniscient narrator provided an 'objective' report of Paul's public impact on 'all the residents of Asia, both Jews and Greeks' (19.10, 17, 26). Now this account is focalized through Paul's own 'subjective' point of view concerned chiefly with pastoral care of the Ephesian believers. Here Paul acknowledges his public witness 'to both Jews and Greeks' but also stresses more intimate instruction 'from house to house' (20.20-21).

Through repetition Paul highlights certain aspects of his exemplary character and ministerial integrity during his years among the Ephesians:

(a) His model conduct and service were displayed consistently throughout his extended stay in Ephesus—every hour of every day for three years.

> You yourselves know how I lived among you *the entire time from the first day that I set foot in Asia* (20.18).

> …remembering that *for three years I did not cease night or day* to warn everyone with tears (20.31).

This perpetual, three-year pastoral ministry complements Paul's daily, two-year formal lecturing in the hall of Tyrannus (19.9-10).

(b) Twice Paul stresses that he served the Ephesians 'with tears' (*meta dakryōn*, 20.19, 31). This image of Paul as an intense, empathetic suffering servant counterbalances the picture of an effortless, spectacular miracle-worker in 19.11-20. Perhaps the best commentary on the pastoral significance of Paul's tears comes from one of his own writings: 'I wrote you out of much distress and anguish of heart and with many tears, not to cause you pain, but to let you know the abundant love that I have for you' (2 Cor. 2.4).

(c) Twice Paul affirms that he 'did not shrink' from relating God's full message to the Ephesians:

> *I did not shrink* (*hypesteilamēn*) from doing *anything* helpful, *proclaiming* (*anangelai*) the message to you and teaching publicly and from house to house, as I testified to both Jews and Greeks about repentance toward God and faith toward our Lord Jesus (20.20-21).

> *I did not shrink* (*hypesteilamēn*) from *declaring* (*anangelai*) to you the *whole* purpose of God (20.27).

The parallel structure of these two statements identifies 'the purpose of God' as the salvific plan of leading all people to experience 'repentance toward God and faith toward our Lord Jesus'. Paul's success in challenging the Ephesians to repentance and faith was dramatically evidenced in the public disclosure of occultic practices and massive burning of magic books by many new believers in the Lord Jesus (19.17-20). The comprehensive scope ('anything'/'whole') of the Pauline message in Ephesus was illustrated in the 'more accurate' instruction supplied to Apollos and the twelve disciples of John (18.24-19.7).

(d) Paul's brief and broad reference to serving the Ephesians 'with all humility' at the beginning of his discourse (20.19) is filled out and exemplified in socioeconomic terms in his concluding remarks: 'I coveted no one's silver or gold or clothing. You know for yourselves that I worked with my own hands to support myself and my companions' (20.33-34). In short, Paul did not exploit the Ephesians for financial gain. His humble disinterest in 'silver'-based wealth sets him apart from the Ephesian magicians (19.19) and shrinemakers (19.24-27). His commitment to self-support through manual labor recalls the tentmaking work with Priscilla and Aquila in Corinth (18.1-3). It also shifts Paul's social location in Ephesus away from 'high society' ties with the Asiarchs (19.31) to more lowly links with Demetrius and fellow-artisans. Ideologically, Paul opposes the fashioners of Artemesian idols, but sociologically he compares with them as a handcraftsman ('gods made with hands' [19.26]/'I worked with my own hands' [20.34]).

As was typical of ancient farewell addresses (see Kurz, *Farewell*, pp. 16-51; Neyrey, *Passion*, pp. 6-8, 43-48), Paul reviews the past not only to set the record straight concerning his conduct, but also to set himself up as a model for his successors to emulate. As he passes on the reins of leadership to the Ephesian elders, he charges them with the duty of carrying on his merciful ministry: 'In all this I have given you an example that by such work we must support the weak' (20.35a). In this way they will follow not only Paul's pattern but also Jesus' motto of service: 'It is more blessed to give than to receive' (20.35b). These precise words never appear on the lips of the Lukan Jesus, but they aptly resonate with his teaching and practice throughout the Gospel, including his own farewell challenge to the disciples matching his own model of sacrificial service: 'the greatest among you must become like the youngest, and the leader like one who serves... But I am among you as one who serves' (Lk. 22.26-27).

The *preview* elements of Paul's parting speech focus on the imminent dangers facing both Paul and the Ephesian church. Rhetorically, these elements are introduced by attention-grabbing transitions—'and now, behold' (*kai nyn idou*) or just 'and now' (*kai nyn*)—and/or the emphatic form of 'I know' (*egō oida*).

(a) '*And now, behold*, as a captive to the Spirit, I am on my way to Jerusalem, not *knowing* what will happen to me there, except that the Holy Spirit testifies to me in every city that imprisonments and persecutions are waiting for me' (20.22-23). Paul's expectation of encountering trials 'in every city' en route to Jerusalem demonstrates that he has become fully aware of 'how much he must suffer' for Jesus' sake (cf. 9.15). This knowledge does not make Paul despondent, however; he still shows signs of hope and confidence. While he anticipates hardship in Jerusalem, he does *not* yet know his complete fate there. Who knows? Perhaps God will again move to his rescue and provide fresh opportunities for witness. In any case, Paul need not fret over impending imprisonments at the hands of human authorities, since his life and ministry are already 'captive' to a higher authority. Dedicated to serving Jesus as Lord (20.19, 21) and 'bound (*dedemenos*) to the Spirit' (20.22; contrast his former 'binding' [*deō*] of believers: 9.2, 14, 21), Paul is wholly consumed with 'finishing the course' which Jesus and the Spirit have laid out for him (20.24).

(b) '*And now, behold, I know* that none of you, among whom I have gone about proclaiming the kingdom, will ever see my face again' (20.25). While Paul does not know exactly how his troublesome venture to Jerusalem will turn out, he does know that this meeting marks the end of his proclamation and presence among the Ephesian church. This sense of finality infuses tremendous pathos into the encounter, culminating in the elders' emotional display of grief before Paul's departure (20.36-38). Their tears (and hugs and kisses) of concern and affection for Paul reciprocate his tears for them throughout his ministry (20.19, 31).

(c) '*I know* that after I have gone, savage wolves will come in among you, not sparing the flock. Some even from your own group will come distorting the truth in order to entice the disciples to follow them' (20.29-30). In the absence of Paul's protective care, he expects that callous opportunists will endeavor to infiltrate the Ephesian church to promote their own agendas, including some 'wolves' in sheep's clothing already in their midst! The prospect of betrayal and apostasy within the believing community has been with us since the closing chapters of Luke and the beginning of Acts, sparked by the tragic cases of Judas, Ananias and Sapphira, and even Peter (temporarily). We should be watchful and wary, but it is easy to become complacent again and let down our guard. And so the narrative brings us back to a state of alert as Paul exhorts the elders to 'keep watch over *yourselves* [as well as] over all the flock' (20.28), just as Jesus roused his drowsy followers on the Mount of Olives and demanded that they prayerfully poise themselves against temptation (Lk. 22.40, 46).

(d) '*And now* I commend you to God and to the message of his grace, a message that is able to build you up...' (20.32). While Paul charges the Ephesian leaders with the future care of the church in his absence, he ultimately places his trust in the nurturing power of God's grace. God will watch over the elders as they watch over the flock. The community, leaders and people together, constitute 'the church of God', purchased at the heavy cost of 'the blood of his own Son' (20.28). God thus has a vested interest in the church's security. Various parallels emerge with the Lukan passion narrative (Neyrey, *Passion*, pp. 43-48): in his farewell supper and address to the disciples, Jesus assured them of their fellowship with God in 'the new covenant' soon to be sealed with Jesus' blood (Lk. 22.20); in addition to imploring his disciples to watch and pray for their own safety, Jesus emphasized that he had already prayed for their perseverance as well (22.31-32)—thus effectively committing them to God's sustaining grace; finally, in his dying breath, Jesus 'commended' (*paratithemai*) his own spirit into God's hands (23.46), just as Paul now 'commends' (*paratithemai*) the threatened Ephesians to God's care.

(3) *On to Jerusalem: 21.1-14.* We leave Miletus in a high state of tension, expecting Paul to begin to face the turmoil 'in every city', as he forecast through the Spirit. However, no such persecution erupts in Paul's next two major stops—at Tyre and Caesarea—before reaching Jerusalem. Still, suspense is maintained through emotional farewell scenes with local believers (21.3-6, 13-14) and another Spirit-inspired prediction of Paul's imprisonment in Jerusalem, this time via the itinerant Judean prophet, Agabus (21.10-12).

This section features a notable shift in itinerary, as Paul visits congregations in Tyre (Phoenicia) and Caesarea which he did not establish. Both areas were initially evangelized by Hellenist missionaries driven from Jerusalem in the wave of persecution surrounding Stephen: an anonymous group in the case of Phoenicia (11.19) and Philip the evangelist in the case of Caesarea (8.1-4, 40). Actually, while Paul cannot be directly credited with starting these churches, he was indirectly instrumental in their foundation, for, of course, *it was he who spearheaded the persecution which propelled the witnesses out of Jerusalem* (8.1-3; 9.1-2). How ironic to see Paul now so warmly received in these communities—even in the home of Stephen's close associate, Philip the evangelist! (21.8-14)—as he himself presses *toward* the persecution awaiting him in Jerusalem. This Paul (Saul) who had previously terrorized Christian disciples by:

(a)   'entering house after house,
(b)   dragging off both men and women... [and]
(c)   commit[ting] them to prison' (8.3)

is now

(a)   graciously welcomed in Christian households (21.4-14),
(b)   embraced by husbands and wives (21.5-6), fathers and daughters (21.8-9), and
(c)   himself under threat of imprisonment in Jerusalem (21.11) (see Spencer, *Portrait*, pp. 258-60).

Further links with previous mission reports are established through the figure of *Agabus*. During Paul's early ministry in Syrian Antioch, Agabus came down from Jerusalem and forecast through the Spirit the onset of a terrible global famine. Consequently, the Antiochene church dispatched Barnabas and Paul to Judea with a charitable offering to help the needy believers survive the coming crisis (11.27-30). Presently, Agabus comes to Caesarea and makes another ominous prediction inspired by the Spirit. However, now the prophecy focuses on Paul's individual fate as a captive in Jerusalem, dramatically punctuated by Agabus' pantomime of fettering his hands and feet with Paul's belt. As a result, the local assembly begs Paul *not* to go to Jerusalem. He determines to go anyway, ready to die in the holy city if necessary (21.10-13). After Agabus' previous prophecy, Paul proceeded on a mercy mission to Jerusalem to provide life-saving material aid to the believing community; now he sets out on a martyr's march to Jerusalem prepared to surrender his life to hostile authorities. This striking change in fortune raises questions concerning the development of Paul's relations with the Jerusalem *church*, which we must consider below. How will the Jerusalem disciples treat him when he returns and comes under attack from unbelieving Jews? Will they remember his earlier beneficence? Will they stick up for him? shelter him? shun him?

The role of Agabus in the present narrative may be further explored in terms of functional gaps with two other prophetic groups. Most immediately, we notice a *vocal* gap with Philip's 'four unmarried daughters who had the gift of prophecy' (21.9). While it seems that we have finally found the prophetic daughters we have been looking for since Peter's Pentecost speech (2.17), they in fact appear as little more than window dressing in the scene set in their home. The visiting male prophet, Agabus, comes in and takes center stage with his dramatic verbal and visual display, while the resident daughters remain silent in the background.

Secondly, we confront a glaring *interpretive* gap with the Spirit-inspired Tyrian disciples. Speaking as the Spirit's mouthpiece, Agabus announces Paul's tragic destiny in Jerusalem (21.11). In the preceding scene in Tyre, however, the believers—also speaking 'through the Spirit'—clearly advised Paul '*not* to go on to Jerusalem' (21.4). To go or not to go: which is the Spirit's will? Prior testimony from the narrator and Paul himself support Agabus' understanding of the Spirit's Jerusalem-oriented plan (19.21; 20.22-23), but the 'we'-party and Caesarean disciples gathered in Philip's home follow the Tyrians in urging Paul to cancel his visit to Jerusalem (21.12). While this latter group does not explicitly speak through the Spirit, their host is a well-known Spirit-guided preacher and table-servant, as the description—'Philip the evangelist, one of the seven'—directly recalls (21.8; cf. 6.3, 5; 8.29. 39). Discerning the Spirit's will is not an easy task, especially when emotions churn over the prospects of human suffering and separation from loved ones (see Shepherd: 235-38; Tannehill, *Narrative*, II, pp. 262-67). The Lukan Jesus wrestled mightily with God over whether he must accept the martyr's 'cup' in Jerusalem, ultimately settling the issue by surrendering to God's purpose, whatever that might be: 'not my will but yours be done' (Lk. 22.42-44). Paul's distraught friends finally come to grips with his perilous fate in Jerusalem in the same way: 'The Lord's will be done' (21.14).

Evaluation in Jerusalem: 21.15-36

Paul's visit to Jerusalem unfolds in three stages of interaction with different groups: (1) Mnason and the brothers (21.15-17); (2) James and the elders (21.18-26); and (3) the Asian Jews and the crowd (21.27-36). Paul's reception among these groups stationed in different locales progressively cools from (1) an initally 'warm welcome' in Mnason's home, to (2) a more cautious, official meeting with church leaders at an unspecified site (James' residence?), and finally to (3) a hostile assault in the temple compound, prompting the closing of the temple doors and the binding of Paul by Roman authorities (as Agabus had predicted). In short, Paul's course in Jerusalem runs between the poles of open house and shut temple.

The conflict which develops in the last two stages concerns Paul's alleged opposition to 'our people, our law, and this place' (21.28). In other words, the *social* ('our people') and *spatial* ('this place') implications of Paul's stance on the Jewish 'law' are brought into question. The *social* issue, concerning the function of the Mosaic law as a boundary marker between Jews and Gentiles in the Diaspora, preoccupies Paul's encounter with James and the elders. The *spatial* issue, focusing on the temple as the sacred center of Jewish faith and practice where the law is most perfectly enacted, dominates Paul's final clash with the Asian Jews in Jerusalem.

As Paul is thrust into these trying situations, he suddenly stands alone. The 'we'-party that accompanies Paul into Jerusalem drops out of the picture in 21.19 and does not reappear as Paul's crisis deepens. The Asian Jews 'supposed' that Paul had brought Trophimus the Ephesian into the temple because they had earlier seen the two men together in the city, but Trophimus is nowhere to be found when the mob attacks Paul and drags him out of the temple (21.29). Like Jesus, whose disciples followed only 'at a distance' during his ordeal of trial and crucifixion (Lk. 22.54; 23.49), Paul is apparently left to face his persecution by himself (see Kurz, *Reading*, pp. 120-21).

(1) *Mnason and the brothers: 21.15-17.* Representatives of the Caesarean congregation accompany Paul and associates into Jerusalem and lead them to the home of a Cypriot named Mnason, identified as 'an early (*archaiō*) disciple' (21.16). Here 'the brothers' gladly receive the Pauline party with open arms (21.17). Mnason's ties with both Cyprus and the primitive Jerusalem church remind us of Barnabas (4.36) and the first Hellenist missionaries to Greeks and Jews in Antioch (11.20). Just like Mnason and the brothers in the present context, these early Cypriot believers welcomed and encouraged Paul (Saul) in the face of other disciples' suspicious response and the outright hostility of certain unbelieving Hellenistic Jews in Jerusalem (9.26-30; 11.20-26).

(2) *James and the elders: 21.18-26.* The next day Paul encounters a more mixed reception with James and the leaders of the Jerusalem

church. On the one hand, they 'praise God' for Paul's detailed report of his missionary expeditions among the Gentiles and address him as 'brother' (21.19-20). This congeniality is overshadowed, however, by their serious concerns over the repercussions of Paul's alleged dealings with Diaspora Jews among the 'many thousands' of Jewish Christians who remain 'zealous for the law' (21.20). They demand that Paul clear his reputation and demonstrate his solidarity among these zealots by participating in and paying for the completion of a purity vow taken by four members of the church (21.23-24). Paul dutifully and promptly ('the next day') complies with their wishes (21.26).

The summary note that Paul 'related one by one' all of his previous missionary exploits and the specific presentation of various characters, decisions, and issues which we have encountered before in Acts invite us to pause and reflect back over the mission story and where it has brought us.

(a) The 'myriads' (*myriades*) of Jewish believers recall the 'three thousand' respondents at Pentecost (2.41) and the 'five thousand' additional believers in Jerusalem not long thereafter (4.4; cf. 6.7). On those occasions, emphasis was placed on their strong devotion to the apostolic 'word' (*logos*), with no mention of their zeal for the Jewish 'law' (*nomos*). (Such commitment was simply assumed.) This legal issue now comes to the fore in Acts 21 because of sweeping changes in the expanding messianic mission since its beginnings in Jerusalem. Throughout the Greco-Roman world, scores of Gentile converts ignorant of the Mosaic law, at best, or prejudiced against it, at worst, have been incorporated into believing communities alongside Jews, thus creating a perceived threat to Jewish identity.

(b) Problems surrounding Jewish-Gentile relations in the Pauline churches were also tackled by James and the elders in a previous Jerusalem conference in Acts 15. There it was decided unanimously that a letter be dispatched to all the churches stipulating that the Gentiles should not be unduly 'burdened' with the Mosaic law, except for keeping a few basic purity regulations as a measure of goodwill toward Jewish believers (15.22-29). In Acts 21, James and associates now refer to this same letter, but they refer only to the restrictive legislation imposed on the Gentiles without the balancing concern to protect the Gentiles' freedom (21.29). Moreover, they inform Paul of this letter *as if he is hearing about it for the first time* and assume full credit for its circulation ('*we* have sent a letter with *our* judgment'), with no acknowledgement of Paul's contribution to this effort clearly reported in 16.4. This rhetoric conveys a mounting mistrust of Paul on the part of conservative Jewish Christians. From their perspective, Paul has not adequately enforced among his Gentile churches the fundamental taboos agreed upon at the first Jerusalem conference; it is as if he had forgotten or disregarded the decision as soon as he heard it.

(c) More than this, the Jewish believers now fear that Paul has taken his commitment to Gentile freedom even further by encouraging *Jews* to abandon the practice of circumcision and other signs of their covenantal heritage, much as certain 'renegade' Jews endeavored to assimilate their compatriots to Greek customs in the period leading to the Maccabean revolt (cf. 1 Macc. 1.10-15, 41-63). Nothing, however, in the preceding mission narratives substantiates this conclusion. Indeed, in the opening verses of ch. 16 immediately following the account of the Jerusalem conference, we recall not only Paul's dissemination of the assembly's decision 'from town to town' (16.4) but also his *circumcision* of a new associate, Timothy, the son of a Jewish mother and Greek father—'because of the Jews who were in those places' (16.3). Obviously, a gap exists between the narrator's earlier report of Paul's sensitivity to the Jews and the 'reading' of this evidence by certain Jewish Christians in Jerusalem.

(d) In a move to bridge this gap, James steps in once again with a diplomatic solution. This time, however, rather than resorting to a *textual* (letter) solution with its attendant risks of mishandling both in terms of delivery and interpretation, James proposes a *ritual* (Nazirite) confirmation of Paul's loyalty to the Jewish law (21.23-24, 26). As interpreters of Paul well know, letters can be 'hard to understand' (2 Pet. 3.16); actions often speak louder and clearer than words. Paul's participation in a purity vow culminating in a hair-cutting ceremony echoes his earlier action in Cenchrea prior to another visit to Jerusalem (18.18-23). Again we note that Paul is having a hard time convincing the Jerusalem church of his faithfulness to Jewish traditions. One purity display is not enough; he must repeat it and, beyond that, pay the expenses for four other devotees (21.24). Previously, Paul conveyed the voluntary gifts of the Antioch church to the poor disciples in Judea as a gesture of benevolent patronage (11.29-30). Now Paul again uses money to strengthen ties with the Jerusalem church, but from a very different position. James and the elders virtually order Paul ('do what we tell you', 21.23) to pay the Nazirite fees, treating him more like their servant than their patron.

(3) *The Asian Jews and the crowd: 21.27-36.* As Paul and the four men fulfill their vow in the temple, the focus suddenly shifts away from the interests of local Jewish Christians to the attacks of unbelieving Asian Jews against Paul. These antagonists seize and accuse Paul of 'defil[ing] this holy place': most immediately, by bringing Greeks into the temple's inner courts, and more broadly, by 'teaching everyone everywhere' against the fundamentals of Jewish religion and society (21.27-28). Before Paul utters a word of defense, support for these charges already appears quite flimsy. Paul's association with the Gentile Trophimus was witnessed 'in the city' (21.29), not in the temple, and the only ones he has brought into the temple are the four devout Jews whom he is helping complete a rite of *purification*. Paul says or does

nothing in the present scene that even hints of temple defilement.

The involvement of Asian Jews connects back to Paul's Ephesian mission in chs. 18–20 and, before that, to Stephen's Jerusalem crisis in chs. 6–7. Paul referred summarily in his Miletus speech to 'the plots of the Jews' against him in Asia (20.19), and the Ephesian narrative reported slanderous opposition to Paul's message from some members of the city's synagogue (19.8-9). But, as we emphasized above, a number of Asian Jews also joined with Greeks in *welcoming* Paul's teaching (19.10, 17-20). Moreover, while Paul clearly undermined the status of the pagan temple in Ephesus devoted to Artemis (19.26-27), he did not, as far as we are told, ever denounce the holy temple in Jerusalem to Asian Jews. (The critique of human-made sanctuaries in 17.24 was also directed to an idolatrous Greek [Athenian] audience.)

Stephen's situation was both similar and different. Like Paul, he was prosecuted in Jerusalem by Jewish immigrants from Asia (and other parts of the Diaspora) for allegedly inveighing against 'this holy place and the law' (6.9-13). Unlike Paul's case, however, there seems to be something to these allegations, especially pertaining to Stephen's views on the Solomonic temple (7.44-50). In any event, it is difficult to imagine the radical Stephen being terribly concerned about temple purity or making concessions to Jewish traditionalists.

Paul appears to be headed toward the same tragic end which befell Stephen, as a mob erupts in response to the calumnies of the Asian Jews, drags Paul out of the temple, and proceeds to beat him to death. He is rescued, however, by a military squad of 'centurions and soldiers' led by a 'tribune' or 'chiliarch' (*chiliarchos*), a high-ranking Roman officer with a cohort of a thousand troops at his disposal (21.30-32). (By striking contrast, neither James nor any other of the 'many thousands' of Jewish believers, nor any of Paul's travelling companions come to his aid.) The tribune has Paul arrested and bound in order to protect him from the crowd and to ascertain the causes of the disturbance (21.33). The prophecy of Agabus is fulfilled, but with a significant amendment. The Jews do not 'hand him [Paul] over to the Gentiles' (21.11). Rather, the Gentiles (Romans) wrest him from the riotous Jews; in fact, the soldiers literally have to carry Paul away because 'the violence of the mob was so great' (21.35).

We have become accustomed by now to mob action against Paul which is quickly resolved in some fashion, enabling Paul to continue on his way. But the white-hot intensity of the present uproar, requiring the intervention of a tribune's cohort, makes us wonder how much further Paul can go. The persisting shouts of 'Away with him!' (21.36) eerily echo the Jerusalem crowd's pleas regarding Jesus, which the Roman governor eventually granted (Lk. 23.18-25). Paul's premonitions about 'finishing his course' seem to be coming to pass.

Acts 21.37-28.15: Prisoner's Progress

Any hopes of Paul's speedy release steadily erode over the final chapters of Acts: he remains a confined prisoner throughout the balance of the story. Yet Paul is by no means defeated, and the mission story of Acts does not end as a terrible tragedy (although there are tragic dimensions, especially concerning Jewish response). Despite his limitations as a prisoner, Paul continues to bear witness to the gospel—finally speaking this word before 'kings' and other high officials, as anticipated in his original commission (9.15; 'King Agrippa', 26.2)—and to save lives and work miraculous cures (27.21-28.10). Although bound in chains, Paul still makes notable *progress* in advancing the Christian mission.

The element of 'progress' in these closing prison narratives may also be charted geographically. While not free to move around as he pleases, Paul the prisoner still remains on the move, journeying from one trial venue to another, presenting his case before progressively higher courts of appeal. Specifically, the route of Paul's trials leads westward through three capital cities: (1) the Jewish religious capital in *Jerusalem* before a general assembly and then the high priest's (Ananias) council; (2) the Roman provincial capital in *Caesarea* before governors (Felix and Festus) and a client-king (Herod Agrippa); and (3) the imperial capital in *Rome* anticipating a hearing before Caesar.

As for the *pace* of these narratives, we detect in the Jerusalem segment (chs. 22-23) a fairly close correspondence between 'discourse time' (how long it takes to relate the account) and 'story time' (how long the events in the story are presumed to transpire) (see Powell, *What Is Narrative?*, pp. 36-39); we receive a detailed, day-by-day report of two trials, a plot against Paul's life, and the transfer to Caesarea (note: 'the next day' [22.30]; 'that night' [23.11]; 'in the morning' [23.12]; 'during the night' [23.31]; 'the next day' [23.32]). In the following segments, however, a greater gap opens between the two temporal perspectives. While discourse time covering three trials remains roughly the same in the Caesarean section (chs. 24-26), story time now extends over several days ('five days later' [24.1]; 'some days later' [24.24]; 'three days after' [25.1]; 'eight or ten days' [25.6]; 'after several days' [25.13]) up to and beyond a period of 'two years', mentioned in a brief summary statement, in which 'Felix left Paul in prison' (24.27). Similarly, the voyage to Rome narrated over chs. 27-28 spans several months of story time ('fourteenth night/day' [27.27, 33]; 'three months later' [28.11]; 'seven days' [28.14]), and Paul's stay in Rome under house arrest, recounted in a comparatively brief report at the end of Acts, is said to stretch over 'two whole years' (28.30). In sum, while we become aware that Paul remained a prisoner for several years, we are not encouraged to dwell on the fact. In no sense does Paul appear to languish in prison. Quite the contrary: the brisk discourse time in which Paul repeatedly speaks and acts with authority creates an overall impression of continuing urgency and dynamism in mission. Far from winding down and stumbling to the end of his course, Paul presses on vigorously to the finish line (cf. Phil. 3.12-14).

The type of material featured in Acts 21–28 alternates between *defense-speeches* before various audiences and judges and *travel-narratives* charting perilous journeys between trial centers:

1. Paul's Defense before the Jerusalem Crowd: 21.37–22.29
2. Paul's Defense before the Jerusalem Council: 22.30–23.10
3. *Perilous Journey from Jerusalem to Caesarea: 23.11-35*
4. Paul's Defense before Felix: 24.1-27
5. Paul's Defense before Festus: 25.1-27
6. Paul's Defense before Agrippa: 26.1-32
7. *Perilous Journey from Caesarea to Rome: 27.1–28.14*

A number of redundant elements tie the *defense-speeches* together, revolving around an evaluation of the *charges* levelled against Paul and the evidence of his exemplary *character* offered in his defense: in other words—'who he was [*character*] and what he had done [*charges*]' (21.33). When the tribune first arrested Paul in the temple compound, he was unable to ascertain the charges brought against Paul amid the confusing shouts coming from the uproarious mob (21.34; cf. the Ephesian riot: 19.29, 32). This uncertainty from the Roman side concerning 'what Paul was being accused of by the Jews' (22.30) continues throughout the trial reports, culminating in Festus's frank admission before sending Paul on to Caesar: 'I have nothing definite to write to our sovereign about him [Paul]…for it seems to me unreasonable to send a prisoner without indicating the charges against him' (25.25-27). Obviously, the Jewish leaders do not present their case against Paul in a clear and persuasive way. They do manage to convey their general annoyance with Paul as 'a pestilent fellow' with unorthodox views concerning the Jewish religion (24.5-9; 25.19), but they offer no hard evidence to the Roman officials of any crimes meriting imprisonment or death. Three times we hear the same verdict:

> *Tribune Claudius Lysias*: 'I found that he was accused concerning questions of their law, but was charged with nothing deserving death or imprisonment' (23.29).

> *Governor Festus*: 'I found that he had done nothing deserving death' (25.25; cf. 25.18-20).

King Agrippa: 'This man is doing nothing to deserve death or imprisonment' (26.30).

In responding to his accusers, Paul flatly denies that he has done anything to undermine the Jewish law or temple (22.3, 17; 24.10-18; 25.8; 26.3-5). But surprisingly, he also shifts the focus again and again to another charge which the Jewish antagonists had not even raised and which Paul, far from denying, fully accepts as the core of his faith: 'I am on trial concerning the hope of *the resurrection of the dead*' (23.6; 24.15, 20-21; 25.19; 26.6-8, 23). Not since his debate with the Athenian philosophers has Paul brought up the topic of the resurrection (17.31-32). Why raise the issue now? As a ploy, perhaps, to deflect attention away from the more pressing question of his transgressing sacred legal and cultic boundaries? Or because in fact he regards his proclamation of the resurrection as the more fundamental dividing point with the Jewish authorities, as it was for the early apostles (cf. 4.1-12; 5.27-33)?

Beyond addressing specific charges, Paul devotes most of his defense to certifying the high caliber of his overall character. Twice he rehearses his dramatic 'heavenly vision' on the road to Damascus as evidence of divine control over his life and ministry (22.3-21; 26.2-29): 'The God of our ancestors has chosen [me] to know his will' (22.14); 'To this day I have had help from God, and so I stand here, testifying to both small and great' (26.22). He thus offers an 'alternative retrospective interpretation' of his career and appeals to a higher authority (God) to neutralize his accusers' claims (cf. Malina and Neyrey, 'Conflict', pp. 108-10, 117-20). Also, following the norms of a 'dyadic' or 'group-oriented' culture in which reputation was strongly tied to the status of the places one came from and the people one associated with (Malina and Neyrey, 'First-Century Personality'), Paul emphasizes his dual citizenship in the 'important' Greek city of his birth, Tarsus (21.39; 22.3), and in the imperial capital of Rome (22.25-29), his upbringing in Jerusalem 'at the feet of Gamaliel' (22.3; 26.4), his affiliation with the Pharisees, 'the strictest sect of our religion' (26.5; 23.6-10), and with 'the Way' (24.14). Before King Agrippa, Paul further defends the integrity of his mission with a well-known spatial image: 'this was not done in a corner' (26.26). By this picture, as Malherbe ('"Not in a Corner"') has shown, Paul claims not simply to have spread his message throughout the Greco-Roman world but to have become engaged in public life as a responsible moral philosopher-teacher. Far from 'worming' his way around 'in a filthy corner', as Celsus would later vilify the activity of Jews and Christians alike (*Against Celsus* 4.23), Paul's noble deeds were open to the light of societal scrutiny.

The two *travel-narratives* also parallel each other in key respects. Both recount Paul's movement from one judicial station to another under a cloud of danger. First, Paul is transferred from Jerusalem to

Caesarea under the threat of violent ambush from Jewish conspirators (23.12-35; cf. 25.1-3). In the second journey, a sea voyage from Caesarea to Rome, Paul's life is again in jeopardy, this time from the natural forces of tempest and viper (27.13–28.6). Dramatic tension is heightened in both crises through the motif of prolonged fasting. In the first scenario, the conspirators bind themselves in solemn 'oath neither to eat nor drink until they kill him [Paul]' (23.12, 14, 21); in the second, the beleaguered sailors are forced to throw the ship's provisions overboard and go without food for fourteen days (27.18-21, 33).

Most importantly, Paul safely makes it through both hazardous treks with the aid of sympathetic characters, both major and minor. Chief assistance comes through a night visitation from God himself or an angel of God:

> That night the Lord stood near him and said, 'Keep up your courage! For just as you have testified for me in Jerusalem, so you must (*dei*) bear witness also in Rome' (23.11).

> For last night there stood by me an angel of the God to whom I belong and whom I worship, and he said, 'Do not be afraid, Paul; you must (*dei*) stand before the emperor; and indeed, God has granted safety to all those who are sailing with you.' So keep up your courage... (27.23-25).

These closely parallel passages establish a vital positive framework for interpreting Paul's final course in Acts as a prisoner. Through his arrest, bondage, multiple trials, and perilous journeys, a higher purpose is at work—the very purpose of God—driving Paul to testify before Caesar in Rome. Nothing can deter the fulfillment of the sovereign divine will: the gospel 'must' (*dei*) extend, if not to the end of the earth, at least to the heart of global power in the known Mediterranean world.

Paul is also supported in both dangerous trips by anonymous family and friends: a nephew warns Paul of the Jewish assassination plot against him (23.16-22), and a group of friends in Sidon 'care for' Paul's material needs en route to Rome (27.3). These intimates have only limited power, however, to save Paul's life. A greater protective role is played by the named Roman officials superintending the prisoner's transfers. In the first case, the tribune *Claudius Lysias* learns of the planned attack from Paul's nephew, marshalls a large military escort, writes a sympathetic letter introducing Paul to the governor, and brings Paul safely to Caesarea (23.18-35; cf. 21.37-40; 22.22-30). In the second instance, a centurion named *Julius*, attached to the Augustan Cohort, 'treat[s] Paul kindly', not only by permitting him to receive help from his friends in Sidon, but also by preventing his soldiers from killing Paul and the other prisoners after the shipwreck at Malta (27.1, 3, 42-44).

This impression of official Roman support for Paul needs to be balanced, however. As a character group, the Roman authorities—including tribune, centurions, governors, and client-king—are more 'dynamic' ('round') than 'static' ('flat') in their treatment of Paul the prisoner (see Powell, *What Is Narrative?*, pp. 54-55). The military officers may thwart plots against Paul's life, but they do not set him free; their task is to deliver Paul alive *as a prisoner* to his next trial. Moreover, at one point the tribune orders Paul to be 'examined by flogging'; only Paul's timely reminder of his Roman citizenship keeps this from happening (22.22-29). Like Julius the centurion, Felix the governor allows Paul to 'have some liberty' and be ministered to by friends, but he also toys with Paul, talking often with him in hopes of eliciting a bribe and leaving him in prison for two years to appease his Jewish opponents (24.23, 26-7). Likewise, the succeeding governor Festus, while convinced that Paul 'had done nothing deserving death' (25.25), also courts Jewish favor by suggesting that Paul be tried back in Jerusalem (25.9) and later labels Paul and his testimony as 'insane' (26.24). Finally, the identity as well as judgment of King Agrippa further demonstrates the ambiguity of official response to Paul the prisoner. While a Roman appointee, Agrippa is also 'King of the Jews' in the Herodian line, 'especially familiar with all the customs and controversies of the Jews' (26.2-3). This profile might lead us to expect him to be violently opposed to Paul and the Christian mission (cf. 12.1-6, 18-19), but in fact, as well as echoing verdicts of Paul's innocence (26.30-31), Agrippa expresses a surprising receptivity to Paul's gospel. Or maybe not. His response to Paul—'Are you so quickly persuading me to become a Christian?' (26.28)—can be taken either way: as an honest admission of dawning interest in Paul's message or as a mocking dismissal of Paul's presumption.

While Paul fulfills God's will and advances Christ's mission as a Roman prisoner in the closing chapters of Acts, this 'progress' does not come easily. Roman officials smooth the way a little but scarcely go out of their way to accommodate Paul. The honor which Paul attains in the eyes of various overseers remains—as always in a competitive, limited-good society—a precarious commodity which can be lost as easily as won (see Tannehill, review of Lentz, pp. 218-19). Paul must proceed with cunning and caution as well as confidence in God's protective care.

Trials in Jerusalem: 21.37-23.10

Paul defends his case in Jerusalem in two stages: first, on the steps of the prison barracks before the popular assembly agitated by Asian Jews (21.37-22.29) and, then, before a formal meeting of the entire high-priestly council (22.30-23.10). Here Paul follows a similar trial course to that of Stephen (6.9-7.1), whom he expressly remembers in the present section as 'your [the Lord's] witness (*martys*)' (22.20). Although Paul's two defense speeches vary in length and content, the first sets the stage for the second in several ways: (1) the mention of Gamaliel's tutelage (22.3) prepares us for Paul's identification with the Pharisees (23.6-9); (2) stress on Paul's strict upbringing 'according to the law' (22.3; cf. v. 12) lays the foundation for specific legal disputes (23.2-5); (3) recollection of the testimony of 'the high priest and the whole council of elders' concerning Paul's former business in Jerusalem (22.4-5) estabishes a shrewd connection with this same council whom he appears before next (22.30–23.2); and, finally (4) the crowd's violent reaction to Paul's witness, requiring the tribune to intervene (again) on his behalf (22.22-24; cf. 21.31-34), previews the similar outcome of Paul's defense before the Jerusalem council (23.10).

Paul's Defense before the Jerusalem Crowd: 21.37-22.29

The extended public defense speech at the heart of this segment (22.1-21) is framed by brief exchanges between Paul and the Roman tribune—the first dealing with Paul's request to speak (21.37-40), the last with the crowd's reaction to the address (22.22-29)—and both featuring significant disclosures of Paul's citizenship status (21.39; 22.25-29). This entire narrative-discourse unit focuses on establishing Paul's Greek, Jewish and Roman credentials as a model witness and citizen on the basis of his associations with exemplary places and people. However, since two of those with whom Paul aligns himself are executed criminals (Jesus and Stephen), his standard of noble character obviously does not always fit conventional norms.

	Places	*People*
(1)	Tarsus	*not* 'the Egyptian'
(2)	Jerusalem	Gamaliel
		High Priest and Council
(3)	Damascus	Jesus the Nazorean
		Ananias
(4)	Jerusalem	Isaiah the prophet
		Stephen the martyr
(5)	Rome	Tribune

(1) *Tarsus: 21.37-40.* Paul first reveals his Greek heritage. When he asks for permission to speak, the tribune registers with some surprise that Paul knows the Greek language and then concludes that Paul must not be (as he had apparently hypothesized) 'the Egyptian' who had recently led a revolt in the area (21.37-38). As John Lentz notes, identifying Paul as a native Egyptian would have been regarded as 'an immense social slur' (p. 29), given this people's stereotypical notoriety in the first century as uncivilized, uneducated barbarians (cf. Strabo, *Geog.* 17.1.12; Philo, *On Dreams* 1.240). Josephus reports that the Romans denied all

citizenship privileges everywhere to Egyptians (*Against Apion* 2.41) (cf. Lentz, pp. 28-30). If Egyptians in general had a bad name, how much more a rabble-rousing captain of 'four thousand assassins' (21.38). The tribune's speculation that Paul might have been this dangerous rebel confirms the size and severity of the tumult surrounding him.

Beyond displaying his ability to speak Greek and dissociating himself from the Egyptian, Paul also declares his standing as a Greek citizen of Tarsus in Cilicia (21.39). Paul's Tarsian roots have already been established in Acts (9.11, 30; 11.25), but this is the first time we learn of his citizenship status there. Such a position commands considerable respect because of Tarsus's reputation as 'no insignificant city', as Paul claims (21.39). The ancient geographer Strabo especially touted Tarsus as an intellectual center nonpareil in the Greco-Roman world:

> The people at Tarsus have devoted themselves so eagerly, not only to philosophy, but also to the whole round of education in general, that they have surpassed Athens, Alexandria, or any other place that can be named where there have been schools and lectures of philosophers... Further, the city of Tarsus has all kinds of schools of rhetoric, and in general it not only has a flourishing population but also is most powerful, thus keeping up the reputation of the mother city (*Geog.* 14.5.12-15; cited in Lentz, p. 31).

Coming from such a place clearly commends Paul's right to speak in his own defense, as the tribune acknowledges.

(2) *Jerusalem: 21.40–22.5.* Paul deftly shifts from appealing to his Roman captor to addressing the Jewish assembly. He switches from speaking Greek to 'the Hebrew language' (Aramaic, 21.40; 22.2) and from stressing his Diaspora origins (which he mentions in passing) to highlighting his traditional upbringing in Jerusalem (22.3-5). Establishing rapport with the audience and presenting one's 'manner of life' as evidence of being a worthy witness were typical features of the opening gambits of forensic defense speeches, as outlined in ancient rhetorical handbooks (see Neyrey, 'Forensic', pp. 210-13).

Paul particularly calls attention to his rigorous education 'according to our ancestral law' under Gamaliel and his zealous persecution of 'this Way' under the auspices of the high priestly council. These connections with Gamaliel and the council evoke memories of the trials of Peter and the Jerusalem apostles in Acts 4–5. Unlike the 'uneducated and ordinary' apostles, however, who both annoyed and amazed the Jewish leaders with their bold witness concerning the risen Jesus (4.1-2, 13), Paul appears as a highly educated man instructed by Gamaliel, a Pharisaic 'teacher of the law, respected by all the people' (5.34). We may also recall that Gamaliel was the member of the council who argued for tolerance in the apostles' case, suggesting that God's judgment concerning the Christian movement would be revealed in due course and warning that if this movement 'is of God', no one can stop it (5.35-39). As it happened, no one proved Gamaliel more right than his zealous student, Paul. No one tried to destroy the church more aggressively or futilely than Paul (with the high priest's backing). And nothing demonstrated God's indomitable purpose to spread the gospel to the ends of the earth more dramatically than Paul's conversion and commission, which he narrates next in his defense speech.

(3) *Damascus: 22.6-16.* While recapitulating the basic plot of his life-changing trek to Damascus reported in ch. 9, Paul adds some interesting new information appropriate to the present situation. For example, he elaborates on the identities of the two figures who ministered to him: Jesus and Ananias. He labels *Jesus*, who appeared and spoke to him on the Damascus road, as 'the Nazorean' (*ho nazōraios*, 22.8) and 'the Righteous One' (*ho dikaios*, 22.14). While neither title occurred in the Acts 9 narrative, both emerged in the testimonies of Peter and Stephen concerning Jesus' rejection and crucifixion by Jewish authorities (2.22; 3.14; 4.10; 6.14; 7.52). In one case Stephen was accused of proclaiming that 'Jesus the Nazorean will destroy this place and will change the customs that Moses handed on' (6.14); such an iconoclastic association with 'the Nazorean' would not seem to be in Paul's best interest in his current defense against charges of subverting the Jewish law and temple. On the other hand, if 'Nazorean' represents more than an alternative spelling for 'Nazarene' (*nazarēnos*)—that is, someone from Nazareth—it may connote something of Jesus' extreme consecration to God, like that of a 'Nazirite' (see Johnson, *Gospel*, p. 284; *Acts*, p. 411). ('Righteous One' carries a similar accent on holiness.) This connection would be more suited to reinforcing the point that Paul had entered the Jerusalem temple not to defile it but to fulfill a Nazirite-purity vow (cf. 21.23-28).

Whatever the meaning of 'Nazorean', Paul clearly shapes the description of *Ananias* to appeal to traditional Jewish opinion: 'Ananias...was a devout man according to the law and well spoken of by all the Jews living there' (22.12). Moreover, beyond the account in ch. 9, Paul announces that Ananias instructed him to 'have [his] sins washed away' through baptism in Jesus' name (22.16). Paul's fellowship with Jesus and his followers intensified rather than diminished his commitment to purity.

At several points, Paul's version of his Damascus road experience deviates from the narrator's earlier account to highlight even more the *visual* dimension of the encounter with the risen Jesus.

(a) Paul notes the time of the heavenly vision as 'about noon' (22.6), the brightest part of the day.

(b) He describes the celestial light which shone around him as 'great' (22.6) and specifies what ch. 9 only implied, that he 'could not see because of the brightness of that light' (22.11).

(c) He inverts his companions' experience of the event: the narrator recounted earlier that 'they heard the voice but saw no one' (9.7), whereas Paul reports that 'they saw the light but did not hear the voice' (22.9).

(d) He doubly stresses the divine commission, relayed by Ananias, that he bear witness to what he has 'seen and heard' (notice the order) concerning Jesus (22.14-15).

While Paul's detractors might quibble over the meaning and significance of words he claims to have heard, it is more difficult to argue against a brilliant heavenly vision he claims to have seen in the presence of other witnesses. Furthermore, beyond the immediate context, the fact that Paul *saw* rather than merely heard about the risen and glorified Jesus confirms his authority as a messianic witness on a par with the apostles (cf. 1.3, 22; 4.20).

(4) *Jerusalem: 22.17-21.* Wisely skipping over his troubles with hostile Jews in Damascus (cf. 9.23-25), Paul moves on to discuss his return to Jerusalem. Here he does acknowledge facing opposition which drove him out of the city, but he presents it in a totally new setting from that described in 9.26-30. Paul now reports that Jesus appeared to him in another vision while he was praying in the temple (22.17) and directed him to 'get out' and 'go away':

> *Get out* of Jerusalem quickly, because they will not accept your testimony about me (22.18).
> *Go*, for I will send you *far away* to the Gentiles (22.21).

Alongside the Damascus-road Christophany, this second experience creates a 'double vision' effect strengthening Paul's testimony. Its setting further demonstrates Paul's dedication to the temple: he came to this place to pray, not stir up trouble. Also, it was here that Paul received his commission to preach to the Gentiles (not in Damascus, as in 9.15). So instead of bringing Gentiles into the temple illegally, as his accusers contend, Paul took the gospel directly to the Gentiles 'far away' from the temple.

Through this report of his visionary call, Paul becomes aligned with two earlier embattled messengers of the Lord: the prophet Isaiah (implicitly) and 'your witness Stephen' (explicitly). *Isaiah* also received a temple vision through which he was 'sent' to preach (Isa. 6.1-9). As he responded with a confession of inadequacy (6.5) and learned that his own people of Judah would resist his message (6.9-13), so Paul doubted his fitness as the Lord's spokesman and learned that the people of Jerusalem would spurn his testimony (Acts 22.18-20). Paul's self-doubt particularly concerned his former career as a persecutor of Christians, including his oversight of the execution of *Stephen*. His admission of 'blood'-guilt over Stephen's death and acknowledgement of Stephen's authority as the Lord's 'witness' (22.20) further solidifies Paul's remarkable reversal, not to mention the fact that he now finds himself in

Stephen's position, pleading his case before a bloodthirsty mob in Jerusalem angry over his supposed denigration of the Jewish law and temple.

(5) *Rome: 22.22-29.* While much of Paul's speech, as we have seen, has bolstered his reputation as a faithful, law-abiding and temple-honoring Jew, his commendation of Stephen and legitimation of his Gentile mission support a more radical image. Accordingly, at this point the assembly interrupts Paul's defense and begins to clamor again for his death (22.22). They punctuate their shouts of condemnation with dismissive gestures of casting off their cloaks and pitching dust (22.23), roughly equivalent, as Lake and Cadbury (p. 282) suggest, to modern shaming tactics of mudslinging or kicking dust on an errant umpire in American baseball.

The tribune leads Paul away from the violent mob once again. But this provides little immediate comfort for Paul, since the tribune orders him to be interrogated by the brutal method of flogging (probably the scourge or *flagellum*; see Bruce, p. 420) (22.24). In this predicament, Paul's Jewish heritage is negligible; so he now appeals to his protective rights as a citizen of *Rome* (22.25-28), as he did in Philippi (16.37-38). We learn for the first time that his Roman as well as his Greek (Tarsian) citizenship was inherited from birth, much to the surprise and dismay of the tribune who had purchased his own citizenship at a heavy price (22.27-29). As a citizen Paul outranks the tribune: his 'ascribed' honor by virtue of kinship ties is greater and more secure than the tribune's 'acquired' honor dependent on the patronage of bureaucrats he had bribed (cf. Malina and Neyrey, 'Honor', pp. 27-29). No wonder that those about to administer the flogging 'immediately' recoil from Paul and the tribune becomes 'afraid' and shifts the burden of examination onto the Jewish council (22.29-30).

Paul's Defense before the Jerusalem Council: 22.30-23.10

Paul begins his address to 'the chief priests and the entire council' with a similar emphasis on the integrity of his manner of life displayed in the previous section (22.30-23.1). The verb he uses (*politeuomai*) particularly continues the idea of 'living as a (good) citizen' (cf. *politēs*, 21.39; *politeia*, 22.28; Johnson, *Acts*, p. 396). Before he can expound this theme, however, Paul is rudely interrupted, forcing him to change his tactics. He goes on the offensive, switching from defendant and apologist to prosecutor and proclaimer, from forensic witness to his own character to heraldic witness to the truth of scripture (23.5) and 'the hope of the resurrection' (23.6). Moreover, Paul's testimony here is notable as much for how he presents it as what he says. He appears as a highly 'resourceful witness', as Robert Tannehill describes him—

perhaps too sympathetically. Less adoring readers might well characterize elements of Paul's rhetoric as volatile, sarcastic, disingenuous and manipulative. In any case, one can scarcely help but admire Paul's gritty performance. Certainly 'Paul the prisoner is not a passive victim' (Tannehill, *Narrative*, II, p. 291).

Paul's witness before the council unfolds in two stages: first dealing with the high priest, Ananias (23.2-5), and then targeting the parties of the Sadducees and Pharisees (23.6-10). In the process Paul takes a 'divide and conquer' approach, effectively writing off the high priest and the Sadducees and reaching out to the Pharisees—his fellow-Pharisees—as we now learn (23.6).

(1) *Before the High Priest, Ananias.* With no explanation, Ananias orders that Paul be struck on the mouth almost as soon as he opens it with a declaration of his 'clear conscience before God' (23.1-2). Paul promptly retaliates with a rhetorical attack in the form of a physical curse—'God will strike you, you whitewashed wall'—and a legal objection—'Are you sitting there to judge me according to the law, and yet in violation of the law you order me to be struck?' (23.3-5). Such a volatile response stands in contrast with Jesus' more restrained bearing before the priestly court (Lk. 22.63-71; cf. Jn 18.22-23) but echoes Stephen's diatribe at the end of his speech (7.51-53), especially at the point of exposing the court's disregard for the law which it should be upholding (7.53; 23.3; Johnson, *Acts*, p. 397). Denouncing the high priest as a 'whitewashed wall', who attempts to mask internal corruption with outward, theatrical displays of piety and authority, comes closer to sounding like Jesus in his sharp 'woes' against Pharisaic hypocrisy (Lk. 11.37-44; cf. Mt. 23.27-28—'you are like whitewashed tombs') as well as Ezekiel's critique of false prophets of his day ('when the people build a wall, these prophets smear whitewash on it', Ezek. 13.10-16).

Paul's direct challenge to the high priest's honor through name-calling and charging him with breaking the law draws a riposte from bystanders questioning Paul's own honor: 'Do you dare to insult God's high priest' (23.4). In other words: 'Do you dare be so shameless as to demean the very honor of God by mocking God's highest representative?' Paul then appears to back down from his challenge, claiming ignorance of Ananias' position as high priest and affirming the scriptural injunction against reviling a leader of God's people (23.5; cf. Exod. 22.28). It is difficult, however, to take Paul's apology with full seriousness: how could he not recognize the high priest in a council setting where one would expect just such an official to be presiding? Perhaps Paul is just trying to save face by pretending that he did not really know what he was doing. Or, more in keeping with Paul's bold rhetoric, perhaps he speaks with sarcastic intent, suggesting that the high priest's whitewashed demeanor has rendered him effectively 'unrecognizable' as a faithful and true leader of God's people (Cassidy, pp. 62-65; Johnson, *Acts*, p. 397).

(2) *Before the Sadducees and Pharisees*. Keenly perceiving the presence of both Sadducees and Pharisees in the council (again, if he 'noticed' this, how could he have missed the high priest?), Paul identifies himself as a Pharisee by birth and belief. We began to suspect his Pharisaic connections by way of his teacher, Gamaliel, mentioned in the previous speech. Now Paul explicitly declares that he was born 'a son of Pharisees' (as surely as he was born a son of a Tarsian and Roman citizen) and is on trial because he shares a cardinal Pharisaic belief 'concerning hope and resurrection of the dead'—which the Sadducees happen to deny (23.6, 8; cf. Lk. 20.27-40). Paul achieves two things by this strategy. First, more than simply diverting attention away from himself by dividing council-members against each other, he gains an important group of allies within the council ('certain scribes of the Pharisees') who staunchly defend his innocence ('we find nothing wrong with this man') against the powerful Saducean party associated with the priestly hierarchy (23.9; cf. 4.1; 5.17).

Secondly, following the convention of forensic defense speeches to define 'the main question' or subject of debate (part of the *narratio* or 'statement of facts' segment), Paul refocuses his examination away from questions concerning law and temple to the issue of resurrection (see Neyrey, 'Forensic', pp. 213-16; Tannehill, *Narrative*, II, pp. 285-92). This change of subject represents more than just a ploy to disrupt the proceedings and split the council. Witnessing to the resurrection is no game for Paul. In the recent rehearsal of his conversion and call, Paul made it clear that proclaiming the risen Jesus whom he has seen and heard marks the core of his mission (22.6-21; cf. 13.29-37; 17.3, 31). Now he formally announces this resurrection testimony as the crux of his trial: this is the word he must continue to preach and for which he must be judged. Still, however serious Paul is about defending his faith in Jesus, he also proceeds with caution and cunning in the present setting. He does not single out Jesus by name but only refers in a general sense to 'the resurrection of the dead (*nekrōn* [plural])'. This allows some of the Pharisees, who might otherwise be alienated by Paul's christological convictions, to support his position and even grant the possibility that 'a spirit or an angel' might have spoken to him (23.6, 9). If they concede this much, the door at least remains open to their becoming believers in the risen Jesus, as other Pharisees in Jerusalem had done (cf. 15.5).

Whatever advantage Paul might have gained among certain Pharisees is eventually lost, however, amid the escalating conflict over Paul's case within the council. Tensions run so high, in fact, that the tribune begins to fear for Paul's life once again and so orders his soldiers to escort the prisoner back to the fortress (23.10).

Trek from Jerusalem to Caesarea: 23.11-35

During the night in prison after his appeal to the Jerusalem council, Paul receives another special visitation from the Lord (23.11). Dramatic visions continue to shape Paul's career as they have since his fateful trip to Damascus (cf. 9.1-19; 16.6-10; 22.6-21). Here the Lord delivers a revealing command and promise. The command to 'keep up your courage' acknowledges Paul's recent troubles in Jerusalem but also implies that more danger lies ahead. Whatever hardship he must endure, however, Paul may rest assured that just as he has testified in Jerusalem, so he 'must bear witness also in Rome'. Paul's status as a prisoner will not deter his continuing mission to spread the gospel beyond Jerusalem to the ends of the earth.

The prophetic vision begins to be realized the very next morning as Paul becomes the target of yet another murderous plot which necessitates his transfer out of Jerusalem to Caesarea, one step closer to Rome. The threat to Paul's life comes from a group of more than forty Jewish conspirators who vow 'neither to eat nor drink until they have killed Paul'. The story calls particular attention to this oath by repeating it three times: first in the narrator's introduction (23.12-13) and then in the reports of the conspirators themselves (23.14) and of Paul's nephew who got wind of the plot (23.21). The element of fasting is strikingly ironic in this context in comparison with previous examples in Acts surrounding Paul. Paul 'neither ate nor drank' for three days after his life-changing vision of Jesus which ended his vicious campaign against the church and launched his career as a Christian missionary (9.9, 19); and later the fasting and praying congregation at Antioch sent Paul out on his first extended missionary expedition (13.2-3). Now, by contrast, instead of defusing persecution and promoting Paul's mission, the Jewish plotters dedicate themselves through fasting to terminating Paul's life and ministry by violent means. Such abuse of the ritual of fasting is reminiscent of that denounced by Third Isaiah: instead of utilizing fasting for sacrificial and compassionate ends, as the Lord desires, 'you serve your own interest on your fast day, and oppress all your workers...you fast only to quarrel and to fight and to strike with a wicked fist' (Isa. 58.3-10).

Other elements pertaining to the plot against Paul's life may be discovered as we follow the course of the narrative structured around three sets of communication between various characters:

(1) Hatching the Plot: The Jewish Conspirators' Proposal to the Chief Priests and Elders

(2) Exposing the Plot: A Young Man's Report to the Roman Tribune

(3)   Preventing the Plot: The Roman Tribune's Letter to Governor Felix.

Hatching the Plot
The Jewish Conspirators' Proposal to the Chief Priests and Elders: 23.14-15

No doubt frustrated by the sympathy of some council-members for Paul and the failure of the council at large to reach a condemnatory verdict, a group of vigilantes seek to manipulate the council and to take justice into their own hands. They go directly to the hierarchy of 'chief priests and elders' (23.14)—who were also prejudiced against Paul (cf. 23.1-5)—and propose that they summon Paul to another council session under the pretext of 'mak[ing] a more thorough (*akribesteron*) examination of his case'. While Paul is en route from the barracks to the court, the conspirators plan 'to do away with him' (23.15).

Again we detect a touch of satirical irony. Jewish aggravation with Paul supposedly centered on his laxness toward the law (21.28; 23.4). Here, however, Paul's opponents make a mockery of the legal system by feigning a commitment to 'stricter' (*akribesteron*) judgment so they might lynch Paul without due process. Such a plan moves beyond striking Paul on the mouth to striking him dead, thus representing an even more egregious 'violation of the law' by those sworn to uphold it (cf. 23.2-3). Its hypocrisy also stands in marked contrast to Paul's sincere witness to his own 'strict' (*akribeian*) education under Gamaliel 'according to our ancestral law' (22.3).

Exposing the Plot
A Young Man's Report to the Roman Tribune: 23.16-22

At this point of extreme threat to the prisoner Paul, we might expect the liberating intervention of another mighty angel or earthquake (cf. 5.18-20; 12.6-11; 16.25-27); but we find instead that assistance comes from a very ordinary human being through very ordinary means. An unnamed 'young man', 'the son of Paul's sister', hears about the scheduled ambush and then relays this information first to Paul and then, at Paul's request, to the Roman tribune (23.16-18). Unlike another 'young man' (Eutychus) who failed to pay attention and consequently required life-saving aid from Paul (20.9-12), this youth shows keen alertness which is instrumental in sparing Paul's life.

In the Pauline letters, we learn of valued colleagues such as Epaphroditus (Phil. 2.25-30) and Onesiphorus (2 Tim. 1.16-18) who ministered to Paul's needs in prison. But in the present situation in Acts, Paul the prisoner seems to have been abandoned by his missionary associates—including the 'we'-party—who came with him to Jerusalem. Only this young nephew, hitherto unknown in the story, comes to Paul's aid. The fact that he is a relative of Paul from his sister's family in

Jerusalem validates Paul's earlier witness to being brought up and schooled in the holy city (22.3).

Despite his youth, anonymity and apparent lack of special social status, Paul's nephew surprisingly enjoys a certain intimacy and assumes a certain authority with the high-ranking Roman tribune. When a centurion (an important official in his own right) brings the young man in, the tribune draws him aside 'by the hand' for a close, private hearing (23.19). The informant then candidly confronts the tribune with his unwitting role in the treacherous plot—as the one proposed to bring Paul out into the open—and with his clear duty to thwart the conspirators' scheme: 'do not be persuaded by them'. What happens now, the young man concludes, is up to the tribune: 'They are ready now and are waiting for your consent' (23.19-21). After receiving this challenge, the tribune dismisses Paul's nephew with orders to 'tell no one that you have informed me of this' (23.22). This intriguing, secretive liaison between a bold youth and a powerful official enhances the story's popular appeal and heightens dramatic tension. We wait on the edge of our seats to see if the tribune will spring into action, at a lad's behest, to save our hero.

Preventing the Plot
The Roman Tribune's Letter to Governor Felix: 23.17-35

We need not wait long. The sense of excitement and 'high adventure', in the mode of ancient Jewish and Greek romances, only intensifies as the tribune promptly arranges a clandestine transfer of the imperiled prisoner to Caesarea (see Pervo, *Profit*, pp. 32-34). An imposing military detail of 'two hundred soldiers, seventy horsemen, and two hundred spearmen'—about half the force under the tribune's command and twelve times larger than the band of forty terrorists—usher Paul under the cover of darkness to Antipatris, and from there, out of harm's way, only the horsemen (all seventy of them!) escort Paul to the governor in Caesarea (23.23-24, 31-35). These lavish measures to protect Paul's life stir our imagination, even as they stretch our credulity, and enhance Paul's profile as a heroic figure worthy of the utmost attention. As Richard Pervo (*Profit*, pp. 32-33) puts it:

> 'Operation Paul' was a bold move, Jerusalem could have gone up in smoke. It required 470 men and two days to rescue Paul from the hands of his co-religionists. Numerous contradictions and improbabilities aside, this tale is a rousing success... While enjoying the excitement, the reader is assured, not for either the first or the last time, that Paul is a VIP.

Paul's importance is also documented in an official letter from the tribune Claudius Lysias (the first mention of his name) to the governor Felix in Caesarea (23.26-30). In this report, Lysias stresses Paul's status as a Roman citizen and for the first time formally declares his opinion of Paul's innocence of any serious crimes meriting death or imprisonment (23.27, 29). Of course, he also presents himself in the best possible light, conveniently omitting any reference to his initial ignorance of Paul's Roman citizenship and his illegal arrangement of Paul's flogging (cf. 22.24-29). In fact he revises the story completely, claiming that he first rescued Paul from a violent Jewish mob precisely because he knew that Paul was a Roman citizen (23.27). We must not romantically transform every official who helps Paul or other missionaries into a devout Christian disciple. Lysias is not Cornelius. His interest in Paul is political not spiritual, running only as far as his self-interest demands.

Trials in Caesarea: 24.1-26.32

Following his appeals to two Jewish assemblies in Jerusalem—an ad hoc gathering of angry citizens and an official meeting of the supreme court—Paul now appears before three powerful individual rulers in Caesarea with strong Roman connections: two successive provincial governors of Judea, Felix and Festus, and an appointed 'king of the Jews', Agrippa. However, Paul is not done yet with hostile Jerusalem Jews. The high priest brings his case against Paul, along with a new prosecuting attorney (Tertullus), to Felix in Caesarea (24.1-9), and conspirators try to enlist Festus's aid in implementing another assassination plot against Paul (25.1-9). While previous business from Jerusalem carries over to Caesarea, the prospect of new opportunity in Rome also arises, as Paul registers a formal appeal to the emperor's tribunal (25.10-12, 21; 26.32). The Caesarean section thus marks a pivotal stage in the progress of Paul the prisoner from Jerusalem to Rome.

The first and third trials (chs. 24, 26) closely parallel each other in terms of structure and perspective. Each begins with the customary courting of the judge's favor through flattery (*captatio benevolentiae*) followed by an alternating pattern of narration and declaration in Paul's defense speech. The *narration* offers another look back at significant past experiences—surrounding either his recent conflict in the temple or his more remote upbringing in Jerusalem and conversion on the Damascus road—while the *declaration* reaffirms Paul's vital hope in the resurrection.

Paul's Trial before Felix: Acts 24

Introduction:	flattering the judge (24.2-4 [Tertullus]; 24.10 [Paul])
Narration:	review of temple incident (24.11-13)
Declaration:	hope of resurrection (24.15-16)
Narration:	review of temple incident (24.17-20)
Declaration:	hope of resurrection (24.21)

Paul's Trial before Agrippa: Acts 26
> Introduction: flattering the judge (26.2-3)
> Narration: review of Jerusalem upbringing (26.4-5)
> Declaration: hope of resurrection (26.6-8)
> Narration: review of conversion/call (26.9-21)
> Declaration: hope of resurrection (26.22-23)

The middle trial (Acts 25) differs from the two surrounding it in terms of the brevity of Paul's defense speech and its orientation forward to Rome rather than backward to Jerusalem or Damascus (25.8-11). Also, Paul makes no mention here of resurrection. In contrast both to Paul's concise testimony in the present hearing and to the brief responses of Felix and Agrippa in the other trials, Governor Festus offers an extended evaluation of Paul's case (25.13-27). As for the substance of their verdicts, after Felix's deliberate procrastination in making a decision (24.22, 25-27), Festus and Agrippa both agree on Paul's innocence, from the standpoint of Roman law, and the superfluity of his appeal to Caesar (25.25-27; 26.30-32). Indeed, as Agrippa tells Festus (with the latter's apparent approval) at the end of this section: 'This man could have been set free if he had not appealed to the emperor' (26.32).

Paul's Trial before Felix: 24.1-27

After reading the letter sent by Lysias and learning of Paul's roots in Cilicia, Felix is impressed enough with the prisoner to grant him a hearing. Protocol demands, however, that he wait for Paul's accusers to arrive (23.33-35). As it happens, this is the first of these final trials in which a prosecutor formally brings charges against Paul before an official magistrate. It also marks the first time that Paul's defense speech does not provoke a violent outburst from the audience. As Lysias intended, changing the venue of Paul's trial to Caesarea brings much-needed peace and order to the proceedings.

(1) *Tertullus's Accusation (24.1-9)*. Having failed to convict Paul in Jerusalem, the high priest and other Jewish leaders enlist a skilled rhetorician (*rhētor*) named Tertullus as a special advocate for their case. Following established conventions of legal argument, Tertullus counterpoints a litany of the judge's noble attributes and achievements with the defendant's dishonorable traits and deeds. He addresses the governor with the lofty title of 'Excellency', as Lysias did in the letter (23.26), extols his virtues of 'foresight' and 'graciousness', and credits him with forging lasting peace and launching salutary reforms within the Jewish nation (24.2-4). While flattering the judge was expected in forensic speeches, Tertullus seems to stretch the limits of credibility here. To put it mildly, not every first-century Judean 'in every way and everywhere' (24.3) was quietly and gratefully at rest during Felix's reign. Josephus characterized this period as one of ceaseless unrest by revolutionaries—

such as the 'dagger-men' (*sicarii*) and Egyptian prophet (for whom Paul had earlier been mistaken [21.28])—on the brink of war (*War* 2.252-70).

From lauding Felix as a peacemaker and reformer among the Jews, Tertullus turns to branding Paul as a disturber of the peace 'throughout the world' and a defiler of the temple in Jerusalem (24.5-6). He thus makes Paul out to be a serious threat to the security of the Roman empire as well as to the sanctity of Judaism's central institution. Suddenly much more is at stake than trifling internal quibbles about the Jewish law. In fact, Paul's inclusion among the Jewish people is called into question by the charge that he is 'a ringleader of the sect of the Nazoreans' (24.5). While 'sect' (*hairesis*) can refer to an established Jewish 'party' or 'group', such as the Sadducees or Pharisees (5.17; 15.5), it can also have a more pejorative, divisive connotation of 'heretical sect' or 'faction', as seems to be the case here (BAGD, pp. 23-24). In Tertullus's mind, the Nazoreans are not a traditional group of Nazarite-purists but rather a radical band of dissidents on the fringes of Judaism, perhaps associated with Jesus' native village of *Nazareth* or with a messianic movement which identified Jesus as the promised Davidic 'shoot' (Hebrew: *nezer*) in Isa. 11.1 (cf. Johnson, *Gospel*, p. 284). In any case, as the ringleader of this faction, Paul must now be regarded as a renegade from the honorable Pharisees.

(2) *Paul's Defense: 24.10-21.* Paul's opening *captatio* is much more restrained than that of Tertullus, simply acknowledging that Felix has governed the Jewish people 'for many years' (24.10). Why this fact should predispose Paul to present his defense 'cheerfully' is not clear; perhaps he anticipates receiving a fairer hearing because of Felix's long experience in dealing with Jewish affairs. As sketched above, Paul's speech alternates between *narrative reviews* of his recent ordeal in Jerusalem and *declarative statements* of his hope in the resurrection.

First he stresses that he came to Jerusalem 'to worship', not to engage in debate or to stir up trouble. In fact, he claims to have initiated no disputes with anyone either in the temple, or 'in the synagogues and throughout the city' (24.12). The type of worship which Paul practiced focused on (a) serving 'the God of our ancestors' revealed in the Jewish scriptures (24.14) and (b) offering 'alms to my nation' and sacrifices in the temple (24.17). This confession of Paul's faithfulness to 'ancestral' tradition echoes previous testimony in 22.3. In the present case, however, he attributes this devotion not to his education under Gamaliel, but to his association with 'the Way, which they call a sect' (24.14). Paul thus denies being involved with a heretical movement, as Tertullus had charged, changing the attorney's sectarian label of 'Nazoreans' to the less divisive 'Way'. This designation, according to Ernst Haenchen,

> describes the new religion of Jesus as an entity in itself and yet does not divorce it from Judaism: indeed it is strongly reminiscent of such

OT expressions as 'the ways of the Lord', which represented Judaism as the beloved true religion (p. 658).

The testimony about almsgiving in the temple introduces a new element into Paul's final Jerusalem visit. The initial story reported Paul's payment of fees for four members of the Jerusalem church to complete their purity vows, but nothing was said about presenting alms to the needy. Offering charitable gifts is more reminiscent of Paul's earlier mission of famine relief, except that such ministry was directed exclusively to the Christian communities in Judea (11.27-30). Now Paul professes an active concern for the material welfare of the entire Jewish nation (*ethnos*) which he still owns as '*my* nation'. Paul also reaffirms his personal commitment to ritual holiness centered in the temple, noting that he (no mention is made of the other four participants) was 'completing the rite of purification' in the sanctuary when his accusers found him (24.18).

In short, Paul claims to have done nothing out of the ordinary to provoke a disturbance in the temple. Thus, within the narrative world of Acts, there is much less reason for Paul's recent arrest than for Peter and John's arrest in the early chapters. This latter pair, we may recall, in lieu of giving alms to a lame beggar at the temple gate, empowered this man to walk and leap through the temple compound in the name of Jesus— thus creating a considerable stir among the crowd and eventually the judicial authorities (3.1-4.22). Paul, by contrast, gave alms to the poor, worked no miracles and bore no witness in Jesus' name on his final temple visit. By all accounts, he was an exemplary worshipper, a model of decorum and devotion.

In declaring his resurrection hope Paul clarifies the identity of 'the dead' destined to be raised. The scope still remains quite broad, however, with no particular focus on the resurrection of Jesus. Paul simply expresses the dualistic notion 'that there will be a resurrection of both the righteous and the unrighteous' (24.15), without singling out the risen Jesus as 'the Righteous One', as he did before the Jerusalem crowd (22.14). By sticking with a general hope in resurrection, Paul can maintain an affinity with some of his accusers ('a hope that they themselves also accept', 24.15; cf. 23.8-9). By implying a destiny of eschatological reckoning for both the righteous and unrighteous, Paul reinforces his belief in God's retributive justice according to the standards of the law (cf. 22.3-5; 23.3-5).

(3) *Felix's Verdict: 24.22-27*. At first our hopes are raised that Felix might render a favorable decision in Paul's case. We learn that the governor is 'rather well informed about the Way' and is prepared to give a verdict when Lysias the tribune arrives. In the meantime, he allows the prisoner to have a measure of freedom and the nurture of friends. He also invites Paul to speak to him again concerning the Way, this time in the company of his Jewish wife, Drusilla (24.22-24). Being married to

such a woman suggests that Felix is also quite knowledgeable of Jewish affairs. Perhaps, then, he will see through the chicanery of Tertullus's argument against Paul. On the other hand, we cannot be certain that Felix cares that much about upholding the Jewish law for Drusilla's sake, since, according to Josephus, he wooed her away from an existing husband, thus causing her 'to transgress the laws of her forefathers' through adultery (*Ant*. 20.141-43).

Any hopes we might have had for Paul's release are soon dashed, as Felix shows his true colors. Whatever knowledge and fairness he might appear to have are overwhelmed by fear, greed, and political expedience, all of which prompt the governor to keep Paul in custody for two years. Felix first becomes anxious over Paul's opening address. Paul changes tack from shrewdly defending his honor as a devout Jew to boldly proclaiming the gospel; in other words, he switches from apologist to prophet. Specifically, he presents Felix and Drusilla with both a doctrinal message 'concerning faith in Christ Jesus' and an ethical challenge concerning matters of 'justice, self-control, and the coming judgment'. Upon hearing these words, Felix 'bec[omes] frightened' and dismisses Paul until a more 'opportune' occasion for further discussion arises (24.24-25). We are not told precisely what scares Felix here, but we may surmise that he feels threatened in some way—perhaps because he *lacked* the virtues of justice and self-control (cf. Tacitus, *Hist*. 5.9)— by the forthcoming judgment which Paul announces.

The governor is not so threatened, however, as to have Paul severely punished or banished forever from his presence. Paul is too valuable to Felix for such harsh treatment. Likely assuming from Paul's earlier testimony concerning almsgiving that he was a man of some means, Felix keeps sending for Paul in the hopes of receiving a generous bribe (24.26). Paul may not have had to buy his citizenship, as Lysias did (cf. 22.27-28), but he is being required to buy the governor's patronage as he bought, in a sense, the favor of James and other church leaders by paying the expenses of the four Nazirites. In this case, however, the price is evidently too high; although frequently entertained by Felix, Paul never bargains for his release, as far as we are told. And so he remains in prison for an extended period.

While frustrated in his greed, Felix tries to exploit Paul in another way. By keeping Paul in custody up to the end of his rule and passing the case on to his successor, Felix aims to ingratiate himself with the Jewish leaders (24.27). Just as they need him to enforce certain judgments, so Felix needs the Jewish authorities to help maintain order in Judea and give favorable reports of his administration to the emperor. (Josephus notes that Felix in fact suffered from *negative* evaluations of his rule brought to Nero by influential Caesarean Jews [*Ant*. 20.182].) Paul the prisoner functions as a dispensable pawn in this political chess match.

Paul's Trial before Festus: 25.1-27

The political maneuvering and favor-mongering at Paul's expense continues with the change in administration. Three days after Porcius Festus replaces Felix as provincial governor, the Jewish leaders petition for Paul's transfer back to Jerusalem 'as a favor to them'. Behind this appeal lies an ulterior motive of arranging another ambush to murder Paul (25.1-3). While careful to assert his ultimate authority over the proceedings (25.4-5), Festus also 'wish[es] to do the Jews a favor'. Thus, after hearing charges against Paul in Caesarea, Festus proposes to conduct the formal trial back in Jerusalem (25.9).

Paul disrupts these plans, however, with a power play of his own. While his fate seems to be cycling back to Jerusalem at the will of manipulative chief priests and a provincial magistrate, he propels his destiny forward to Rome by appealing to the highest earthly ruler of the day, the emperor himself (25.10-11). The matter is taken out of Festus's hands; he has no choice but to extradite Paul to 'his Imperial Majesty' (25.12, 21, 25). Still, Festus politically exploits the situation further before sending Paul on to Rome. When the prominent Herodian king Agrippa and his sister Bernice come to Caesarea 'to welcome Festus' to his new office, the governor reciprocates this tribute by seeking Agrippa's counsel concerning Paul's case. Festus also takes the opportunity of the king's arrival to highlight his exemplary handling of Paul's examination according to standard Roman legal procedure (25.13-27).

(1) *The Jewish Leaders' Plot: 25.1-5.* This plot against Paul's life follows the basic pattern of the previous scheme in 23.12-15: Jewish leaders petition a Roman official to bring Paul to the Jerusalem court, with the secret intention of assassinating the prisoner en route (25.2-3). Among the differences which emerge between the two cases, the priestly rulers in the present situation directly instigate the plot without the prompting of a separate band of conspirators, and there is now no informant like Paul's nephew to expose the plot.

Fortunately for Paul, Festus does not comply immediately with the chief priests' request. Although he will later offer to try Paul's case in Jerusalem, he first insists that the Jewish authorities come with him to Caesarea and present their charges before his tribunal there (25.4-5). While wanting to appease the Jerusalem hierarchy, Festus cannot afford to accede to their demands too easily. This early in his tenure, he must firmly establish his own rule on his own turf.

(2) *Paul's Defense: 25.6-11.* In contrast to the detailed record of Paul's previous trial before Felix, the hearing before Festus is recounted in summary fashion. All we learn about the prosecutors is that they brought 'many serious charges against him [Paul], which they could not prove' (25.7). For his part, Paul simply denies again that he has done anything contemptible 'against the law of the Jews or against the temple'. But he also adds an important third dimension to his denial: he

has done nothing disloyal 'against the *emperor*' (25.8). In this testimony he finally rebuts Tertullus's allegation—no doubt implicit in the current 'serious charges'—that he was a pernicious agitator throughout the empire (cf. 24.5). He also sets the stage for his sudden appeal to Rome (25.10). Confident that he has done nothing to offend the emperor, Paul is happy to have the emperor decide his case.

Once again Paul's trials take an ironic turn. He calculates that he has a better chance of receiving justice before the highest secular court in the Roman empire than before the chief Jewish religious council in Jerusalem—where Paul was raised as a devout Pharisee—or before the Roman governor of Judea wishing to appease this council. And just as Festus and the Jewish leaders appear to control Paul's fate for their own advantages, he makes a strategic move to break loose from their trap. The imperiled pawn in the political chess match manages to survive a while longer by appealing to the king for refuge.

(3) *Festus's Verdict: 25.12-27*. At base, Festus's decision is crisp and uncomplicated: 'You have appealed to the emperor; to the emperor you will go' (25.12). Beyond this, however, Festus uses the occasion of Agrippa and Bernice's visit to review his administration of Paul's case at some length. Ultimately, he seems insecure about passing this case on to the emperor and thus seeks Agrippa's advice and legitimation (25.25-27). Various self-interested accents and new pieces of information surface in Festus's account of recent proceedings.

(a) Festus stresses his strict handling of Paul's case from the beginning according to proper Roman legal procedure. Whereas the narrator previously reported that the Jewish leaders in Jerusalem sought Paul's transfer back to their city (25.3), Festus indicates that they actually demanded a judicial 'sentence against him [Paul]', whereupon the governor formally cited the established 'custom of the Romans' that the accused had the right to confront his accusers and defend himself against their charges (25.15-16). In short, Festus claims to have conducted a fair trial.

(b) He also claims to have 'lost no time' in getting underway with Paul's trial the very next day after the Jewish prosecutors arrived in Caesarea (25.17). This speedy judicial action stands in contrast with the previous governor's dilatory approach, implicitly recalled in Festus's introduction of Paul as 'a man left in prison by Felix' (25.14; cf. 24.25-27).

(c) In detailing the charges levied against Paul which the narrator had only vaguely described as 'serious' (25.7), Festus mentions nothing about any alleged crimes against the Roman state or any disruption of the *pax Romana*. He focuses instead on the accusers' internal squabbles with Paul over 'their own [Jewish] religion', as Lysias did in his letter to Felix (23.29), and on a personal dispute—which Festus makes explicit for the first time in Paul's recent trials—'about a certain Jesus, who had died, but whom Paul asserted to be alive' (25.19). We have noted Paul's determined shifting of the main topic of investigation to his belief in the general 'resurrection of the dead' (23.6; 24.21) and the 'resurrection of the righteous and unrighteous' (24.15). We have assumed an underlying debate about the risen Jesus in particular, so central to Paul's personal history (cf. 22.6-21), but not until now has this issue come to fore. It is interesting that the matter is first brought up by a Roman magistrate and even more interesting that he seems not to be perturbed about it. Festus does not really understand the Jesus question, any more than he apprehends other intra-Jewish religious arguments (25.20), but he remains convinced that none of these conflicts implicate Paul in any criminal action meriting death (25.25).

(d) Festus attributes his proposal to try Paul's case back in Jerusalem solely to his ignorance concerning Jewish affairs (25.20), conveniently passing over his motivation to placate the Jewish authorities in Jerusalem, which the narrator previously stressed (25.9). Again, the governor highlights his magnanimous commitment to fair and equitable justice. His only interest, he would have us believe, was to insure the most enlightened hearing and evaluation of Paul's testimony. Whether or not Agrippa and Bernice are taken in by such posturing, we know better. Paul's case has been subject as much to the whims of Judean politics as to the canons of Roman law.

Paul's Trial before Agrippa: 26.1-32

Beyond recounting his own assessment of Paul's case for Agrippa's approval, Festus also brings Paul before Agrippa, at the king's request, for a personal hearing (25.22-23). Although Paul will address his defense directly to the king, it is important to appreciate the wider setting for this speech. It does not take place in a private chamber but rather in a public 'audience hall' where Agrippa and Bernice make a grand entrance in the presence of the governor, 'military tribunes [note the plural] and the prominent men of the city' (25.23-24). Such an august assembly further intimates Paul's 'VIP' status and provides an appropriate audience for his climactic defense speech: a grand gallery for a grand finale.

However, in the context of the larger Lukan narrative, the scenario of a double-trial before the Roman governor of Judea and the Herodian client-king also hints at a more precarious situation for the prisoner. The present King Agrippa (Herod Agrippa II) was the son and successor of Herod Agrippa I, whom we last encountered as a smitten diet for worms following a cruel reign of terror against the leaders of the Jerusalem church (12.1-11, 18-23). Before that, Herod the tetrarch (Antipas) had made his malevolent mark in Luke's Gospel as an enemy of Israel's prophets: imprisoning and eventually decapitating John the baptizer for denouncing his irregular marriage to his brother's wife Herodias (Lk. 3.19-20; 9.7-9), seeking to kill Jesus in Galilee and drawing Jesus' rebuke of his vicious, fox-like schemes (13.31-32), shaming Jesus during his final trials in Jerusalem and, though determining along with Pilate that Jesus 'had done nothing to deserve death', still allowing him to be crucified (23.1-25). The Herodian image is scarcely a benevolent one in Luke–Acts (see Darr, pp. 127-68).

With this developed profile, we wonder about Paul's fate. Is Paul now about to reprise the role of fiery prophet to a Herodian king, condemning, for example, Agrippa's liaison with his sister Bernice—widely scandalized as incestuous (cf. Juvenal, *Satires* 6.156-160)—as John had denounced the Antipas-Herodias union? Is he about to receive derisive treatment from the governor-king tandem of judges and, despite their verdicts of innocence, be handed over to Roman soldiers for execution, as Jesus was? Is he about to be miraculously freed by an angel of the Lord, as Peter was, while another Herod Agrippa feels the lethal force of the angel's wrath? We turn now to examine Paul's appearance before Agrippa to see to what extent our accumulated fears and expectations are fulfilled and/or overturned.

(1) *Introduction: 26.1-3*. Far from opening with a rebuke of Agrippa's relationship with Bernice or with any critique of Agrippa's rule, Paul commences with a conventional *captatio benevolentiae* honoring the king before whom he is 'fortunate' to appear. In particular, Paul commends Agrippa's deep knowledge of 'all the customs and controversies of the Jews' (26.2-3). In contrast to Festus, who distanced himself from Judaism by dubbing it 'their own religion' about which he knew nothing (25.19-20), Agrippa, while a loyal agent of Rome, still embraces the Jewish faith and people as his own. Paul hopes that this Jewish connection with the king will facilitate a 'patient', if not sympathetic, hearing of his case (26.3).

(2) *Narration: Pharisaic Background: 26.4-5*. Having extolled Agrippa's Jewish heritage, Paul now certifies his own. Again he recounts his devout Jewish upbringing in Jerusalem as a Pharisee. This time he adds a description of the Pharisaic party as 'the strictest sect of our religion' (26.5), which recalls various elements in the preceding trial speeches. Paul's expressed affiliation with the 'strictest' (*akribes tatos*) group in Judaism echoes his earlier testimony concerning his 'strict' (*akribeia*) legal education under Gamaliel (22.3). His use of the term 'sect' (*hairesis*) in its positive sense of an established, respected 'party' offsets Tertullus's charge that he spearheaded a dangerous 'heretical' movement (24.5). And Paul's reference to '*our* religion' reinforces the bond between him and Agrippa and resists Festus's dismissive designation of Judaism as '*their* religion' (25.19). Terminology may also come into play here as Paul opts for a more neutral word for 'religion' (*thrēskeia*) than the one employed by Festus (*deisidaimonia*), which can carry the derogatory tone of 'superstition' (see Johnson, *Acts*, p. 426).

Previously, Paul highlighted his Pharisaic background before exclusively Jewish audiences (crowd and council) in Jerusalem well-acquainted with the reputation of the Pharisees as a group and of the venerable teacher Gamaliel in particular (22.3; 23.6). How would the present mixed audience—including Roman noblemen and military officers as well as the Jewish-informed King Agrippa—view Paul's Pharisaic connections? John Lentz suggests that in Greco-Roman society Paul's professed association with the Pharisees 'bespeaks a solid pedigree in what might have been recognized as a type of philosophical school' (p. 53). A similar pedigree was claimed by the first-century Jewish apologist, Flavius Josephus; writing for the Roman aristocracy, Josephus regarded the Pharisees as the most popular and enlightened party in Judaism (*Ant.* 13.288, 297-98, 401-406; 17.41-46; *Life* 191). It is possible, then, that Paul impresses Governor Festus and the other attendant civic and military officials from Caesarea—as well as King Agrippa—with his roots in a strict philosophical-religious sect.

(3) *Declaration: Resurrection Hope: 26.6-8.* Yet again Paul insists that the crux of his trial is his hope in God's power and purpose to raise the dead. Given Festus's recent disclosure of Paul's particular interest in the resurrection of 'a certain Jesus' (25.19), we might expect Paul himself now to expound this emphasis. For the moment, however, he retains his focus on a general resurrection of 'the dead' (plural, 26.8). Still, Paul does add a significant clarifying point related not to Jesus' unique experience, but to the entire history of the people of Israel. Paul avers that his present hope in the resurrection carries on the ancestral hope in God's promised restoration of 'our twelve tribes' (26.6-7). This idea is similar to that dramatically conveyed in Ezekiel's exilic vision of the revived multitude of dry bones (Ezek. 37.1-14): raising the dead means restoring the people of God to new life.

(4) *Narration: Conversion and Call: 26.9-21.* Although Paul does not specifically refer to Jesus when he broaches the question of 'God['s] rais[ing] the dead' (26.8), it is clear that Jesus is not far from Paul's mind as he directly turns to recall his former antipathy to 'the name of Jesus the Nazorean' (26.9), transformed by a brilliant visionary encounter with the exalted 'Jesus whom [he had been] persecuting' (26.14). Of course, we are already familiar with this story from Paul's first defense speech in ch. 22 and the narrator's original report in ch. 9. But certain fresh elements come to light in this re-telling appropriate to the present context.

First, Paul accentuates the tyranny of his former persecution campaign against the church. For example, Paul now tells us that he not only shut up many believers in prison, but also sought the death penalty against them. Moreover, he hunted Christians down 'in all the synagogues' (as well as 'house after house', 8.3) in 'foreign cities' as well as in Jerusalem, trying to coerce them into 'blasphemy' against God (26.10-11). Paul's current audience of powerful Herodian and Roman officials are certainly no strangers to violent measures of enforcing one's interests. Paul is speaking their language here—but only to subvert it. For ultimately Paul admits that his cruel and zealous pursuit of the early disciples sprang not from sober concerns for justice, but from 'maniacal' (*emmainomai*) paroxysms of rage (26.11).

Paul goes on to stress the dramatic turnaround in his conduct triggered by his shattering encounter with the risen Jesus on the road to Damascus. While previously Paul focused on the visual-illuminating effects of Jesus' brilliant appearance (cf. 22.6-16), here he concentrates more on the *aural-instructional* effects of Jesus' authoritative word. He notes for the first time in Acts that Jesus spoke to him 'in the Hebrew language' (Aramaic) (26.14a), thus suggesting Jesus' capture of Paul's attention as a Jewish compatriot, much as Paul himself had silenced the angry Jewish mob in Jerusalem by 'addressing them in Hebrew' (21.40–22.2). Paul also reports a proverbial addendum to Jesus' rhetorical query concerning his persecution: 'Saul, Saul, why are you persecuting me? *It hurts you to kick against the goads*' (26.14b; cf. Euripedes, *Bacchae* 794-95). In other words, Paul's plan to exterminate the church was doomed to fail because it was 'kicking against' the irresistible purpose of God (cf. Gamaliel's warning in 5.38-39). Such a purpose applied not only to the survival and growth of the church, but also to the life and career of Paul. The Lord was 'goading', prodding him in another direction which he had no choice but to follow—the path of proclaiming this same Jesus he had been attacking.

Paul heightens the authority of his call to preach by presenting it as a direct mandate from the risen Jesus himself on the Damascus road rather than a message mediated later through Ananias in the city (26.16; cf. 9.15-16; 22.12-16). As in the earlier commission accounts, Paul underscores the fact that the Lord sent him to evangelize the Gentiles outside of Judea as well as his own Jewish people. He also proceeds, however, in the present speech to elaborate on the nature of the Gentile mission, especially its redemptive aims. Jesus made it quite clear that he was sending Paul to enlighten the Gentiles 'so that they may turn (*epistrepsai*) from darkness to light and from the power of Satan to God...and receive forgiveness of sins and a place among those who are sanctified by faith in me' (26.18). Paul understood this goal of conversion not only in terms of forgiveness and faith, but also in terms of a full ethical transformation. Above all, Paul tells Agrippa, he sought to turn the Gentiles to God, as Jesus commanded, by bringing them to *active repentance*: 'I...declared...to the Gentiles that they should *repent* (*metanoiein*) and *turn (epistrephein) to God* and do deeds consistent with *repentance* (*metanoias*)' (26.20). Paul's fraternization with foreigners had touched off the trouble with hostile Jews in Jerusalem (26.21; cf. 21.27-36; 22.21-24). What his accusers had failed to appreciate, however, was that Paul reached out to the Gentiles not to flout the

Jewish law or temple, but to *convert* the Gentiles to a new way of life befitting the restored holy people of God.

(5) *Declaration: Resurrection Hope: 26.22-23.* At the climax of this final defense speech, Paul makes explicit the critical connection, which he has been building to throughout his trials, between Israel's scriptural hope and the resurrection of Jesus. Earlier in this present speech, Paul intimated the link between Israel's hope of restoration and the general notion of God's resurrection of the dead (26.6-8). Now he specifies that such a hope, outlined in the biblical witness of 'the prophets and Moses', has been fulfilled first and foremost in the experience of Jesus Messiah—'the first to rise from the dead' (26.22-23). In other words, to borrow language from Paul's writings, Christ is the 'first fruits' or 'first born' of 'a large family' of God brought to new life (Rom. 8.29; 1 Cor. 15.20, 23; Col. 1.15, 18). Simply put: Christ's resurrection inaugurated the promised restoration of God's people.

And yet again the Lukan Paul insists, in the familiar tones of Isaiah, that this revitalized, en*light*ened community includes Gentiles (*ethnē*) as well as 'our people (*laos*)' (Jews) (26.23; cf. 13.47; Lk. 2.31-32; Isa. 49.6). But he adds a new twist: the living Christ catalyzes the restoration of God's people not only through his resurrection, but also through *his proclamation* of 'light' to both Jews and Gentiles (26.13). Jesus not only commissions Paul as a witness to his resurrection; he continues to participate with him in this witness. We can now trace over the course of the speech a developing pattern of this dynamic union between Paul and the risen Jesus around the motif of 'light':

(a) The risen Jesus originally revealed himself to Paul as a blinding, enveloping '*light* from heaven' (26.13).

(b) The risen Jesus commissioned Paul to testify to what he had seen before Gentiles (as well as Jews) in order that 'they may turn from darkness to *light*', as Paul had done (26.16-17).

(c) The risen Jesus continues to 'proclaim *light*' to both Jews and Gentiles—the same mission he had assigned Paul (26.23).

(6) *Reaction: 26.24-32.* Paul's testimony draws somewhat mixed responses from both Festus and Agrippa. The governor, for the most part, reacts in a negative way—not changing his mind about Paul's innocence—but suddenly questioning Paul's *sanity*! Twice he exclaims that Paul, with all his strange talk about visions and resurrections, appears to be 'out of his mind', in the grips of 'mania' (*mainē/eis manian*, 26.24). There is also a positive side, however, as Festus attributes Paul's madness to excessive 'learning' (*grammata*). Thus Festus supports Paul's earlier claim to be a highly educated man (22.3) (unlike the obviously 'unlearned' [*agrammatoi*] Peter and John in 4.13), even if he thinks Paul has taken matters too far. As for Paul's riposte to Festus's challenge, he insists that he is only 'speaking the sober truth' in the mode of a wise

philosopher, not uttering crazy nonsense (26.5). Paul had been plagued with a 'maniacal' condition, we may recall, manifested in fits of uncontrollable rage toward the early disciples (*emmainomai*, 26.11). But that affliction was a thing of the past from which the risen Christ had delivered him.

Paul quickly turns his attention back to Agrippa, expressing his confidence that the king would certify his status as a sober, honorable philosopher-teacher—not a madman slinking around despicably 'in a corner' (26.26; see Malherbe, '"Not in a Corner"', and discussion above, p. 206). He then attempts to resume his speech, picking up the thread of scriptural-prophetic witness which he is sure that Agrippa believes (26.27). At this point, however, Agrippa interjects his own ambiguous response, querying Paul's apparent aim to convince him 'quickly...to become a Christian' (26.28). It appears that Agrippa is being more dismissive than receptive here, particularly concerning the pressure he feels to make a hasty decision, but still in some sense Paul has obviously struck a nerve with the king. What is important, in any case, is that Paul continues aggressively to bring the light of salvation to Jews like Agrippa and Gentiles like Festus, to incorporate them into the renewed people of God. As he announces in his closing statement: 'Whether quickly or not, I pray to God that not only you [Agrippa] but also all who are listening today might become such as I am—except for these chains' (26.29). Despite the tendency of Herodian rulers throughout Luke–Acts, along with certain Roman officials, to imprison and execute the Lord's prophets and apostles, Paul reaches out to the present Herodian king and Roman governor—while they have him in chains!—earnestly desiring their conversion.

The ambivalence of Festus and Agrippa towards Paul culminates in their final joint verdict. Although they might question both Paul's sanity and audacity, they agree (again) that he 'is doing nothing to deserve death or imprisonment' (26.31). In fact they would be willing to release him had Paul not appealed to Rome (26.32).

Trek from Caesarea to Rome: 27.1-28.15

Paul the prisoner is transferred, as he requested, from the provincial to the imperial capital (Caesarea to Rome) via an extended westward voyage through the Mediterranean Sea. This section reinforces various patterns developed in preceding trial and travel scenes. For example, at the outset of Paul's first defense speech in Jerusalem, he emerged as a cultured speaker of the Greek language and citizen of the important Greek maritime city of Tarsus (21.37-39). Now Paul's Greek identity is further enhanced by his depiction as a confident, experienced seafarer within a narrative rich in nautical detail. As Loveday Alexander has noted in comparing the sea adventure in Acts 27-28 with similar voyages recounted in classical Greek epics and in the more contemporary

Greek romances of Chariton and Xenophon: 'the Mediterranean is seen as "the Greek sea", the area where...Greek characters feel at home...a cultural territory which many readers, both Greek and Judaeo-Christian, would perceive as inherently "Greek"' (pp. 34, 37). Also, Paul's course as a prisoner continues to be directed from the human side by Roman officers. In this case, a centurion named Julius superintends Paul's transfer and, like previous Roman overseers, helps Paul by allowing friends to minister to his needs and by intervening to spare his life (27.1-3, 42-43; cf. 21.33; 22.24; 23.23-35; 24.23). Finally, from the divine side Paul again receives a nocturnal epiphany amid a period of crisis, exhorting him to maintain his courage and assuring him that he 'must' testify in Rome (27.22-25; cf. 23.11).

In addition to showing these continuities with the preceding trial accounts, the narrative of Paul's overseas trek to Rome also evinces some notable changes in Paul's status as a prisoner. For several chapters now Paul has been under attack from Jewish prosecutors and conspirators and defended himself in a series of five forensic speeches. To a certain extent he has been treated respectfully by elite officers and judges as an educated Pharisee and Roman citizen, but he has also been toyed with as a pawn and dismissed as an eccentric. He has continued to proclaim the gospel, particularly bearing witness to the resurrection of the dead, but the results have been minimal. While stirring some interest and even sympathy, Paul has nonetheless made no new converts, as far we know, during this imprisonment (unlike at Philippi; cf. 16.25-34). He has also offered no benevolent service to others, although he himself apparently received some aid from unnamed friends in Caesarea (24.23). Moreover, apart from these friends and a nephew in Jerusalem, he has been entirely on his own throughout the trials, separated from all Christian communities. (James and the Jerusalem church have nothing to do with him, for example, after his arrest.) In short, Paul appears in Acts 22–26 as an isolated and restricted, even if somewhat valuable, political prisoner.

Now, however, in Acts 27–28, although technically remaining a prisoner and defendant, Paul re-establishes his role as a *dynamic prophet and servant* in the mold of Jesus. With his voyage to Rome, it is almost as if he embarks on another missionary expedition. This resumption of Paul's missionary career after a lengthy hiatus may be charted in three areas:

(1) First, Paul is associated with a wider *company* of people. Instead of being isolated as a 'VIP' prisoner, he is now lumped together with 'some other prisoners' on the journey to Rome (27.1) and is thus in a situation closer to that of the Lukan Jesus who, fulfilling the role of Isaiah's suffering servant, 'was counted among the lawless' (Lk. 22.37; Isa. 53.12; cf. Lk. 23.32-43). Also, in addition to visiting friends at the ports of Sidon (27.3) and Puteoli (28.13-14), Paul is accompanied

throughout the voyage by the *'we'-party* (27.1-8, 18-20, 37; 28.1-2, 7, 10), which suddenly emerges again for the first time since 21.18—just before Paul's arrest and trials. The reunion of this group with Paul on a westward sea voyage recalls the beginning of a previous missionary expedition (16.10-12). The re-appearance of another former associate, a Thessalonian named *Aristarchus* (27.2; cf. 19.29; 20.4) also suggests a fresh opportunity for mission.

(2) Paul further regains his *authority* over the course of the voyage to Rome. As the violent tempest threatens the safety of the ship and everyone on board, Paul takes charge of the crisis, effectively becoming captain of the expedition as he did with his first missionary journey starting on the island of Cyprus (see discussion, p. 139 on 13.4-12). In a striking reversal of roles, the centurion and the entire crew essentially come under Paul's command as the storm hits (27.21-28). Of course, Paul's superior authority derives, as always in Acts, from his special position as the servant of the Most High God. This God—'to whom I [Paul] belong and whom I worship' (27.23)—is the supreme Heavenly Patron whose purpose to reach Rome and power to control the sea Paul mediates (brokers) to the distressed sailors and passengers.

(3) Finally, Paul resumes his active *ministry* of salvation to the destitute and infirm. Instead of simply testifying to his personal belief in the hope of resurrection, as he did throughout his trials, Paul now provides tangible, life-giving aid to many others in a desperate situation where 'all hope of our being saved was at last abandoned' (27.20). He sees to it that all 276 storm-tossed passengers 'take some food', after two weeks of fasting, to restore their strength (27.33-36) and that all are finally 'brought safely to land' (27.44). Moreover, coming ashore at Malta, Paul begins again to work miracles of healing—which we have not seen since his Ephesian mission in 19.11-12. He cures not only the feverish father of 'the leading man of the island', which may be viewed as a reciprocal act of favor towards this prominent figure who had graciously hosted Paul and his companions for three days (28.7-8); he also channels healing power to 'the rest of the people on the island who had diseases' (28.9), thus mirroring the inclusive, compassionate ministry of Jesus (cf. Lk. 4.38-41; 7.21-22).

This dramatic transformation in Paul's status—from political prisoner back to dynamic missionary—is appropriately staged in an extraordinary, *liminal setting* (see Turner, pp. 166-72; Malina, *Christian Origins*, pp. 139-43; McVann). *Temporally*, the stormy crisis in which Paul re-asserts his leadership occurs during a standard 'time-out' period. The narrator dates the turbulent sea voyage in relation to 'the Fast' or the annual autumn observance of the Day of Atonement on the tenth of Tishri (September/October) (27.9). The mention of an important Jewish holiday alerts us to the possibility of an unusual turn of events, such as the outpouring of the Spirit on Pentecost or Peter's miraculous prison-break during Passover. But more significant in the present story is the focus on the period *following* the festival ('even the Fast had already gone by'), namely, 'the winter' season when the sea becomes hazardous to navigate (27.10-12). As Luke Timothy Johnson notes, 'the Mediterranean was considered "closed" during the winter months...because of the severe weather' (*Acts*, p. 447). Despite Paul's warning, however, the pilot and owner of the vessel, along with Julius the centurion, decide to push their luck and keep sailing (27.10-12). When trouble strikes during this 'closed' period—creating a long stretch of bleak darkness 'when neither sun nor stars appear' (27.20)—the time is ripe for a change in Paul's role on the voyage.

The *spatial* coordinates of this final journey also appear to be situated 'out of bounds', certainly from a Jewish perspective. As comfortable as the Greeks may have felt sailing the sea and hopping from island to island, the landlubbing Jews felt quite the opposite. In any case, both Jews and Greeks would have preferred to steer clear of the path of a violent sea storm, such as that which engulfs the sailing party in Acts 27. This turbulent, chaotic environment, however, provides an apt setting for reconfiguring status relations between Paul and his shipmates. Likewise, the isolated island havens rising out of the sea—where Paul asserts himself both before (Crete, 27.8-12) and after (Malta, 28.1-10) the shipwreck—represent suitable stages for exhibiting Paul's elevation in status, as we saw earlier at his pioneering missionary venture on the island of Cyprus (see discussion, p. 142, on 13.4-12).

Having taken a broad look at Paul's transformation during his final trek from Jerusalem to Rome, we now get on board with Paul to chart the course of this change in status in more detail, as it unfolds.

Embarking for Rome: 27.1-6
The first leg of the voyage follows the Mediterranean coastline north and west from Caesarea, calling at the ports of Sidon in Phoenicia and Myra in Lycia. During this segment Julius the centurion, an officer of the 'Augustan' division (named after Caesar Augustus), clearly controls the course of the ship and passengers as an agent of imperial authority. Specifically, he functions as *patron*, permitting Paul to be tended to by friends in Sidon (27.3), and *captain*, procuring a vessel in Myra destined for Italy and 'put[ting] us on board' (27.6). At this stage, Paul remains a passive prisoner, saying nothing and taking no initiative.

Endangered at Crete: 27.7-13
From the southwestern coast of Asia Minor, the journey moves out into the heart of the Mediterranean Sea towards the island of Crete. As stiff winds impede this voyage and create increasingly dangerous sailing conditions around the island, Paul's role begins to change. 'Sailing...with difficulty', the travellers manage to reach 'a place called *Fair Havens*' on

the southern coast of Crete, ironically named in the present context where the weather is anything but fair and doubts are raised about the suitability of the place as a winter haven (27.7-9, 12). Paul finally speaks up in prophetic style, forecasting the dire hazards of continuing the voyage and implying that they would be better off staying put at Fair Havens (27.10). Julius, however, discounts Paul's warning and, heeding the opinion of the ship's pilot and owner together with 'the majority' of the crew, sets sail under a more moderate breeze for the harbor of Phoenix further west along the Cretan shore (27.11-13). For the moment Paul stands alone as a rejected prophet.

Pounded at Sea: 27.14-38

As the lighter wind suddenly gives way to the turbulent gale of 'the northeaster, rush[ing] down from Crete' (27.14), Paul is promptly vindicated. As he predicted, the situation becomes desperate. Brutally 'pounded' by 'no small tempest', the sailors are forced to jettison the ship's cargo and gear (27.18-19). 'For a long time', then, they drift precariously on the stormy sea without light from sun or stars, without food, and, consequently, without hope of survival (27.20-21). This black and bleak oceanic environment is reminiscent of the primordial chaos at the beginning of the creation myth in Genesis 1. There God spoke to bring light and life out of the dark deep (Gen. 1.1-3). Now Paul, inspired by a vision in the night, speaks of God's purpose to sustain him and everyone else on board through the tempest. Whereas in the earlier vision at Caesarea, the Lord exhorted Paul individually to 'keep up your [sing.] courage' (23.11), in the present situation Paul relays the visionary message to his travelling companions, urging them (twice) to 'keep up your [pl.] your courage' (27.22, 25).

Paul not only encourages the passengers; he also insists that they follow his plan if they want to stay alive. When the crew attempts to leave the ship on an auxiliary lifeboat, Paul speaks directly 'to the centurion and the soldiers' in no uncertain terms: 'Unless these men stay in the ship, you cannot be saved' (27.30-31). The soldiers duly respond this time to Paul's warning by setting the boat adrift (27.32). Apparently, the centurion has finally come around to acknowledge Paul's authority as director of the journey and mediator of salvation. We may recall how another centurion in the midst of darkness also changed his mind about the honor of a condemned Jewish prophet (cf. Lk. 23.44-47).

Paul takes charge of the crisis not only with words of hope and guidance, but also with life-sustaining actions related to nourishment. On the fourteenth day 'without food, having eaten nothing', Paul takes some bread, offers thanks to God, breaks it and starts to eat. The other passengers then follow Paul's lead and eat until 'they ha[ve] satisfied their hunger' (27.33-38). The sudden availability of food—including surplus wheat which is thrown overboard after everyone has their fill (27.38)—

is puzzling in view of the earlier report that 'they had been without food for a long time' (27.21). Perhaps they had been fasting (Gaventa, p. 2110), along with praying (27.29), in hopes of eliciting divine sympathy. If this were the case, such fasting was designed to avert a threat to the lives of Paul and companions, in diametric contrast to the fasting connected with the previous transfer journey, which signified the conspirators' solemn resolve to assassinate Paul (cf. 23.12-15).

The gap in the narrative regarding food supply also invites a more mystical-symbolic reading in light of the foundational Lukan story of Jesus. Paul's taking, blessing and breaking of bread, leading to the full feeding (with leftovers) of all 276 passengers stranded at sea, recalls, albeit with a larger group on land, Jesus' miraculous provision for 5000 men 'in a deserted place' (Lk. 9.10-17). Such actions also evoke memories of Jesus' special revelations to his disciples concerning his death (22.14-19) and resurrection (24.28-35). As Jesus was 'made known to them in the breaking of the bread' at the close of the Gospel (24.35), so in the context of table-service amid his own life-and-death struggle, Paul is revealed afresh to us readers at the end of Acts as a model minister of the crucified and risen Jesus.

Aground at Malta: 27.39-28.10

Precisely following Paul's forecast, the beleaguered seafarers 'run aground on some island' (27.26)—Malta, as it happens, due south of Italy (28.1)—and, despite wrecking their ship, they all manage to reach the shore safely (27.39-44; cf. 27.22, 24, 34). With Paul's benevolent authority so clearly vindicated, we might expect a smooth course to Rome from this point on. But in fact Paul must overcome further threats and trials which confront him on the island. Specifically, he faces another murderous plot against his life (27.42) as well as a charge that he himself 'must be a murderer' (28.4).

Worried that the prisoners might flee amid the confusion of the shipwreck, the soldiers hatch a 'plan' (*boulē*) to kill all of them (27.42)—in direct opposition to the Lord's plan that Paul testify in Rome and to Paul's prophecy that no one on board would 'lose a hair from [their] heads' (27.34). The centurion, however, blocks their scheme, permitting everyone to reach land safely on account of his particular desire 'to save Paul' (27.43-44). Apart from certifying the centurion's respect for Paul, this action also intimates Paul's indirect role in saving the lives of his fellow prisoners. Numbered with them on the brink of death, Paul ultimately insures the prisoners' salvation, as did the dying Jesus for the criminal hanging at his side (Lk. 23.39-43). If not the eternal, heavenly 'paradise' of which the Lukan Jesus spoke, Malta at least represents for the moment an island paradise providing refuge from the deadly storm.

Just as the turbulent story appears to settle down around a soothing fire prepared by hospitable natives of the island (28.1-2), it becomes suspenseful again. For just as the fire attracts bedraggled sailors, it also draws out from the underbrush a poisonous viper which latches on to Paul's hand. This scenario prompts the islanders to change their opinion about Paul, assuming that he 'must be a murderer' under judgment from the sea goddess, 'Justice' (*Dikē*). When Paul suffers no ill effects from the snakebite, however, they change their minds again and begin to proclaim Paul 'a god' (28.3-6). Thus Paul encounters an inversion of earlier events at Lystra (14.8-20; see Krodel, pp. 479-80). Whereas the Lystran citizens first adulated Paul as a pagan deity but then turned violently against him (at the instigation of visiting Jews) and left him for dead, in the present story, the Maltan natives initially regard Paul as a criminal condemned to die but then come to praise him as a divine being. We are reminded that human opinion about Paul is often fickle and fraught with misunderstanding.

Another apparent contrast with the Lystran episode concerns Paul's response to being deified by an awe-struck assembly. At Malta, we see no rending of garments and hear no vehement objections nor attempts to convert the crowd to the true God (cf. 14.14-17). Neither, however, does Paul say or do anything to encourage the crowd; in fact, no reaction is recorded. We may fill in this blank with reference to the preceding narrative in ch. 27 in which Paul clearly voices his dependence on God's protective care ('I have faith in God'; 27.24-25, 35). The natives may have changed their minds about Paul, but there is no reason to think that Paul has altered his view of himself as the humble servant of the one sovereign God. Also, in the context of the larger Lukan story, Paul's immunity to the viper's venom derives not from his own innate strength, but from the delegated authority of Jesus the Lord. When 70 commissioned disciples of Jesus returned to report their success in casting out demons in his name, Jesus replied:

> I watched Satan fall from heaven like a flash of lightning. See, I have
> given you authority *to tread on snakes* and scorpions, and over all
> the power of the enemy; and nothing will hurt you (Lk. 10.17-19).

Like the Seventy, Paul conquers destructive forces (tempest and snakebite) by way of Jesus' supreme authority 'given' to him. Moreover, the metaphorical link between overcoming the sting of serpents and the power of Satan reinforces the cosmic effects of Paul's mission. As he dynamically defeated the 'son of the devil' (Bar-Jesus) during his inaugural missionary venture on the island of Cyprus (13.9-11), so Paul reasserts his control over satanic agents (represented by the viper) on the island of Malta.

More than withstanding serious threats against his own life, Paul actively reaches out to relieve the suffering of other island residents. And once again he follows the commission and example of the Lukan Jesus. As Jesus' disciples were sent to administer healing in those households which received them (Lk. 9.1-6; 10.1-9), so Paul repays the hospitality of Malta's leading citizen (Publius) by curing his bedridden father of fever and dysentery (Acts 28.7-8). And as Jesus himself healed many diseased townfolk in Capernaum who were brought to him after he had relieved the 'high fever' of Peter's mother-in law (Lk. 4.38-41), so Paul heals 'the rest of the [infirm] people on the island' who come to him following the cure of Publius' feverish father (Acts 28.9). In turn the indebted islanders bestow 'many honors' and abundant supplies on Paul and his party (28.10). Paul the prisoner is thus confirmed as the esteemed captain and patron of the journey to Rome. Accordingly, Julius the centurion has dropped out of the picture altogether.

Arriving in Italy: 28.11-14

After passing the three winter months at Malta, the travel party sets sail again, heading to Syracuse on the southeastern corner of Sicily and then on to the Italian mainland, calling first at Rhegium on the toe of the boot, then up the western coast at Puteoli from where they proceed overland to Rome. Again it is noteworthy that Paul and the 'we'-group now seem free to chart their own course without permission or interference from the centurion or any other soldiers or crew. Notice the consistent use of the first person plural subject controlling the plot:

> *We* set sail...
> *we* put in at Syracuse and stayed there...
> *we* weighed anchor and came to Rhegium...
> *we* came to Puteoli...
> *we* found believers...
> And so *we* came to Rome (28.11-14).

Also of interest in this brief travelogue is the suggestive counterpointing of family images, particularly involving 'brothers'. The new vessel which transports Paul and his companions has a *Dioskuri* insignia associated with the figures of the 'Twin Brothers', Castor and Pollux, sons of Zeus and patron deities of ships thought to ensure smooth sailing (28.11; BAGD, p. 199). Implied readers can only smirk at such a reference in the present narrative, since it has become abundantly clear that Paul's security at sea has everything to do with the benevolence of his God and nothing to do with the whims of pagan deities, whether *Dikē* ('Justice', 28.4) or *Dioskuri* ('Twin Brothers'). Moreover, in contrast to these useless mythological brothers, Paul is sustained in his journey to Rome not only by God who reveals himself in visions but also by real, flesh-and-blood 'brothers' (*adelphoi*) in the faith, who entertain him for several days at Puteoli (28.14) and come out from Rome to embrace him and his companions and escort them into the city (28.15). Indeed, Paul views the presence of these brothers as another manifestation of God's grace ('on seeing them, Paul thanked God'), preparing him to face his final ordeal in Rome with 'courage' (28.15).

Acts 28.16-31:
Reorientation: The Journey Concludes

The account of Paul's final witness in Rome marks the conclusion not only of his 'prisoner's progress' begun in ch. 21, but also of the entire Acts journey: hence our focus on this material as a distinct unit. This closing narrative unfolds in three scenes, each opening with key disclosures of spatial, temporal and social settings:

> *Scene 1*: When we came into Rome, Paul was allowed to live by himself, with the soldier who was guarding him. Three days later he called together the local leaders of the Jews (28.16-17).

> *Scene 2*: After they [the Jewish leaders] had set a day to meet with him, they [the Jewish people] came to him at his lodgings in great numbers. From morning until evening he explained the matter to them... (28.23).

> *Scene 3*: He lived there two whole years at his own expense [or] in his own hired dwelling and welcomed all who came to him (28.30).

(1) All three episodes occur in the same *place*: Paul's private quarters where he was allowed to dwell under house arrest and to host numerous visitors interested in his message. Although still a prisoner under guard, Paul continues to assert his authority and create opportunities for ministry. He summons the local Jewish leaders to come 'to him', not vice versa, and 'welcomes' a multitude of other inquirers at his residence. Although Paul the prisoner does not establish a house church per se in Rome, he does conduct a thriving, house-based mission here similar to that carried out in other cities. This one who had often proclaimed the gospel as a guest in others' homes now ministers in the role of host (cf. 16.14-15, 40, 17.7; 18.3, 7-8; 20.20; 21.8-14).

(2) The *timing* of these reports of Paul's Roman mission stretches from a few days after his arrival in the city—including one very intense day when he debates with a throng of Jewish visitors 'from morning until evening'—to 'two whole years' of persistent witnessing. As noted in previous segments of Paul's ministry (e.g. 20.17, 31), this temporal spectrum conveys a sense of both urgency and consistency, depth and breadth: Paul both makes the most of every moment and perseveres faithfully over an extended period to maximize the impact of his outreach.

(3) The *social* contours of Paul's mission in Rome also expand progressively. The first picture portrays Paul in isolation—living by himself

under the surveillance of a single soldier. But soon various audiences of increasing magnitude gather at Paul's residence, beginning with local Jewish leaders, followed by 'great numbers' of Jewish people and, finally, 'all' types of seekers, both Jew and Gentile (cf. 28.28, 30). Although Paul's movements are restricted physically, he continues to advance the universal mission of the gospel up to the end of Acts. Interestingly, while the scope of Paul's ministry expands, the particular focus on his dealings with Roman officials dissipates. Julius the centurion does not reappear in the story, and Paul never appears before Caesar. The anonymous soldier in 28.16 stands as the lone, last representative of imperial authority.

Paul's witness in Rome centers on the familiar nexus of themes concerning the hope of Israel, the kingdom of God, and the gospel of Jesus.

> *Scene 1*: For the sake of the *hope of Israel*... I am bound with this chain (28.20).

> *Scene 2*: He explained the matter to them, testifying to the *kingdom of God* and trying to convince them about *Jesus* both from the law of Moses and from the prophets (28.23).

> *Scene 3*: He...welcomed all who came to him, proclaiming the *kingdom of God* and teaching about the *Lord Jesus Christ* (28.30-31).

At the beginning of Acts, the apostles asked Jesus—'Lord, is this the time when you will restore the kingdom to Israel?'—to which Jesus responded by commissioning his followers to bear witness to him in the power of the Spirit from Jerusalem out to the ends of the earth (1.6-8). In sum, Israel would be restored not through a restrictive, nationalistic revolution, but through an expansive global mission of salvation in the name of Jesus Messiah. Now at the end of Acts, Paul's preaching suggests a significant culmination of these restoration hopes. Paul has brought the gospel from Jerusalem to Rome; although not the end of the earth, Rome marks the new center (displacing Jerusalem) from which the entire known world may be reached. In the heart of the global mundane empire ruled by Caesar, Paul heralds the universal messianic kingdom of God. Within this kingdom, 'salvation' (restoration) is extended to the whole people of God, Jews and Gentiles alike, all who 'hear' and 'believe' the gospel of Jesus Christ (cf. 28.24-28).

Additional features of Paul's testimony in Rome along with the responses of various groups to his message may be charted in a brief sequential survey of the concluding narrative in Acts.

Scene 1: Reporting to the Jewish Leaders: 28.16-22

Although Paul has come to Rome to defend himself before the emperor, the narrative focuses more on his apologetic appeal to the local Jewish community. Paul first summons the Jewish authorities and provides them a brief review of his case, concentrating on the falsity of the charges pressed against him by Jerusalem Jews and the verdicts of innocence pronounced by Roman examiners. Above all, he takes this opportunity to reaffirm his adherence to Jewish tradition and his solidarity with the Jewish people. He addresses the Jewish leaders as 'brothers' and flatly claims to have 'done nothing against *our* people or the customs of *our* ancestors' (28.17). Paul also insists that, although certain Jewish compatriots have wrongly accused him, he has no intention of lodging any complaints 'against *my* nation' before the emperor's tribunal (28.19); quite the contrary, he reiterates that he is on trial precisely because of his fundamental commitment to Israel's renewal ('the hope of Israel' [28.20]).

While most Jewish leaders have been hostile to Christian witnesses throughout Acts, some notable exceptions have emerged, such as Gamaliel and other Pharisaic members of the Jerusalem court (5.33-39; 23.6-10) and Crispus the synagogue ruler in Corinth (18.8). The present group of Jewish officials in Rome adds to these exceptions. Although aware of the nasty rumors circulating 'everywhere' about 'this sect' which Paul represents, these leaders admit that they have received no direct negative reports about Paul, whether in writing or in person, from Judea (28.21-22). Moreover, they express what seems to be a sincere interest in hearing Paul's views first-hand, going so far as to 'set' a future meeting date for such a purpose (28.23).

Scene 2: Dividing the Jewish People: 28.23-28

On the appointed day of discussion, the Jewish leaders come to Paul's quarters along with 'great numbers' of other members of the Jewish community. Paul follows the same preaching pattern in his Roman residence as he did in the Diaspora synagogues, grounding his message concerning Jesus and the kingdom of God on the witness of the Jewish scriptures ('the law of Moses and…the prophets', 28.23; cf. 13.15-41; 17.2-3, 10-11).

The mixed reception of Paul's gospel among the Jews at Rome also fits the pattern of previous missions: some are 'convinced' (*epeithonto*; cf. 'some of them [Thessalonian Jews] were persuaded [*epeisthēsan*], 17.4), 'while others refuse to believe' (28.24). Those who become believers join the ranks of other Roman Jewish-Christians encountered in Acts, including the 'brothers' who ushered Paul into the city (28.15), the married couple, Priscilla and Aquila, who aided Paul in his Aegean mission (18.1-3, 18-26), and part of the throng of worshippers converted at Pentecost (2.10, 41). This latter group from the beginning of Acts comprised Roman Jews who came as pilgrims to Jerusalem and heard the gospel there. Now at the end of Acts, the direction has been reversed: Paul journeys from Jerusalem to bring the gospel to fellow Jews residing in Rome.

As for those who reject the Christian message in Rome, they do not turn to attack Paul, as we have come to expect, but simply enter into debate with those who believe (the Jews 'disagree *with each other* [*allēlous*]', 28.25). Somewhat surprisingly, then, as his disputing visitors are leaving, Paul, appropriating the prophetic voice of Isaiah, issues a stinging critique of the Jews' stubborn refusal to hear and understand the liberating word of God (28.25-27; cf. Isa. 6.9-10). Moreover, in introducing his scriptural citation Paul links his present audience with '*your* [rebellious] ancestors' whom Isaiah denounced—thus distancing himself from '*our* ancestors' whom he had openly embraced in the previous scene (28.25; cf. 28.28.17)—and following the quotation Paul moves directly to announce that, because of the Jews' recalcitrance, God's message of salvation has been sent to more receptive Gentiles (28.28).

Is Paul signalling with these words at the close of Acts a *final* turning of the Christian mission away from the Jews to the Gentiles because *some* Jews persist in disbelief? Early in his first missionary expedition (at Antioch in Pisidia), Paul also borrowed Isaianic language to declare a similar shift in outreach from his own people to the Gentiles, from the Jewish synagogue to the ends of the earth (13.46-47). From that point on, however, we witnessed not only an expansion of the Gentile mission but also a continued programme of reaching out *first* to Jews and sympathetic God-fearers in local synagogues—with a measure of success as well as frustration. Since the days of Isaiah up to the time of Paul, God's gracious plan to save Jews as well as Gentiles has remained in force. Prophetic warnings have always been designed to prepare God's people for renewal; judgment leads to hope—the 'hope of Israel'. There is no reason to think that this hope has suddenly been abandoned at the end of Acts.

Scene 3: Welcoming All People: 28.30-31

The final picture in Acts displaying Paul's open witness to 'all' (*pantas*) who come to him reinforces the sense that he continues to evangelize both Jews and Gentiles. We also discover in the book's closing words two critical elements concerning how Paul conducts this mission: 'with all boldness (*parrēsias*) and without hindrance (*akōlytōs*, unhinderedly)' (28.31).

Both of these elements prompt a brief look back over the foregoing Acts narrative. 'Boldness' (*parrēsia/parrēsiazomai*) characterized the preaching of the Jerusalem apostles in the face of obstructive temple authorities (4.13, 29, 31) and the witness of Paul in Jerusalem and throughout the Diaspora before antagonistic synagogue audiences (9.27, 28; 13.46; 14.3; 19.8). Now yet again, as the mission story concludes in Rome, Jewish resistance does nothing to dampen the courageous proclamation of the gospel. Overcoming social and religious barriers 'hindering' (*kōlyō*) the full acceptance of God-fearing Gentiles into the fellowship of God's household characterized the baptismal missions of Philip and Peter to the Ethiopian eunuch and Roman centurion (Cornelius), respectively (8.36; 10.47). And now we are assured one more time of Paul's boundary-breaking mission, inviting all to come freely into the kingdom of God via the Way of Jesus Christ.

As the very last words in the narrative, 'with all boldness and without hindrance' also prepare us to exit the narrative and look ahead. Actually, their focus on open, dynamic, unimpeded witness suggests that Acts' mission story does not so much end as simply break off in mid-stream. Resisting its own intimations of Paul's trial before Caesar and ultimate fate of martyrdom (which was probably already a fait accompli by the time Acts was written; cf. 20.22-25; 21.13; 25.10-11; 27.24), the narrative leaves Paul with a hopeful future filled with fresh opportunity for vigorous mission. To be sure, there is a two-year limit to this scenario. But 'two *whole* (*holēn*) years' (28.30) is a long time, and whatever happens to Paul the prisoner after this stretch, we are left with a strong impression that the gospel of Jesus Christ which he proclaims will remain fruitful and unfettered. The missionary journey of Acts continues 'unhinderedly'.

Bibliography

Alexander, L., '"In Journeyings Often": Voyaging in the Acts of the Apostles and in Greek Romance', in C.M. Tuckett (ed.), *Luke's Literary Achievement: Collected Essays* (JSNTSup, 116; Sheffield: Sheffield Academic Press, 1995), pp. 17-49.

Alter, R., *The Art of Biblical Narrative* (New York: Basic Books, 1981).

Anderson, J.C., 'Reading Tabitha: A Feminist Reception History', in E.V. McKnight and E.S. Malbon (eds.), *The New Literary Criticism and the New Testament* (Valley Forge, PA: Trinity Press International, 1994), pp. 108-44.

Barrett, C.K., *The Acts of the Apostles* (2 vols.; ICC; Edinburgh: T. & T. Clark, 1994, forthcoming).

—*Freedom and Obligation: A Study of the Epistle to the Galatians* (London: SPCK, 1985).

Brawley, R.L., *Centering on God: Method and Message in Luke–Acts* (Literary Currents in Biblical Intepretation; Louisville, KY: Westminster/John Knox Press, 1990).

—*Luke–Acts and the Jews: Conflict, Apology, and Conciliation* (SBLMS 33; Atlanta: Scholars Press, 1987).

Brodie, T.L., 'Luke–Acts as an Imitation and Emulation of the Elijah–Elisha Narrative', in E. Richard (ed.), *New Views on Luke and Acts* (Collegeville, MN: Liturgical Press, 1990), pp. 78-85.

—'Towards Unraveling the Rhetorical Sources in Acts: 2 Kgs 5 as One Component of Acts 8, 9-40', *Bib* 67 (1986), pp. 41-67.

Brown, R.E., and J.P. Meier, *Antioch and Rome: New Testament Cradles of Catholic Christianity* (London: Geoffrey Chapman, 1983).

Bruce, F.F., *The Book of Acts* (NICNT; Grand Rapids, MI: Eerdmans, rev. edn, 1988).

Cassidy, R.J., *Society and Politics in the Acts of the Apostles* (Maryknoll, NY: Orbis Books, 1987).

Cohen, S.J.D., *From the Maccabees to the Mishnah* (Library of Early Christianity, 7; Philadelphia: Westminster Press, 1987).

Crossan, J.D., *Jesus: A Revolutionary Biography* (San Francisco: HarperSanFrancisco, 1994).

D'Angelo, M.R., 'Women in Luke–Acts: A Redactional View', *JBL* 109 (1990), pp. 441-61.

Darr, J.A., *On Character Building: The Reader and the Rhetoric of Characterization in Luke–Acts* (Literary Currents in Biblical Interpretation; Louisville, KY: Westminster/John Knox Press, 1993).

Douglas, M., *Natural Symbols: Explorations in Cosmology* (New York: Pantheon Books, 1982).

—*Purity and Danger: An Analysis of the Concepts of Pollution and Taboo* (London: Routledge, 1966).

Downing, F.G., 'Theophilus's First Reading of Luke–Acts', in C.M. Tuckett (ed.), *Luke's Literary Achievement: Collected Essays* (JSNTSup, 116; Sheffield: Sheffield Academic Press, 1995), pp. 91-109.

Elliott, J.H., 'Temple versus Household in Luke–Acts: A Contrast in Social Institutions', in J.H. Neyrey (ed.), *The Social World of Luke–Acts: Models for Interpretation* (Peabody, MA: Hendrickson, 1991), pp. 211-40.

Esler, P.F., *Community and Gospel in Luke–Acts: The Social and Political Motivations of Lucan Theology* (SNTMS, 57; Cambridge: Cambridge University Press, 1987).

Evans, C.A., 'Luke's Use of the Elijah/Elisha Narratives and the Ethic of Election', *JBL* 106 (1987), pp. 75-83.

Felder, C.H., 'Racial Motifs in the Biblical Narratives', in R.S. Sugirtharajah (ed.), *Voices from the Margin: Interpreting the Bible in the Third World* (Maryknoll, NY: Orbis Books, 1991), pp. 172-88.

Ferguson, E., *Backgrounds of Early Christianity* (Grand Rapids, MI: Eerdmans, 1987).

Fitzmyer, J.A., 'The Authorship of Luke–Acts Reconsidered', in *Luke the Theologian: Aspects of His Teaching* (New York: Paulist Press, 1989), pp. 1-26.

Freyne, S., *Galilee, Jesus and the Gospels: Literary Approaches and Historical Investigations* (Philadelphia: Fortress Press, 1988).

Garrett, S.R., *The Demise of the Devil: Magic and the Demonic in Luke's Writings* (Minneapolis, MN: Augsburg/Fortress Press, 1989).

Gaventa, B.R., 'The Acts of the Apostles', in W.A. Meeks (gen. ed.), *The Harper Collins Study Bible: New Revised Standard Version* (New York: HarperCollins, 1993), pp. 2056-2113.

Gill, D.W.J., 'Acts and Roman Religion. A. Religion in a Local Setting', in D.W.J. Gill and C. Gempf (eds.), *The Book of Acts in its First-Century Setting. II. The Book of Acts in its Graeco-Roman Setting* (Grand Rapids, MI: Eerdmans; Carlisle: Paternoster Press, 1994), pp. 79-92.

Gill, D.W.J., and C. Gempf (eds.), *The Book of Acts in its First-Century Setting. II. The Book of Acts in its Graeco-Roman Setting* (Grand Rapids, MI: Eerdmans; Carlisle: Paternoster Press, 1994).

Gilmore, D.D., 'Introduction: The Shame of Dishonor', in D.D. Gilmore (ed.), *Honor and Shame and the Unity of the Mediterranean* (Washington, DC: American Anthropological Association, 1987), pp. 2-21.

Gowler, D.B., 'Characterization in Luke: A Socio-Narratological Approach', *BTB* 19 (1989), pp. 54-62.

—*Host, Guest, Enemy and Friend: Portraits of the Pharisees in Luke and Acts* (Emory Studies in Early Christianity; New York: Peter Lang, 1991).

Gunn, D.M., 'Narrative Criticism', in S.R. Haynes and S.L. McKenzie (eds.), *To Each Its Own Meaning: An Introduction to Biblical Criticisms and Their Application* (Louisville, KY: Westminster/John Knox Press, 1993), pp. 171-96.

Gunn, D.M., and D.N. Fewell, *Narrative in the Hebrew Bible* (The Oxford Bible Series; Oxford: Oxford University Press, 1993).

Haenchen, E., *The Acts of the Apostles: A Commentary* (Oxford: Basil Blackwell, 1971).

Hanson, P.D., *The People Called: The Growth of Community in the Bible* (San Francisco: Harper & Row, 1986).

Hengel, M., *Earliest Christianity* (London: SCM Press, 1986).

Hemer, C.J., *The Book of Acts in the Setting of Hellenistic History* (ed. C.H. Gempf; Winona Lake, IN: Eisenbrauns, 1990).

Hock, R.F., *The Social Context of Paul's Ministry: Tentmaking and Apostleship* (Philadelphia: Fortress Press, 1980).

Horsley, R.A., and J.S. Hanson, *Bandits, Prophets, and Messiahs: Popular Movements at the Time of Jesus* (New Voices in Biblical Studies; San Francisco: Harper & Row, 1985).

Jeremias, J., *Jerusalem in the Time of Jesus: An Investigation into Economic and Social Conditions during the New Testament Period* (Philadelphia: Fortress Press, 1969).

Johnson, L.T., *The Gospel of Luke* (Sacra Pagina, 3; Collegeville, MN: Liturgical Press, 1991).

—*The Acts of the Apostles* (Sacra Pagina, 5; Collegeville, MN: Liturgical Press, 1992).

Kennedy, D., 'Roman Army', *Anchor Bible Dictionary*, V, pp. 789-98.

Krodel, G.A., *Acts* (Augsburg Commentary on the NT; Minneapolis, MN: Augsburg, 1986).

Kurz, W.S., *Farewell Addresses in the New Testament* (Zacchaeus Studies; Collegeville, MN: Liturgical Press, 1990).

—*Reading Luke–Acts: Dynamics of Biblical Narrative* (Louisville, KY: Westminster/ John Knox Press, 1993).

Lake, K., and H.J. Cadbury, *The Beginnings of Christianity*. I. *The Acts of the Apostles*. IV. *English Translation and Commentary* (London: Macmillan, 1933).

Lentz, J.C., Jr, *Luke's Portrait of Paul* (SNTSMS, 77; Cambridge: Cambridge University Press, 1993).

Longenecker, R.N., 'The Acts of the Apostles', in F.E. Gaebelein (ed.), *The Expositor's Bible Commentary*, IX (Grand Rapids, MI: Zondervan, 1981), pp. 207-573.

Malherbe, A.J., 'The Cultural Context of the New Testament: The Graeco-Roman World', in *The New Interpreter's Bible*, VIII (Nashville, TN: Abingdon Press, 1995), pp. 12-26.

—'"Not in a Corner": Early Christian Apologetic in Acts 26:26', *SecCen* 5 (1986), pp. 193-210.

—*Paul and the Thessalonians: The Philosophic Tradition of Pastoral Care* (Philadelphia: Fortress Press, 1987).

Malina, B.J., *Christian Origins and Cultural Anthropology: Practical Models for Biblical Interpretation* (Atlanta, GA: John Knox Press, 1986).

—*The New Testament World: Insights from Cultural Anthropology* (Louisville, KY: Westminster/John Knox Press, rev. edn, 1993).

—'Reading Theory Perspective: Reading Luke–Acts', in J.H. Neyrey (ed.), *The Social World of Luke–Acts: Models for Interpretation* (Peabody, MA: Hendrickson, 1991), pp. 3-23.

Malina, B.J., and J.H. Neyrey, 'Conflict in Luke–Acts: Labelling and Deviance Theory', in J.H. Neyrey (ed.), *The Social World of Luke–Acts: Models for Interpretation* (Peabody, MA: Hendrickson, 1991), pp. 97-122.

—'First-Century Personality: Dyadic, Not Individualistic', in J.H. Neyrey (ed.), *The Social World of Luke–Acts: Models for Interpretation* (Peabody, MA: Hendrickson, 1991) pp. 67-96.

—'Honor and Shame in Luke–Acts: Pivotal Values of the Mediterranean World', in J.H. Neyrey (ed.), *The Social World of Luke–Acts: Models for Interpretation* (Peabody, MA: Hendrickson, 1991), pp. 25-66.

Marshall, I.H., 'Acts and the "Former Treatise"', in B.W. Winter and A.D. Clarke (eds.), *The Book of Acts in its First-Century Setting*. I. *The Book of Acts in its Ancient Literary Setting* (Grand Rapids, MI: Eerdmans; Carlisle: Paternoster Press, 1993), pp. 163-82.

—*The Acts of the Apostles: An Introduction and Commentary* (Tyndale NT Commentaries; Leicester: Inter-Varsity Press; Grand Rapids, MI: Eerdmans, 1980).

Martin, C.J., 'The Acts of the Apostles', in E.S. Fiorenza (ed.), *Searching the Scriptures*. II. *A Feminist Commentary* (New York: Crossroad, 1994), pp. 763-99.

McVann, M., 'Rituals of Status Transformation in Luke–Acts: The Case of Jesus the Prophet', in J.H. Neyrey (ed.), *The Social World of Luke–Acts: Models for Interpretation* (Peabody, MA: Hendrickson, 1991), pp. 333-60.

Meeks, W.A., *The First Urban Christians: The Social World of the Apostle Paul* (New Haven: Yale University Press, 1983).

—*The Origins of Christian Morality: The First Two Centuries* (New Haven: Yale University Press, 1993).

Metzger, B.M., *A Textual Commentary on the Greek New Testament* (London: United Bible Societies, 1975).

Moessner, D.P., *Lord of the Banquet: The Literary and Theological Significance of the Lukan Travel Narrative* (Minneapolis, MN: Fortress Press, 1989).

Moore, S.D., *Literary Criticism and the Gospels: The Theoretical Challenge* (New Haven: Yale University Press, 1989).

Moxnes, H., 'Patron–Client Relations and the New Community in Luke–Acts', in J.H. Neyrey (ed.), *The Social World of Luke–Acts: Models for Interpretation* (Peabody, MA: Hendrickson, 1991), pp. 241-68.

Neyrey, J.H., 'Ceremonies in Luke–Acts: The Case of Meals and Table-Fellowship', in J.H. Neyrey (ed.), *The Social World of Luke–Acts: Models for Interpretation* (Peabody, MA: Hendrickson, 1991), pp. 361-87.

—'The Forensic Defense Speech and Paul's Trial Speeches in Acts 22-26: Form and Function', in C.H. Talbert (ed.), *Luke–Acts: New Perspectives from the Society of Biblical Literature Seminar* (New York: Crossroad, 1984), pp. 210-24.

—'Luke's Social Location of Paul: Cultural Anthropology and the Status of Paul in Acts', in B. Witherington (ed.), *History, Literature, and Society in the Book of Acts* (Cambridge: Cambridge University Press, 1996), pp. 251-79.

—*The Passion according to Luke: A Redaction Study of Luke's Soteriology* (New York: Paulist Press, 1985).

—'The Symbolic Universe of Luke–Acts: "They Turn the World Upside Down"', in J.H. Neyrey (ed.), *The Social World of Luke–Acts: Models for Interpretation* (Peabody, MA: Hendrickson, 1991), pp. 271-304.

Neyrey, J.H. (ed.), *The Social World of Luke–Acts: Models for Interpretation* (Peabody, MA: Hendrickson, 1991).

Nobbs, A., 'Cyprus', in D.W.J. Gill and C. Gempf (eds.), *The Book of Acts in its First-Century Setting*. II. *The Book of Acts in its Graeco-Roman Setting* (Grand Rapids, MI: Eerdmans; Carlisle: Paternoster Press, 1994), pp. 279-90.

Nock, A.D., 'Paul and the Magus', in K. Lake and H.J. Cadbury (eds.), *The Beginnings of Christianity*. I. *The Acts of the Apostles*, V (London: Macmillan, 1933), pp. 164-88.

O'Day, G.R., 'Acts', in C.A. Newsom and S.H. Ringe (eds.), *The Women's Bible Commentary* (Louisville, KY: Westminster/John Knox Press; London, SPCK, 1992), pp. 305-12.

Parsons, M.C., *The Departure of Jesus in Luke–Acts: The Ascension Narratives in Context* (JSNTSup, 21; Sheffield: JSOT Press, 1987).

Parsons, M.C., and R.I. Pervo, *Rethinking the Unity of Luke and Acts* (Minneapolis, MN: Fortress Press, 1993).

Pereira, F., *Ephesus: Climax of Universalism in Luke–Acts: A Redaction-Critical Study of Paul's Ephesian Ministry (Acts 18:23–20:1)* (Jesuit Theological Forum Studies, 1; Anand, India: Gujarat Sahitya Prakash, 1983).

Pervo, R.I., *Profit with Delight: The Literary Genre of the Acts of the Apostles* (Philadelphia: Fortress Press, 1987).

Powell, M.A., *What Are They Saying About Acts?* (New York: Paulist Press, 1991).

—*What Is Narrative Criticism?* (Minneapolis, MN: Fortress Press, 1990).

Reimer, I.R., *Women in the Acts of the Apostles: A Feminist Liberation Perspective* (trans. L.M. Maloney; Minneapolis, MN: Fortress Press, 1995).

Rhoads, D., 'Social Criticism: Crossing Boundaries', in J.C. Anderson and S.D. Moore (eds.), *Mark & Method: New Approaches in Biblical Studies* (Minneapolis, MN: Fortress Press, 1992), pp. 135-61.

Rousseau, J.J., and R. Arav, *Jesus and his World: An Archaeological and Cultural Dictionary* (Minneapolis, MN: Fortress Press, 1995).

Sanders, J.T., *The Jews in Luke–Acts* (London: SCM Press, 1987).

Sawicki, M., *Seeing the Lord: Resurrection and Early Christian Practices* (Minneapolis, MN: Fortress Press, 1994).

Schottroff, L., *Let the Oppressed Go Free: Feminist Perspectives on the New Testament* (trans. A.S. Kidder; Gender and the Biblical Tradition; Louisville, KY: Westminster/John Knox Press, 1992).

Seim, T.K., *The Double Message: Patterns of Gender in Luke and Acts* (Nashville, TN: Abingdon Press; Edinburgh: T. & T. Clark, 1994).

Shepherd, W.H., Jr, *The Narrative Function of the Holy Spirit as a Character in Luke–Acts* (SBLDS, 147; Atlanta, GA: Scholars Press, 1994).

Smith, A., 'A Second Step in African Biblical Interpretation: A Generic Reading Analysis of Acts 8:26-40', in F.F. Segovia and M.A. Tolbert (eds.), *Reading from this Place. I. Social Location and Biblical Interpretation in the United States* (Minneapolis, MN: Fortress Press, 1995), pp. 213-28.

Soards, M.L., *The Speeches of Acts: Their Content, Context, and Concerns* (Louisville, KY: Westminster/John Knox Press, 1994).

Spencer, F.S., 'Acts and Modern Literary Approaches', in B.W. Winter and A.D. Clark (eds.), *The Book of Acts in its First-Century Setting. I. The Book of Acts in its Ancient Literary Setting* (Grand Rapids, MI: Eerdmans; Carlisle: Paternoster Press, 1993), pp. 381-414.

—'The Ethiopian Eunuch and his Bible: A Social-Science Analysis', *BTB* 22 (1992), pp. 155-65.

—'Neglected Widows in Acts 6:1-7', *CBQ* 56 (1994), pp. 715-33.

—*The Portrait of Philip in Acts: A Study of Roles and Relations* (JSNTSup, 67; Sheffield: Sheffield Academic Press, 1992).

Talbert, C.H., *Literary Patterns, Theological Themes, and the Genre of Luke–Acts* (SBLMS, 20; Missoula, MT: Scholars Press, 1974).

Tannehill, R.C., '"Cornelius" and "Tabitha" Encounter Luke's Jesus', *Int* 48 (1994), pp. 347-56.

—'The Gospels and Narrative Literature', in *The New Interpreter's Bible*, VIII (Nashville, TN: Abingdon Press, 1994), pp. 56-70.

—*The Narrative Unity of Luke–Acts: A Literary Interpretation* (2 vols.; Philadelphia: Fortress Press, 1986, 1990).

—'Review of *Luke's Portrait of Paul*' by J.C. Lentz in *Critical Review of Books in Religion* 7 (1994), pp. 218-20.

Taylor, L.R., 'The Asiarchs', in K. Lake and H.J. Cadbury (eds.), *The Beginnings of Christianity*. I. *The Acts of the Apostles*, V (London: Macmillan, 1933), pp. 256-62.

Trebilco, P., 'Asia', in D.W.J. Gill and C. Gempf (eds.), *The Book of Acts in its First-Century Setting*. II. *The Book of Acts in its Graeco-Roman Setting* (Grand Rapids, MI: Eerdmans; Carlisle: Paternoster Press, 1994), pp. 291-362.

Tyson, J.B. (ed.), *Luke–Acts and the Jewish People: Eight Critical Perspectives* (Minneapolis, MN: Augsburg, 1988).

Turner, V., *The Ritual Process: Structure and Anti-Structure* (Ithaca, NY: Cornell University Press, 1977).

Vermes, G., *The Dead Sea Scrolls: Qumran in Perspective* (Philadelphia: Fortress Press, rev. edn, 1977).

Wall, R.W., 'Peter, "Son" of Jonah: The Conversion of Cornelius in the Context of Canon', *JSNT* 29 (1987), pp. 79-90.

—'Successors to "the Twelve" According to Acts 12:1-17', *CBQ* 53 (1991), pp. 628-43.

Weeks, H.R., 'Sharon', *Anchor Bible Dictionary*, V, pp. 1161-63.

Wenham, D., 'Acts and the Pauline Corpus II. The Evidence of Parallels', in B.W. Winter and A.D. Clarke (eds.), *The Book of Acts in its First-Century Setting*. I. *The Book of Acts in its Ancient Literary Setting* (ed. Grand Rapids, MI: Eerdmans; Carlisle: Paternoster Press, 1993), pp. 215-58.

Winter, B.W., *The Book of Acts in Its First-Century Setting*. 6 vols. (Grand Rapids, MI: Eerdmans; Carlisle: Paternoster Press, 1993-).

Winter, B.W., and A.D. Clarke (eds.), *The Book of Acts in its First-Century Setting*. I. *The Book of Acts in its Ancient Literary Setting* (Grand Rapids, MI: Eerdmans; Carlisle: Paternoster Press, 1993).

Index of References

Old Testament

New Testament

Other Ancient Sources

Index of Authors

DATE DUE